Rethinking Modern Polish Identities

Rochester Studies in East and Central Europe

Series Editor: Timothy Snyder, Yale University

Additional Titles of Interest

*Seeking Accountability for Nazi and War Crimes in East and Central Europe:
A People's Justice?*
Edited by Eric Le Bourhis, Irina Tcherneva, and Vanessa Voisin

*Great Power Competition and the Path to Democracy:
The Case of Georgia, 1991–2020*
Zarina Burkadze

*Toward Xenopolis:
Visions from the Borderland*
Krzysztof Czyżewski
Edited by Mayhill C. Fowler
With a Foreword by Timothy Snyder

*The Universe behind Barbed Wire:
Memoirs of a Ukrainian Soviet Dissident*
Myroslav Marynovych
Translated by Zoya Hayuk
Edited by Katherine Younger
With a Foreword by Timothy Snyder

*Borders on the Move:
Territorial Change and Ethnic Cleansing in the Hungarian-Slovak Borderlands,
1938–1948*
Leslie Waters

*Beyond the Pale:
The Holocaust in the North Caucasus*
Edited by Crispin Brooks and Kiril Feferman

*Polish Literature and National Identity:
A Postcolonial Perspective*
Dariusz Skórczewski
Translated by Agnieszka Polakowska

A complete list of titles in the Rochester Studies in East and Central Europe series
may be found on our website, www.urpress.com.

Rethinking Modern Polish Identities

Transnational Encounters

Edited by Agnieszka Pasieka and Paweł Rodak

UNIVERSITY OF ROCHESTER PRESS

The University of Rochester Press gratefully acknowledges generous support from the Stefan and Lucy Hejna Endowment for Polish Studies at the University of Illinois Chicago Department of History, the College of Letters and Science at the University of Wisconsin-Madison, and the University of Michigan.

Copyright © 2023 The Editors and Contributors

All rights reserved. Except as permitted under current legislation, no part of this work may be photocopied, stored in a retrieval system, published, performed in public, adapted, broadcast, transmitted, recorded, or reproduced in any form or by any means, without the prior permission of the copyright owner.

First published 2023

University of Rochester Press
668 Mt. Hope Avenue, Rochester, NY 14620, USA
www.urpress.com
and Boydell & Brewer Limited
PO Box 9, Woodbridge, Suffolk IP12 3DF, UK
www.boydellandbrewer.com

ISBN-13: 978-1-64825-058-3
ISSN: 1528-4808

Library of Congress Cataloging-in-Publication Data

Names: Pasieka, Agnieszka, 1983– editor. | Rodak, Paweł, 1967– editor.
Title: Rethinking modern Polish identities : transnational encounters / edited by Agnieszka Pasieka and Pawel Rodak.
Description: Rochester : University of Rochester Press, 2022. | Series: Rochester studies in East and Central Europe, 1528-4808 ; 30 | Includes bibliographical references and index.
Identifiers: LCCN 2022028736 (print) | LCCN 2022028737 (ebook) | ISBN 9781648250583 (hardback) | ISBN 9781800108592 (pdf) | ISBN 9781800108608 (epub)
Subjects: LCSH: National characteristics, Polish. | Polish people—Ethnic identity. | Nationalism—Poland—History—20th century. | Poland—History.
Classification: LCC DK4121 .R48 2022 (print) | LCC DK4121 (ebook) | DDC 943.8—dc23/eng/20220812
LC record available at https://lccn.loc.gov/2022028736
LC ebook record available at https://lccn.loc.gov/2022028737

A catalogue record for this title is available from the British Library.

This publication is printed on acid-free paper.

Printed in the United States of America.

Contents

Acknowledgments — vii

Introduction
Polishness: A Story of Sameness and Difference — 1
Agnieszka Pasieka

Part One: Redefining Polishness

1. The Birth of the "Polak-Katolik" — 19
   Brian Porter-Szűcs

2. Vita Magistra Historiae? The Case of A. B. — 37
   Paweł Bukowiec

3. An Anti-Imperial Civilizing Mission: Claiming Volhynia for the Early Second Polish Republic — 50
   Kathryn Ciancia

4. Suspicious Origins as a Category of Polish Culture — 74
   Irena Grudzińska-Gross

5. Redefining Polishness through Jewishness — 92
   Geneviève Zubrzycki

Part Two: Identity in the Making

6. Human Mobility and the Creation of a Transatlantic Polish Culture — 113
   Keely Stauter-Halsted

7. "Good Americans" and Polish Modern Identity Construction after World War I — 133
   Krystyna Lipińska Illakowicz

8. From "True Believers" to "Cultural Feminists": Polish Identity and Women's Emancipation in post-1945 and post-1989 Poland — 161
   Magdalena Grabowska

9. Labor, Gender, and Interethnic Relations among Polish-American Communities in Rural Massachusetts — 191
Agnieszka Pasieka

10. Being European in Poland and Polish in Europe: Transnational Constructions of National Identity — 208
Marysia Galbraith

Part Three: Portraits and Performances

11. Views of Polishness: Style and Representation in Local and National Exhibitions — 237
Małgorzata Litwinowicz

12. Plebeian, Populist, Post-Enlightenment: Mass Sarmatism and Its Political Forms — 256
Przemysław Czapliński

13. The Polish Connection: Lithuanian Music and the Warsaw Autumn Festival — 277
Lisa Jakelski

14. Performing Polishness Abroad: (Non-)Polish Actors and the Construction of (Trans)National Identities in European Cinema — 304
Kris Van Heuckelom

15. "Poles—Their Own Portraits" Revisited: Taking a Critical Stand — 324
Ryszard Koziołek

Afterword
Polishness: A Time of Deconstruction, a Time of Reconstruction — 348
Paweł Rodak

Notes on the Contributors — 359

Index of Names — 365

Index of Subjects — 373

Acknowledgments

Every book project is a collective endeavor, shaped by numerous conversations and inspirations. This could not be truer for an edited volume.

We would like to thank all the authors for their willingness to join our book project and for their support during all the stages of work on the volume. Special thanks go to Kathryn Ciancia, Brian Porter-Szűcs, Keely Stauter-Halsted, and Geneviève Zubrzycki—not only did they contribute fantastic chapters but they also helped to secure funding for the book's publication.

Further, we would like to thank: Sonia Kane and Tracey Engel from the University of Rochester Press, for their excellent advice and for all their efforts to make this book happen; Timothy Snyder, the editor of the series Rochester Studies in East and Central Europe, for his interest in our project; two anonymous reviewers who helped the contributors to improve their essays and the editors to ensure the volume's coherence; and our language editor Paweł Markiewicz and copyeditor Michael Sandlin for their careful reading of the text. Finally, we would like to extend our special thanks to Maria Anna Ciemerych-Litwinienko for her splendid cover artwork.

We would also like to thank the University of Warsaw and the Institute of Polish Culture, University of Warsaw, for financial help as well as the Institute of Slavic Studies, Polish Academy of Sciences, which organized the conference that generated the idea for this volume.

Agnieszka dedicates this volume to her father, Dariusz Pasieka, teacher of Polish literature. Discussions with him mark every page of her work.

Agnieszka Pasieka
Paweł Rodak

* * *

Chapter 4, by Irena Grudzińska-Gross, is a revised and translated version of the author's Polish-language version published in her collection of essays entitled "Honor, horror i klasycy," Pogranicze, Sejny, 2012.

Chapter 5, by Geneviève Zubryzcki, is adapted from "Nationalism, 'Philosemitism' and Symbolic Boundary-Making in Contemporary Poland," *Comparative Studies in Society and History*, 58:1, 66–98.

Chapter 15, by Ryszard Koziołek, is adapted from his essay in Polish that appeared in the book *Migracyjna pamięć, wspólnota, tożsamość*, edited by Ryszard Nycz, Tomasz Sapota, and Roma Sendyka (Warsaw: Instytut Badań Literackich, 2017). Translated by Leszek Drong.

Introduction

Polishness

A Story of Sameness and Difference

Agnieszka Pasieka

> –In a word, it's all, always, unchangingly—Poland, of Poland, for Poland, to Poland . . .
> –That's right. Here in this country we were and are impaired in that respect. We're born with the defect of Polishness.
> –I'm not talking about Poles being Poles, but rather the essential defect that arises when philosophical and sociological discussions end with a *deus ex machina*: Poland. There's a well-known joke about elephants—that when a Pole has to follow the other nations in writing an essay about elephants, he immediately begins: 'The Elephant and the Polish Question.'"[1]
> —Stefan Żeromski, *The Coming of Spring*

Only a decade ago, a PhD candidate in anthropology wanting to study "identity" would most likely have been met by ironic smiles from search committee members. They would have pointed out the need to move "beyond identity,"[2] to focus on "identity performances" or competing constructions of the self, as

---

[1] Original version: "— Słowem wszystko, zawsze i niezmiennie — Polska, Polski, Polsce, Polskę . . ." "— Tak. My tutaj byliśmy i jesteśmy na tym punkcie ułomni. Jesteśmy urodzeni z defektem polskości." "— Nie o tem mówię, że Polacy są Polakami, lecz o istotnym defekcie, jeżeli w rozważaniach filozoficznych i socyologicznych wynika *deus ex machina*: — Polska. Znana jest anegdota o temacie "Słoń." Polak, mający po innych nacyach napisać rozprawę o słoniu, napisał bez wahania: "Słoń a Polska." (Żeromski, *Przedwiośnie*).

[2] Cf. Brubaker and Cooper, "Beyond 'Identity,'" 1–47.

discussed within the emerging field of cognitive anthropology.[3] To many, "identity" appeared to be yesterday's news, an issue unsuited to the postideological era, characterized by deconstructionism, self-criticism, and a reluctance to make "big claims." Many wished to bury "identity" together along with other "essentializing" concepts such as "culture."[4] Beyond scholarship, "identity politics," the key terrain of identity, had also lost its vigor and was increasingly criticized for ineffectiveness in addressing the problems faced by individuals and groups it purportedly aimed to support.

But today, the question of identity seems to be returning with renewed force in cultural, social, and political contexts. It reemerges as a subject of debates—tackling the "identity issue" supposedly offers possibilities for understanding disquieting sociopolitical developments: from a wave of right-wing populism to growing political radicalization. Also, today, "identity" is no longer neatly associated with various strands of "identity politics" and, instead, it is being increasingly appropriated by various right-wing groups (among them, *nomen omen*, or "Identitarians"[5]). Whether the topic of discussion is a farmers' strike, changing voting patterns among the middle class, or protests against a daring theater piece by outraged citizens, we hear much about cultural identities being at stake.[6] Consequently, the scholarly gaze has turned again toward identity/identities. Yet rather than searching for alternative, less "essentializing" concepts, scholars increasingly recognize the potential afforded by the coexistence of the scholarly/constructivist conception of identity with its reified usage in popular discourses.[7]

Can a collection of essays discussing "Polishness" contribute to these debates and shed light on current identity questions, whether by offering a comparative perspective or simply fostering reflection on the problems of identity formation, negotiation, and relevance? What does the story of a priest from a borderland locality, a conversation with a country dweller, correspondence between

---

3   See, for example, Holland and Lave, *History in Person*.
4   See, for example, Abu-Lughod, "Writing against Culture," 137–62; Hann, "All 'Kulturvölker' Now?" 259–76.
5   Identitarians are an international, far-right movement, composed primarily of young people, which calls for a defense of European/Western/white identities, while employing anti-Islam and anti-immigration discourses.
6   Russian aggression on Ukraine in the spring and summer of 2022, the questioning the existence of Ukrainian national identity by the Russian authorities, and the Ukrainian heroic defense are perhaps the most dramatic proof of the continuous relevance of "identity issue."
7   Sökefeld, "Reconsidering Identity," 538.

political émigrés, or a music competition verdict contribute to our understanding of why identity matters beyond specifically Polish matters? After all, considering the title of this volume, one could assume that this book constitutes yet another attempt to demonstrate Poland's "exceptional" trajectory, a (perhaps unwitting) illustration of the "defect of Polishness."

Inspired by new scholarship in the humanities and social sciences as well as drawing on a rich tradition of critical examination of the idea of Polishness, this volume seeks to do the opposite. In offering a diversity of case studies and methodological-theoretical approaches, it demonstrates a profound connection between the national and the transnational by placing the case of Poland in a larger context and in doing so demonstrates that Poland is better seen as a "perfectly normal country," to use Brian Porter-Szűcs's formulation. Stressing Poland's "normalness" or perhaps "usualness"[8] is a continuously important task given that the "Polish question" tends to be dealt with in studies and discussions in much the same way. In a volume on religion, the Polish case is supposed to illustrate a divergent path of secularization (or, rather, its lack of secularization); in a publication related to the nineteenth-century "national awakenings," it will likely feature in the context of religious-political mythologies. And in a consideration of the violent twentieth century, it most likely will be related to anti-Semitism, ethnic cleansing, and resistance to Nazi Germany and Soviet communism. Similarly, "typical" characters of such accounts are a (backward) peasant, a freedom fighter, and the Virgin Mary (or her earthly equivalent—*Matka Polka*). Far from ignoring these issues and protagonists, in this volume we encourage different perspectives on these issues by looking for "less obvious" connections and identifying previously neglected themes and their interpretations. We thus ask: What about philo-Semitism? Convinced communists? Cosmopolitan peasants? What do we gain and lose by rejecting long-established topoi? In asking these questions, we strive to move the discussion beyond the analysis built on dichotomies: showing different paths to and different agents of modernity, indicating interdependencies between resistance and domination and unveiling exclusionary undertones of supposedly egalitarian strands. It is in this way that we strive to contribute to a broader scholarly reflection.

---

8   The subtitle of Brian Porter-Szűcs's book in Polish is: "Całkiem zwyczajny kraj." "Zwyczajny" corresponds with both "normal" and "usual." The notion of "normal" tends to have strong implications (normal as opposed to pathological), and it is certainly important to use it cautiously; at the same time, the question of the mechanisms behind establishing what is normal, or what is the norm, is definitely one of the key preoccupations of this volume. See also Rodak, this volume.

To date, investigations into the idea of Polishness constitute a rich body of literature, from sociological and anthropological studies of Polish identities and Polish culture[9] through historical works[10] and abundant literary works, which are perhaps the best testimonies of "wresting with Polishness" (as a matter of fact, literary works are so numerous that making a list of "representative contributions," covering the terrain from Wacław Potocki to Ziemowit Szczerek, is a quixotic task). This long history notwithstanding, in recent decades particularly far-reaching examinations have appeared. The emergence of this new strand of work might be seen partly as a specific regional, postsocialist development: it is plausible to assume that after years of examining political-economic aspects of the post-1989 transformation and Poland's accession to the European Union, a turn toward a sociocultural dimension was inevitable. But it is only a partial explanation, as this shift is also related to the previously mentioned "return of identity" on the global scene. At any rate, this turn brought about fascinating research on Polish history and Polish society, spurring many long overdue debates[11] and a new wave of literary works.[12] Paweł Rodak discusses these developments in detail in his afterword, showing how the chapters gathered here enter into a dialogue with recent literature on "Polishness," broadly understood. In this introduction, I want to highlight instead three key dimensions—old/new, plural/uniform, mainstream/marginal—that the contributions in this volume are built around and that provoke debates on issues central to the exploration of *any* identity. These dimensions are discussed in the following sections alongside a brief presentation of the volume's contents.

The Old and the New

Growing "interconnectedness," increased "globalization," the "acceleration" of the pace of life, "transnational" networks—these and parallel terms have featured frequently in recent academic discussions, at times becoming, in a sense, sine qua non expressions that are supposed to guarantee a publication's or grant application's success. Scholars have frequently pointed to the unprecedented

---

9 For a canonical work, see: Kłoskowska, *Oblicza polskości*.
10 For example, Kleinmann at al., *Imaginations and Configurations of Polish Society*.
11 The most important being works and debates on Polish coresponsibility for the Holocaust. For a discussion see Rodak, this volume.
12 Such as by Masłowska, "Między name dobrze jest"; Varga, "Trociny"; Twardoch, "Morfina," Ziemowit Szczerek's "Siwy dym," to mention but a few.

nature of the events analyzed, whether the phenomena at issue are migratory processes, new tools of communication, or rapid transformations of socioeconomic structures.[13] Those (still) using the concept of identity have talked about "dialogical selves" and "multiple identifications" as characteristic of globalized, multicultural environments.[14] And as a consequence, many scholars have argued that new sources, methodologies, and theoretical approaches are necessary to best grasp the changes that individuals and communities are undergoing as a result of such processes.

The essays collected here demonstrate that explorations of Polish identities, on the one hand, perfectly exemplify the aforementioned phenomena, perceived as emblematic of the twenty-first century, yet, on the other, problematize the idea of their novelty. Let us look at a few examples. Focusing on Polish American encounters, Keely Stauter-Halsted and Krystyna Illakowicz reflect upon long roots of "transnational Polishness," demonstrating the ways in which various US images and narratives shaped Poles' self-perception in the interwar era. Illakowicz analyzes popular culture, advertising, and literature to demonstrate that the models of "modernity" those media conveyed were not passively accepted but transformed and used strategically by Polish recipients in their identity-building processes. Stauter-Halsted is more concerned with the individual dimension, embodied by migrants who went back and forth between their native Polish villages and the United States and who, in so doing, became not only nationally conscious but critical and politically active subjects. Paweł Bukowiec's essay also sets out an individual case: his reconstruction of the life and output of the Catholic bishop Antanas Baranauskas/Baranowski/Барановский—an example par excellence of (possible) "multiple identification"—demonstrates the futility of considering such complexities a staple of postmodernity. In turn, Małgorzata Litwinowicz and Przemysław Czapliński discuss what can be described as elite identity projects. In her discussion on the attempts to create emblematic "views of Polishness" by nineteenth- and twentieth-century intellectuals, Litwinowicz illustrates acute tensions between what was perceived as "local" (or "domestic") and what was considered "modern" (or foreign). By analyzing the long trajectory of Sarmatian ideology,

---

13 For a poignant criticism of this kind of approach to transnationalism, see: Green, *Limits of Transnationalism*.

14 Van Meijl, "Multiple Identifications and Dialogical Self," 917–33.

Czapliński shows how Sarmatism has, through its various adaptations and reincarnations, remained a fundamental tool of Polish identity creation.

The authors thus demonstrate that an understanding of modern Polish identity means crossing not only historical but also geographical boundaries, placing the question of Polish identity in a broader context. This encompasses everything from a more generalized Eastern European context, a usual frame of comparison, to overseas immigrant communities. Migrant experiences play a vital role in shaping both national imaginaries and images of a nation. Given the symbolic weight of the nineteenth-century Great Emigration and post–World War II political émigré milieus in shaping the discourse on Polishness, this observation might seem obvious. However, our volume contributes to the scholarship on this subject by broadening the *social* context and the recognition of a variety of agents who shaped representations and understandings of Polishness. The recognition of the foundational nature of the migration experience constitutes a point of departure in Kris Van Heuckelom's study about "on-screen Polishness," a subject hitherto neglected in discussions on expatriate Polishness. His diachronic analysis of film productions featuring Polish migrants demonstrates the role of varied transnational encounters, increased mobility, and hyphenated identifications in reshaping both the perception of emigration (against the Romantic-era model) and the reconfiguration of Poland/Poles on the European map. Similarly, Agnieszka Pasieka's study of three generations of Polish American farmers in rural Massachusetts demonstrates the ways in which Polish identity has reconfigured in a broader ethnic landscape, this time through strategic use of ethnic references and stretched between concealing and bolstering. In short, in our discussion on "transnational" identities and "interconnected" communities we do not approach these questions as "old" or "new" but rather as questions that are part of a continuous conversation and with numerous actors involved.

Between Plurality and Uniformity

The aforementioned phenomena of "interconnectedness" and "acceleration" tend to be associated with newly emerging social networks and sharing platforms that allow for circulation and exchange of news, quotes, and accompanying images. Widespread and encouraged "hashtagging" well illustrates the emphasis on the collective creation of social phenomena, including those of national culture and heritage. This collective production is supposedly more democratic and less elitist. As the very title of this volume suggests—where we speak about "identities" rather than "identity"—these issues are of key importance for our collection. Indeed, our goal is to come to an understanding of plural conceptualizations of identities by examining to what extent the discussion about "Polishness" has been an *open* one. More precisely, in analyzing the gradual construction of a modern—unified and bounded—idea of Polishness, we do examine the practices that constantly challenged those "attempts at uniformity," but we are sensitive to questions of structure and power that circumscribe those practices.

The "grand narrative" on the creation of modern Polish identity is built around several milestones, the most important being the move from civic conceptualizations characteristic of the First Polish Republic (when Polishness was a category defining representatives of the nobility) toward an "ethnically narrow" but "socially deep" understanding, to use Rogers Brubaker's terms.[15] The new definition of nationhood, which included all social classes but excluded the nonethnic Polish populations, shaped the politics of the Second Republic. It was only fully realized in the post-World War II ethnically and religiously homogenous state. As such, this narrative often constitutes a sort of teleological account in which ethnic and religious "others" gradually disappear while new social classes enter the scene, becoming citizens of a homogenous nation-state (with Catholicism as one of the *national* characteristics). A lot of ink has been spilled in an attempt to problematize this account, mostly by showing various "dark" sides of Polish national developments: colonial aspects, the legacy of serfdom, the violence of assimilatory policies, the relationship between the Jews' and gentry's annihilation and postwar modernization, as well as the discriminatory aspects of the new Polish postsocialist neoliberal system.[16] Other works have tackled often taken-for-granted aspects of Polish history, such as the

---

15   Brubaker, "Nationalizing States in the Old 'New Europe,'" 411–37.
16   On serfdom and peasantry, see: Pobłocki, "How Poles Become White"; Pobłocki, *Chamstwo*; Sowa, *Fantomowe ciało króla*; Engelking, "<Poleszczuk> nieoswojony." On minorities, see: Chu, *The German Minority in Poland*; Mędrzecki, *Kresowy kalejdoskop*; Linkiewicz, *Lokalność i nacjonalizm*; "Studies of Nationality Issues in the Interwar Poland"; On anti-Semitism, see Krzywiec, "Polska bez Żydów"; Leder, *Prześniona rewolucja*. On postsocialism in Poland, see: Buchowski, *Czyściec*.

presumed endurance of the Polish-Catholic connection[17] and the alleged "multiculturality" of the First and Second Polish Republics.[18]

Authors of this volume corroborate these scholarly observations by telling the stories of perhaps less known Polish identity carriers, negotiators, and creators. To start with the religious-national nexus, Brian Porter-Szűcs's and Geneviève Zubrzycki's contributions expose the arbitrariness and the (un)making of Polish Catholic identities. They can be read as sort of parallel stories, as Porter-Szűcs discusses the clergy's and right-wing ideologists' attempts to create a uniform model of *"Polak katolik"* while Zubrzycki shows Polish non-Jews' attempt to stretch the boundaries of Polishness. A similar question, regarding the process of negotiating the confines of "Polish culture," constitutes the background of Lisa Jakelski's contribution, which shows the profound effect of one musical piece—Lithuanian *Last Pagan Rites* performed during the Warsaw Autumn International Festival of Contemporary Music—on the perception of Polish identity, Polish-Lithuanian relations and, more broadly, on cultural relations during the Cold War era. In so doing, Jakelski situates the Polish identity question in the context of an East-West dynamic, and more specifically Polish elites' attempts to cast Polishness as the Western civilization's "carrier" and to prove Poland's "belonging" to the West. (How central this question continues to be is demonstrated by the contributions tackling contemporary developments: van Huckelom's analysis of film productions and Marysia Galbraith's study of perceptions of Europe.)

As these examples suggest, acknowledging plurality means taking into account a variety of voices and experiences, but our contributions show more than that. On the one hand, they indicate potential traps that accounts of Poland's past or present diversity may fall into. As such, they enter into discussion with post-1989 scholarship, which promoted the idea of *"tutejsi,"*[19] "borderlands," and any other testimonies of past diversity—and of different faces of Polishness. Even if this kind of scholarship was meant as a reminder and a corrective of the works written in the times of People's Poland, it often merely constituted a nostalgic illustration of a local *"koloryt"* (local flavor).

---

17   Bjork, "Bulwark or Patchwork?"; Porter, "The Catholic Nation"; Zubrzycki, *The Crosses of Auschwitz*.
18   Augustyniak, "Wielokulturowość Wielkiego Ksiestwa Litewskiego"; see also Pasieka, "Neighbors: About the Multiculturalization of the Polish Past."
19   Meaning literally "people from here," *tutejszy* was a self-identification in ethnically and religiously mixed areas in today's Poland, Belarus, and Lithuania. Cf. Engelking.

Sometimes idealizing, at times nostalgic, accounts of—metaphorical and factual—"margins" too often treated them as isolated from centers of power and control. Our analyses show that accounts of plurality simultaneously reveal the extent of normative expectations and exclusionary mechanisms that are to be found even in supposedly affirmative and egalitarian projects. Remarkable in this regard is Irena Grudzińska-Gross's essay on "suspicious origins" where she describes public disputes over acclaimed writers' rights to "Polishness" and, at the same time, a hierarchical gradation of their "other" identity components. In hers and Jakelski's accounts diversity appears to be accepted when it is "exotic" and, hence, attractive but not threatening; contrary to the difference represented by "Jewishness," an everlasting feature of anti-Semitic accounts in Poland and in Polish diaspora milieus (see chapters by Grudzińska-Gross, Porter-Szűcs, Zubrzycki). The question of hierarchies is developed in a novel way also by Kathryn Ciancia in her case study of Volhynia. Ciancia argues for the importance of "civilization rhetoric" in the Second Polish Republic, proving that it was accepted even by those state representatives who purportedly rejected the imperialist discourse of the partition powers and national democrats' discriminatory politics. Ciancia, Jakelski, and Litwinowicz also make evident an interdependence of different hierarchies, in that they demonstrate the coexistence of the images of rurality, backwardness, otherness, and the East. Finally, Zubrzycki's account of the attempts to redefine and pluralize Polishness through an inclusion of "the Others"—represented by Jews—reveals how the success of this inclusive attempt is contingent on Jews *remaining Others*.

On the other hand, however, we do not aim to use reflections on hierarchies and normative expectations, which are intrinsic to any national project, to depict "totalizing" power and helpless individuals. That good scholarship ought to examine tensions between people's agency and structural forces is by now a given. We attempt to address it precisely by highlighting the validity of identity as an emic category—one that individuals and collectivities mobilize for different purposes. Sometimes this usage is more akin to the "strategic essentialism" discussed by Gayatri Spivak,[20] sometimes it simply appears to be an interpretative scheme through which social actors engage the immediate world; in one way or another, the relevance of identity as an emic category is precisely proof of identity's plural composition. The question of mobilizing particular identities, or its aspects, appears extremely important for a discussion on gender vis-à-vis national/ethnic identity. Grabowska demonstrates the ways in which female activists, by endorsing particular ideas of gender, fought against

---

20   Spivak, *Subaltern Studies*.

a narrow definition of not only "feminism" but also "Polishness." In his analysis of female film protagonists, van Hueckelom illustrates attempts at recasting the "traditional" image of Polish women as models of resistance and contestation. Illakowicz, instead, in her treatment of gender models imported from the United States, shows how certain ideas of modernity were rendered compatible with more traditional conceptualizations of gender-cum-national identity.

There is yet another way in which this volume contributes to a plural understanding of Polish identity. While taking into account the output of different disciplines—history, anthropology, sociology, literature, cultural studies, musicology—our edited collection does not limit itself to offering an overview of the state of the art in these different fields, but it puts them into dialogue. This dialogue is further enriched by the fact that the authors not only represent different disciplines but also come from different countries and academic settings. Although often taken for granted in the era of—supposedly overwhelming—transnationalism and interconnectedness, joint ventures as the one reflected in the volume remain scarce. Our "transnational encounter" is a venture of immense value yet also a very challenging one due to the fact that the scholarship we produce cannot but bear marks of the authors' personal experiences, the genres of writing that dominate in their country/discipline, and, last but not least, questions of one's background and language. This challenge is well summarized in the concluding essay by Ryszard Koziołek, who uses the case study of a famous 1979 exhibition "Poles' Self-portrait" to reflect on a possibility of "taking a critical position" toward one's identity. Focusing on the final part of the display, a mirror in which each visitor could see his or her face, the author contends that even a critic cannot avoid the questions that standing in front of a mirror provokes, due to the inescapability of one's own language.

The Mainstream and the Marginal

Increased awareness of plurality is related to yet another aspect of scholarly production, namely attempts to uncover experiences and narratives of those people who had been excluded from mainstream national narratives. The memory studies boom characteristic of the 1990s, growing interest in oral histories, rediscovery and restudy of peasants' and workers' diaries, letters, and the above-mentioned studies of national processes "at the margins" have all contributed to this shift.[21] Although attention to the "margins" rather than to the centers and a

---

21   Some recent works exemplifying new sources and novel methodologies: Jaroszyńska-Kirchmann, *Letters from Readers in Polish American Press*,

grassroots perspective have always been defining features of some disciplines—such as anthropology—what is relatively new are the ways in which such stories are set in relation to mainstream ones. Anthropological contributions are an important reference because anthropologists have long warned against idealizing the voices of the "subordinated" and their perception as more "authentic" or "real" ones.[22]

The contributors to this volume also offer a critical view. While entering into conversation with those scholarly approaches that reach for vocabulary and tools developed within the fields of "postcolonial" and "race" studies, they also call for cautiousness and attention to historical and disciplinary specificities. Rather than reproducing the idea of the Polish state as a colonial one, Ciancia proposes a set of original concepts that permit us to better understand the Polish case of a "post-imperial" state *and* open it for comparisons. The question of proper conceptualization returns also in the essay by Bukowiec, who reminds us of the risk of presentism if we try to fit historical cases into present-day schemes of thought and analysis, leading not only to wrong answers but also to wrong questions. Koziołek's point of departure is a rejection of psychoanalytical analyses offered in widely cited works by Jan Sowa and Andrzej Leder,[23] whom he accuses of examining their own theoretical models instead of real objects. He relates these analytical flaws to the scholars' unawareness of their own (ideological) positions. Galbraith, who discusses Poles' conceptualizations of Europeanness and Polishness, focuses instead on the relevance of research participants' concepts. Thanks to her attentiveness to and a detailed explanation of the notions used by her interlocutors, she unveils different layers of the "taken-for-grantedness" that characterize people's considerations of Polish-European connections.

Additionally, the gathered contributions demonstrate the carefulness required in interweaving grassroots narratives with broader ones. Stauter-Halsted's case study perfectly exemplifies that understanding the micro domain of peasants' making of "transnational Polishness" is possible only if

---

1902–1969; Kubica, *Śląskość i protestantyzm. Antropologiczne studia o Śląsku Cieszyńskim*; Linkiewicz, Olga. *Lokalność i nacjonalizm. Społeczności wiejskie w Galicji Wschodniej w dwudziestoleciu międzywojennym*. Universitas. Lebow, "Autobiography as Complaint: Polish Social Memoir Between the Two World Wars," 13–26; Filipkowski, "Historia mówiona jako historia faktyczna; Filipkowski, "Historia mówiona jako hermeneutyka losu. Doświadczenie Przedtekstowe."

22 Ortner, "Resistance and the Problem of Ethnographic Refusal."
23 He refers here to two works in historical sociology, which drew on psychoanalysis and postcolonial theory and had a huge impact on the discussions in Poland.

we take into consideration a macro picture of migration patterns. Galbraith interweaves the analysis of in-depth interviews with a broader set of data in order to explore the complexities of Polish citizens' approaches to Europe. In Grabowska's essay, the relevance of the pre-1989 Polish activists' emancipatory projects comes into full light thanks to her original diachronic and synchronic comparative analysis. Czapliński situates the ideology of Sarmatism in a broad context, showing how its different variations enter into dialogue with popular culture and late modernity. In a similar vein, Illakowicz analyzes US socioeconomic and cultural developments and their impact on Polish society at large and the multiplicity of voices contributing to the process of mythologizing and demythologizing "America."

As this short summary demonstrates, our analyses draw on a variety of sources: from interviews and archived documents through literary works and film to exhibitions and festivals, which afford multiple stories and images. But to contribute to a discussion of the methodologies and analytical approaches which became important, if not dominant, in examinations of collective identities means also acknowledging these approaches' limitations. It has been widely recognized that—let us repeat it once again—we need to include previously excluded voices, unveil ideological biases, and, more generally, recognize and acknowledge diversity. Paweł Rodak discusses such various "attempts at inclusion" in the volume's afterword. But can we be satisfied with simply concluding that "Polishness can be understood in multiple ways"? Put differently: how do we prevent the "multiplicity" of voices from transforming into a "cacophony" that would make our examinations worthless? Even if we are reluctant to say that "Polishness" is X or Y, and we prefer to state instead that "Polishness" may mean X but may also mean Y, we still operate in the domain of historically determined symbols, cultural idioms, linguistic tropes that have become key points of reference for generations, "determining the situation called Polishness."[24] Rather than restating the observation on multiple understandings, a more important task seems to be examining the perseverance, relevance, and strength of those specific aspects of identity not *despite of* but *due to* the multiplicity of the actors involved.

---

24 We are referring here to the article by Mieczysław Porębski ("Polskość jako sytuacja", ZNAK, nr 690, 2012) in which he suggests: "Sytuację, zwaną polskością, warunkuje—tak bym to przynajmniej widział—istnienie po części zwartej, po części żyjącej w diasporze wspólnoty duchowej, która skupia się wokół pewnych historycznie uwarunkowanych symboli, z symbolami tymi identyfikuje swe trwanie, trwania tego ciągłość i godność."

Therefore, in this volume we strive to highlight those narratives and practices that shed light on Polishness as an emic category—understood both as strategy and framework of experiences—yet also keep an analytical focus on identity. The volume's organization is meant to reflect this attempt. The first part, entitled "Redefining Polishness," tackles the issue of who, what, when and on what grounds "has counted" as Polish and how those understandings relate to the problem of class background, social status, religious belonging, and role performed in the society. In so doing, the essays reflect on the breadth of Polishness: its potential to be inclusive and open to diversity and changes, whether diversity is manifested in a dialect, regional specificity, or creation of new traditions. In the second part, "Identity in the Making," we continue this discussion on another level, exploring Polishness betwixt and between various contexts, emphasizing a need to perceive changing constructs of Polishness through an interplay of Polish "abroad" and "at home." The notion of *interplay* I am using here is to suggest the importance of multidirectional transfers of ideas as well as the ongoing nature of this process. The last part, entitled "Portraits and Performances," likewise engages with the ideas of "foreign"/"domestic" and the tension between universal/idiosyncratic marking any identity project. In exploring the ways in which particular models of Polish "identity" and "culture" have been crafted, represented, and performed, the essays ask whether (and how and at what cost) it is possible to "escape" an identity and a culture. What these essays show is that the ways national/ethnic/cultural identities are employed enable processes of political contestation, cultural change, and socioeconomic transformation—and open vistas into a study of larger processes.

Poland, of Poland, for Poland—and Beyond?

This introduction opened with a quote from *Coming of Spring*, in which Stefan Żeromski derides Poles' tendency to connect everything with Poland. His novel is often described as a critical commentary on the shape of the newly independent state and the main protagonist's discovery of his (national) identity (cf. discussion on Żeromski in Illakowicz's chapter). But is this book indeed about Polishness and Poland's trajectory? Or would it be fairer to say that it describes this *and* much more: a battle for a more equal society, the fate of revolutions, the clash between old and new social structures, and finally—the aspirations and dreams of a young man (an individual)? We would certainly like this volume to foster precisely these kinds of reflections: linking the specific with the general and enabling a recognition of the general through a careful examination of the particular.

Speaking on a similar matter, anthropologist Michael Jackson has recently criticized contemporary discussions of identity by observing that in these debates "difference" takes precedence over "sameness." Referring specifically to anthropology, he noted that when <anthropos> becomes less relevant than <ethnos>, when the discipline practitioners delight in drawing distinctions and downplaying similarities, they lose the ability to understand the human condition (while the term "human condition" becomes discarded as a peculiar product of Western modernity).[25] The examples Jackson provides in offering an alternative approach are personal stories of refugees and migrants—the people who embody, in his view, something universally human: experimentation, improvisation, strategic negotiating of one's place, and moving between structural constrains and personal imperatives. I conclude with this reference not (only) to counter the opening account on the current wave of exclusionary policies (so often driven by anti-immigrant sentiments) but to invite readers to read the contributions with these reflections in mind. Czapliński's "postmodern Sarmatian" calling for a moral revolution, Zubrzycki's "philo-Semits" acting against the odds, Grudzińska-Gross's "suspects" struggling to prove their right to belong, Ciancia's "others" striving to fit in, Stauter-Halsted's "unappreciated modernizers," Grabowska's "forgotten *emancypantki*": all of these characters may well inhabit other locales and other times. Their stories and other compelling analyses gathered in our volume will, we hope, become a lens through which to investigate other contexts and a source of reflection on identities as encompassing both sameness and difference.

Bibliography

Augustyniak, Urszula. "Wielokulturowość Wielkiego Księstwa Litewskiego i idea tolerancji, a praktyka stosunków miedzywyznaniowych w XVI–XVIII w." In *Lietuvos Didžiosios Kunigaikštijos tradicija ir tautiniai naratyvai*, edited by A. Bumblauskas and G. Potašenko. Vilnius: Vilniaus universiteto leidykla, 2009.
Bjork, Jim. "Bulwark or patchwork?: religious exceptionalism and regional diversity in postwar Poland." In *Christianity and modernity in Eastern Europe*, edited by B. R. Berglund and B. Porter-Szűcs, 129–58. Budapest: Central European University Press, 2010.

---

25 Jackson, "Existential Mobility."

Brubaker, Rogers, and Frederick Cooper. "Beyond "Identity," *Theory and Society* 29, no. 1 (2000): 1–47.

Buchowski, Michał. *Czyściec. Antropologia postsocjalistycznego neoliberalizmu.* Poznań: Wydawnictwo UAM, 2018.

Chu, Winson. *The German Minority in Poland.* Cambridge: Cambridge University Press, 2012.

Engelking, Anna. "<Poleszczuk> nieoswojony. Wokół funkcji chłopskości w konstruowaniu polskości," *Teksty drugie,* 6 (2017): 68–94.

Filipkowski, Piotr. "Historia mówiona jako historia faktyczna. Albo jak „odantropologizować" opowieści o przeszłości?" *Rocznik Antropologii Historii,* 2 (2016).

Filipkowski, Piotr. "Historia mówiona jako hermeneutyka losu. Doświadczenie Przedtekstowe," *Teksty Drugie,* 1 (2018): 40–60.

Green, Nancy. *Limits of Transnationalism,* Chicago: Chicago University Press, 2019.

Holland, D. and J. Lave, eds. *History in Person: Enduring Struggles, Contentious Practice, Intimate Identities.* Albuquerque: School of American Research Press, 2001.

Kleinmann Yvonne, Heyde Jürgen, Hüchtker Dietlind, Kałwa Dobrochna, Joanna Nalewajko-Kulikov, Steffen Katrin, and Tomasz Wiślicz, eds. *Imaginations and Configurations of Polish Society: From the Middle Ages through the Twentieth Century.* Göttingen: Wallstein, 2017.

Kłoskowska, Antonina, ed. *Oblicza polskości.* Warsaw: Wydawnictwo Uniwersytetu Warszawskiego, 1990.

Krzywiec, Grzegorz. "Polska bez Żydów. Polska bez Żydów Studia z dziejów idei, wyobrażeń i praktyk antysemickich na ziemiach polskich początku XX wieku. Wydawnictwo IH PAN, 2017.

Kubica, Grażyna. *Śląskość i protestantyzm. Antropologiczne studia o Śląsku Cieszyńskim.* Kraków: Wydawnictwo Uniwersytetu Jagiellońskiego, 2011.

Lebow, Kate. "Autobiography as Complaint: Polish Social Memoir Between the Two World Wars." *Laboratorium: Russian Review of Social Research* 6, no. 3 (2014): 13–26.

Leder, Andrzej. *Prześniona rewolucja. Ćwiczenia z logiki historycznej.* Warsaw: Wydawnictwo Krytyki Politycznej, 2014.

Letters from Readers in Polish American Press, 1902–1969: A Corner for Everybody, edited by Anna D. Jaroszyńska-Kirchmann, translated by Theodore L. Zawistowski. Lanham, MD: Lexington Books, 2014.

Linkiewicz, Olga. *Lokalność i nacjonalizm. Społeczności wiejskie w Galicji Wschodniej w dwudziestoleciu międzywojennym.* Kraków: Universitas, 2018.

Meijl, Toon van. "Multiple identifications and dialogical self: Maori youngsters and the cultural renessaince," *Journal of Royal Anthropological Institute* 12, no. 4 (2006): 917–33.

Mędrzecki, Włodzimierz. *Kresowy kalejdoskop. Wędrówki przez Ziemie Wschodnie Drugiej Rzeczypospolitej 1918–1939.* Kraków: Wydawnictwo Literackie, 2018.

Ortner, Sherry. "Resistance and the Problem of Ethnographic Refusal." *Comparative Studies in Society and History* 37, no. 1 (1995): 173-93.
Pasieka, Agnieszka. "Neighbors: About the Multiculturalization of the Polish Past." *East European Societies and Politics* 28, no. 1 (2014): 225-51.
Porębski, Mieczysław. "Polskość jako sytuacja." ZNAK, nr 690, 2012. https://www.miesiecznik.znak.com.pl/porebski-polskosc-jako-sytuacja/. Accessed July 24, 2022.
Pobłocki, Kacper. "How Poles Become White." In *Halka/Haiti 18°48'05"N 72°23'01"*, edited by C.T. Jasper and J. Malinowska, 107-19, Warsaw: Inventory Press, 2015.
Pobłocki, Kacper. *Chamstwo*, Wołowiec: Wydawnictwo Czarne, 2021.
Porter-Szűcs, Brian. "The Catholic Nation: Religion, Identity, and the Narratives of Polish History," *The Slavic and East European Journal* 45, no. 2 (2001): 289-99.
Porter-Szűcs, Brian. *Całkiem zwyczajny kraj. Historia Polski bez martyrologii*. Translated by Anna Dzierzgowska and Jan Dzierzgowski. Warsaw: Filtry, 2021.
Sökefeld, Martin. "Reconsidering Identity." *Anthropos* 96, no. 2 (2001): 527-44.
Sowa, Jan. *Fantomowe ciało króla. Peryferyjne zmagania z nowoczesną formą*, Kraków: Universitas, 2011
Spivak, Gayatri C. *Subaltern Studies. Deconstructing Historiography*. London: Routledge, 1988
Zubrzycki, Geneviève. *The Crosses of Auschwitz. Nationalism and Religion in Postcommunist Poland*. Chicago; Chicago University Press, 2007.
Żeromski, Stefan. *The Coming of Spring*. Budapest: Central European University Press, 2007.

Part One
Redefining Polishness

Chapter One

The Birth of the "Polak-Katolik"

Brian Porter-Szűcs

The title of this essay refers not to the historical, sociological, anthropological, or demographic questions surrounding how Poles became Catholics. The links between these two categories have ebbed and flowed over the years, so we should not conceive of a linear story according to which a Catholic Polishness was formed and then maintained.[1] Instead, we should recognize that the relationship between religious faith (or devotional practice) and ethno-national identification is in constant flux. Moreover, the *meaning* of Catholicism within Polish nationalism (or vice versa) has always been contested, so generalizations are risky. Separate from that complicated problem, however, is a somewhat simpler but nonetheless important question: when did the *rhetorical* practice of linking Polishness and Catholicism emerge, and what did that linkage signify? Although Polish Catholics and Catholic Poles have been around for a very long time, the hyphenated "*Polak-katolik*" was only born at the very end of the nineteenth century. An inquiry into the origins of this phrase will help us think more systematically about the place of religion in various ideologies of identity in Poland and about the multiple ways in which Catholicism and Polishness can overlap.

The phrase "*Polak-katolik*" does not easily translate into English. The hyphen links two masculine singular nouns, thereby differing from alternatives like *polski katolik* (Polish Catholic), "*katolicki Polak*" (Catholic Pole), or

---

[1] See Porter-Szűcs, "Marking the Boundaries of the Faith." For a more thorough presentation, see Porter-Szűcs, *Faith and Fatherland*.

"*polskokatolicki*" (Polish-Catholic, as an adverb-adjective hybrid).[2] The noun-noun construction is relatively uncommon in Polish; for example, it would be unusual to write about a hyphenated "*Niemiec-protestant*" (German-Protestant) or "*Syryjczyk-muzułmanin*" (Syrian-Muslim). By contrast, *Polak-katolik* is a common expression, particularly in debates about the meaning and content of Polish national identity. It can be used today both to identify oneself with pride (on the right), and to mock people for "backward" or "provincial" views (on the left). Either way, it implies an inseparable bond between these two communities of belonging, most commonly posited as an ideal (be it utopian or dystopian) rather than as a description.

In the nineteenth century, we can find many uses of the paired nouns "*Polak*" and "*katolik*," but without the hyphen. In these earlier texts the phrase was employed to clarify that an author was writing about a particular kind of Pole who just happened to be Catholic, and the ideological valance that "*Polak-katolik*" would gain in the twentieth century was absent. For example, a contributor to a Catholic magazine from Poznań, *Obrona Prawdy*, wrote in 1845 (regarding a particular point of doctrine) that "this problem cannot be answered by a *Polak protestant* . . . it can only be solved by a *Polak katolik* who, alongside a living faith in the basic dogma of Christ's Church, believes that outside that Church there is no salvation."[3] Similarly, Eustachy Iwanowski wrote in his 1876 memoirs about his Siberian exile that among the Poles in his particular district, one was a "*Polak katolik*." Here the descriptor was used to distinguish

---

2   The capitalization rules in Polish differ from English, often leading to confusion. Nouns referring to national groups are capitalized, but nouns referring to religions are usually not. *Polak-katolik* is sometimes (but not always) an exception in this regard. Adjectives and adverbs are not capitalized when referring to either nationalities or religions. In older texts the capitalization is irregular, and I will maintain the original orthography throughout this article. The term "polskokatolicki" has a very specific usage, as the name for the Polish Catholic Church, a group of Catholic immigrants to the United States who broke from the Roman Catholic Church at the end of the nineteenth century, mostly because of arguments about administration and authority with the (Irish-dominated) US Catholic hierarchy. In 1919, some people returning to Poland brought this denomination back with them. The Church has about twenty-six thousand members today, and is affiliated with the so-called Old Catholics of the Union of Utrecht. See Elerowski, *Zarys historii Kościoła Narodowego Polskokatolickiego*; Küry and Wysoczański, *Kościół starokatolicki*.

3   *Obrona Prawda* 1 (January 1845): 26.

one specific individual from other Polish residents of that region.⁴ Another nineteenth-century memoirist recounted the story of a Polish soldier exiled to Ekaterinburg who managed to attain great respect within a community of Orthodox Old Believers, despite being a *"Polak katolik."*⁵ In 1869, an author described Russian misrule in Lithuania, complaining that the only way to pursue a career in the state service was to *either* convert to Orthodoxy *or* "become a traitor or persecutor of one's own nation." Given that situation, he wrote, "What can a *Polak katolik* expect?"⁶ In all these cases, the two nouns were paired in order to distinguish a Catholic Pole from other sorts of Poles, or to emphasize the particularly difficult fate confronted by those who exemplified both of these identities.

A noteworthy use of the unhyphenated phrase *Polak katolik* comes from a booklet distributed in Germany during WWI. This richly illustrated text featured a group of stereotypical Poles praying to the Virgin Mary and included several quotations aimed at inspiring Polish loyalty to the German state. Kaiser Wilhelm was quoted as saying, "Let every *Polak katolik* know that his religion will always be honored in my realm, and that no one will hinder him in his religious practice." Pope Leo XIII appeared on the Virgin's left, affirming that Germany's Catholic subjects "will always be faithful subjects of the German Emperor and the Prussian King." Finally, toward the bottom of the poster was an injunction from Archbishop Edward Likowski of Poznań/Gniezno for Poles to join the "holy struggle against the schismatic *Moskcle*."⁷ In other words, this document stressed the linkage between Catholicism and Polishness in order to remind Poles of the well-established Church principle mandating that *as Catholics* they should be loyal to their legitimate ruler and fight the enemies of the Church and the empire. Leo XIII's words were taken out of context here, but the basic message had been consistently preached throughout the nineteenth century by the Catholic hierarchy, both in Rome and in northeastern Europe, so equating Polishness and Catholicism could serve the cause of loyalism just as well as it could be used to spark national insurgencies.

---

4   Iwanowski, *Wspomnienia*, 2:251.
5   Piotrowski, *Pamiętnik z pobytu na Syberyi*, 2:335.
6   Czaplick, *Moskiewskie na Litwie rządy*, 204.
7   Anonymous, *Zmartwychwstanie Polski* (1914). Leo XIII had died in 1903, but he was both more beloved (and more pro-German) than Pius X. The phrase "Moskal" was a derogatory label for Russians, and "schismatics" was a derogatory label for Eastern Orthodox.

Figure 1.1. *Zmartwychwstanie Polski* (anonymous pamphlet, Germany, 1914). Biblioteka Kórnicka Polskiej Akademii Nauk.

Such appeals were potent because the hierarchy of the Roman Catholic Church (with a few exceptions) did indeed oppose the Polish national movement in the nineteenth century, just as it opposed the Italian national movement. This goes all the way back to Gregory XVI's encyclical *Cum Primum* from 1832, which stated, "We are taught most clearly that the obedience which men are obliged to render to the authorities established by God is an absolute precept which no one can violate."[8] It was awkward for nineteenth-century national activists to emphasize religiosity in their appeals because in all three partitions Catholic grievances and national grievances only partially—and inconsistently—overlapped. In Germany, the Kulturkampf linked Polish and German Catholics in a common cause, and in Galicia, Catholicism tied the Poles to the Habsburgs. The convergence between national separatism and religious identity was a bit clearer in the Russian Empire, where the Catholics were either Polish, Lithuanian, or (Eastern-Rite) Ukrainian. But the Church hierarchy in the Russian partition adhered to the Ultramontane hostility toward revolutionary nationalism, and insofar as leading members of the clergy expressed a Polish identity, it was emphatically depoliticized.[9] In most cases, resistance to imperial rule as a Catholic lined up only imperfectly and sporadically with resistance to imperial rule as a Pole.

That left the Polish-Catholic equation (insofar as it was expressed at all prior to the twentieth century) to develop somewhat independently from the politicized rhetoric of the Polish national movement. There were plenty of references to Polish Catholics and Catholic Poles; in fact, the phrase "Polish therefore Catholic" (*Polak więc katolik*) was often described as an "axiom" or a "stubborn assertion."[10] But these were merely affirmations of a demographic assumption, typically evoked only so as to be debunked. For example, the journalist Maurycy Mann wrote in 1849, "I do not at all accept the axiom, assumed around nearly the whole world: Polish therefore Catholic. I perceive no differences in terms of religious denomination when it comes to patriotism, and in my opinion a *Polak niekatolik* can be, as they say, a truly excellent Pole, just as much as a *Polak katolik* can be."[11]

This passage hints at debates that arose occasionally among Poles in the nineteenth century (most fatefully with the positivists, starting in the 1870s) but only in the twentieth century would these issues truly rise to prominence

---

8   Gregory XVI, *Cum Primum*, June 9, 1832.
9   Porter-Szűcs, "Thy Kingdom Come."
10 For example see "Charitas o emigracyi polskiej," 299.
11 Mann, *Liga i doświadczenie*, 24.

in the broader public realm.[12] It was then that that hyphen was added, implying that the *Polak-katolik* had to be named precisely because of the conviction that the notion *ought* to be hegemonic but was not. The hyphenated *Polak-katolik* implied that a Catholic was the only proper Pole, that the opposite of the *Polak-katolik* was the foreigner, not another kind of Pole.

The earliest usage of the hyphenated phrase *Polak-katolik* that I have found comes from this 1893 speech by Stanisław Tarnowski:

> What is the condition of Catholic sentiment and conviction in our nation? What is the level of its strength and fortitude? Every thoughtful *Polak-katolik* who is concerned about the value of his nation, who cares about its future, considers and explores these questions, seeks answers to them. Only He who sees into the mysteries of the heart—God—knows how we are in this regard.[13]

The phrase spread in popularity very gradually over the coming years, receiving a boost in 1905 when it was adopted as the title of a short-lived magazine from Lublin, as well as the printing house that produced it. The Polak-katolik firm was quite active, releasing a steady supply of devotional books, catechisms, and saints' lives.[14] A few years later, the Archdiocese of Warsaw sponsored the creation of the Polak-katolik Press [*Tłocznia Polaka-Katolika*], which released a similar array of religious books, along with the daily newspaper *Polska* and one of the most important Catholic magazines of the early twentieth century, *Przegląd Katolicki*.[15]

After the First World War the political and polemical edge of the phrase *Polak-katolik* sharpened. During the debates surrounding the creation of the first Polish constitution in 1921, the Christian Democratic Party introduced an amendment stating that only a *Polak-katolik* could be eligible for the presidency.[16] That proposal didn't pass, though the issue (and the phrase) was part of the heated debates surrounding the election and subsequent assassination

---

12 On some of the earliest arguments about the role of religion in Polish society, see Jaszczuk, *Spór pozytywistów z konserwatystami o przyszłość Polski*.

13 Tarnowski, "Niebezpieczeństwa grożące Kościołowi w naszym kraju," 2:25.

14 For example, *Pierwsze początki katechizmu*; Woroniecki, *Historja katolickiej akcji społecznej w XIX wieku*; *Żywot błogosławionej Bronisławy Norbertanki*; *Żywot św. Stanisława biskupa Męczennika*; *Żywot św. Wojciecha biskupa Męczennika*.

15 Among their books were Bełza, *Katechizm polskiego dziecka*; Hołowiński, *Życie mojej matki*.

16 An interesting discussion of this proposal can be found in the Protokół narad Komitetu Biskupów z dniu 4 i 5 marca 1921 roku, Archiwum Archidiecezji Warszawskiej, Sygn. 2642 / A II 1.1.

of President Gabriel Narutowicz. Politicians of the nationalist right, along with most members of the clergy, were bitterly opposed to Narutowicz because the electoral coalition that put him in office included a wide diversity of parties from the center-right to the center-left, including the so-called Minorities Bloc that represented Jews, Germans, Belarusians, and Ukrainians. Nationalists insisted that the president should be chosen by the majority of Poles (which they understood in the narrowest ethno-linguistic sense), not merely the majority of Polish citizens.[17] During all the election campaigns of the 1920s there were frequent appeals to the *Polak-katolik* voter, and advocates of a more inclusive vision of Polish multiculturalism often argued against the implications of the phrase.[18] As the interwar years progressed the phrase became increasingly common. In the novel *Kłamca* [The liar] by Jerzy Kossowski, a character identifies himself as Catholic and is asked in return, "Więc *Polak* [So, a Pole]?" He responds, "No tak, *Polak-katolik* [Of course, yes, a Pole-Catholic]."[19]

The hyphen in this expression did a lot of work, and it is no coincidence that it began to link the nouns *Polak* and *katolik* around a century ago. The aforementioned speech by Tarnowski helps us see precisely what this new expression signified. The basic message of that 1893 speech was that a Pole who truly cared about his nation should also care about the fate of the Church, which Tarnowski thought was threatened by the failure of Poles to take their religious duties seriously enough. In Galicia, he believed, Catholicism was weak precisely because the Poles were *not* good Catholics.[20] In other words, the *Polak-katolik* was not a descriptive term but a prescriptive one: it was not something that existed but something Tarnowski wanted to cultivate. This implication has remained true to this day: the phrase *Polak-katolik* does not signify a sociological or anthropological reality but a project. Embedded in the term is a perceived problem, and its very use marks an uncertainty, a point of discomfort, an undesirable ambiguity. There would be no need for the expression if the fusion between Polishness and Catholicism was truly obvious and universal. In other words, the precise form of the expression *Polak-katolik* emerged during a moment when Polish

---

17 These debates are covered in depth by Brykczynski, *Primed for Violence*.
18 See for example, Czarnowski, *Polacy prawosławni*; Hulka-Laskowski, *Czem Ewangelicyzm dla Polski jest*.
19 Kossowski, *Kłamca*, 110.
20 In fact, Catholicism was quite strong in Galicia by almost any standard. Religious rituals accompanied most state functions, mass attendance was very high, and the clergy enjoyed a great deal of prestige. Tarnowski's concerns seem to have been based on the conviction that all this apparent devotion was superficial.

Catholics perceived a necessary link between their faith and their nation, *and* felt that this connection was frayed.

To clarify what was happening with this term, it helps to pull back even further, all the way to the sixteenth century. Poles are justly proud of a text from the Warsaw Confederation of 1573. During an interregnum that year there was a serious danger of political instability or even violence, particularly given the backdrop of the Protestant Reformation. With this in mind, the delegates to the electoral *sejm* (an assembly of the nobility) began their discussions of succession by issuing the following pledge:

> We promise each other pro nobis et successoribus nostris in perpetuum sub vinculo iuramenti, fide, honore et conscientiis nostris, that although we are dissidentes de religione, we will preserve peace among ourselves and not shed blood because of differences in faith or variety of church.[21]

A version of this oath was repeated by future electoral *sejms*, but not without some important modifications. In 1632 the text was altered to read "that we who are divided by faith will keep peace among ourselves, and not shed blood on account of difference in our *Christian* faith or church." Sixteen years later it was changed yet again, this time stating that "in matters concerning Christian religion, peace should be among the dissidents in the Christian religion, which we pledge to maintain ... provided that the rights of the Roman Catholic Church were not violated in this peace and security of the dissidents in Christian religion." Finally, in 1733, the pledge almost completely inverted the original intent:

> Because the foundation and longevity of all states are grounded in the true God and Holy religion, so through our confederation of this year we prohibit anyone from restricting the rights and privileges of the true Roman Catholic and Greco-Uniate churches. And indeed, since in this faithful country we detest strange cults, we pledge and oblige ourselves to stand by the Holy Roman Catholic Church and defend its freedoms.[22]

---

21 The text of the Warsaw Confederation can be found at http://www.literatura.hg.pl/varsconf.htm (accessed May 27, 2016). The blend of Latin and Polish marked the entire document and was typical of Polish rhetoric from that time. On the background to the Warsaw Confederation, see Salmonowicz, "Geneza i treść uchwał konfederacji warszawskiej."

22 Teter, *Jews and Heretics in Catholic Poland*, 46–48.

All of these successive revisions set the stage for the formulation of article one of the Polish Constitution of May 3, 1791, which affirmed that "the ruling national religion is and will be the Holy Roman Catholic faith, with all its laws."[23]

So we can observe a gradual but steady shift between the sixteenth and eighteenth centuries, from a strong proclamation that Poles can be of different faiths to the establishment of Catholicism as an official state religion and a condemnation of "strange cults." It is impossible to extrapolate from legal texts like these to matters of personal identity, but we can say that *rhetorically* it was possible to include non-Catholics in the community of enfranchised nobles of the Polish-Lithuanian Republic during the early decades of the Reformation, but much more difficult to do so on the eve of that state's destruction. This is not quite the same thing as proclaiming a multicultural and inclusive *Polish* identity, but rather an inclusive membership in the elite of the First Republic. Nonetheless, it seems clear that there was a relationship between a sort of national-political identity and religion. In the sixteenth century, this was expressed in the form of a negation: a recognition that others in Europe merged religion and citizenship, but that the signatories of the Warsaw Confederation would be more inclusive. In the eighteenth century, the linkage was articulated as a positive affirmation that in Poland too these two categories were merged.[24]

This progression of texts makes it clear that the linkage of Polishness and Catholicism long predated the emergence of the phrase *Polak-katolik*. Moreover, after the destruction of the First Republic in 1795, the movement to restore the country's independence frequently utilized religious iconography. Even that ultimate expression of Polish inclusiveness, the famous 1830 battle flag reading FOR OUR FREEDOM AND YOURS, was prefaced by the invocation IN THE NAME OF GOD and adorned with a cross. Nonetheless, mid-nineteenth-century texts tended to reflect not a continuity with prepartition ideas about the religious

---

23 On the background to this article, see Butterwick. *The Polish Revolution and the Catholic Church*. The text of the 1791 constitution is available at http://www.polishconstitution.org/Konstytucja-PL.html (accessed May 27, 2016).

24 The context for this shift is multifaceted, and a full explanation would go beyond both the space limitations of this chapter and the expertise of this author. Suffice it to say that the supporters of the counter-reformation gained power in the seventeenth century, particularly during the reign of King Jan Kazimierz (1648–1660). The protracted wars of that era set the Polish-Lithuanian Republic against Protestant Sweden and Orthodox Russia, thus reinforcing the linkage between Catholicism and Polishness. Finally, the rise of Enlightenment ideas in the eighteenth century was met with an increasingly militant Catholic response, and in that heightened polemical atmosphere expressions of religious tolerance (or "indifference," as it was increasingly labeled) became more difficult.

identity of the national "we," but an evocation of a broader community that harkened back to the sixteenth-century attitudes expressed by the Confederation of Warsaw. Later, the emergence of the phrase *Polak-katolik* in the twentieth century marked the pendulum's swing back toward a more religiously homogenous vision of the nation, one which set up new barriers to outsiders and demanded conformity among insiders.[25] The hyphenated expression denoted a moment of transition and rhetorical contestation, when multiple ideas about who was a Pole vied for supremacy in a dynamically expanding modern public sphere. In that environment, the hyphen asserted a bond that others were repudiating; it was a polemical boundary marker between those who wanted the modern Polish nation to be pluralistic and those who did not.

To understand that argument, it is important to distinguish between the various ways in which Pole and Catholic might be equated. I see at least five distinct implied meanings to the assertion that "Poland is Catholic."

1. The most obvious way in which these two ideas can be linked is through the law, by officially proclaiming that Catholicism is the official religion of the Polish state. This was the claim of article one in the 1791 constitution, and even today some Polish politicians (and even more members of the clergy) would like to see this link reestablished. Indeed, with state support of religious education and with crosses or pictures of Pope John Paul II hanging in most government offices, many would argue that the state does, in fact, have an official religion (particularly since the elections of 2015). As we have seen, one of the earliest deployments of the *Polak-katolik* idea was in a demand to make only Catholics eligible for election to the Polish presidency.
2. On another register, the relationship between Polishness and Catholicism could be a mere demographic observation. In statistical terms, the dominance of Catholicism is hard to overstate: 99 percent of all children in Poland are baptized, 92.8 percent of all marriages are accompanied by a church wedding, and between 90 percent and 98 percent of the population will answer "Roman Catholic" when asked about their religion (depending on how the question is posed).[26] Historically the issue has been more complex. Before the Second World

---

25 See Porter, *When Nationalism Began to Hate*.
26 Bożewicz, "Religijność Polaków w ostatnich 20 latach"; and *Wyznania religijne*. For more on the demography of religion in contemporary Poland, see Borowik and Doktór, *Pluralizm religijny i moralny*; Borowik, *Procesy instytucjonalizacji i prywatyzacji religii*; Ciupak, *Katolicyzm ludowy*; Koseła, *Polak i katolik*; Piotrowski,

War about two-thirds of the population of Poland was Catholic, giving some justification to article 114 of the constitution of 1921, which stated, "The Roman-Catholic denomination, being the religion of the overwhelming majority of the nation, occupies in the State a leading position among the denominations, which all have equal rights."[27] While a reader today might interpret that clause as a thinly veiled way to make Catholicism the implied official religion, it was understood by Church leaders at the time as an unacceptably weak endorsement that reduced Poland's Catholicity to mere demography. Bishop Józef Pelczar captured a common reaction in an open letter to the parliamentary delegates from his diocese, when he complained that "under the name of a 'denomination,' [the Church] was positioned equal to Judaism and the a-Catholic sects. Let's hope a future sejm fixes that mistake."[28] Anticlericalism remained a prominent strain in Polish politics in the interwar years, and there was much debate at the time about integrating (or not) and labeling the third of the population that was *not* Catholic. But for now let us simply recognize that even in the 1920s and 1930s Catholicism was indisputably the "religion of the overwhelming majority" of the population of Poland, regardless of the ideological, sociological, anthropological, or political consequences one might derive from that demographic reality.

3. Related to the population statistics is a historical claim that would seem to be an equally unproblematic empirical statement: the Catholic Church has played an important role in Polish history. This can be stated in the mystical framing of John Paul II, who said in 1979 that "without Christ it is impossible to understand the history of Poland."[29] Or it can be phrased in a more secular fashion, as when Jan Józef Lipski (who can hardly be considered an apologist for Catholicism) wrote, "The formation of our culture was produced by a synthesis with Christianity, adopted from the West in the tenth century, and the percolation of the Renaissance, the Enlightenment, and Romanticism."[30] Whether in the

---

Na przełomie stuleci; Zdaniewicz and Zembrzuski, *Kościół i religijność Polaków*; and Zdaniewicz, *Religijność Polaków*.

27 The text of the constitution can be found at http://isap.sejm.gov.pl/DetailsServlet?id=WDU19210440267 (accessed February 9, 2021).

28 Pelczar, *List otwarty do posłów diecezji przemyskiej*, 3.

29 John Paul II, *Return to Poland*, 28.

30 Lipski, *Dwie ojczyzny, dwa patriotyzmy*, 13. Though Lipski used the word "Christian" rather than "Catholic," it is clear from the context of this passage that he

realm of high politics or popular culture, whether considering matters of international diplomacy or *alltagsgeschichte*, no historian of Poland can afford to ignore Catholicism. Setting aside all the ideological baggage and all the layers of subtext, it is indisputable that the Catholic Church has been important throughout Poland's past.

4. The fourth way to approach the connection between Catholicism and Polishness is to look at the ways in which religion serves as a marker of identity in daily life. This anthropological frame is exemplified by the work of scholars like Agnieszka Pasieka, who has shown how assumptions equating Poles with Catholics are embedded in the quotidian practices of a small multidenominational community in the southeastern part of the country.[31] Significantly, in the context of such scholarship, the *Polak-katolik* is not explicitly evoked but tacitly assumed. In other parts of Poland, or in other historical eras, this might not be the case. For example, in Silesia, Catholicism could never serve as a sufficient marker of Polishness because the local German speakers were also Catholic. The same would have been true in the northeast, where Catholic Polish speakers mixed with Catholic Lithuanian speakers. Similarly, in specific neighborhoods where *everyone* was both Polish and Catholic (ironically, in precisely the spots where the *Polak-katolik* equation really was universal), religion was less likely to serve as a means of differentiating and identifying people. This might seem counterintuitive, but it is difficult to use something that is experienced as universal for delineating and sustaining a community, precisely because of the absence of any visible "other" against whom to distinguish "us." In the modern era this has been complicated by the presence of virtual "others" presented through mass media and political ideologies, though even today the importance of such "imagined communities" in the realm of everyday life cannot be simply assumed. The work of Kate Brown reminds us that even in the twentieth century there were spaces in Eastern Europe where the ideologies of identity were slow to penetrate, and the means of community differentiation were fluid and not always in accordance with the ethno-religious categories that outsiders wanted to impose.[32] More

---

was referring to the Roman Church. Until very recently, the words "Catholic" and "Christian" were used interchangeably in most Polish texts. Although nowadays one encounters references to a "Judeo-Christian" heritage, this phrase is a neologism. Even in the United States, the expression only dates from the post-WWII era.

31 Pasieka, *Hierarchy and Pluralism.*
32 Brown, *A Biography of No Place.*

recently, Tara Zahra, Nathan Wood, and others have explored the idea of "national indifference," drawing our attention to the ways in which ideologies of identity can fade entirely into the background when we move beyond the sphere of politics and look instead at popular culture and everyday social practice.[33] Every Polish historian is familiar with stories from the prepartition era that divided the First Republic into a "naród szlachecki" and a "naród plebejski" (noble nation and plebian nation); in that mapping of the social world either both communities were Catholic or religion was irrelevant.[34] In all these contexts we may nonetheless note an ethnographic overlap between Polishness and Catholicism (according to *our* categories), but without cultural activation such an intersection might have little significance. In other words, the ethnic markers that *we* identify may or may not have been relevant to the historical actors we are studying.

5. The final means of merging Catholicism and Polishness is in the realm of ideology (both formalized and quotidian), and this at last brings us to the slogan of the *Polak-katolik*, with all of its nationalistic baggage. This usage, as I suggested earlier, is not descriptive but prescriptive: it entails a claim that Poland and the Poles *should* be Catholic, even if they are not entirely faithful to the Church at any particular moment. This is a sense captured by a joint pastoral letter of the Polish episcopate from 1955 proclaiming that *all* Poles shared Catholic principles and customs because these came to us

> as if in the blood, becoming the common property of the nation and an essential value that is not subject to any discussion. In this case we are no longer talking about Poles in this or that percentage but of the entire nation, understood morally, for even people who do not fully accept the faith of the Church rarely reject this moral unity with us. Indeed, they usually accept it with genuine pride and sympathy.... The Church and Poland have been so tightly bound through the centuries, their moral and spiritual roots have grown so deeply with each other that they can hardly be separated.[35]

This doubtlessly would sound aggressive and exclusionary to those outside the Church, but ironically it reflected a sense of weakness. We do not find such assertions from the clergy when their authority was simply taken for granted; instead, the *explicit* insistence that Poles must be Catholic rises to the surface

---

33   Wood, *Becoming Metropolitan*; Zahra, *Kidnapped Souls*.
34   This characterization of the social landscape of the First Republic is evoked so frequently that its origins are obscure. See, for example, Łepkowski, *Polska*, 10.
35   "List biskupów polskich o działalności Kościoła," 152.

at times of institutional or cultural insecurity within the Church (and we can certainly understand why Catholics might have felt insecure during the Stalinist era). When it is truly "axiomatic" that "*Polak więc katolik*," there is no need to put forth the ideological figure of the *Polak-katolik*. That powerful hyphen, with its implication of an essential fusion as opposed to a mere demographic pattern, appeared when the unspoken verities of nineteenth-century popular religiosity and clerical authority were weakened by the disruptions of urbanization and industrialization. That was the period when millions of Poles left their home parishes for employment in Warsaw or Łódź, only to find a near total absence of pastoral care in their new neighborhoods. In 1860 there were 1,527 Catholics per priest in the Kingdom of Poland, but a half-century later this figure had increased to 2,857. The statistics were similar in Poznania (increasing from 1,576 to 2,505) and even worse in Galicia (2,837 to 4,362).[36] The decline in the size of the clergy relative to the booming population was a problem for countryside and city alike, but the issues were made acute in the new urban agglomerations because of the Church's failure to adjust to the era's huge population shifts. By the start of WWI, one working-class parish in the Warsaw district of Praga had 82,000 parishioners, and within the boundaries of the Holy Cross parish in Łódź there were 142,000 souls.[37] These distortions were in part due to the reluctance of the Russian authorities to approve new church construction, but oppression does not fully explain this phenomenon because things were just as bad in autonomous Galicia. In fact, the problem existed throughout Europe: at the start of the twentieth century the average Parisian parish had 36,000 members, the average Berlin parish 31,000, and the average Viennese parish 22,500. Warsaw's figure of 34,000 parishioners per parish fits into this pattern (though Łódź's 50,000 to 1 ratio remained an outlier).[38] Moreover, the situation improved only slightly after Poland regained independence, and in some regions of the country it continued to get worse.[39] The ensuing erosion of the more intimate forms of pastoral work once typical of Polish villages only exacerbated the sense among many Catholics that "modernity" (whatever might be subsumed under that amorphous label) constituted a grave spiritual danger. It was at this same time, not coincidentally, when old stereotypes and prejudices

---

[36] On the Kingdom, see Kumor, *Ustrój i organizacja Kościoła polskiego*. These figures encompass the dioceses of Warsaw, Włocławek, Płock, Lublin, Sandomierz, Sejny, Janów, and Kielce. See also Olszewski, "Okres wzrastającego ucisku," 481.

[37] Kłoczowski, *A History of Polish Christianity*, 234; Olszewski, *Polska kultura religijna na*, 481.

[38] For comparative statistics on urban parish sizes, see Olszewski, *Polska kultura religijna*, 65–66.

[39] Stanowski, "Diecezje i parafie polskie," 1635, 1637.

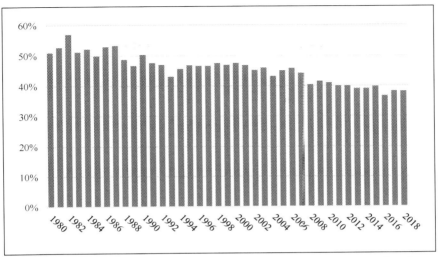

Figure 1.2. Percentage of Polish Catholics who attend mass on an average weekend. Based on data from Annuarium Statisticum Ecclaesiae in Polonia (Instytut Statystyki Kościoła Katolickiego, 2020), 28–29.

against the Jews were transformed into modern anti-Semitic conspiracy theories, and when the Catholic hierarchy's condemnation of the Polish national movement was transformed into a tacit alliance with the Endecja.[40]

If this interpretation is correct, one would expect the term "*Polak-katolik*" to appear with more frequency in times of crisis and danger for the Church and become somewhat less common during times of Catholic hegemony. It is therefore no surprise that expressions of Catholic exclusivity were less insistent during the 1970s and 1980s, when (despite ongoing harassment from the communist state) the Church enjoyed unprecedented cultural respect and institutional power. Conversely, accompanying the steady erosion of the Catholicism's social position in the Third Republic we have seen ever more vocal claims that only the *Polak-katolik* is a genuine Pole. This helps us reconcile the enduring strength (in fact, the renewed strength) of political Catholicism, even in the face of statistics like those in figure 1.2.[41]

---

40 I have written about this shift in several articles: "Anti-Semitism and the Search for a Catholic Modernity," in Blobaum, *Antisemitism and Its Opponents in Modern Poland*; "Making a Space for Anti-Semitism"; and "Marking the Boundaries of the Faith."

41 These figures represent *dominicantes*—those who attend mass on an ordinary Sunday. See *Annuarium Statisticum Ecclaesiae in Polonia*, 28–29.

The paradox of the hyphenated *Polak-katolik*, then, is that it appears most insistently when Catholicism in Poland is weak, not when it is strong. Genuine hegemony renders superfluous the emphasis of orthography.

Bibliography

Annuarium Statisticum Ecclaesiae in Polonia. Instytut Statystyki Kościoła Katolickiego, 2020.

Bełza, Władysław. *Katechizm polskiego dziecka*. Warsaw: *Polak-Katolik*, 1917.

Borowik, Irena, Doktór, Tadeusz. *Pluralizm religijny i moralny w Polsce: Raport z badań*. Kraków: Nomos, 2001.

Borowik, Irena. *Procesy instytucjonalizacji i prywatyzacji religii w powojennej Polsce*. Kraków: Wydawnictwo Uniwersytet Jagielloński, 1997.

Bożewicz, Marta. „Religijność Polaków w ostatnich 20 latach," *Komunikat z Badań CBOS* 63 (2020).

Brown, Kate. *A Biography of No Place: From Ethic Borderlands to Soviet Heartland*. Cambridge, MA: Harvard University Press, 2005.

Brykczynski, Paul *Primed for Violence: Murder, Antisemitism, and Democratic Politics in Interwar Poland*. Madison: University of Wisconsin Press, 2016.

Butterwick, Richard. *The Polish Revolution and the Catholic Church, 1788-1792*. New York: Oxford University Press, 2012.

Catalogue of the Antykwariat 'Rara Avis', *95 Aukcja Antykwaryczna: Książki – Fotografie – Plakaty* (Kraków, 21 Maja 2011).

"Charitas o emigracyi polskiej," *Przegląd Powszechny* 67, 17 (July/August/September 1900).

Ciupak, Edward. *Katolicyzm ludowy w Polsce*. Warsaw: Wiedza Powszechna, 1973.

Czaplicki, Władysław. *Moskiewskie na Litwie rządy, 1863-1869*. Kraków: Jan Siedlicki, 1869.

Czarnowski, Olgierd. *Polacy prawosławni w Polsce*. Self-published, 1930.

Gregory XVI. *Cum Primum* (June 9, 1832). http://www.papalencyclicals.net/Greg16/g16cumpr.htm. Accessed May 27, 2016.

Elerowski, Eugeniusz. *Zarys historii Kościoła Narodowego Polskokatolickiego*. Warsaw: n.p., 1997.

Helenijusz [Eustachy Iwanowski]. *Wspomnienia lat minionych*. Kraków: Księgarnia Katolicka, 1876.

Hołowiński, Ignacy. *Życie mojej matki*. Warszawa: *Polak-Katolik*, 1915.

Hulka-Laskowski, Paweł. *Czem Ewangelicyzm dla Polski jest; czem być powinien*. Warszawa, Koło Studiów Ewangelików 'Filadelfja', 1929.

Jaszczuk, Andrzej. *Spór pozytywistów z konserwatystami o przyszłość Polski, 1870–1903*. Warsaw: PWN, 1986.

John Paul II. *Return to Poland: The Collected Speeches of John Paul II*. New York: Collins, 1979.
Kłoczowski, Jerzy. *A History of Polish Christianity*. Translated by Małgorzata Sady. Cambridge: Cambridge University Press, 2000.
Koseła, Krzysztof. *Polak i katolik: splątana tożsamość*. Warsaw: Instytutu Filozofii i Socjologii PAN, 2003.
Kossowski, Jerzy. *Kłamca*. Warszawa: Gubethner i Wolff, 1923.
Kumor, Bolesław. *Ustrój i organizacja Kościoła polskiego w okresie niewoli narodowej 1772-1918*. Kraków: Polskie Towarzystwo Teologiczne, 1980.
Küry, Urs, Wysoczański, Wiktor. *Kościół starokatolicki: historia, nauka, dążenia*. Warszawa: Chrześcijańska Akademia Teologiczna, 1996.
Łepkowski, Tadeusz. *Polska: narodziny nowoczesnego narodu 1764–1870*. Warsaw: PWN, 1967.
Lipski, Jan Józef. *Dwie ojczyzny, dwa patriotyzmy: Uwagi o megolomanii narodowej i ksenofobii Polaków*. Warszawa: Otwarta Rzeczpospolita, 1992
"List biskupów polskich o działalności Kościoła." (Jasna Góra, 15 IX 1955). In *Listy pasterskie Episkopatu Polski, 1945-1974*. Paris: Éditions du Dialogue, 1975.
Mann, Maurycy. *Liga i doświadczenie*. Poznań: Księgarnia Jana Konstantego Żupańskiego, 1849.
Olszewski, Daniel. "Okres wzrastającego ucisku i głębokich przemian społecznych (1864–1914)." In *Chrześcijaństwo w Polsce: zarys przemian, 966-1979*, edited by Jerzy Kłoczowski. Lublin: Towarzystwo Naukowe Katolickiego Uniwersytetu Lubelskiego.
Olszewski, Daniel. *Polska kultura religijna na przełomie XIX i XX wieku*. Warsaw: PAX, 1996.
Pasieka, Agnieszka. *Hierarchy and Pluralism: Living Religious Difference in Catholic Poland*. London: Palgrave, 2015.
Pelczar, Józef Sebastjan. *List otwarty do posłów diecezji przemyskiej, a pośrednio do wszystkich posłów Sejmu Ustawodawczego* (n.p. 1921).
Pierwsze początki katechizmu dla małych dziatek. Lublin: Polak-Katolik, 1906.
Piotrowski, Mirosław, ed. *Na przełomie stuleci: Naród - Kościół - Państwo w XIX i XX wieku*. Lublin: Klub Inteligencji Katolickiej, 1997.
Piotrowski, Rufin. *Pamiętnik z pobytu na Syberyi*. Poznań: Księgarnia Jana Konstantego Żupańskiego, 1861.
Porter-Szűcs, Brian. "Anti-Semitism and the Search for a Catholic Modernity." In *Antisemitism and Its Opponents in Modern Poland*, edited by Robert Blobaum, 103–123. Ithaca, NY: Cornell University Press, 2005.
Porter-Szűcs, Brian. *Faith and Fatherland: Modernity, Catholicism, and Poland*. Oxford: Oxford University Press, 2011.
Porter-Szűcs, Brian. "Making a Space for Anti-Semitism: The Catholic Hierarchy and the Jews in the early 1900s," *Polin* 16 (2003): 415–29.

Porter-Szűcs, Brian. "Marking the Boundaries of the Faith: Catholic Modernism and the Radical Right in Early Twentieth-Century Poland." In *Studies in Language, Literature and Cultural Mythology in Poland: Investigating "the Other*," edited by Elwira M. Grossman, 261–86. Lewiston-Lampeter, UK: Edwin Mellen Press, 2002.

Porter-Szűcs, Brian. "Thy Kingdom Come: Patriotism and Prophecy in 19th Century Poland." *Catholic Historical Review* 89, no. 2 (2003): 213–38.

Porter-Szűcs, Brian. *When Nationalism Began to Hate: Imagining Modern Politics in 19th century Poland*. New York: Oxford University Press, 2000.

Protokół narad Komitetu Biskupów z dniu 4 i 5 marca 1921 roku, Archiwum Archidiecezji Warszawskiej, Sygn. 2642 / A II 1.1.

Salmonowicz, Stanisław. "Geneza i treść uchwał konfederacji warszawskiej," *Odrodzenie i Reformacja w Polsce* 19 (1974): 7–30.

Stanowski, Adam. "Diecezje i parafie polskie w XIX i XX wieku," *Znak* 17 (1965).

Tarnowski, Stanisław. "Niebezpieczeństwa grożące Kościołowi w naszym kraju: Mowa na wiecu katolickim dnia 7 lipca 1893 roku." In *Studia Polityczne*. Vol. 1, Kraków: Wydawnictwo Polskie, 1895.

Teter, Magda. *Jews and Heretics in Catholic Poland: A Beleaguered Church in the Post-Reformation Era*. Cambridge: Cambridge University Press, 2006.

The text of the 1791 constitution: http://www.polishconstitution.org/Konstytucja-PL.html. Accessed May 27, 2016.

The text of the constitution: http://isap.sejm.gov.pl/DetailsServlet?id=WDU19210440267. Accessed February 9, 2021.

The text of the *Warsaw Confederation*: http://www.literatura.hg.pl/varsconf.htm. Accessed May 27, 2016.

Wood, Nathaniel D. *Becoming Metropolitan: Urban Selfhood and the Making of Modern Cracow*. Bloomington: Northern Illinois University Press, 2010.

Woroniecki, Adam. *Historja katolickiej akcji społecznej w XIX wieku*. Lublin: Polak-Katolik, 1906.

Wyznania religijne w Polsce w latach 2015-2018. Warsaw: Główny Urząd Statystyczny, 2019.

Zahra, Tara. *Kidnapped Souls: National Indifference and the Battle for Children in the Bohemian Lands, 1900–1948*. Ithaca, NY: Cornell University Press, 2009.

Zdaniewicz, Witold ed. *Religijność Polaków 1991–1998*. Warsaw: Instytut Wydawniczy PAX, 2001.

Zdaniewicz, Witold, Zembrzuski, Tadeusz, eds. *Kościół i religijność Polaków 1945-1999*. Warsaw: Pallotinum, 2000.

Żywot błogosławionej Bronisławy Norbertanki. Lublin: *Polak-Katolik*, 1907.

Żywot św. Stanisława biskupa Męczennika. Lublin: *Polak-Katolik*, 1907.

Żywot św. Wojciecha biskupa Męczennika. Lublin: *Polak-Katolik*, 1907.

Chapter Two

Vita Magistra Historiae? The Case of A. B.

Paweł Bukowiec

There is no need to explain the benefits that result from knowing history. The world of Latin civilization likes to repeat Cicero's words that "history is life's teacher."[1] No one doubts the key role assigned to impressions of the past in shaping, strengthening, and transforming the standards of collective identity such as Polishness. If this process requires critical thinking, then this is primarily because it is a hermeneutic circle—the representations of the past developing our identity are shaped by said identity as well, under the acute influence of the present, from its perspective and in the name of today's collective and individual interests.

I describe this inevitable entanglement of historical representations with the present by reversing Cicero's formula. Life is the teacher of history: it constantly shapes and changes images of the past. This means, of course, that historical truth (i.e., the meaning of past events) must be pragmatic, and not necessarily consistent with the correspondence theory of truth. What was in the past acquires its current meaning according to what is now.

The main character of my article—A. B., mentioned in the title—is a key figure of Lithuanian literature, the most important (next to Maironis) Lithuanian poet of the long nineteenth century, and author of a classic Lithuanian poem *Anykščių šilelis* [The forest of Anykščiai]. A Catholic priest and the bishop of Sejny (a small town in present day Poland in Podlasie Voivodeship), A. B. was also active in the area of linguistics, mathematics, and of course pastoral ministry (Aleksandravičius 2014, Mikšytė 2001, Vanagas 1997, Mikšytė 1964).

---

1 Cicero, *De Oratore*, 110.

CHAPTER TWO

Addressing him, I limit myself to the initials because the questions I ask in this text are: What is this man's *proper* name? How and in what way is such a name *proper*?

This question is not only historical but also doubly paradigmatic. Firstly, because A. B. was one of a number of Lithuanian intellectuals whose names still occur in Polish, Lithuanian, and sometimes other (e.g., Russian) versions. In archival sources as well as Polish and Lithuanian publications on this subject, one can find both the Lithuanian and Polish versions of names of numerous prominent writers and people active in Lithuanian culture during the nineteenth century: Antoni Drozdowski (Antanas Strazdas), Sylwester Walenowicz (Silvestras Valiūnas), Szymon Dowkontt (Simonas Daukantas), Wawrzyniec Iwiński (Laurynas Ivinskis), Mikołaj Akielewicz (Mikalojus Akelaitis), Maciej Wołonczewski (Motiejus Valančius), Jonas Mačiulis (Jan Maculewicz), Ludmila Malinauskaitė (Ludmiła Malinowska), Józef Żelwowicz (Juozapas Želvys-Želvavičius), Juozapas Miliauskas (Józef Milewski), Konstantinas Mikalojus Čiurlionis (Konstanty Mikołaj Czurlonis), Aleksandras Dambrauskas (Aleksander Dąbrowski), Meczysław Dowojna Sylwestrowicz (Mečislovas Davainis-Silvestraitis), to provide a dozen or so examples. In Lithuanian works, one may also come across the Lithuanian names of Polish writers associated with Lithuania.

Secondly, the choice of a *proper* version is paradigmatic because each and every possible choice is an indication of the attitude toward the complicated history of Lithuanian-Polish relations in the long nineteenth century and later.

The long nineteenth century is an epoch in the history of Europe beginning with the French Revolution and lasting until the First World War. Although this periodization may seem controversial in relation to the history of the continent as a whole, it undoubtedly makes sense in relation to Polish and Lithuanian history. It is an epoch of the nonsovereign, beginning with the collapse of the Polish-Lithuanian Commonwealth and ending with the establishment of the independent Lithuanian and Polish states.

In the history of Lithuania, this is also a time of national revival. From 1795 to 1918, Lithuanian lands were part of Russia's empire. Before that, the independent Grand Duchy of Lithuania was for centuries part of the Polish-Lithuanian Commonwealth and subject to the Polonizing pressure of the stronger "partner." Somewhat surprisingly, after the First World War the newly independent Republic of Lithuania turned out to be inhabited by Lithuanians, a modern ethnic nation speaking one language and culturally cohesive. This nation came into being during the Russian partition (regardless of and even contrary to the predominantly anti-Lithuanian orientation of the policies of successive tsars). This process has been comprehensively described by Lithuanian and Polish historians. The modern Lithuanian nation is the result of the culture-creating activities of a small group of writer-intellectuals, one of whom was A. B.

Their creative activity was concentrated in three major fields. Firstly, they created a national history, referring above all to the past glory of the Grand Duchy of Lithuania. Secondly, they constructed a national literature based on folk songs and transformed romantic patterns. Thirdly, they developed a mother tongue, taking advantage of the enormous linguistic differences separating Lithuanian from Polish and Russian, and slowly transforming the various oral dialects used by the peasants into a language with a set of grammatical norms, writing, and stable institutions of printing (books, newspapers, illegal and legal printing houses, etc.). Of course, all this came about in close contact with the dominant Polish culture. Poles, undergoing a similar transition from a civic to an ethnic nation, long claimed (some still do) some form of cultural supremacy over the Lithuanians, treating this culture as a class (peasant) or regional variant of Polishness.

This is why the choice of a name variant for a nineteenth-century poet writing in Lithuanian and Polish has emancipatory or hegemonic consequences and is a decision that summarizes the history of this part of the world. And such a decision is never a simple one. As an example, let us consider a commemorative book published over two decades ago by the publishing house of the Polish parliament, entitled *Biskup Antoni Baranowski (Antanas Baranauskas) 1835–1902* (Bishop Antoni Baranowski [Antanas Baranauskas] 1835–1902). The book includes four articles regarding A. B.'s public and literary activity, written by researchers from Poland and Lithuania, all published in Polish (one translated from Lithuanian): Piotr Łossowski's "Dwie drogi odrodzenia kulturalnego i narodowego Litwinów: Baranauskas i Basanavičius" (Two paths of Lithuanians' cultural and national revival: Baranauskas i Basanavičius); Bronisław Makowski's "Antanas Baranauskas—niezrozumiany intelektualista i biskup" (Antanas Baranauskas—a misunderstood intellectual and bishop); Witold Jemielita's "Biskup sejneński Antoni Baranowski" (Bishop of Sejny Antoni Baranowski); and Regina Mikšytė's "Antanas Baranauskas wśród Litwinów i Polaków" (Antanas Baranauskas among Lithuanians and Poles). One immediately notices that the name of the bishop in the quoted titles is written in Polish or Lithuanian. The anonymous editor of the book did not choose to standardize the notation but gave both versions side by side in the titles throughout (with the Polish one as the primary and the Lithuanian one in parentheses). So, once again: which one of them is *proper* and why?

I am restating the question not in order to answer it. Instead, my aim is a critical reflection on the answers (both those suggested by the way the question is posed and those actually given), and on the question itself in its historical and anthropological context—to show the ahistorical and forced assumptions that underlie it. The answer to the question regarding A. B.'s *proper* name seems to be less important than the recognition of the Lithuanian literary culture of his times. Numerous factors—the lack of general norms of Lithuanian language at that time, the absence of a writing standard, the atomization of the literary life related to prohibition of printing, the influences of the Romantic model of nationalism (with its emphasis on treating language as a core value for the Lithuanian nation)—are attributed to why the *proper* name of a man living over one hundred years ago should be replaced with a question regarding the ways in which this appropriateness and its political dimension are developed. Having in mind the titles quoted above, it seems that four different answers to the question regarding A. B.'s *proper* name are possible:

1. Both versions mentioned in the above works are correct, but for some reason one is "better" and more suitable than the other, which would match either the predominance of the formula used in the title of the book—the Polish version as the main one, the Lithuanian as the secondary—or the opposite hierarchisation.
2. Only the Lithuanian version is correct (as in the titles of the articles by Łossowski, Makowski, and Mikšytė).
3. Only the Polish version is correct (as in the title of Jemielita's article).
4. Neither are correct.

From the point of view of biographical studies as well as biographically oriented historical and literary research, there is no significant difference between Antanas Baranauskas and Antoni Baranowski. Imitating this style of thinking, one might ask if there is any point at all in wondering about the spelling of the name since both versions represent the same person, as Baranauskas turns out to be Baranowski, and Baranowski is simply Baranauskas. In fact, colonial-like symbolic violence underpins this seemingly commonsense question. Most likely, Ngũgĩ wa Thiong'o and James Ngugi are the same person, Крим and Крым (Crimea) are the same peninsula, but the identity of a referent is not tantamount to the interchangeability of its names. A sound or an echo can be sensed with each of them where one can clearly hear the language from which it originates. Proper nouns, which are what we deal with here, indicate and unify rather than produce meaning. What is really meaningful can be found in their acoustic and graphical spheres—this is also why surnames are usually not translated. The disregard for the political dimension of writing as a system of representation, which is particularly characteristic of Polish historical literary studies, leads to a failure to notice the performative dimension of spelling.

Baranauskas is obviously the same person as Baranowski. Nevertheless, maintaining that "Baranauskas" is the same as "Baranowski" in the reality of Polish historical discourse is tantamount to neglecting the cultural separation of Lithuanians and, as a result, also refusing their right to participate in the heritage of the Polish-Lithuanian Commonwealth. If there is no *significant* difference between the two surnames, there is also no *significant* difference between the "immemorial" Polish nation and the Lithuanian nation developed in the nineteenth century. "Język żmudzki *ni sioje, ni toje*" (The Samogitian[2] language is neither fish nor fowl)—the Polish clergyman wrote at the beginning of the eighteenth century. These words were considered print worthy in the middle of the next century[3] when there were already people for whom the Samogitian dialect of the Lithuanian language was not only a tool of spoken communication but who also took conscious steps to standardize it into a written language.[4]

Stating that "Baranauskas" *means* the same as "Baranowski" and therefore the latter can be replaced by the former is equally as anachronic, absurd, and offensive for Lithuanians as stating (in a "humorous" or serious way) that since the name of the former president of Lithuania is Gribauskaitė, she may as well be named "Grzybowska."[5] This way of treating Lithuanian versions of surnames that have (or potentially have) Polish equivalents echoes extreme trends of Polish nationalism (both in its nineteenth-century and contemporary versions) that seem to treat Lithuanians as colonials, as younger siblings whose separate identity is regional or class based, not national (*My historyczni, prawdziwi Litwini, jesteśmy Polakami, a nie Żmudzinami*, 2014). Such views have not been present in Polish public mainstream discourse until recently. After 1989 there were no voices in the Polish political debate calling for the "recovery" of Vilnius or Lviv. It was decided by the Polish political elites' adoption of Jerzy Giedroyc and Juliusz Mieroszewski's argument that the contemporary borders of Poland

---

2   Samogitia (Lit. Žemaitija, Pol. Żmudź) is an ethnographically distinct western part of Lithuania. At the beginning of the nineteenth century the Lithuanian language was alive only there, and that is why it was called "Samogitian."
3   Bagiński, "Chorografia, czyli opisanie Żmudzi," 138.
4   Subačus, *Žemaičių bendrinės kalbos idėjos*.
5   I did not invent this example but took it from an article by a Polish journalist. See Ikonowicz 2009. The "translation" of the Lithuanian surname to Polish is here accompanied by much more common lack of respect for Lithuanian diacritical signs, which is typical of multiple mainstream media in Poland.

are inviolable while the existence of independent and democratic states of Lithuania, Belarus, and Ukraine is compliant with Polish national interest.[6]

While the reduction to "Baranowski" is characteristic of Polish humanities, examples of the opposite can be found on the Lithuanian side. This option perceives Lithuanian and Polish matters as a sphere of conflict, a clash of two unified qualities: the essentially understood Lithuanian "nature" with the Polishness that puts it at risk. The logic of "if you are not with us, you are against us" is involved here, according to which the poet and his legacy are considered within a simplified opposition. In fact, A. B. himself, as a social activist, had huge problems with this line of thinking, especially at the end of his life when he was misunderstood and marginalized by fellow believers because of his unwillingness to approach the complicated social and cultural reality in a binary way. Literary studies also seem to operate according to the same pattern when posing the question of whether the bishop was a Lithuanian *or* a Polish writer. From the philological point of view, the case seems rather clear: with few exceptions, we are either dealing with a text written in Lithuanian or a text written in Polish, period. All nineteenth-century Lithuanian literature is characterized by linguistic purism, striving to purge the language from traces of Slavonic, especially Polish, influences. The text written in Polish is—or may be—naturally an object of interest for Polish philology that has been researching works written in Polish and educates specialists in the scope of researching texts written in Polish. The same applies to Lithuanian works and Lithuanian philology. One may say that, from a philological point of view, Antanas Baranauskas starts where Antoni Baranowski ends.

A. B. wrote in Lithuanian and Polish throughout his entire career and at times also in Latin and Russian. A review of the texts recorded in his lifetime is not just an insight into the wide variety of this man's interests and duties but, more importantly, it will enable us to realize how wrong logical predictions may be if they are not supported by historical facts.

A. B. debuted with Polish poetry in *Teka Wileńska* ("Vilnius File") magazine (Baranowski 1857). In the next decade, the poet printed his most important Lithuanian poem, entitled "Anykščių šilelis": the first part was anonymous ([Baranauskas] 1860), while the other was published under a pseudonym along with two of his other poetry works (Jurrksztas Smałausis, 1860a, 1860b, 1860c). More than ten years later, the poem was published again (Baranowski 1875) and after another seven years it was presented to the public for a third time (Baranowski 1882). The next editions are Baranauskas 1892c and

---

6   See Bumblauskas 2014.

Baran<auskas> 1893. This text (or actually most of it) was published for the last time in A.B.'s life in the twentieth century (Варановскій 1901).[7]

Another poetry-related achievement of A. B., known from numerous publications, was a Lithuanian cycle of five religious songs entitled—in contemporary spelling—*Artojų giesmės šventos* ("Pious songs for ploughmen"), often included as part of a renewed hymnal entitled *Kantyčkas* ("Pious songs"). The first publication was anonymous ([Baranauskas] 1862) while in the later editions, poems were more often signed "Baranauskis" (the first such edition was most likely Baranauskis 1867). Furthermore, in 1865 the hymnal was released as a Cyrillic print (still in the Lithuanian language) with the following title: Кантычкасъ (Варанаускисъ 1865). At the beginning of the 1860s, A. B. released two more religious songs (Baranauskis 1862).

New publications by A. B. were not released until the 1880s. At this time, several texts were printed: poems signed with the initials A. B., one under the incipit "Kogi spaudze man szirdiałe" ("for whom my heart longs"; B<aranauskas> 1882), and the other known today under the incipit-based title "Dainu dainelę" ("I'm singing a song"; B<aranauskas> 1883); an anonymous fragment of a poem entitled "Kelionė Peterburkan"[8] ("A journey to Petersburg"; [Baranauskas] 1887, while another edition followed, signed by his initials: B<aranauskas> 1892d); also an anonymous book containing Christian teaching about death ([Baranauskas] 1889); and a press article dedicated to the Catholic Church's approach to Lithuanians (Baranowski 1883). More of A. B.'s prints were published in the subsequent decade.[9]

---

7 This is a publication in Latin font. The title and name of the author were specified by means of the Cyrillic script on the page header. The table of contents presents the name in Cyrillic script, while the title is in Latin (*Anykszczu Szilēlis*). On the other hand, the footnote on p. 475 includes the name written in Latin ("A. Baranowfki"). In 1864–1904, in the Russian empire (of which the majority of ethnographically Lithuanian lands were a part in 1795–1918) there was a ban on printing Lithuanian text in Latin font (see Merkys 1994). The Lithuanians dealt with this problem in various ways, usually falsifying publishing information of books and/or importing books from abroad, but also, as in this case, naming the publication with the use of a "dialectological transcription" ("въ діалектологической транскрипціи", Варановскій, 1902, 475).

8 First full edition only after the author's death.

9 At that time he released: an anonymous poetry volume entitled *Tevyniszkos giesmės* ([Baranauskas], 1892b); a poem entitled "Szirdies jausmai", signed with the initials A.B. (B<aranauskas> 1892a); a short anonymous epic verse entitled *Pasikalbėjimas giesmininko su Lietuva* ([Baranauskas] 1895); an anonymous Lithuanian language-learning handbook ([Baranauskas] 1896); an anonymous

After doing away with the pseudonym ("Jurrksztas Smałausis") and abbreviations ("A. B.," "Ant. Baran."), there are six different formats for writing A. B.'s surname, confirmed in his own texts printed during his lifetime. They are four Latin forms (1. "Baranowski" 2. "Baranauskis" 3. "Baranauskas" 4. "Baranauckas") and two Cyrillic ones (5. "Барановскій" 6. "Баранаускисъ"). It is important to mention that in various manuscripts and printed sources regarding A. B. from that epoch one may also come across the following formats: 7. Baronovskas and 8. Baronas (Biržiška 1990, 381). Format 1 is Polish in terms of the writing method and language. Format 5 is its Russian "mirror"—the alphabet and word form are both Russian here (cf. "Dostojewski" and "Достоевский"). Formats 2, 3, 4, 7, and 8 are Lithuanian (whereas one of them, namely format 2, has its Cyrillic "mirror," i.e., format 6).

The multiplicity of Lithuanian formats is a very characteristic exhibit of changes taking place in the Lithuanian language at that time. Similar processes regarding the Polish or Russian language took place earlier and in a significantly less rapid way. At the beginning of the nineteenth century, the Lithuanian language was used mostly by peasants. It did not feature general inflection rules or an orthographic standard. There was also no "material database" in the form of dictionaries and grammar textbooks. The climate of opinion in Lithuania, which prevailed in all of Europe at the turn of the nineteenth century (regionalisms inspired by Herder's thought, growing interest in native past and language, etc.), favored the appearance of writers and cultural activists convinced of the need for research on the Lithuanian language, writing, and native culture (Bukowiec 2008). They created the basis for the national revival movement developing in the mid-nineteenth century (Ochmański 1965; Aleksandravičius, Kulakauskas 1996, 236–307). A. B. was active in a period when the so-called literary language (i.e., the general standard of Lithuanian) was developing, while work on adjusting the Latin alphabet to its needs was also being performed (Zinkevičius 1992). In such conditions, the multiplicity of the formats of A. B.'s surname cannot be surprising—it is a sign of efforts by elites of a developing nation to create standards. They generated results shortly after A. B.'s death—the Lithuanian nation experienced independence in 1918 not only with stable institutions of

---

collection of religious songs ([Baranauskas] 1899); three documents that are closely associated with his bishop service: a pastor's letter in Polish (Baranowski [1897a]), a pastor's letter in Lithuanian (Baranauckas 1899), as well as a directorium prepared for the diocese he managed (Baranowski 1897b); two scientific works in Polish: one was strictly mathematical (Baranowski 1895), while the other regarded mathematics, philosophy and theology (Baranowski 1897c); and a Russian linguistic study about the Lithuanian language (Барановскій 1898).

literary life (writers with the status of classicists, literary press, publishing market) but also with a standardized language.

It should also be noted that this multiplicity of the written (and printed) versions of A. B.'s name raises doubts about the possibility of finding his *proper* surname in the depths of archival collections. It is not easy to favor any of these variants if all of them together demonstrate the incompatibility of writing with language at that time. There is no single document proving that "Baranauskas"—currently a primary version of A. B.'s surname—was the name of the bishop's great-grandfather. Moreover, any document, whether relating to the poet's ancestors or to himself, would be written in Polish, Russian, or Latin and not in Lithuanian! "Baranauskas" is his *proper* surname not because it's authentic and confirmed in the course of archival queries but due to pragmatic reasons. The same applies to all other Lithuanian surnames from the nineteenth century—those listed above and the ones that were not mentioned. All of them occurred in different varieties, whereas one of them was considered the most Lithuanian as time passed and eventually became his *proper* one.

Nevertheless, one must realize that the "Baranowski" format was also imposed, albeit ineffectively. If you were to imagine an alternative version of the history of Central Europe in the nineteenth century, a version within which nation-creating processes in this century were put on hold, it could actually turn out that the format "Baranowski" is used as primary in catalogues, bibliographies etc. Or perhaps "Барановскій." But Lithuanians effectively shaped their history as that of a revived nation—once marginalized, dominated—and brought to the brink of extinction before regaining independence and becoming proud of their linguistic and cultural distinctiveness.

A. B. himself saw it very differently—and his view of the past will prove surprising to anyone with even a cursory interest in Lithuanian historical scholarship. A. B. avoided talking about the Polish-Lithuanian past in terms of conflict and growing Polish domination. He wrote, for example:

> Litwa nigdy nie była prowincją polską, ale narodem z Polską połączonym, z zachowaniem zupełnego samorządu. . . .Polacy wprawdzie języka litewskiego się nie wyuczyli i literatury litewskiej nie uprawiali, ale . . . nie było wydane na Litwie ani jedno rozporządzenie zakazujące języka litewskiego lub nakazujące polski. . . . Szkoła na Litwie nie była . . . ani w ręku Polaków, ani środkiem ustanowionym dla spolszczenia Litwinów
>
> (Lithuania was never a Polish province, but a nation united with Poland, with full self-government. . . . Although Poles did not learn the Lithuanian language or practice Lithuanian literature, . . . there was not a single decree issued in Lithuania forbidding the Lithuanian language or ordering Polish. . . . The school

in Lithuania was ... neither in the hands of Poles nor was it a means established to Polonize Lithuanians) (Baranowski 1883, 605–7).

A. B. approaches the Lithuanian language differently from his compatriots: not as a nineteenth-century Lithuanian but as a Lithuanian citizen of the Commonwealth. It is not that he is wrong when he reasonably points out the objective factors not necessarily caused by Poles, which brought the language to the brink of decline; however, he does not link the language with the nation and does not think of it in terms of the metaphysics of national identity. His poetry deals with Lithuania's sad present and tries to inspire religious rather than nationalist hope. In other words, A. B. defined the group for whom and on whose behalf he acted primarily through religion.

It seems, therefore, that A. B. himself, by signing his Polish texts with the Polish version of his surname and his Lithuanian ones with the Lithuanian versions, not only opposed the dominant paradigm linking identity with language but also failed to see the political dimension of the very gesture of signing.

When speaking and writing about nineteenth-century Lithuanian literature, I try to use both versions of Lithuanian writers' names (Baranowski and Baranauskas, Paszkiewicz and Poška, etc.) interchangeably, thereby always taking into account the danger of linguistic simplification of the complicated reality of their times. However, refraining from answering the question about the *proper* version of a given name (corresponding to point 4 in the enumeration above) has hardly anything in common with the apparently analogous behavior of A. B. Even if there are some reasons to make A. B. a model of contemporary Lithuanian-Polish rapprochement, cooperation, or even the ethos of multiculturalism, it is necessary to remember that what was in a sense natural for him is irrevocably political for us. When he alternated between two versions of his name, he did so because he alternated between two languages. When I refer to him as "Baranauskas" in my Polish texts, I do so in order to emphasize his strangeness and remoteness and to mark the otherness of his being a Lithuanian and his being a Pole and to escape from simplistic projections of *vita* into *historia*. History should never be shaped according to the contemporary image and analogies. In order for it to teach us something, history has to remain foreign. It has to be *testis temporum*[10]—witness to the past and not the present day.

---

10   Cicero, *De Oratore*, 110.

Bibliography

Baranauckas, A. 1899. "Piemeniszkas laiszkas Seinų vyskupo, apėmus rundyjimą diecezijos." *Tėvynės Sargas* (Bitėnai) no. 6, 3–10.

[Baranauskas, A.] 1860. "Anikszcziu siłelis." In *Kalendorius arba metskajtlus ukiszkasis nuog užgimima Wieszpaties 1860 metu pribuwiniu, turenčziun 366 dienas, paraszitas par Ł. Iwiński*, Wilniuje: Kasztu ir spaustuwe Juozapa Zawadzkia, 61–61 [verses 1–176].

[Baranauskas, A.] 1862. "Artoju giesmes szwentos." In *Kantyczkas, arba Kninga giesmiu, par Moteju Wołonczewski Źemajcziu Wiskupa parwejzieta ir isznauje iszspausta*, Vilnius: Kasztu ir spaustuwi Jozapa Zawadzkia, 695–712.

B<aranauskas>, A. 1882. "Kogi spaudze man szirdiałe", *Lietuwiszka ceitunga* [in Gothic script] (Klaipeda) no. 25, 3.

B<aranauskas>, A. 1883. "Lietuvôs senowês paminejimas." *Auszra. Laikrasztis iszleidźiamas Lietuvos milêtoju* (Ragainė [Nowadays Neman in Kaliningrad District, Russian Federation]) no. 1, 8–10.

[Baranauskas, A.] 1887. "Su Diev' Lietuva", *Szviesa. Laikrasztis Žemaicziu ir Lietuvos mylėtoju iszleidžiamas*, no. 1, 42–43.

[Baranauskas, A.] 1889. *Paskutinis pamoksłas wiena żemajcziu kuniga priesz smerti*. Plymouth, PA: spaustuweje Juozapa Paukszczio.

B<aranauskas>, A. 1892a. "Szirdies jausmai." *Žemaicziu ir Lietuvos apžvalga* no. 20, 157.

[Baranauskas, A.] 1892b. *Tevyniszkos giesmes*. Vilnius: Iszduotos per K. Žalvarį.

Baranauskas, A. 1892c. "Anykszcziu szilelis." *Vienybė Lietuvininkų. Literaturos, mokslo ir polytikos nedėlinis laikrasztis* (Plymouth, PA), 7:168, 181, 192, 229, 240.

B<aranauskas>, A. 1892d. "Sudiev' Lietuva." In *Lietuvos kanklės*. Tilžėje: Išleido V. Kalvaitis, 60–61.

Baran<auskas>, A. 1893. "Anyksczių szilelis." In "*Lietuviszkos" dainos isz visur surinktos*, 144–54. Plymouth, PA: Kasztu ir spaustuvėje Jūzo Paukszczio.

[Baranauskas, A.]. 1895. "Pasikalbėjimas giesmininko su Lietuva." *Žemaiczių ir Lietuvos apžvalga* (Tilžė Nowadays Sovetsk in Kaliningrad District, Russian Federation]) no. 12, 90–91.

[Baranauskas, A.] 1896. *Kalbomokslis lietuviszkos kalbos*, Tilžėje: Spauda E. Jagomasto.

[Baranauskas, A.] 1899. *Graudųs verksmai ir kitos naujosios giesmės žinotinos žmonėms katalikams, ypacziai-gi izsdavėjams maldakningių*. Tilžė: Tėvynės sargas.

Baranauskis, [A.]. 1862. "Giesme padekawones uż błajwisti. Sweika Marija, danguj iszauksztinta." In *Kalendorius ukiszkasis nuog uźgimima Wieszpaties 1863 metu paprastunju, turenčziun 365 dienas, paraśzitas par Ł. Iwiński*, 30–31. Vilnius: Kasztu ir spaustuwe Juozapa Zawadzkia.

Baranauskis, A. 1867. "Artoju giesmes szwentos." In *Kantyczkas, arba Kninga giesmiu, par Moteju Wołonczewski Źemajcziu Wiskupa parwejzieta ir isznauje iszspausta*, Tilžė: J. Zabermanno lėšos, 1867.

Baranowski, [A.]. 1857. "Wiersz młodego poety Baranowskiego do Karoliny P<roniewskiej>." *Teka Wileńska wydawana przez Jana ze Śliwina* [real name: Adam Honory Kirkor], no. 2, 62.

Baranowski, A. 1875. "Anikszcziu szilelis." In *Litauische Studien. Auswahl aus den ältesten denkmälern, dialectische beispiele, lexikalische und sprachwissentschaftliche beiträge*, von Dr. Leopold Geitler. Prague: Verlag von Teodor Mourek Buch- & Kunsthandlung, 40–48.

Baranowski, A. 1882. "Anykszczū sziłêlys." In *Ostlitauische Texte mit einleitungen und anmerkungen*, herausgegeben von Anton Baranowski und Hugo Weber, erstes Heft. Weimar: Hermann Böhlau, 2–23.

Baranowski, A. 1883. "Czy Kościół katolicki wynaradawiał Litwinów?" *Przegląd Katolicki* (Warsaw), no. 38: 605–8.

Baranowski, A. 1895. "O wzorach służących do obliczenia liczby liczb pierwszych nie przekraczających danej granicy." *Rozprawy Wydziału Matematyczno-Przyrodniczego Akademii Umiejętności w Krakowie*, vol. 28: 192–210.

Baranowski, A. [1897a]. [pastoral letter], [Suwałki]: Tip. Suw. Gubiernsk. Prawl.

Baranowski, A. 1897b. *Directorium Divini Officii ad usum universi cleri saecularis Dioecesis Sejnensis seu Augustoviensis*, Varsaviae: typis filiorum St. Niemira [druk łaciński, fragmenty po polsku i rosyjsku].

Baranowski, A. 1897c. *O progresji transcendentalnej oraz o skali i siłach umysłu ludzkiego. Studium matematyczno-filozoficzne*, Warsaw: Druk K. Kowalewskiego.

Jurrksztas Smałausis [A. Baranauskas]. 1860a. "Anikszciu szitelis." In *Kalendorius ukiszkasis nuog użgimima Wieszpaties 1861 metu paprastunju, turenčziun 365 dienas, paraśzitas par Ł. Iwiński*, Vilnius: Kasztu ir spaustuwe Juozapa Zawadzkia, 59–60 [verses 177–322].

Jurrksztas Smałausis [A. Baranauskas]. 1860b. "Suwejga girtoklu." In *Kalendorius ukiszkasis nuog użgimima Wieszpaties 1861 metu paprastunju, turenčziun 365 dienas, paraśzitas par Ł. Iwiński*, Wilniuje: Kasztu ir spaustuwe Juozapa Zawadzkia, 51–58.

Jurrksztas Smałausis [A. Baranauskas]. 1860c. "Diewo rikszte ir małone." In *Kalendorius ukiszkasis nuog użgimima Wieszpaties 1861 metu paprastunju, turenčziun 365 dienas, paraśzitas par Ł. Iwiński*, 51. Vilnius: Kasztu ir spaustuwe Juozapa Zawadzkia.

Баранаускисъ А. 1865. "Артою гысмесъ швеинтосъ." In *Кантычкась, арба Книнга гесмю*, паръ Мотыю Волончевски вискупа парвейзета иръ ишнауе ишспауста Вильнюй: спаустувенъ А. Сыркина, 709–724.

Барановскiй, А. 1898. *Замѣтки о литовскомъ языкѣ и словарѣ*, Санктпетербургъ: Типографiя Императорской Академiи Наукъ.

Барановскiй, А. 1901. "Оникштенскiй боръ." In Е. Вольтер = E. Volteris, *Литовская хрестоматiя = Lietùviška chrestomatija*, 475–83. Санктпетербургъ: Типографiя Императорской Академiи Наукъ.

Aleksandravičius, E. 2014. *Antanas Baranauskas: Droga wieszcza*, trans. Jadwiga Rogoża, Tomasz Błaszczak, Sejny: Pogranicze.

Aleksandravičius, E., and A. Kulakauskas. *Carų valdžioje: XIX amžiaus Lietuva*, Baltos lankos: [Vilnius] 1996.

Ankersmit, F. 2001. *Historical Representation*. Stanford, CA: Stanford University Press.

Bagiński, K. 1845. "Chorografia, czyli opisanie Żmudzi świętej około roku 1780 sporządzona." In *Athenaeum*, 135–43. Vol. 4. *Pismo zbiorowe poświęcone historii, filozofii, literaturze, sztukom itd.*
Biržiška, V. 1990. *Aleksandrynas: Senųjų Lietuvių rašytojų, rašiusių prieš 1865 m., biografijos, bibliografijos ir biobiliografijos*. Vol. 3. Vilnius.
Biskup Antoni Baranowski (Antanas Baranauskas) 1835-1902: Orędownik pojednania litewsko-polskiego. 1998. Warsaw: Wydawnictwo Sejmowe:
Bukowiec, P. 2008. *Dwujęzyczne początki nowoczesnej literatury litewskiej: Rzecz z pogranicza polonistyki*, Kraków: Universitas, 2008.
Bumblauskas, A. 2014. "Koncepcja ULB Jerzego Giedroycia: Spojrzenie z Litwy." In *Dialog kultur pamięci w regionie ULB*, edited by A. Nikžentaitis, M. Kopczyński, 40–60. Translated by B. Kowal. Warsaw: Muzeum Historii Polski.
Cicero. 1862. *De Oratore*, für den Schulgebrauch erklärt von K.W. Piderit, Leipzig: B.G. Teubner.
Ikonowicz, P. 2009. *Gorzkie prawdy pani Grzybowskiej*. https://www.tygodnikprzeglad.pl/gorzkie-prawdy-pani-grzybowskiej/.
Jemielity, W. *Biskup sejneński Antoni Baranowski*, 44–53.
Łossowski, P. *Dwie drogi odrodzenia kulturalnego i narodowego Litwinów: Baranauskas i Basanavičius*, 13–33.
Makowski, B. *Antanas Baranauskas-niezrozumiany intelektualista i biskup*, 34–43.
Merkys, V. 1994. *Knygnešių laikai. 1864-1904*. Vilnius: Valstybinis leidybos centras.
Mikšytė, R. n.d. *Antanas Baranauskas wśród Litwinów i Polaków*, 54–62.
Mikšytė, R. 2001. "Antanas Baranauskas." In *Lietuvių literatūros istorija: XIX amžius*, edited by J. Girdzijauskas, 707–26. Vilnius: Lietuvių literatūros ir tautosakos institutas.
Mikšytė, R. 1964. *Antano Baranausko kūryba*. Vilnius: Vaga.
My historyczni, prawdziwi Litwini, jesteśmy Polakami, a nie Żmudzinami, 2014. http://narodowikonserwatysci.pl/2014/02/23/my-historyczni-prawdziwi-litwini-jestesmy-polakami-a-nie-zmudzinami/.
Ngugi, James. 1967. *A Grain of Wheat*. London: Heinemann.
Ngugi, James. 1970. *A Grain of Wheat*. London: Heinemann.
Ngugi wa Thiong'o. 1994. *Decolonizing the Mind: The Politics of Language in African Literature*, 2nd ed. Harare: Zimbabwe.
Ochmański, J. 1965. *Litewski ruch narodowo-kulturalny w XIX wieku do 1890 r.*, Białystok–Warsaw: Białostockie Towarzystwo Naukowe—Państwowe Wydawnictwo Naukowe.
Subačus, G. 1998. *Žemaičių bendrinės kalbos idėjos: XIX amžiaus pradžia*, Mokslo ir enciklopedijų leidybos institutas: Vilnius.
Vanagas, V. 1997. "Literature at the Crossroads of Enlightenment and Romanticism." In *Lithuanian Literature*, edited by V. Kubilius, 66–70. Translated by R. Dapkutė. Vilnius: Vaga.
Zinkevičius Zigmas. 1992. *Lietuvių kalbos istorija*, Vol. 5. *Bendrinės kalbos iškilimas*, Vilnius: Mokslo ir enciklopedijų leidybos institutas.

Chapter Three

An Anti-Imperial Civilizing Mission

Claiming Volhynia for the Early Second Polish Republic

Kathryn Ciancia

In November 1918, the Second Polish Republic emerged from the wartime implosion of the Habsburg, Russian, and German empires. As they celebrated this historic moment, even in the midst of ongoing border wars, Poles seemed to reject not only the particular empires that had oppressed them but the very concept of empire itself. The new Poland was to be a democracy, a state based both on the principle of national self-determination and on the idea that even the 30 percent of its citizens who identified as non-Polish would have their rights codified in a new liberal constitution.[1] Poles could claim, therefore, that their state embodied a prescription most famously attributed to the American president Woodrow Wilson: empires no longer had any place on the European continent.[2]

Many historians subsequently agreed with this characterization of the Second Republic as an anti-imperial nation-state, labeling it, among other

---

1   On the entangled histories of self-determination and democracy, see Weitz, "Self-Determination."
2   On Wilson's ideas of an anti-imperial Europe, see Wolff, *Woodrow Wilson and the Reimagining of Eastern Europe*. On the disappointment of the non-European people for whom imperial rule continued, see Manela, *The Wilsonian Moment*.

things, a "decolonial state" or an "Other of Empire."[3] Yet some scholars have returned to another argument that was also made during the interwar period: that the eastern European successor states, including Poland, functioned not so much as *anti*-empires but as *aspiring* empires that oppressed the multiethnic minority populations living within their borders. David Reynolds argues, for example, that these states were "not so much nation-states as mini empires," while Istvan Deak labels them "miniature multinational empires."[4] For Pieter Judson, the fact that representatives of the post-Habsburg states had a vested interest in denigrating empire and promoting the links between democracy and national self-determination should not blind us to the continuities in practice across the apparent break of the First World War. Each of these states, Judson tells us, acted like "a small empire," in that it tried to grab and integrate territories where the population did not belong to the ruling national group.[5]

Reflections on whether the Second Polish Republic functioned as an empire speak to a broader set of questions about the comparative frameworks in which Polish history should be understood. Indeed, debates over Poland's relationship with empire extend far beyond studies of the Second Republic. Scholars who argue that the early modern Polish-Lithuanian Commonwealth was an empire, for instance, point to what they see as that state's violent eastern conquests and the unequal power relations between a Polish center and a non-Polish periphery, while their opponents accuse them of anachronistically projecting modern colonialism onto a very different kind of state.[6] Historians of the long nineteenth century have similarly debated the relationship between Poland and imperialism, albeit in the absence of a Polish state. On the one hand, they have highlighted how German discursive tropes of "dirty" and "uncivilized" Poles echoed depictions of non-European colonial populations.[7] More recently, however, a new wave of scholarship has shown that Poles who worked within the interstices of the German empire both utilized racist colonial tropes and

---

3 Snyder, *Black Earth*, 31; Smith, "Empires at the Paris Peace Conference," 259.
4 Reynolds, *The Long Shadow*, 12; Deak, "How to Construct a Productive, Disciplined, Monoethnic Society," 212.
5 Judson, *The Habsburg Empire*, 448.
6 On viewing the Commonwealth within a colonial framework, see Sowa, *Fantomowe ciało króla*. Hieronim Grala criticized this approach in "Kolonializm alla polacca." On debates around the Commonwealth's status as an empire, see Nowak, "From Empire Builder to Empire Breaker, or There and Back Again," 255–61.
7 Ureña Valerio, *Colonial Fantasies, Imperial Realities*; Kopp, *Germany's Wild East*; Liulevicius, *The German Myth of the East*.

claimed that they could better understand colonized peoples because of their own colonial victimhood, dynamics that continued into the interwar years, as Poland pushed for overseas colonies.[8] Moreover, sociologists, historians, and literary scholars have argued over whether postwar Poland's relationship with the Soviet Union can be captured within a postcolonial framework. Although some have proposed that such an approach illuminates hitherto overlooked parallels with the histories of other oppressed peoples, skeptics suggest that it provides a way of emphasizing Polish victimhood.[9]

While an awareness of such debates is critical for understanding the various modes in which we might think about Polish history, the scholarly utility of characterizing the Second Republic as *either* an empire *or* a nation-state is limited. In fact, advocating for one side or the other necessarily involves holding Poland up against a checklist of imperial characteristics and ignores the blurring between these two "types" of state in the wake of the First World War.[10] Instead, we might normalize Polish history by acknowledging that Poles were part of a broader patchwork of interwar political projects around the world by which European elites mobilized a common argument to justify rule in contested territories: they were carrying out a civilizing mission toward a less advanced group that was undeserving of national self-determination. This idea was used to rationalize both the ongoing reach of the British and French empires and the new League of Nations mandate system, by which the sovereignty of postimperial countries, such as Iraq, Syria, and Palestine, was seen in temporal terms, their populations deemed not yet able to govern themselves as part of the civilized world.[11] But it also informed dynamics in the civilizationally in-between

---

8   Ureña Valerio, *Colonial Fantasies, Imperial Realities*, 116–47. On interwar Polish colonialism, see Puchalski, *Poland in a Colonial World Order*; Grzechnik, "The Missing Second World."

9   Those who have promoted the idea of postcolonial Poland include Cavanagh, "Postcolonial Poland"; Thompson, "Whose Discourse? Telling the Story in Post-Communist Poland." Critics include Snochowska-Gonzalez, "Postcolonial Poland"; Kołodziejczyk, "Postkolonialny transfer na Europę Środkowo-Wschodnią." Good overviews of the debate include Zarycki, "Debating Soviet Imperialism in Contemporary Poland"; Kola, *Socjalistyczny postkolonializm*; Grzechnik, "The Missing Second World."

10   For an overview on the blurring of these types of state in eastern Europe specifically, see Miller and Berger, eds., *Nationalizing Empires*. More generally, see Kumar, "Nation-States as Empires, Empires as Nation-States."

11   Pedersen, *The Guardians*. On temporality and "non-synchronous sovereignties," see Wheatley, "Legal Pluralism as Temporal Pluralism."

region of eastern Europe where political elites fended off accusations that they were acting imperialistically, while simultaneously claiming to be carrying out a civilizing mission toward citizens whose national "backwardness" made them ineligible for self-rule.[12] In short, Poland's story speaks to the inner tensions of the post–First World War moment more broadly, when imperialism was simultaneously rejected in Europe and recast in new forms beyond Europe's shores and when elites often viewed internal borderlands and colonial spaces within a shared framework.[13]

Although less attention-grabbing than the Poland-as-empire thesis, this approach nonetheless marks a fundamental shift in how we write the story of interwar Poland, particularly when it comes to the issue of so-called national minorities. Historians of the Second Republic, a state where people who spoke Polish as their mother tongue constituted just 69 percent of the total population on the 1931 census (the rest speaking a mixture of languages, including Yiddish, Russian, Hebrew, Ukrainian, Lithuanian, German, Belarusian, and Czech), have generally focused either on *relations* between different national groups or on the state's policies toward various national *questions*.[14] But taking a more global approach indicates how discussions about national groups—and indeed the very construction of these groups in the first place—were never isolated from broader claims about which nations had the civilizational right to rule over others. This was particularly true in the multiethnic and nationally contested eastern borderlands (*kresy*), which had, prior to the First World War, been part of the western borderlands of the Russian empire. While some historians have been inclined to label the interwar *kresy* as an internal Polish colony, the story is,

---

12 Porter-Szűcs thinks through the idea of Poland's in-between status in *Poland in the Modern World*, 3. A comparative case is Czechoslovakia, where elites deemed the area of sub-Carpathian Rus, which had a Rusyn majority, to be less civilized than the rest of the country and therefore in need of a Czech modernizing and democratizing mission. See Holubec, "We Bring Order."

13 One recent work on the links between conceptions of national and imperial space is Roberta Pergher's book on Italy's relationship with both South Tyrol and Libya. Pergher, *Mussolini's Nation-Empire*. See also Pergher and Payk, *Beyond Versailles*.

14 Tomaszewski, *Rzeczpospolita wielu narodów*, 35. Examples of this literature, which transcends 1989, include Tomaszewski, *Ojczyzna nie tylko Polaków*; Chojnowski, *Koncepcje polityki*; Potocki, *Polityka państwa*; Mironowicz, *Białorusini i Ukraińcy*; Papierzyńska-Turek, *Sprawa ukraińska*; Torzecki, *Kwestia ukraińska*.

in fact, more complicated—and more interesting.[15] Here, Poles walked a tightrope: they claimed to be mounting an anti-imperial civilizing mission by both reclaiming land from the Russian empire and bringing European modernity, democracy, and civilization to a "backward" region.

This chapter explores how various Poles deployed the idea of a civilizing mission in the first few years of the Second Republic as they sought to fashion a state from various imperial fragments. It begins by tracing how Polish elites on the global stage reckoned with the tensions of 1919, as they argued that Poles constituted the sole agents of civilization in the lands to the east of ethnographic Poland, with a particular focus on the Polish-occupied region of Volhynia (Wołyń in Polish).[16] I then discuss two sets of nationalizing actors that engaged with Volhynia from very different political perspectives: the first, activists with a democratizing and nominally inclusive agenda who worked in Volhynia in 1919–20; the second, supporters of the right-wing National Democracy movement (Endecja) who were based in the western city of Poznań and became locked in a power struggle with the government in Warsaw during the early-to-mid-1920s. Despite their competing, even antithetical, political projects, these actors all employed the framework of civilizational development not only to put Poles at the top of an imagined hierarchy but also to create hierarchies between groups of Poles.

1919 and the Meanings of Polish Imperialism

The Paris Peace Conference, which opened at the beginning of 1919, occurred against a backdrop of both heated international debates about the correct location for Poland's borders and a series of ongoing wars with other emerging states. Such questions about which lands belonged to the Polish nation were not new, particularly in a place like Volhynia where a long history of dynastic, imperial, and national competition had created both possibilities and anxieties for Polish elites. During the nineteenth century, Polish nationalists had already claimed that the region was historically connected to Poland, rather than to the Russian empire that had ruled here following the late eighteenth-century partitions, citing the fact that Volhynia had been part of the Polish-Lithuanian

---

15   Roshwald, *Ethnic Nationalism and the Fall of Empires*, 168; Mick, "Colonialism in the Polish Eastern Borderlands, 1919–1939."
16   Note that I use the Polish spellings of place names throughout this chapter. This does not imply any argument about their "correct" national identity.

Commonwealth since the latter's foundation in 1569. While the mid-to-late nineteenth century had witnessed the intensification of so-called Russification policies that targeted the Roman Catholic Church and the Polish language, national challenges did not come from the Russian empire alone.[17] By the late nineteenth century, Russian imperial authorities and nationally minded Polish elites alike faced competition from leaders of an emerging Ukrainian nationalist movement who claimed that the "Little Russian" majority constituted a separate Ukrainian nation.[18] With the outbreak of the First World War, these debates transitioned onto the battlefield, as borders were quickly redrawn and states competed for newly obtainable territory. The Austro-Hungarian army captured the western part of the Russian imperial governorate of Volhynia in 1915, only for the Russian army to partially recapture the area the following year. As the empires collapsed, Volhynia became the site of ongoing battles between a dizzying array of competing groups: Russian Bolsheviks and their White opponents, a fledgling Ukrainian People's Republic, a German-backed Ukrainian Hetmanate, and an emerging Polish state.

Once the Paris Peace Conference was in session, various national groups mounted intense international campaigns to claim these contested lands. In appeals to Western audiences, Ukrainian nationalists built a case for statehood by drawing on the prevailing Wilsonian rhetoric of self-determination: put simply, if the majority population in Volhynia was Ukrainian—rather than "indisputably Polish," as per President Woodrow Wilson's formulation—these lands surely belonged to a sovereign Ukrainian state.[19] But Polish commentators, who readily admitted that Poles did not constitute a numerical majority in Volhynia (even in the western areas of the former Russian governorate occupied by the Polish army in the spring of 1919), rested their claims on the widely held Western idea that civilizational quality could trump demographic

---

17 For an overview of Russian policies in the western borderlands more broadly, see Weeks, *Nation and State in Late Imperial Russia*.

18 On the emergence of a Ukrainian movement among intellectuals in the empire's western borderlands, see Plokhy, *Unmaking Imperial Russia*; on the "Little Russian" national movement, see Hillis, *Children of Rus'*.

19 The phrase "indisputably Polish populations" comes from President Woodrow Wilson's Fourteen Points (1918). Ukrainian booklets include Shelukhin, *Ukraine, Poland and Russia and The Right of the Free Disposition of the Peoples*. Maps provided by the Ukrainian delegation depicted the whole of the Russian governorate of Volhynia, as well as some areas farther west, as part of Ukraine. See *Mémoire sur l'indépendance*.

quantity.[20] In this "backward" region, with its low literacy rates and underdeveloped agriculture, Poles argued that they were the only competent agents of modern civilization.

The claim that Poles possessed higher levels of civilization than the *kresy*'s non-Polish majority transcended traditional ideological camps. Historians have long drawn a distinction between the national visions of Józef Piłsudski and Roman Dmowski, with the former attempting to create a federation of friendly eastern nations that would act as a buffer against Russia and the latter favoring a border based on a narrower concept of the nation that would extend only as far as assimilable "Ruthenian" (i.e., not nationally conscious Ukrainian) populations.[21] Despite their considerable differences, however, supporters of both approaches based their claims on a shared idea of Polish civilizational superiority. The federalist Oskar Halecki's assertion that in Ruthenia (a region that included Volhynia) "civilization and the social order find their principal support in the Polish element" relied on the same basic logic as the National Democrat Joachim Bartoszewicz's argument that a Polish "*mission civilisatrice*" had continued under the Russian empire.[22]

Even as they appealed to the language of a Polish civilizing mission, however, Poles found themselves fending off accusations that they were acting as imperialists. For one, non-Polish national elites saw Piłsudski's "invitation" to join a federation of nations, which was nominally based on inclusive ideas of civic nationalism, as an excuse for a Polish land grab, since Lithuanians, Ukrainians, and Belarusians were making their own claims to the very same territory.[23] Representatives of the short-lived Ukrainian state, for instance, accused Poland of being an imperialist power (like Russia) and depicted Ukraine, rather than

---

20   On statistics, see Maliszewski, "Żywioł polski na Wołyniu," 621.
21   For a summary of the basic distinction, see Davies, *Heart of Europe*, 113–29. Historians disagree on the extent to which Piłsudski was fully committed to federalism. On how policies toward federalism changed after August 1919, see Conrad, "Das Ende der Föderation." See also Wandycz, *Soviet-Polish Relations, 1917–1921*, 90–117; Dziewanowski, *Joseph Piłsudski*.
22   For Halecki, see "Les confins orientaux de la Pologne"; for Bartoszewicz, see "Mémoire sur les frontières nord et sud-est de la Pologne restaurée". On the similarities between the approaches, see Benecke, *Die Ostgebiete der Zweiten Polnischen Republik*, 22.
23   As Brian Porter has argued, by the late nineteenth century, pluralistic concepts of the Polish nation were already beginning to look like an excuse for irredentism. Porter, *When Nationalism Began to Hate*, 173.

Poland, as a nation with democratic and anti-imperial traditions.[24] Polish politicians pushed back, arguing that Polish imperialism could only ever be oxymoronic, since Poland had historically expanded eastward in a peaceful fashion and was now simply claiming back regions that empires had illegitimately snatched away at the end of the eighteenth century.[25]

The concept of Polish imperialism became more complicated still from the perspective of the Entente's leaders and regional experts who were simultaneously architects of the political map of the new eastern Europe and advocates for imperial systems of rule in non-white areas across the globe. On the one hand, some external commentators argued that Poland's role in the east was analogous to that of the Western powers in their imperial territories—and that this was an acceptable, even natural, phenomenon. Denying that Polish claims represented "imperialistic folly," the Cambridge historian Harold Temperley stated that Poles should not be accused of "criminal ambition" by taking the "intermediate peoples" of the east "under their protection" and introducing "such order and institutions as were suitable for their needs."[26] Others took a more critical stance. One member of Wilson's delegation in Paris drew on what Susan Pedersen has called "nineteenth-century ideas about the relative value of different European peoples and civilizations" when arguing that it would be better to have Poles under German rule than the other way around.[27] The South African Jan Smuts even floated the idea that the eastern European states should themselves be put under a mandate system, since they were "mostly untrained politically" and "either incapable or deficient in the power of self-government."[28]

Some representatives of the Western powers saw in Poland a dangerous combination of uncivilized behavior and tinpot imperialism, particularly when it came to Polish actions toward national minorities.[29] If this attitude stemmed from deeper assumptions about eastern European backwardness, stories in the

---

24   *Les problèmes nationaux de l'Ukraine à la Conférence de Paris*, 7; Leuthner, "The End of the Idea of a Polish Empire." For a Ukrainian perspective that contrasted democracy and self-determination with Polish imperialism, see Shelukhin, *Ukraine, Poland and Russia*.

25   As one Polish MP stated in parliament in April 1919, Polish colonization in the east could not be regarded as imperialism. See *Sprawozdanie stenograficzne z 24 posiedzenia*, 32.

26   Temperley, ed., *A History of the Peace Conference of Paris*, 276–77.

27   Pedersen, *The Guardians*, 18.

28   Smuts is cited in Judson, *The Habsburg Empire*, 444.

29   The minority treaties, the first of which was signed by Poland in June 1919, provided evidence of Western doubt that the successor states could be trusted to

Western press about the looting, rape, and shooting of Jewish civilians, most infamously in the Galician city of Lwów (November 1918) and the more northerly city of Pińsk (April 1919), did little to suggest that Poles could run a civilized state.[30] Indeed, many British politicians who did not favor an expansive Polish state in the east argued that Poles were acting as the worst kind of imperialists—aggressive, reckless, and oppressive. Britain's prime minister David Lloyd George told the Polish statesman and federalist Ignacy Jan Paderewski that members of "small nations" like Poland were "more imperialist... than either England and France [sic], than certainly the United States," while the British Zionist Lewis Namier accused the anti-Semite Dmowski of supporting "Polish imperialism which desires to extend its dominion over non-Polish races at the expense of Russia."[31] Even as the British and the French extended their imperial holdings abroad, Polish imperialism became an accusation to be rebutted—in response to Lloyd George's comment, Paderewski "protested vehemently against the imputation that Poles were animated by imperialistic ambitions."[32]

Anti-Imperial Democracy and Civilizational Hierarchies

Critical questions about the nature of civilization, imperialism, and democracy animated discussions at a local level, too, as more of Volhynia came under Polish military occupation in the first half of 1919. Between December 1918 and May 1919, some five thousand Polish troops pushed the fledgling Ukrainian People's Republic out of the western part of Volhynia, and by the end of August, Poles had captured the towns of Krzemieniec, Dubno, and Równe.[33] In February 1919, Poland's head of state Józef Piłsudski created a Civil Administration for the Eastern Lands (Zarząd Cywilny Ziem Wschodnich) to administer the occupied territories in the east. Although the question of who actually held power on the ground did not yield a clear answer, one influential group that sought

---

   exercise sovereignty and to protect vulnerable minority populations who lived within their emerging borders. See Mazower, "Paved Intentions," 78.

30 Fink, *Defending the Rights of Others*: on Lwów, see 101–132; on Pińsk, see 171–208.

31 Lloyd George, *The Truth about the Peace Treaties*, 998. Namier is cited in Hanak, *T.G. Masaryk (1850–1937)*, 96.

32 Lloyd George, *The Truth about the Peace Treaties*, 998.

33 Davies, *White Eagle, Red Star*, 58.

to shape the nature of the new state was the Borderland Guard (Straż Kresowa, hereafter "the Guard"), whose activists moved into the region with the Polish army and who worked alongside (although not always in harmony with) the civil administration.[34] Its so-called instructors, young men who had cut their teeth in Piłsudski-inspired conspiratorial student organizations in Warsaw, aimed to convince the *kresy*'s multiethnic population of the benefits of the Polish state.[35] By November 1919, twenty-seven Guard employees were active in Volhynia.[36]

In line with the language of 1919, the Guard was avowedly anti-imperial. Its national and local journals valorized the early modern Commonwealth and argued that Piłsudski's approach constituted the solution to the ongoing threats of both Russian and German imperialism.[37] When they explained their anti-imperial vision to local populations, Guard activists relied on a bifurcated distinction between an outdated, violent, and oppressive model of empire and a modern system of democracy that operated in the name of "the people" (*lud*). While Russian imperialism had relied on the will of the tsar "who, with just a stroke of the pen, settled the fate of millions and didn't consider if his law was good or bad for the *lud*," one activist explained to local people at a meeting in September 1919, the ballots in Polish elections were secret, meaning that factory owners and landowners could not control the votes of their employees.[38] Indeed, the idea of popular consent—another key Wilsonian principle—was central to their project.[39] In a report from October 1919, the head instructor of Łuck County stated that the eastern borderlands could be incorporated into Poland only "with the consent (*zgoda*) of at least the significant part of this population and the absence of opposition openly expressed by the remaining

---

34   A historical overview of the Guard can be found in Zielińska, *Towarzystwo Straży Kresowej*.
35   Nowacki, *ZET w walce o niepodległość i budowę państwa*, 130–41; for potted biographies of the major instructors, see 544–68.
36   Schenke, *Nationalstaat und nationale Frage*, 71.
37   "Od Redakcji," *Wschód Polski*, 3.
38   "Protokuł zjazdu delegatów północnych części powiatów Łuckiego i Rówieńskiego dnia 28 września 1919 r. w Sarnach."
39   Weitz, "From the Vienna to the Paris System," 1328; Getachew, *Worldmaking after Empire*, 37–70.

part."[40] In their minds, local people would benefit from the "democratic mechanisms" offered by the new government in Warsaw.[41]

The Guard also perpetuated the idea that Volhynia's multiethnic populations—Polish and non-Polish alike—were covictims of imperial oppression and that they therefore needed to work together. In June 1919, as part of the celebrations for the 350th anniversary of the Union of Lublin, by which Volhynia had become part of the Polish-Lithuanian Commonwealth, the Guard's local newspaper emphasized non-Polish support for Polish-Volhynian reunification. One article stated that in the town of Łuck "Ruthenians" carried signs that read FOR OUR FREEDOM AND YOURS in the Cyrillic script, evoking a Polish slogan from the 1830–31 anti-Russian insurrection, while another stated how satisfying it was to see Jews in Kowel participate enthusiastically in the celebrations.[42] While Polish-orchestrated pogroms against Jews had damaged Poland's reputation abroad, the author referred instead to prewar pogroms in the Russian empire and to those carried out by Ukrainians and White imperial forces. Jews, he argued, would not have to worry about such imperialistic violence in the Polish state.[43]

Even as they rejected both Russian imperialism and the ethnically based Polish nationalism that they associated with the right, however, the Guard's paternalistic claims that only Poles had the knowledge to import democracy rested on the assumption that most Volhynians were not nationally developed enough to rule themselves. At meetings, "Ruthenian" speakers who complained about abuses at the hands of the Polish civil administration were told that, as "guests," their complaints mattered less than those of local Poles and that they should instead be grateful that they were now under Polish rule. "When this was Russia, you were subjects," one activist told a group of "Ruthenians" who aired their grievances at a meeting in the town of Kowel, adding that Poland instead offered them citizenship.[44] By depicting Poles as a true nation and "Ruthenians" as nationally underdeveloped children who needed to be guided by a more advanced parent—an idea that historians have generally associated with the Polish right—Guard activists evoked language that was concurrently circulating

---

40 "Memoriał w sprawie położenia na Wołyniu."
41 Ibid., 91.
42 On Ruthenians, see "Obchody narodowe na Wołyniu," 2; on Jews, see "Obchód narodowy w Kowlu," 4.
43 "Obchód narodowy w Kowlu," 4.
44 "Protokół zjazdu delegatów ludności polskiej pow. Kowelskiego w dniu 14.9.1919 r."

in reference to populations in European-ruled empires and mandates.[45] Even if the Polish army entered Volhynia under "the banners of fraternal unity," as the Guard claimed on the front of an issue of its local newspaper, the older brother demanded a certain type of behavior from his allegedly less civilized sibling.[46]

Yet if Poles were the only national group that could act as conduits for anti-Russian, Western civilization in the Volhynian borderlands, the question of which Poles were able to carry out the task received diverse local answers. Most importantly, the Guard criticized Volhynia's Polish elites, including those who had trained as lawyers, doctors, and engineers, as well as large landowners, claiming that they were remnants of the Russian imperial system and therefore fundamentally antithetical to the democratizing national project.[47] As they sought to replace the manor house with the new institutions of democracy (or at least their version of democracy), Guard activists argued that life in the Russian empire had caused the once "sincerely Polish" landowners to lose their Polishness altogether and that landowners' attempts to undermine the civil administration by stymieing acts of land reform constituted a challenge to incoming state power.[48] While the landowners had their own claims to an age-old civilizing mission in the *kresy*, the Guard suggested that this was little more than a smokescreen for ongoing imperialism.[49] As such, the Guard's activists used charges of imperialism as a weapon in the fight to realign political power, wresting it not simply from an abstract (and now largely defunct) polity called the Russian empire but from those Poles whom they depicted as imperial remnants.

---

45   On the idea that "Poland is a mother who loves all her children equally," see "Obywatele!"; on paternalistic colonial language, see Singh Mehta, *Liberalism and Empire*, 31–33.
46   "Wielki święto Wołynia," 1. On the historical development of the "older brother" image in reference to Ruthenians from the 1890s, see Porter, *When Nationalism Began to Hate*, 182–88.
47   Mędrzecki, *Inteligencja polska na Wołyniu*, 46–49; Beauvois, *La bataille de la terre en Ukraine 1863–1914*. An interesting reflection is Petersen, "'Us' and 'Them'? Polish Self-Descriptions."
48   "Memoriał w sprawie położenia na Wołyniu."
49   On the Polish landowners' own version of the civilizing mission in the *kresy*, see Gosk, "Polski dyskurs kresowy w niefikcjonalnych zapisach międzywojennych."

Civilizing Poles, Removing Jewishness

As the borderland wars raged on, members of the Guard were not the only ones who aimed to assert their power over both non-Polish populations and their fellow Poles by drawing on the idea of an anti-imperial civilizing mission. Indeed, a look at another group that suggested a competing vision for Volhynia indicates how civilizational frameworks could accommodate antithetical political projects. In Poznań, a city that had been under German rule prior to the First World War and was home to almost 170,000 people by 1921, supporters of the right-wing Endecja were heavily critical of the deleterious effects of Germanizing policies on Polish cultural, economic, and political development.[50] But while the Guard saw Russian imperialism—and imperialism more broadly—as antithetical to Polish nationalism, Poznanian elites held a more ambivalent view of the German empire under which they had lived. Even if German administrators had described Poles through the language of backwardness, Poznanians argued that Polish experiences under German imperial rule, including their own practices of so-called organic work, made Poles from the formerly German lands the most effective carriers of Western civilization in the new state, particularly when compared to their fellow Poles from the Russian empire.[51] In fact, the Poznań-based National Democrats were less likely to reject imperialism per se and more inclined to criticize the specific characteristics of Russian imperialism and to emphasize its damaging effects on their nominal compatriots.

Such civilizational framings were part of an internal power struggle between Poznań and Poland's capital city, Warsaw. According to the Endecja-supporting Poznanians, Warsaw was not only dominated by supporters of their rival Piłsudski but was also lower down on the civilizational hierarchy, its wastefulness, incompetence, and lack of patriotism the woeful legacies of Russian influence.[52] The National Democrat Stanisław Kozicki's claim that Poznań had closer links than Warsaw did with Western European civilization reflected a broader set of opposites: Poznań was Western and civilized; Warsaw was Eastern and

---

50 Zalewski, "Rezultaty rządów niemieckich w Poznaniu," 209–15.
51 Hagen, "National Solidarity and Organic Work in Prussian Poland, 1815–1914."
52 On Dmowski's position, see Dmowski, "Społeczeństwo Poznańskiego i Pomorza w odbudowanej Polsce," 2. On Poznanian regionalism against Warsaw, see Wysocka, *Regionalizm wielkopolski w II Rzeczypospolitej 1919–1939*, 22; Moskal, *Im Spannungsfeld von Region und Nation*, 40–1.

backward.[53] As they competed for power against Warsaw, representatives of Poznań and the broader region of Greater Poland (Wielkopolska) to which it belonged also proposed a rival civilizing mission in the *kresy*. Even before Poland's eastern border had been set, plans were made for people from the *kresy* to journey to Greater Poland to learn about higher levels of farming culture, while both policemen and agricultural tools went eastward from Poznań.[54]

While the Guard's civilizing mission ostensibly relied on gaining the consent of the region's national minorities, the civilizational vision proposed by supporters of the Endecja instead combined aggressively assimilationist policies toward "Ruthenians" and explicit anti-Semitism. With Poznań's Jewish population sitting at just over 1 percent in 1921, right-wing Poznanians argued that the towns of eastern Poland, where Jews often made up a majority of the population, were dominated by "foreign" Jewish influences that they linked to Russian imperialism.[55] If in their most violent form such sensibilities resulted in Poznanian troops carrying out anti-Semitic attacks against eastern Jews, there were also calls to transform ethnic and religious demographics by sending Polish traders and artisans from Poznań to eastern towns to break up the "Jewish monopoly."[56] Significantly, those on the right did not limit their criticisms to Jews. In fact, they made a broader case against their fellow Poles from the former Russian partition whom they accused of having been corrupted by Russian and Jewish influences.[57] As one article in the *Greater Poland Messenger (Goniec Wielkopolski)* argued in 1919, "Polish society in the Russian partition did not manage to resist unfavorable eastern influence," especially that of Jews.[58] Once again, arguments about civilization and imperialism were deployed to frame struggles between people who nominally identified as Polish—and who were competing for power in the new state.

---

53 Kozicki, *Pamiętnik, 1876–1939*, 468. On pairs of opposites, see Moskal, *Im Spannungsfeld von Region und Nation*, 36.

54 On the visit, see Letter from the Society of the Former Prussian Partition for the North-Eastern Borderlands to the Ministry of Farming and State Lands in Poznań. On police, see "Protokuł zjazdu Instruktorów Straży Kresowej Okręgu"; on tools, see "Raport tygodniowy za czas od 16/X do 23/X.1919."

55 Wróbel, "Auswanderung," 81.

56 Borzęcki, "German Anti-Semitism à la Polonaise"; on attempts to damage Jewish trade, see Witos, *Moje wspomnienia*, 398.

57 Moskal, *Im Spannungsfeld von Region und Nation*, 34.

58 Cited in ibid., 36–7.

Even after the end of the Polish-Bolshevik war, the Endecja's idea that Poznań would play a civilizing role in combating Russian imperial remnants in the "backward" and "Jewish" eastern borderlands persisted. Everything—they argued—was topsy turvy, with Poles being undermined and marginalized, in spite of their civilizational superiority. In Volhynia, which became a formal province (województwo wołyńskie) of the Second Republic in February 1921, not only did Poles constitute less than 17 percent of the province's population according to the 1921 census, but the province did not elect a single ethnically Polish representative to parliament in the 1922 elections, stoking right-wing fears that "today these lands are more foreign to us than they were before the war."[59] During the early 1920s, Endecja journals continued to accuse Jews of perniciously influencing Ruthenians (and urging them to vote for the national minorities bloc), resisting the modernizing influences of the Polish state, and acting as the agents of both imperial and Bolshevik rule.[60]

As a way of combating these supposed problems, Poznań's elites pushed the idea that their city—not Warsaw—constituted Volhynia's civilizational savior. A February 1924 article written by the Poznanian Jan Biliński, which was published in the Endecja's *Poznań Courier* (*Kurjer Poznański*) and then reprinted in Volhynia's right-wing weekly *Volhynia Life* (*Życie Wołynia*), painted a picture of a weak and overwhelmed Polish minority that suffered both materially and spiritually as a consequence of neglect from the "motherland" (*macierz*), wartime destruction, and the influence of eastern Jews. Polish schoolchildren in the eastern borderlands, he argued, were becoming denationalized and, if they were not exposed to Polish schools, would "surrender to the foreign influences of our national enemies, becoming indifferent and lost for the nation."[61] Importantly, Biliński offered the antidote: the best way to give these easterners a sense of "absolute oneness with the motherland" was by bypassing Warsaw entirely and abandoning "the principles of centralization."[62] One of the programs mentioned by Biliński was a book drive, which was organized by the pro-Endecja Society for the Welfare of the Eastern Borderlands (Towarzystwo Opieki nad Kresami) and was depicted elsewhere as part of a broader project to prove Poznań's role as a "patron" for Volhynia and to reconstruct "the Polish spirit and significance

---

59 Budzyński, "Kiedy kres tej kresowej gospodarce?" 7.
60 On the reaction to the elections in the Poznanian press, see Figura, *Konflikt polsko-ukraiński*, 271–76.
61 Biliński, "Kresy Wschodnie—najżywotniejsze zagadnienie," 4.
62 Ibid.

in the east."[63] In calling for the western provinces to take up the "guardianship" of their eastern counterparts, with Poznań protecting what he called the "most endangered province" of Volhynia, Biliński invoked the German example to which Poznanians had been exposed. The only difference, he stated, was that the Germans had gained land through the "trick" of the partitions; Poles, on the other hand, were doing little more than recovering what was theirs.[64]

Plans to forge connections between urban populations—particularly between Poles in Poznań and Poles in Volhynia's provincial capital Łuck—gained momentum by the mid-1920s. At an international fair that was held in Poznań in 1925, the city's leaders staked out a rhetorical claim for their unique civilizing role in Łuck, the only town from the formerly Russian *kresy* to take part. Volhynia's provincial capital was a historically Polish settlement, the exhibition's catalog noted, but it had been severely damaged by Russian rule and, like other *kresy* towns, lacked the hallmarks of civilization that Poznań boasted: a sewer system, municipal parks, and paved roads and sidewalks.[65] Indeed, according to the catalog, even the "poor" paved streets in the towns of the former German partition were in a better state than the poor ones in areas formerly under Russian rule.[66]

Far from constituting a neutral comparison, observations of eastern backwardness provided the rationale for the initiation of a program of "fraternal patronage" by which Poland's "leading cities" would select a "younger brother" from among "less developed towns" within the state's borders.[67] On the final day of the exhibition, the president of Poznań stated that his city would act as a protector over Łuck, much to the delight of Volhynia's right-wing newspaper. Importantly, this relationship was to be achieved not only through the efforts of municipal administrators but also via a range of social and sporting organizations and an exchange between school-aged children.[68] The familial metaphors of brothers and sisters implied an intimate (although by no means equal) relationship between Poles from western and eastern Poland. Moreover, the fact

---

63 "O kresach i na kresach," 7. *Życie Wołynia* reprinted part of an article that had been originally published in *Kurjer Poznański*.
64 Biliński, "Kresy Wschodnie," 4.
65 *Katalog Wystawy Związku Miast Polskich na Międzynarodowym Targu w Poznaniu 1925*, 14–15.
66 Ibid., 31.
67 "Łuck pod patronatem Poznania," 3. The article in *Przegląd Lubelsko-Kresowy* was reprinted from *Życie Wołynia*.
68 Ibid.

that this relationship was imagined as one between ethnic Poles meant that Łuck's Jewish majority, which the National Democrats believed had no place in the Polish nation, was excluded from the civilizing mission.

Conclusion: Globalizing Polish Civilizing Missions

This chapter began with a simple premise: that any attempt to categorize interwar Poland as either an empire or a nation-state tells us more about our own rigid conceptualizations of these types of states than it does about the complex claims to sovereignty made in the Second Republic—and in the interwar world more generally. In the wake of the First World War, Polish elites participated in global conversations that transcended the traditional empire/nation-state divide. Although they deliberately distanced themselves from imperialism and argued that they were establishing democratic practices, they simultaneously based their claims to contested territories in the east on the broader global idea that a "civilized" minority had the right to rule over a "backward" majority. In the early years of the Second Republic, as the demographically non-Polish region of Volhynia was contested at both international and local levels, Polish statesmen, Borderland Guard activists, and Poznanian Endeks alike navigated and shaped civilizational gradients, arguing that Poles were worthy of self-rule here in a way that non-Poles were not, even as they accused their enemies of constituting the remnants of imperialism. Although they had very different ideas of what the Polish nation should look like—with Guard activists more closely aligned with Piłsudski's inclusive (civic) nationalism and Poznanians in favor of Dmowski's exclusionary (ethnic) version—they agreed on one thing: Poles, in some shape or form, were more civilized than the non-Polish populations of the east.

A consideration of these stories allows us to challenge some oversimplified models that linger in the historiography. Most notably, while much of the scholarship has focused on binary relations between seemingly clear-cut national or ethnic groups—such as Poles, Jews, and Ukrainians—these groups were themselves constructed within the framework of civilizational hierarchies. Moreover, this process involved differentiating *between* people *within* the ruling national group, as Polish elites competed against one another to shape the postimperial state. The geographical vectors of these processes were never clear-cut. As the example of Poznań reveals, civilizing missions did not always radiate out from Warsaw but were also framed in ways that attempted to marginalize the capital by tarring it with the brush of Russian imperialism. Such dynamics continued throughout the interwar years as a multitude of Polish stakeholders—from border guards and scouts to health workers and teachers—made a case for their own importance in Volhynia, both in managing the non-Polish majority and in deciding who got to claim the coveted role of the "civilized Pole" at a local level.[69]

Although the main focus here has been on how a range of actors shaped prevailing global justifications for sovereignty within the Second Republic, the approach also invites us to think about how interwar Poland's domestic and external dynamics might be understood within a common conceptual framework.[70] This is especially important as scholars begin to look more closely at Poland's colonial ambitions, a subject that has received limited attention until recently.[71] How did Polish internal plans to settle people from more "civilized" (western) areas into less "civilized" (eastern) regions interact with Polish projects to gain colonial territories and develop emigration practices across the globe? How did ideas of civilizational gradients within the state correspond with various policies toward the so-called Polish diaspora?[72] And how might studying the multiple images of Jews—as an "uncivilized" and antimodern population within the eastern borderlands and as a potential civilizing force in non-white colonial spaces—help us to gain a more complex understanding of both Polish nationalism and lived Jewish experiences between the wars?[73]

Historians have certainly conceptualized other European states through the framework of both empire and nation-state—viewing interwar France as an "imperial nation-state" and Mussolini's Italy as a "nation-empire," for instance.[74] What, we might ask, can we gain by placing Poland, a country with global aspirations (if no formal imperial holdings) within a similar hybrid framework?

---

69   Ciancia, *On Civilization's Edge*.

70   Historiography on Poland during the Cold War, and particularly communist Poland's relationship to the Global South, is already beginning to move in this direction. See, for instance, Stanek, *Architecture in Global Socialism*, especially 97–168; Mazurek, "Polish Economists in Nehru's India."

71   Grzechnik, "The Missing Second World"; Puchalski, *Poland in a Colonial World Order*; Balogun, "Polish *Lebensraum*."

72   In established "civilized" nation-states like France, Poles were said to be susceptible to the same kinds of foreign-imposed denationalization as they were in the *kresy*. In "semi-civilized" places, like Brazil, Poles depicted themselves as European colonizers outside a formal colonial framework. For an overview of the various categories of Polonia as conceptualized during the interwar period, see Jarzębecki, *Polonia zagraniczna*.

73   On Polish policies toward the emigration of Jews, see Snyder, *Black Earth*, 58–76.

74   Wilder, *The French Imperial Nation-States*; Pergher, *Mussolini's Nation-Empire*.

And yet, we should not simply offer Poland up as another version of a universal phenomenon. Instead, studying a state that was both created through imperial implosion and entangled in ongoing global practices of empire allows us to escape the bifurcated language of empire and nation-state altogether. It thus provides a potentially generative case for scholars interested in understanding how interwar actors made sense of the bumpy nature of sovereignty in multiple locations across the world.

Bibliography

Balogun, Bolaji. "Polish *Lebensraum*: The Colonial Ambition to Expand on Racial Terms." *Ethnic and Racial Studies* 41, no. 14 (2018): 2561–79.

Beauvois, Daniel. *La bataille de la terre en Ukraine 1863-1914: Les Polonais et les conflits socio-ethniques*. Lille: Presses universitaires de Lille, 1993.

Benecke, Werner. *Die Ostgebiete der Zweiten Polnischen Republik: Staatsmacht und öffentliche Ordnung in einer Minderheitenregion 1918-1939*. Cologne: Böhlau Verlag, 1999.

Biliński, Jan. "Kresy Wschodnie—najżywotniejsze zagadnienie." *Życie Wołynia*, February 17, 1924.

Borzęcki, Jerzy. "German Anti-Semitism à la Polonaise: A Report on Poznanian Troops' Abuse of Belarusian Jews in 1919." *East European Politics and Societies and Cultures* 26, no. 4 (2012): 693–707.

Budzyński, Władysław. "Kiedy kres tej kresowej gospodarce?" *Myśl Narodowa*, October 27, 1923.

Cavanagh, Clare. "Postcolonial Poland." *Common Knowledge* 10, no. 1 (2004): 82–92.

Chojnowski, Andrzej. *Koncepcje polityki narodowościowej rządów polskich w latach 1921-1939*. Wrocław: Zakład Narodowy im. Ossolińskich, 1979.

Ciancia, Kathryn. *On Civilization's Edge: A Polish Borderland in the Interwar World*. New York: Oxford University Press, 2020.

Conrad, Benjamin. "Das Ende der Föderation: Die Ostpolitik Piłsudskis und des Belweder-Lagers 1918–1920." In *Kommunikation über Grenzen: Polen als Schauplatz transnationaler Akteure von den Teilungen bis heute*, edited by Lisa Bicknell, Benjamin Conrad, and Hans-Christian Petersen, 11–32. Berlin: LIT Verlag Dr. W. Hopf, 2013.

Davies, Norman. *Heart of Europe, The Past in Poland's Present*. Oxford and New York: Oxford University Press, 2001.

Davies, Norman. *White Eagle, Red Star: The Polish-Soviet War, 1919-20*. New York: St. Martin's Press, 1972.

Deak, Istvan. "How to Construct a Productive, Disciplined, Monoethnic Society: The Dilemma of East Central European Governments, 1914–1956." In *Landscaping the Human Garden: Twentieth-century Population Management in a Comparative Framework*, edited by Amir Weiner, 205–17. Stanford, CA: Stanford University Press, 2003.

Dmowski, Roman. "Społeczeństwo Poznańskiego i Pomorza w odbudowanej Polsce." *Głos Lubelski*, December 9, 1925.

Dziewanowski, Marian Kamil. *Joseph Piłsudski: A European Federalist: 1918–1922*. Stanford, CA: Stanford University Press, 1969.

Figura, Marek. *Konflikt polsko-ukraiński w prasie Polski Zachodniej w latach 1918–1923*. Poznań: Wydawnictwo Poznańskie, 2001.

Fink, Carole. *Defending the Rights of Others: The Great Powers, the Jews, and International Minority Protection, 1878–1938*. New York: Cambridge University Press, 2004.

Getachew, Adom. *Worldmaking after Empire: The Rise and Fall of Self-Determination*. Princeton, NJ: Princeton University Press, 2019.

Gosk, Hanna. "Polski dyskurs kresowy w niefikcjonalnych zapisach międzywojennych. Próba lektury w perspektywie postcolonial studies." *Teksty Drugie*, no. 6 (2008): 20–33.

Grala, Hieronim. "Kolonializm alla polacca." *Polski Przegląd Dyplomatyczny* (2017), no. 4: 93–117.

Grzechnik, Marta. "The Missing Second World: On Poland and Postcolonial Studies." *Interventions* 21, no. 7 (2019): 998–1014.

Hagen, William W. "National Solidarity and Organic Work in Prussian Poland, 1815–1914." *Journal of Modern History* 44, no. 1 (1972): 38–64.

Hanak, Harry. *T.G. Masaryk (1850–1937)*. Vol. 1. *Thinker and Politician*. Basingstoke, UK: Palgrave Macmillan, 1990.

Hillis, Faith. *Children of Rus': Right-Bank Ukraine and the Invention of a Russian Nation*. Ithaca, NY: Cornell University Press, 2013.

Holubec, Stanislav. "'We Bring Order, Discipline, Western European Democracy, and Culture to this Land of Former Oriental Chaos and Disorder': Czech Perceptions of Sub-Carpathian Rus and Its Modernization in the 1920s." In *Mastery and Lost Illusions: Space and Time in the Modernization of Eastern and Central Europe*, edited by Włodzimierz Borodziej, Stanislav Holubec, and Joachim von Puttkamer, 223–50. Munich: De Gruyter, 2014.

Jarzębecki, Witold. *Polonia zagraniczna: o Polakach żyjących poza granicami Rzeczypospolitej słów kilka*. Warsaw: Komitet Dnia Polaka Zagranicą, 1934.

Judson, Pieter M. *The Habsburg Empire: A New History*. Cambridge, MA: Harvard University Press, 2016.

Katalog Wystawy Związku Miast Polskich na Międzynarodowym Targu w Poznaniu 1925. Poznań, 1925.

Kołodziejczyk, Dorota. "Postkolonialny transfer na Europę Środkowo-Wschodnią." *Teksty Drugie* 2010, no. 5: 22–39.

Kola, Adam. *Socjalistyczny postkolonializm: Rekonsolidacja pamięci.* Toruń: Wydawnictwo Naukowe Uniwersytetu Mikołaja Kopernika, 2018.

Kopp, Kristin. *Germany's Wild East: Constructing Poland as Colonial Space.* Ann Arbor: University of Michigan Press, 2012.

Kozicki, Stanisław. *Pamiętnik, 1876–1939.* Słupsk: Wydawnictwo Naukowe Akademii Pomorskiej, 2009.

Kumar, Krishan. "Nation-States as Empires, Empires as Nation-States: Two Principles, One Practice?" *Theory and Society* 39, no. 2 (2010): 119–43.

"Les confins orientaux de la Pologne," Archiwum Akt Nowych, Warsaw, Delegacja Polska na Konferencję Pokojową w Paryżu 153.

Les problèmes nationaux de l'Ukraine à la Conférence de Paris: Interview de M. Sydorenko, Président de la Délégation de la Republique Ukrainienne. Paris: Bureau Ukrainien de Presse, 1919.

Letter from the Society of the Former Prussian Partition for the North-Eastern Borderlands to the Ministry of Farming and State Lands in Poznań (April 3, 1920), Archiwum Państwowe w Poznaniu 53/295/0/1/80.

Leuthner, Carl. "The End of the Idea of a Polish Empire." In *Ukraine's Claim to Freedom: An Appeal for Justice on Behalf of Thirty-Five Millions,* 41–52. New York: Ukrainian National Association, 1915.

Liulevicius, Vejas Gabriel. *The German Myth of the East: 1800 to the Present.* New York: Oxford University Press, 2009.

Lloyd George, David. *The Truth About the Peace Treaties: Volume II.* London: Victor Gollancz, 1938.

"Łuck pod patronatem Poznania." *Przegląd Lubelsko-Kresowy,* June 5, 1925.

Maliszewski, Edward. "Żywioł polski na Wołyniu." *Ziemia* 5, no. 44–52 (December 1919).

Manela, Erez. *The Wilsonian Moment: Self-Determination and the International Origins of Anticolonial Nationalism.* New York: Oxford University Press, 2007.

Mazower, Mark. "Paved Intentions: Civilization and Imperialism." *World Affairs* 171, no. 2 (2008): 72–84.

Mazurek, Małgorzata. "Polish Economists in Nehru's India: Making Science for the Third World in an Era of De-Stalinization and Decolonization." *Slavic Review* 77, no. 3 (2018): 588–610.

Mędrzecki, Włodzimierz. *Inteligencja polska na Wołyniu w okresie międzywojennym.* Warsaw: Neriton, 2005.

Mémoire sur l'indépendance de l'Ukraine présenté à la Conférence de la paix par la délégation de la république ukrainienne. Paris: Imp. Robinet-Houtaix, 1919.

"Mémoire sur les frontières nord et sud-est de la Pologne restaurée." Archiwum Akt Nowych, Warsaw, Komitet Narodowy Polski w Paryżu 317.

"Memoriał w sprawie położenia na Wołyniu, zadań administracji i Straży Kresowej" (Antoni Zalewski, 18.X.19). Archiwum Akt Nowych, Warsaw, Towarzystwo Straży Kresowej 217.

Mick, Christoph. "Colonialism in the Polish Eastern Borderlands, 1919–1939." In *The Shadow of Colonialism on Europe's Modern Past*, edited by Róisín Healy and Enrico Dal Lago, 126-41. Basingstoke, UK: Palgrave, 2014.

Miller, Alexei, and Stefan Berger, eds. *Nationalizing Empires*. Budapest: Central European University Press, 2014.

Mironowicz, Eugeniusz. *Białorusini i Ukraińcy w polityce obozu piłsudczykowskiego*. Białystok: Wydawnictwo Uniwersyteckie Trans Humana, 2007.

Moskal, Anna. *Im Spannungsfeld von Region und Nation. Die Polonisierung der Stadt Posen nach 1918 und 1945*. Wiesbaden: Harrassowitz, 2013.

Nowacki, Tadeusz. *ZET w walce o niepodległość i budowę państwa: Szkice i wspomnienia*. Warsaw: Wydawnictwo Naukowe PWN, 1996.

Nowak, Andrzej. "From Empire Builder to Empire Breaker, or There and Back Again: History and Memory of Poland's Role in Eastern European Politics." *Ab Imperio* (2004), no. 1: 255–89.

"O kresach i na kresach." *Życie Wołynia*, March 16, 1924.

"Obchody narodowe na Wołyniu." *Polak Kresowy*, June 22, 1919.

"Obchód narodowy w Kowlu." *Polak Kresowy*, July 20, 1919.

"Obywatele!" (Borderland Guard in Równe, August 1919). Derzhavnyi arkhiv Rivnenskoi oblasti, Rivne, 30/1/2.

"Od Redakcji." *Wschód Polski* 1, no. 1 (December 1919).

Papierzyńska-Turek, Mirosława. *Sprawa ukraińska w Drugiej Rzeczypospolitej, 1922–1926*. Kraków: Wydawnictwo Literackie, 1979.

Pedersen, Susan. *The Guardians: The League of Nations and the Crisis of Empire*. New York: Oxford University Press, 2015.

Pergher, Roberta. *Mussolini's Nation-Empire: Sovereignty and Settlement in Italy's Borderlands, 1922–1943*. New York: Cambridge University Press, 2018.

Pergher, Roberta, and Marcus M. Payk, eds. *Beyond Versailles: Sovereignty, Legitimacy, and the Formation of New Polities after the Great War*. Bloomington: Indiana University Press, 2019.

Petersen, Hans-Christian. "'Us' and 'Them'? Polish Self-Descriptions and Perceptions of the Russian Empire between Homogeneity and Diversity (1815-1863)." In *Empire Speaks Out: Languages of Rationalization and Self-Description in the Russian Empire*, edited by Ilya Gerasimov, Jan Kusber, and Alexander Semyonov, 89–119. Leiden: Brill, 2009.

Plokhy, Serhii. *Unmaking Imperial Russia: Mykhailo Hrushevsky and the Writing of Ukrainian History*. Toronto: University of Toronto Press, 2005.

Porter, Brian. *When Nationalism Began to Hate: Imagining Modern Politics in Nineteenth-Century Poland*. New York: Oxford University Press, 2000.

Porter-Szűcs, Brian. *Poland in the Modern World: Beyond Martyrdom*. Chichester, UK: Wiley-Blackwell, 2014.

Potocki, Robert. *Polityka państwa polskiego wobec zagadnienia ukraińskiego w latach 1930–1939*. Lublin: Instytut Europy Środkowo-Wschodniej, 2003.

"Protokół zjazdu delegatów ludności polskiej pow. Kowelskiego w dniu 14.9.1919 r." Archiwum Akt Nowych, Warsaw, Towarzystwo Straży Kresowej 239.

"Protokuł zjazdu delegatów północnych części powiatów Łuckiego i Rówieńskiego dnia 28 września 1919 r. w Sarnach." Archiwum Akt Nowych, Warsaw, Towarzystwo Straży Kresowej 239.

"Protokuł zjazdu Instruktorów Straży Kresowej Okręgu Wołyńskiego z dnia 5/V 1920 r." Archiwum Akt Nowych, Warsaw, Towarzystwo Straży Kresowej 240.

Puchalski, Piotr. *Poland in a Colonial World Order: Adjustments and Aspirations, 1918–1939*. London: Routledge, 2022.

Reynolds, David, *The Long Shadow: The Legacies of the Great War in the Twentieth Century*. New York: W. W. Norton, 2015.

"Raport tygodniowy za czas od 16/X do 23/X.1919" (Kowel, dnia 23.X.1919). Archiwum Akt Nowych, Warsaw, Towarzystwo Straży Kresowej 214.

Roshwald, Aviel. *Ethnic Nationalism and the Fall of Empires: Central Europe, Russia, and the Middle East, 1914-1923*. London and New York: Routledge, 2001.

Schenke, Cornelia. *Nationalstaat und nationale Frage: Polen und die Ukrainer 1921–1939*. Hamburg: Dölling und Galitz, 2004.

Shelukhin, S. *Ukraine, Poland and Russia and The Right of the Free Disposition of the Peoples*. Washington, DC: Friends of Ukraine, 1919.

Singh Mehta, Uday. *Liberalism and Empire: A Study in Nineteenth-Century British Liberal Thought*. Chicago: University of Chicago Press, 1999.

Smith, Leonard V. "Empires at the Paris Peace Conference." In *Empires at War, 1911–1923*, edited by Robert Gerwarth and Erez Manela, 254–76. New York: Oxford University Press, 2014.

Snochowska-Gonzalez, Claudia. "Post-colonial Poland—On an Unavoidable Misuse." *East European Politics and Societies and Cultures* 26, no. 4 (2012): 708–23.

Snyder, Timothy. *Black Earth: The Holocaust as History and Warning*. New York: Tim Duggan, 2015.

Sowa, Jan. *Fantomowe ciało króla: Peryferyjne zmagania z nowoczesną formą*. Kraków: Universitas, 2011.

Sprawozdanie stenograficzne z 24 posiedzenia Sejmu Ustawodawczego z dnia 3 kwietnia 1919 roku.

Stanek, Łukasz. *Architecture in Global Socialism: Eastern Europe, West Africa, and the Middle East in the Cold War*. Princeton, NJ: Princeton University Press, 2019.

Temperley, H. W. V. ed. *A History of the Peace Conference of Paris*. Vol. 6. London: Hodder and Stoughton, 1924.

Thompson, Ewa M. "Whose Discourse? Telling the Story in Post-Communist Poland." *The Other Shore: Slavic and East European Cultures Abroad, Past and Present*, no. 1 (2010): 1–15.

Tomaszewski, Jerzy. *Ojczyzna nie tylko Polaków: Mniejszości narodowe w Polsce w latach 1918-1939*. Warsaw: Młodzieżowa Agencja Wydawnicza, 1985.

Tomaszewski, Jerzy. *Rzeczpospolita wielu narodów*. Warsaw: Czytelnik, 1985.

Torzecki, Ryszard. *Kwestia ukraińska w Polsce w latach 1923–1929*. Kraków: Wydawnictwo Literackie, 1989.
Ureña Valerio, Lenny A. *Colonial Fantasies, Imperial Realities: Race Science and the Making of Polishness on the Fringes of the German Empire*. Athens: Ohio University Press, 2019.
Wandycz, Piotr. *Soviet-Polish Relations, 1917–1921*. Cambridge, MA: Harvard University Press, 1969.
Weeks, Theodore R. *Nation and State in Late Imperial Russia: Nationalism and Russification on the Western Frontier, 1863–1914*. DeKalb: Northern Illinois University Press, 2008.
Weitz, Eric D. "From the Vienna to the Paris System: International Politics and the Entangled Histories of Human Rights, Forced Deportations, and Civilizing Missions." *American Historical Review* 113, no. 5 (2008): 1313–43.
Weitz, Eric. D. "Self-Determination: How a German Enlightenment Idea Became the Slogan of National Liberation and a Human Right." *American Historical Review* 120, no. 2 (2015): 462–96.
Wheatley, Natasha. "Legal Pluralism as Temporal Pluralism: Historical Rights, Legal Vitalism, and Non-Synchronous Sovereignty." In *Power and Time: Temporalities in Conflict and the Making of History*, edited by Dan Edelstein, Stefanos Geroulanos, and Natasha Wheatley, 53–79. Chicago: University of Chicago Press, 2020.
"Wielki święto Wołynia." *Polak Kresowy*, June 9, 1919.
Wilder, Gary. *The French Imperial Nation-State: Negritude and Colonial Humanism between the Two World Wars*. Chicago: University of Chicago Press, 2005.
Witos, Wincenty. *Moje wspomnienia*. Vol. II. Paris: Instytut Literacki, 1964.
Wolff, Larry. *Woodrow Wilson and the Reimagining of Eastern Europe*. Stanford, CA: Stanford University Press, 2020.
Wróbel, Piotr J. "'Auswanderung': The Exodus of Jews from Greater Poland (Wielkopolska), 1918–1921." *Studia Judaica* 34 (2014): 57–83.
Wysocka, Barbara. *Regionalizm wielkopolski w II Rzeczypospolitej 1919–1939*. Poznań: Wydawnictwo Naukowe Uniwersytetu im. Adama Mickiewicza, 1981.
Zalewski, Zygmunt. "Rezultaty rządów niemieckich w Poznaniu." *Kronika Miasta Poznania*, November 30, 1923, 209–15.
Zarycki, Tomasz. "Debating Soviet Imperialism in Contemporary Poland: On the Polish uses of Postcolonial Theory and their Contexts." In *Empire De/Centered: New Spatial Histories of Russia and the Soviet Union*, edited by Sanna Turoma and Maxim Waldstein Kupovykh, 191–215. New York: Routledge, 2013.
Zielińska, Nina. *Towarzystwo Straży Kresowej, 1918–1927*. Lublin: Verba, 2006.

Chapter Four

Suspicious Origins as a Category of Polish Culture

Irena Grudzińska-Gross

Polish literature always contains the traces of the often stateless but—until the second half of the twentieth century—always multinational Poland. These heterogenic traces undermine the easy closure of a national community. The work of the Polish national poet, Adam Mickiewicz, embraces a universe much larger than an ethnically "pure" Poland. He invited into his poems not only the Polish Mother but also the innkeeper Jankiel, the turncoat Wallenrod, people celebrating Belorussian pagan rites, Lithuanians, Greek Catholic priests, and even ghosts. Mickiewicz's generosity and that of other Romantics built contemporary Poland on a literature of otherness and heterogeneity. It is an open Poland, embedded in world history not as a tight-knit and separate national unit of one ethnicity and one religion but as a multinational community. It is this heterogeneity that, like a permanent blemish, is visible each time the white tablecloth is spread for a national banquet.

This chapter is concerned with a moment in Polish cultural history when the issue of national identity was being clarified anew. It looks at the Polish books and newspapers appearing around the year 2000 (i.e., when Poland, already a member of the NATO, was eagerly preparing to join the European Union). It was a country that during the ten years of its new freedom openly debated its history and identity. These debates often paid close attention to the genealogy of various important Polish personalities. In the model of nativist culture, it is the mother who guarantees belonging. The origin of Frederic Chopin, Adam Mickiewicz, and Juliusz Słowacki became a topic of newspaper and media interest. Today we can clearly see that the intense focus on that issue was pointing the way toward rampant nationalism.

The issue was the ethnic or religious origin of these cultural icons. One could detect three types of reactions to this dilemma. First, the Jewishness of a person is discussed, suggested, or implied, but not made explicit. The second denies a person's Jewish origins. The third reaction involves a particular public figure's non-Polish origins being acknowledged but explained away as not Jewish but Tartar or Armenian. In each of these types of reactions, the matter of foreign origin is treated with utmost importance even though the persons in question declare themselves Polish and have been active participants in Polish culture. It is not the individual's consciousness or religious practice that worry the critics. It is simply a matter of purity of roots.

This chapter will not inquire about people's ethnic or religious origins: such an inquiry could not be helpful or practical. In many wars and disasters in Polish history archives were lost—it is enough to point out that during the Warsaw Uprising of 1944, 90 percent of all the documents in the main Polish archive were burned. What I am interested in is the ongoing attention paid to the problem of origins and what exactly this persistent line of questioning is attempting to accomplish. As professor Maria Janion wrote: "I do not analyze the evidence or rebuttals about Barbara Majewska presented by the supporters or critics of the hypothesis about the Jewish origin of the mother of Mickiewicz. I am interested in the legend. I am interested in the tone of debate."[1]

And that tone is indeed very interesting. Although, as a result of the Holocaust, the changing of borders, and postwar ethnic cleansing Poland became a country of one religion and one ethnicity[2], the issue of genealogical origin shows a strong continuity not only with prewar Poland but even with the nineteenth century.

This chapter is based on several books and media sources, some of them dating to early 2000. I am interested in the way the authors of the texts referenced here arrive at their conclusions; hence, some words are italicized to attract the reader's attention to that process. I want to show not only how these texts establish the predetermined status of some of the most important figures in Polish culture but also how inconclusive this line of inquiry always remains.

---

1   Janion, *Do Europy, tak, ale z naszymi umarłymi*, 190. All translations are mine unless otherwise indicated.
2   According to the 2011 Polish census 97.10 percent of the population claim sole or partial Polish nationality, 98.19 percent declare that they speak Polish at home.

Inexpressible

In May 2000, in what was then Poland's largest daily newspaper, *Gazeta Wyborcza*, a letter appeared titled: "Jan Brzechwa—simply a Polish patriot." Brzechwa, a beloved author of children's literature, had already been dead for twenty-five years. The letter, a kind of clarification, was written by Brzechwa's daughter, Krystyna Brzechwa, in rebuttal to protests against the idea of naming an elementary school after her father. The protesters denounced the Jewish origins of Brzechwa as well as his past affiliation with the communist regime. Defending her father against "barely responsible concepts," she explained that the family of Lesman , which her father and his cousin, the great poet Bolesław Leśmian, came from (both "Brzechwa" and "Leśmian" were literary pseudonyms) was "totally Polonized"; just like their parents, one of them was buried in a Catholic cemetery and the other in an evangelical one. "Though the fathers of Leśmian and Brzechwa were brothers," she wrote, "the circumstance that one is reposing at the Catholic cemetery and the other at an evangelical one results from, if I may say so, the tribulations of the heart. As is well known, the Catholic Church does not condone divorce. In the situation of the intention to change one's life partner one sometimes relied on the change of confession. Such a situation, usually unmentioned, touched rather numerous and even very well-known people in Poland." She then described the patriotic, military, and literary activities of her father. As for the accusation of Stalinism, she declared: "I am unable to meaningfully understand His rather short as far as time is concerned but verbal submission in some of his poems to the pressure of the communist authorities." And in conclusion she wrote: "My father was simply a Polish patriot."[3] The word "Jew" or "Jewish" do not appear in the letter at all.

"Jew, what a strange word it is," wrote Tadeusz Konwicki. "Before one pronounces it there is a short moment of fear."[4] This is why, even with the best of intentions, the word is often redacted. As an example, I will quote from letters exchanged between Jerzy Giedroyc and Melchior Wańkowicz. Giedroyc, the editor of the most important émigré monthly, *Kultura*, asked Wańkowicz, a well-known writer, to respond to a text written by another writer, Gustaw Herling-Grudziński, published in the London émigré periodical *Wiadomości* under the title "On Jewish Topics" (*Wiadomości*, March 12, 1950). While working on the reply, Wańkowicz wrote to Giedoryc: "Józio [Czapski] . . . told me to cross out these two points. The one on page 18 I crossed out, but that on page 5 I don't

---

3   Brzechwa, "Jan Brzechwa—po prostu polski patriota."
4   Konwicki, *Bohiń*, 153–54.

want to. Herling, a colleague of my daughters, was widely known as a Jew. He should not think that I am undermining him. I do not like unclear situations. It depends on you. But I prefer not to cross it out."[5]

Giedroyc replied, "As regards his origin, I leave it totally to your decision. My first reaction was like Józio's, but after reflection I do not insist. First of all, I do not see in this *anything ignominious* (*hańbiący*), and secondly, on this particular topic this fact has a certain importance" (italics mine).[6]

Yet a month later Giedroyc returned to the issue: "I received your 'Tragedy of Koestler' [the title of Wańkowicz's article] together with corrections. I have a great request for you to cut out the sentence about the Jewishness of Herling and to edit out in some points his last name. I think the article will only improve by it."[7] Wańkowicz agreed.[8] Nine years later, in a letter to Giedroyc about other matters, Wańkowicz wrote: "People were afraid of [Jewish] subject matters. We are not afraid of dead matter. So, this matter is alive."[9]

Such well-intentioned omissions of the word "Jew" or "Jewish" were also present in Polish political life. Right after 1989, during the first free presidential campaign, the ethnic and religious background of the candidate Tadeusz Mazowiecki was scrutinized. (Accusations of being Jewish were, at that time, a frequent occurrence in Polish political life and were directed at practically everybody, including Lech Wałęsa and John-Paul II.) Accused of being Jewish, Mazowiecki chose not to reply. Then a priest from the Płock parish publicly declared that he was in possession of the Mazowiecki family's baptism certificates dating back to the sixteenth century—in this way rebutting the accusation. The running joke was that Mazowiecki was a "convert." A similar situation marked the 1995 presidential campaign of Jacek Kuroń, who met accusations of Jewishness with silence. His political colleague Henryk Wujec, during one of Kuroń's campaign meetings, replied to the question of whether Kuroń was Jewish with his own question: "And a Jew cannot be a president?" All three

---

5   All underlining in this and other quotations is mine. Letter from May 4, 1950, 140.
6   Letter from May 8, 1950. Ibid., 140–41.
7   Letter from June 12, 1950, 154.
8   Letter from June 18, 1950, 159.
9   Letter from October 6, 1959, 212. In a very interesting article, Danuta Szajnert calls the act of exposing the Jewish origins of Herling-Grudziński in a 1968 communist article attacking him "a delation." See Szajnert, "Gustaw Herling-Grudziński i Żydzi. Rekonesans," 261–74.

politicians—Mazowiecki, Kuroń, and Wujec—as far as I know, were not Jewish. And all three obviously considered a denial undignified and inexpressible.

Another example of such inexpressibility related to questions concerning the origins of Jan Tomasz Gross. When his book *Neighbors*[10] was being hotly debated, the historian Andrzej Paczkowski wrote: "Among [the arguments for the rejection of the content of that book] are the mistakes (or as it is usually written—lies) of the author of *Neighbors* in his other books, in addition to the display of his ethnic origin (by the way, those who lay down such a charge diverge from truth)."[11] The convoluted structure of the sentence is due to its avoidance of using the word "Jew." Everybody understood what the charge was.

Corrections

The word "Jewish" is not always monopolized by those who use it as an accusatory term. I will again use a letter from someone clarifying the origin of a parent. The weekly *Polityka* published a letter by Krzysztof Tatarkiewicz, son of the philosopher Władysław Tatarkiewicz. The letter was a reply to a column by Ludwik Stomma in which professor Tatarkiewicz was included on a list of Poles of Jewish origin.[12] This list illustrated Stomma's unsustainable thesis that in the independent Poland (1918–1939), Polish citizens of Jewish origin were not discriminated against by the authorities. "Unfortunately," Krzysztof Tatarkiewicz wrote, "my Father Władysław Tatarkiewicz, in sacred memory, would not be entitled to be listed among such deserving Poles of Jewish origin, since the only admixture of 'foreign blood' our family owes to the Morchonowiczes, Polish Tartars."[13] He then explained that professor Tatarkiewicz was an object of many "pieces of gossip and even *legends*" (italics mine); this commentary about the Jewish origin likely came from the book by Mateusz Mieses *From the Jewish Kin.*"[14] "Unfortunately," Krzysztof Tatarkiewicz reiterated, "all inquiries about that issue (even though I was helped in them by Poles of Jewish origin)[15] did

---

10   Gross, *Sąsiedzi*.
11   Paczkowski, "Debata wokół *Sąsiadów*, próba wstępnej typologii," 4–5.
12   Tatarkiewicz, "A może jeszcze . . . ," 54; Stomma, "A może jeszcze. . . ," 114.
13   Ibid.
14   See Mieses, *Polacy-chrześcijanie pochodzenia żydowskiego*. The book was republished after WWII as *Z rodu żydowskiego*.
15   It is an interesting way of valorizing Jewish origin while denying it.

not bring any result.... I have received numerous questions about the list of Mr. L. Stomma. This is why, though with substantial delay, I am writing this letter."[16]

I am quoting this letter extensively because it contains the most important denials of Jewish origins. First of all, the issue of origin is considered important enough to require public explanation. One can easily imagine that such an "inquiry" would not be very important and would not require a special letter, or that such a letter would not find its place among the very few printed in a weekly. As a reason for his written explanation, Tatarkiewicz cited the "numerous questions" he received, though we do not know what for him "numerous" meant. However, the indication of Jewish roots did attract attention. It seems that the matter was still alive and well. Secondly, and also typically, the correction pertained only to Jewish origins and not to the admixture of "foreign blood." Tatars or Armenians bring to mind past military battles since in common knowledge both minorities had distinguished themselves as members of Polish military units. And in the end, there is a third element of such corrections: nothing is definitive. Not finding any Jewish ancestors may simply lead to another search. In the Polish history of wars, disasters, and migrations it is difficult to know anything for sure. The inquiries continue.

The Case of Lechoń

Not only are the inquiries never-ending, the corrections and clarifications are never final. In a 2000 letter to the culture section of the daily *Rzeczpospolita*, a reader named Lech Warzyniak from Ostrów Wielkopolski wanted to correct, "for the sake of historical truth," the claim mentioned in that section (in another article about the origin of Brzechwa!) that the poet Jan Lechoń who died in 1956 in New York, was of Jewish origin. Lechoń's nonliterary name was Leszek Serafinowicz and, according to Warzyniak, he had Tartar, not Jewish roots.[17] The editors, however, must have forgotten about this correction since six months later in the same daily Lechoń again was mentioned as a writer of Jewish origin.[18]

And Mr. Warzyniak's correction was one of many. In 1993 important Warsaw publishing house Czytelnik produced a book by Józef Adam Kosiński entitled *Family Album of Jan Lechoń*. Kosiński, on his mother's side, had also descended

---

16 Tatarkiewicz, "A może jeszcze..."
17 Warzyniak, "Plus Minus." The letter was written in response to a column by Rosalak, "Pochodzenie Lisa Witalisa."
18 Stańczyk, "Rozszerzanie perspektywy."

from the Serafinowicz family. In this book he devotes an entire chapter to prove that his family did not come from Jews. The preface to the volume, written by another author, declared that the essential point of the book is "the probably final annulment of the here and there still repeated version about the Jewish origin of Lechoń."[19] Yet Mr. Warzyniak had to pen his correction seven years after these words were published, and even then it did not stick. In prewar Poland, Lechoń himself declared that he was Jewish. Kosiński alluded to this in his book saying that "not only Lechoń's adversaries stubbornly disseminated the story about his Jewish origins."[20]

Even though Kosiński had difficulty finding Lechoń's familial ties to Tartars, this did not slow him down. In the chapter "Lechoń's Great-Grandfather and His Origin" Lechoń's ancestral roots are presented. The chapter and its conclusions are based on the only existing document pertaining to the great-grandfather: his wedding certificate. The certificate stated that Serafin Serafinowicz married a Marianna and gave their address. Kosiński developed these two pieces of information in an elaborate reasoning written in a stilted and convoluted style. "The fact that he was a long-lived inhabitant of Podlasie *because* he originated from Żmudź, *provokes suspicion* that he was of noble origin. It is because in Żmudź there was a noble family of Serafinowicz, coat of arms Pobóg, descending from Żmudź Tatars settled there already during the Jagiellonian reign who converted to Catholicism" (italics mine).[21]

Żmudź (or today Lithuanian Samogitia) should not be conflated with Podlesie, where Serafin Serafinowicz was married to Marianna, and the "because" in the first sentence is a jump that leads to the transformation of free-floating suppositions into "facts": that he lived for a long time in Podlesie and that his origins were further east where Tartars lived and were Catholic and noble. The tenuousness of this reasoning troubles even the author himself.

"Of course, the similarities in the last names do not yet prove anything, and one could treat the above information with skepticism. I thought so myself, until 1976, when the secretary of the board of the Międzyrzec Scientific Society

---

19   Kaszyński, "Wstęp," 10. Kaszyński writes that Lechoń's life is surrounded by other "mysteries": he probably has in mind Lechoń's homosexuality and his death by suicide. The family story of Kosiński ends with young, thirteen-year-old Serfinowicz before he became Lechoń.
20   Kosiński, *Album rodzinne Jana Lechonia*, 26.
21   "To, że Podlasiakiem był wmieszkałym, bo wywodził się ze Żmudzi, budzi podejrzenie, iż był pochodzenia szlacheckiego. Na Żmudzi bowiem istniała szlachecka rodzina Serafinowiczów, herbu Pobóg, pochodząca z osiedlonych jeszcze za Jagiellonów Tatarów żmudzkich, którzy przeszli na katolicyzm." Ibid., 23.

(and director of the local dairy), Mr. Jan Chmielarski, responded to the question of whether he knew anything about the Serafinowiczes: Serafinowiczes? There is more than a few here in the neighborhood. They are boyars. They originate from Lithuanian Tatars. Till today they have prominent cheekbones. I capitulated in my skepticism. Since the views of the local population, not inspired by anyone (the existence of the poet Lechoń was known only to the ladies in the Międzyrzec library) line up with historical sources and what is known of the family tradition, then the correct reasoning can lead only to one thing: Serafim Serafinowicz, living in Międzyrzec, of the Żmudź Serafinowicz family and coat of arms Pobóg, originated from Tatars."[22]

The family tradition mentioned by the author was not known to Lechoń himself, as he, according to the writer Ferdynand Goetel "traced his pedigree back to the ancient Jewish aristocracy." Feeling a bit confused, I found these words quoted by Kosiński himself who then adds to my confusion by writing: "And Lechoń could as well point to a printed source, which was also talked about in the family, mentioning that this text has been found by [the poet Julian] Tuwim." So, besides the Żmudź Tartars, there were also Jewish aristocratic roots in the family. But Kosiński, after his disquisition about the boyars, declares without blinking:

> All this longish historical argument would probably not have been needed in the case of any other writer. It would be enough to write: the founder of the family was such and such, living in such and such years, in such and such town. But with Lechoń the situation is of a different order. The issue of his origin and the social status of his parents, around which ... so much falsehood, misunderstanding and *balderdash* had accumulated, required final clarification without leaving any vagueness.[23]

For Kosiński there is no doubt that Lechoń comes from the Żmudź Tatars. For the poet Maria Pawlikowska-Jasnorzewska, like Goetel Lechoń's contemporary, his origin was Armenian. But Armenian and Tatar seem here equivalent—it is "foreign blood" but acceptable as long as it is not Jewish.

I am presenting this case not to prove that Lechoń was of Jewish origin. I remember short satirical poems that Tuwim wrote to Lechoń making fun of the whole question (and the document attesting to his Jewish aristocratic origin could have been a practical joke as well: "Jewish" is rarely used in Polish to

---

22   Ibid., 24.
23   Ibid., 25–26.

describe "aristocracy").[24] I was interested in this quick and decisive finding of Żmudź boyars in Międzyrzec Podlaski, which used to be an important spiritual center for the Jews who lived there at least from the 1600s and constituted a substantial majority of the population by 1827. Perhaps one could find some Jewish Serafinowiczes among the people with or without high cheekbones.

Mothers: Słowacki

If we accept Maria Pawlikowska-Jasnorzewska's suggestion that Lechoń was of Armenian origin, his roots would be perhaps similar to those of Juliusz Słowacki, one of the greatest Romantic Polish poets. According to the late Janusz Odrowąż-Pieniążek, literary scholar and former director of the Warsaw Museum of Literature, the mother of the poet Salomea Januszewska, *primo voto* Słowacka, *secundo voto* Bécu, "had a not-too-small admixture of the Armenian blood, which is . . . certain."[25] I was puzzled by this certainty, after all Mrs. Bécu (1772–1855) lived in an era afflicted by numerous difficulties as far as reliable documentation is concerned. I therefore reached for the available information about the ancestors of the family of Januszewskis. The history of the family goes back only to the father of Salomea; his first name was Teodor, and we do not know if he was or wasn't a nobleman. "There are *certain indications*," the text continues, "that the family was of Armenian origin. Such a *hypothesis*[26] has been proposed among others by J. Talko-Hryncewicz in his talk based on the report by professor Papillault from the exhumation of the body of Słowacki. (Reprint from the reports of Polish Academy of Learning, v. XXXII, nr. 10.) *There are however no documented proofs that can be quoted in support of this hypothesis.*"[27] How could an exhumation of a son prove the Armenian origin of his mother? One could also ask how her own exhumation could have proven such an origin. Also consider the proofs of the no doubt distinguished professor Papillaut.

The text then presents the details of the life of Salomea Bécu, which could arouse suspicion that she was of Greco Catholic persuasion (she celebrated family and church holidays according to a different calendar, in a letter to Odyniec dated December 19–31, 1827, she called her family "believers of different

---

24 See Tuwim, *Listy do przyjaciół—pisarzy*, 64, 68.
25 Odrowąż-Pieniążek, "Mickiewicz ciągle pisze," conversation with Krzysztof Masłoń. It is a part of an argument against the book by Jadwiga Maurer about the Jewish origin of the mother of Mickiewicz: *Z matki obcej*.
26 Today, this hypothesis is given as a fact in Polish school textbooks.
27 Sawrymowicz, *Kalendarz życia i twórczości Juliusza Słowackiego*, 670.

religions," and she was buried in the Tunicki cemetery in Krzemieniec (where the Unites and Christian orthodox were buried). However, these suspicions are faulty: the term "believers of different religions" has a humorous character.[28]

The note ends with the translation of her death certificate which *"solves the issue with total certainty.* The priest who buried her was a parish priest and deacon of the Catholic Church."[29]

Mothers: Chopin

The mother of Frederic Chopin (Fryderyk Szopen) also had to deal with confusion surrounding her origins, although not any related to religious Catholic orthodoxy. This was discussed in an article by Jacek Marczyński called "Family Secrets" and published in the cultural section in *Rzeczpospolita*.[30] It was a review of a new book by Andrzej Sikorski and Piotr Mysłakowski titled *The Family of the Mother of Chopin. Myths and Reality*.[31] The book was awarded a prize given by the Polish Heraldic Society for the best books in the domain of "heraldry and related disciplines." As the second part of the title indicates, the book has a polemical aim. Its objective is to refute the myths about the "neophyte" origin of Tekla Justyna Chopin (Szopen), born Krzyżanowska. On the basis of a very large and, it seems to me, thorough "sources inquiry," the authors established or confirmed some of the facts from the biography of the father of Justyna, Jakub Krzyżanowski, and of her mother, Antonina Kołomińska. They also studied many families named Krzyżanowski and chose the one with which Jakub could have been linked. In the preface to the volume, Professor Stefan Kuczyński declared that *"only one link is missing"* for Jakub to be proven as part of that family. The authors expressed the same thought in the following words: "As we proved above, it is most probable that the father of Justyna Chopin came from the Wielkopole family of Krzyżanowski, coat of arms Świnka. *It needs to be repeated however that in the light of today's knowledge it remains only a hypothesis*" (italics mine).[32] So as usual, we have an effort to find noble relations but with no success. The book is illustrated with the coats of arms and genealogical trees of many Krzyżanowski families, nevertheless the table "Lineage of the ancestors of Fryderyk Chopin" does not have the shape of a tree but of a bend-in-the-wind

---

28   The term is "różnowierca." Ibid.
29   Ibid., 671.
30   Marczyński, "Rodzinne tajemnice."
31   Sikorski and Mysłakowski, *Rodzina matki Chopina*.
32   Ibid., 119.

CHAPTER FOUR

bush: on the (French) Chopin side we have many ancestors, on the side of the mother are only her parents.

The authors write: "As is clear from the above overview, there were many noble families living in the second half of the 18th century in Respublica [Poland] and named Krzyżanowski. Most of them were of neophyte or unknown origin."[33] That statistical opportunity does not compel the authors to look for connections with "neophyte" families. Yet the last name Krzyżanowski comes from either a place or from the word for a cross—*krzyż*—which was often given as a last name to Jewish families who had been baptized: "Rather early, maybe already in the 19th century, it was asserted that Justyna Krzyżanowska came from a neophyte family. At the beginning of the 20th century in some circles this was considered certain."[34] As an example they quote the words of "a great supporter of the Jewish assimilation," the poet Antoni Lange (1861–1929): "In any case at the head of this new race [the assimilated Jews] there are the two greatest men Poland brought forth. One of them by his mother Barbara Majewska—with greatest probability; the second by his mother Justyna Krzyżanowska, without any doubt—belong in half to the Jewish tribe. Their names: Adam Mickiewicz and Fryderyk Szopen."[35] They also quote Mateusz Mieses, who used the "Jewish look" argument: "Chopin, with his nose and the expression of his eyes on his portraits strongly resembles a Jew."[36]

To contradict such a notion, the authors pointed to Frederic's passport data, which stated that the composer had blond hair; they also summarized for the reader the anthropological research conducted by a well-known Marxist musicologist Zofia Lissa (1908–1980), interested in the influence of folklore on Chopin's work. Her "anthropological" work in this matter was published in 1938 and 1939, an era in which racial issues were at the forefront of cultural discourse. This work was based on portraits of the composer and his mother, as well as his one photo and his death mask. The authors of the book on the origin of Tekla Justyna Krzyżanowska approved the finding of Zofia Lissa and wrote emphatically: "*It turned out* that Fryderyk belonged to the Dinaric type, which unites the Armenoid and Nordic types. His father, Mikołaj Chopin *obviously* belonged to the Armenoid type and Justyna indeed to the Nordic type,

---

33 Ibid, 51.
34 Ibid, 36.
35 Lange, *O sprzecznościach sprawy żydowskiej*, 77. Quoted in Sikorski and Mysłakowski, *Rodzina matki Chopina*, 36–37.
36 Mieses, 1:77. Quoted in Andrzej Sikorski and Mysłakowski, *Rodzina matki Chopina*, 37.

which is to be visible on her preserved portrait."[37] And then the authors added: "Thanks to the anthropological studies of Professor Rosiński we can describe the external appearance of Justyna.... In anthropological terms she belonged to the sub-Nordic type, which is a combination of the Nordic and Laponoidal elements (so a bit different than declared by Zofia Lissa on the basis of an anthropological analysis of the image of Justyna)" (italics mine).[38] Here we need to underscore that professor Bolesław Rosiński (1884–1964) was a priest who published his analysis in 1951; by then the portrait of Justyna did not exist, as it had been destroyed in a fire during World War II; yet even before the war, "the portrait was submitted to the conservatory procedures which to a certain degree 'evened' her features." The authors also state that it was difficult to say anything about "the state of her bone remains."[39] These remains, too, were destroyed during the war. It must have been difficult to ascertain without a portrait, and any "bone remains" showed that Justyna belonged not to the Nordic but sub-Nordic type.

Before World War II, the atmosphere surrounding such anthropological questions was rather violent. As the authors of the book write, the suggestions about the Jewish origins of Chopin or Mickiewicz were "immediately sharply criticized by national circles." As an example, they quoted the title of an article from a provincial newspaper: "End Jewish gossiping! The Mothers of Chopin and Mickiewicz did not have in them any Jewish blood" (*Dziennik Zachodni*, Bydgoszcz, January 20, 1939).[40] That knowledge did not prevent the authors of the heraldic book from presenting in all seriousness the typologies that proved so deadly. Their 201-page effort to prove that the mother of Chopin was not Jewish was, predictably, inconclusive. Again, it was one link short of success in joining Jakub Krzyżanowski with the Krzyżanowski family, coat of arms Świnka.

In 2010, the government spent a massive amount of funds to celebrate the two hundredth anniversary of the birth of Chopin. In all official publications his mother was described as a noble woman from an impoverished family and related to the noble Skarbek family she worked for. There is no proof that the Krzyżanowskis were noble, as we have seen, nor that Justyna was related to the Skarbek family; however, if she were related to the Skarbeks, she did not

---

37 Sikorski and Mysłakowski, *Rodzina matki Chopina*, 39.
38 Ibid., 55–56. See Rosiński, "O szczątkach kostnych rodziców Chopina," 1951; Lissa, "W sprawie 'rasy' Fryderyka Chopina,"
39 Sikorski and Mysłakowski, *Rodzina matki Chopina*, 56.
40 Ibid., 38–39.

have family ties to the nobleman Skarbek but to his (divorced) wife, a nonnoble daughter of an evangelical banker Jakub Fenger. He was said to be of German origin.

Mothers: Mickiewicz

The authors of this book could not stop themselves from pronouncing a judgment on the origin of the second great Pole indicated by the aforementioned assimilationist poet Antoni Lange as probably born to a "foreign mother" (the words are Adam Mickiewicz's own). And they write: "As a side note we will add that the *legends* around the issue of the origin of the mother of Mickiewicz were *incisively clarified* by professor Stanislaw Pigoń already in 1922, indicating their speculative character, and the newest archival research *confirmed beyond any doubt* that the family of the mother of Mickiewicz did not come from neophytes" (italics mine).[41] Obviously, Professor Pigoń "clarified" and "confirmed" that the mother of Mickiewicz could not have been Jewish. In a footnote they provide the bibliography for the quoted sources ending with an article published a year before their book appeared. The "newest information" was gleaned from an article published in 1999 by Belorussian archivist Sergiusz Rybczonek, in a bulletin issued by the Warsaw Museum of Literature directed then by the already-quoted Janusz Odrowąż-Pieniążek.[42] It was the director himself that had the article translated from Belorussian, commented on it, and then went to the media. Mickiewicz was, in the end, found to be non-Jewish. And it was the director who drew this conclusion, not Rybczonek.

Rybczonek had mentioned that his research on the family Majewski, coat of arms Starykoń, is linked to the fact that it is from this family "that the mother of Adam Mickiewicz Barbara was supposed to originate."[43] The article contains genealogical data related to that family ending with this conclusion: "As we can see, for the moment there is no Barbara Majewska in this family tree. In general, it can be said that Mickiewiczes *twice came in contact* with the said Majewskis. The first time Mikołaj Mickiewicz [the father of Adam] as a lawyer validated a certificate by the functionaries and citizens given to Ignacy Majewski, which took place in November 1801. Barbara herself was mentioned in relation to our

---

41   Ibid., 39–40.
42   Ibid., 40. See Rybczonek, "Przodkowie Adama Mickiewicza po kądzieli," 177–186.
43   Rybczonek, idem., 177.

Majewskis only once, in January of 1805. I am attaching the copy of this document for the moment without any commentary."[44]

The language of the article—saying that the two families "came in contact"—does not indicate that they were united. This is not the way to speak about a married couple, as the father and mother of Adam were at the time of the said contact. Mr. Odrowąż-Pieniążek, however, gave the article the title "Maternal Ancestors of Adam Mickiewicz" and, in his introduction, spelled out his conclusions. "On the basis of the materials uncovered by Sergiusz Rybczonek, let's determine the genealogy of Adam Mickiewicz on his mother's side. Barbara née Majewska Mickiewicz was a daughter of Mateusz mentioned in official acts as a cavalry captain from Nowogródek, married to Anna née Orzeszko."[45] Just before coming to this conclusion he indicated the reasons for his interest in the matter:

> The inquiries into the genealogy of the family of Majewski, coat of arms Starykoń, lately have become especially important since so <u>much fantasy and balderdash</u> has been written and is continuously being written about the allegedly Jewish origins of the poet's mother,—based, by the way, on what one court (Zygmunt Krasiński) said to another count (Ksawery Branicki), who years later added something to this and published it in 1879 in order to annoy a third count (Stanisław Tarnowski).[46]

He then reviews what other people wrote about "the alleged" Jewish origins of Mickiewicz's mother, and who debunked this "balderdash," each time in a definitive manner. He is especially emphatic about the findings of Andrzej Syrokomla-Bułhak, who "set out to determine the last name of the maternal grandmother of Mickiewcz, wife of Michał Majewski" and, "on the basis of knowledge of the last names of nobility settled in the neighborhood of Nowogródek," established it as Barbara Tupalska. And Odrowąż-Pieniążek continues with a certain urgency: "'Please notice,' Bułhak wrote, 'that the Tupalskis were a nobility of Tartar origin and that up till the middle of the 19th century they were noted as Muslims.' *As transpires from the materials here published*—he was right. So Mickiewicz would be a descendant, though rather distant, not of Jews, but of

---

44 Ibid., 186.
45 Odrowąż-Pieniążek, "Od Redaktora," 189.
46 Ibid., 188. The thesis that the Jewish origin of Mickiewicz was to be a method to annoy the three counts, and the term "balderdash" (bałamuctwo) are taken from the 1922 Pigoń essay. I omitted the declarations on that topic of this eminent professor of Polish literature as they go back to 1922, much earlier than the writings discussed in this article.

Tartars. Such relations were not rare among the nobility of the Great Lithuanian Duchy" (italics mine).[47] And he concludes: "No trace of house Jews, Turkish Jews, or Frankists in this genealogy."[48]

On the basis of the same "excellent knowledge" of the names of nobility from around Nowogródek, Andrzej Syrokomla-Bułhak maintained that Mickiewicz's father had falsified the proof of his nobility. The father, being a lawyer, invented all of his ancestors, including their first and last names, as was frequently done by those who were forced by the Russian authorities to prove their nobility or be reduced to a peasant state. But this finding, though very convincingly argued by Syrokomla, was rejected out of hand by Odrowąż-Pieniążek.[49]

The sensational discovery was first described by the director and printed in its entirety in the aforementioned cultural section of the daily *Rzeczpospolita*. The other big newspaper—*Gazeta Wyborcza*—also informed its readers about the conclusive proof that Mickiewicz's mother was not Jewish. "Rybczonek's publication refutes the thesis about the Jewish roots of the Majewskis, it confirms however the Tartar origin of the grandmother of Mickiewicz, Barbara née Tupalska," announced *Gazeta Wyborcza* on October 25, 2000. I have also seen a note about this discovery in a Catholic weekly *Niedziela*, and it was probably widely shared in other publications. It seems therefore that this "final proof" was quite newsworthy. Accepting the "finding" of Rybczonek, the writer and translator Zygmunt Kubiak removed his essay about Mickiewicz's mother from the second edition of his collection of essays titled *The Breviary of a European* (2001).

What is interesting here is the lack of a next phase related to this discovery. If Barbara Tupalska, mother of Adam's mother (also named Barbara), was of Tartar origin, and her family, the Tupalskis, as Odrowąż-Pieniążek said, "till the middle of 19th century" (i.e., during Adam's entire life; he died in 1855) were Muslims, the mysterious words from Mickiewicz's best-known play, *The Forefathers*, that he or his literary alias was "born from a foreign mother": these are the words that for more than two centuries fueled a search for his roots, and they would open a new interpretative space. But nobody ever asked about the influence of Muslim culture or religion on the work of the Polish bard. Quite the opposite. Though Kubiak withdrew the essay about his mother and accepted "the finding" that Mickiewicz was not Jewish, he declared that it did not change

---

47   Ibid, 188–89.
48   Tamże, s. 190.
49   Syrokomla-Bułhak, *"Mistyfikacja*, czyli rzecz o pochodzeniu Mickiewiczów," 181– 86. Prof. Odrowąż-Pieniążek rejected these findings in the obituary of Syrokomla-Bułhak in the same issue of *Blok—Notes*.

his ideas about the link between the poet and Jewish thought. The discovery of the Muslim religion's pervasiveness in Mickiewicz family did not bring about any questions or corrections. Its meaning was only one: that he was not Jewish.

This was one more success for the director Odrowąż-Pieniążek, who also wrote a letter to the same newspaper protesting that the creation of the Jewish Legions would be attributed to Mickiewicz. Odrowąż-Pieniążek said this was simply a regiment attached to Polish Legions.[50] He declared in another article that he would "always fight against the pinning of Jewishness on Mickiewicz."[51] And he did.

The Missing Link

As we have seen, no stone has been left unturned in rooting out the ancestry of these cultural icons, but there is always one link missing. The genealogical trees of Mickiewicz, Słowacki, and Chopin are stunted on their mothers' sides. That does not affect the biographical information about these three men, which can be found, in one form or another, in textbooks, articles, and movies. Yet the doubts regularly resurface and fuel the never-ending return of questions once thought to be conclusively answered.

The interest in the origin of writers had and is having practical consequences. Almost every minister of education in post-1989 Poland tries to modify the literary canon in school curricula. Here I will mention just one example of such consequences, from the same period of the first decade of free Poland. In 2007, Tomasz Kalita, spokesman of the Democratic Left Alliance (SLD), then an opposition party, declared that the minister of education, Roman Giertych, had removed from school curricula poets Jan Lechoń and Kazimierz Wierzyński, as well as the writers Maria Konopnicka, Bruno Schulz, Witold Gombrowicz, and Stanisław Lem because of their Jewish origin or pro-Jewish leanings. "All these writers," the article reported, "besides Konopnicka, are of Jewish origin. Konopnicka, however, was very active in the defense of the Jews—Kalita said. And he added that *the suppositions in that matter are confirmed by Polonists [Polish literature specialists] and the experts of the ministry of education*"(italics mine).[52]

Two days later corrections appeared. In response to the argument that Gombrowicz came from nobility (coat of arms Ostoja) Kalita (who, I repeat, was in a postcommunist party and not in the government that ethnically cleansed

---

50   The letter was published in "Plus Minus," *Rzeczpospolita*, February 3–4, 2001.
51   Odrowąż-Pieniążek, *Mickiewicz ciągle pisze*, ibid.
52   Bielecki, "Jak politycy SLD tropili Żydów na liście lektur," 7.

school curricula), replied: "If you examine well the family of Gombrowicz on the side of his father, <u>one can detect Jewish blood</u>."[53] Piotr Paziński, editor in chief of *Midrasz*, the monthly magazine for Polish Jews, clarified that Kazimierz Wierzyński and Jan Lechoń were not Jewish. Of course, Lechoń was of Tartar origin, was he not? (and Wierzyński of German, hélas).

In 2017, new changes to the school curricula were introduced. A couple of poems by Wierzyński and Lechoń were included, as well as a fragment from a novel by Gombrowicz. Bruno Schulz has been removed from required reading lists and moved to the recommended readings. The former minister of education, Roman Giertych, the one who removed Gombrowicz, is now a persecuted lawyer opposing the right-wing government. In October of 2020, a new education minister, Przemysław Czarnek, was appointed; he has a comprehensive plan to reform the Polish school system. He promises a "conservative counterrevolution" in schools, that is, a return to the pre–World War II ways of teaching that will stress "the values that formed the Poles throughout 1050 years (from the baptism of Poland) and include patriotism and respect for one's country."[54] The value of family and the works of John Paul II will be prioritized. Mickiewicz, Słowacki, and Chopin will of course remain in the canon and, with them, the issue of suspicious origins.

Bibliography

Bielecki, Jędrzej. "Jak politycy SLD tropili Żydów na liście lektur." *Dziennik* 9, no. 7 (2007).
Brzechwa, Krystyna. "Jan Brzechwa – po prostu polski patriota." *Gazeta Wyborcza*, May 8, 2000.
Giedroyc, Jerzy, and Melchior Wańkowicz. *Listy 1945–1963*. Edited and introduction by Aleksandra Ziółkowska-Boehm. Warsaw: Czytelnik, 2000.
Gross, Jan Tomasz. *Sąsiedzi. Historia zagłady żydowskiego miasteczka*. Sejny: Pogranicze, 2000.
Janion, Maria. *Do Europy, tak, ale z naszymi umarłymi*. Warsaw: Sic!, 2000.
Kaszyński, Stanisław. "Wstęp." In Józef Adam Kosiński, *Album rodzinne Jana Lechonia*. Warsaw: Czytelnik,1993.
Konwicki, Tadeusz. *Bohiń*. Warsaw: Czytelnik, 1987.
Lange, Antoni. *O sprzecznościach sprawy żydowskiej*. Warsaw: Skład główny w księgarni G. Centnerszwera i S-ki, 1911.

---

53   Ibid., 7.
54   Słowik, *Konserwatywna rewolucja' ministra Czarnka*.

Lissa, Zofia. "W sprawie 'rasy' Fryderyka Chopina." *Wiadomości Literackie*, no. 38 (1938).
Marczyński, Jacek. "Rodzinne tajemnice," "Plus Minus," cultural section of *Rzeczpospolita*, November 25–26, 2000.
Maurer, Jadwiga. *Z matki obcej . . . Szkice o powiązaniach Mickiewicza ze światem Żydów*. London: Polska Fundacja Kulturalna, 1990.
Mieses, Mateusz. *Polacy-chrześcijanie pochodzenia żydowskiego*. 2 vols. Warsaw: M. Fruchtman, 1938.
Mieses, Mateusz. *Z rodu żydowskiego. Zasłużone rodziny polskiej krwi niegdyś żydowskiej*. Warsaw: Wema, 1991.
Odrowąż-Pieniążek, Janusz. "Mickiewicz ciągle pisze." Conversation with Krzysztof Masłoń, *Plus Minus*, cultural section of *Rzeczpospolita*, July 13–14, 1996.
Odrowąż-Pieniążek, Janusz "Od Redaktora." Blok – Notes Muzeum Literatury im. A. Mickiewicza, no. 12–13 (1999): 189.
Paczkowski, Andrzej. "Debata wokół Sąsiadów, próba wstępnej typologii." "*Plus Minus*," cultural section of *Rzeczpospolita*, March 24–25, 2001, 4–5.
Rosalak, Maciej. "Pochodzenie Lisa Witalisa." "*Plus Minus*," cultural section of *Rzeczpospolita*, April 15–16, 2000.
Rosiński, Bolesław. "O szczątkach kostnych rodziców Chopina." *Przegląd Antropologiczny* 17 (1951).
Rybczonek, Sergiusz. "Przodkowie Adama Mickiewicza po kądzieli." Translated by E. Dąbkowska. *Blok – Notes Muzeum Literatury im. A. Mickiewicza*, no. 12–13 (1999): 177–86.
Sawrymowicz, Eugeniusz. *Kalendarz życia i twórczości Juliusza Słowackiego*. Wrocław: Zakład Narodowy im. Ossolińskich, 1960.
Sikorski, Andrzej, Mysłakowski, Piotr. *Rodzina matki Chopina. Mity i rzeczywistość*. Warsaw: Studio Wydawnicze Familia, 2000.
Słowik, Karolina. "Konserwatywna rewolucja' ministra Czarnka. Są szczegóły w sprawie lektur, historii i wychowanie do życia w rodzinie." http://www.wyborcza.pl. Accessed May 28, 2021.
Stańczyk, Tomasz. "Rozszerzanie perspektywy." "*Plus Minus*," cultural section of *Rzeczpospolita*, April 27–28, 2001.
Stomma, Ludwik. "A może jeszcze . . ." *Polityka* 44 (2269): 114.
Syrokomla-Bułhak, Andrzej, "Mistyfikacja, czyli rzecz o pochodzeniu Mickiewiczów." In *Gustaw i Peri. Ich kraj rodzinny*, 181–86. Zielona Góra: Self-published, 1998.
Szajnert, Danuta. "Gustaw Herling-Grudziński i Żydzi. Rekonesans," *Studia Litteraria Universitatis Iagellonicae Cracoviensis*, no. 10 (2015): 261–74.
Tatarkiewicz, Krzysztof. "A może jeszcze . . . List," *Polityka* 9 (2287) (2001): 54.
Warzyniak, Lech. "Letter," *Plus Minus*, cultural section of *Rzeczpospolita*, April 22–24, 2000.
Tuwim, Julian. *Listy do przyjaciół – pisarzy*, ed. Tadeusz Januszewski. Warsaw: Czytelnik, 1979.

Chapter Five

Redefining Polishness through Jewishness?

Geneviève Zubrzycki

There are currently more than forty festivals of Jewish culture throughout Poland, most of them initiated in the mid-2000s.[1] The interest in Jewish culture is noticeable all year long, however, as can be observed from the commercial success of klezmer music, the proliferation of Judaica bookstores and Jewish-style restaurants, the opening of new museums, memorials and memory

---

This chapter is adapted from "Nationalism, 'Philosemitism' and Symbolic Boundary-Making in Contemporary Poland," *Comparative Studies in Society and History*, 58:1, 66–98. I'm grateful to Cambridge University Press for allowing to reproduce portions of the article here.

[1] The largest and most famous is that of Kraków. Founded in 1988 as a modest two-day local affair consisting primarily of films and lectures with limited public appeal, by the middle of the first decade of the twenty-first century, it had become a major national and international festival, gaining renown as one of Poland's calling cards. Under the patronage of the president of the Republic of Poland since 2001, the festival now lasts ten days and is attended by some thirty thousand people from Poland and abroad. The popularity of the Kraków Festival and a collective awakening to Poland's Jewish past prompted the creation of many other festivals spread across the country such as the Simcha festival in Wrocław (1999) and the Singer's Days in Warsaw (2004). While festivals are more prevalent and important in larger cities, they are hardly restricted to urban metropolitan areas. Many modest festivals are held in smaller towns and play a significant educational function, teaching local populations the forgotten history of their towns and region such as in Chmielnik. See Zubrzycki (2022, 118–133) for a discussion of the Kraków Festival of Jewish Culture and the development of Jewish festivals throughout Poland.

spaces, the growing engagement of artists and public intellectuals with Poland's Jewish past and Polish-Jewish relations more broadly, and the emergence of Jewish studies programs at multiple universities (Gruber 2002; Lehrer 2013; Waligórska 2013; Wodziński 2011; Zubrzycki 2016).[2] The historian and Jewish studies scholar Marcin Wodziński (2021) found that between 2011 and 2021, approximately one hundred books and several hundred articles on Jewish topics were published *every year*, many written to be accessible to a broader public.[3] The last indicator of this cultural phenomenon, about which there are no official statistics, is the modest but rising number of conversions to Judaism. These converts are often people who discover Jewish roots and feel compelled to "return to the source," but sometimes they are Poles without Jewish ancestry who are nevertheless called or seduced by the appeal of Judaism.[4]

To be sure, the twin rebirth of Jewish communal life and non-Jewish Poles' interest in all things Jewish are facilitated by the specific historic juncture brought about by the fall of communism and EU accession, which I discuss elsewhere (2016, 2022). My focus here, however, is on non-Jewish Poles' rediscovery of Poland's Jewish past and their resurrection of Jewish culture in contemporary Poland. That process cannot be reduced to the commodification of Jewish culture, nor does it merely mark the anti-Semitic folklorization of Jews and things Jewish—a point Erica Lehrer has convincingly drawn out in her work (2003, 2013). Neither should it be read as a solely Polish outlet to address

---

2   The last two decades have witnessed a significant museological boom in Poland. Several museums of Jewish history or Jewish culture have opened in that period: Kraków's *Galicja Jewish Museum* was founded in 2003; *Schindler's Factory Museum* on occupation in World War II Kraków opened in 2010; the Museum of Kraków's Ghetto, *The Eagle Pharmacy,* opened in 2013; and the *Museum of the History of Polish Jews in Warsaw* opened the building in April 2013 and its main exhibit in October 2014. There are many other smaller Jewish museums and educational centers throughout Poland, such as the *Świętokrzyski shtetl* in Chmielnik, which opened in 2014.

3   Those numbers are similar to those for the previous decade: Wodziński (2011) noted, for example, that between 2006 and 2009, 365 books on Jewish themes were published in Poland.

4   Personal interviews with Rabbis Schudrich, Pash, Herberger, Horovitz, and Segal in 2012 and 2013, as well as with converts in March 2011 and March 2013. While I name public figures I formally interviewed, I have changed the names of interviewees who were not representing institutions in order to preserve their anonymity. See Reszke (2013) on the third post-Holocaust generation's return to Judaism, as well as documentary films by Kerstner (2013), Zuckerman (2013), and Zucker (2014).

cultural trauma or reckon with a difficult past. No doubt some of these feelings fuel the multipronged Jewish turn, but I find it is primarily related to a broader attempt and long-standing efforts by both Jewish and non-Jewish cultural elites, social activists, ordinary citizens, and some state agencies to expand the symbolic boundaries of Polishness that the political right seeks to harden and shrink using a conservative, nationalist version of Catholicism as its primary tool. It is a means to symbolically reclaim the pluralistic society that was eradicated during World War II.[5]

Symbolic National Boundaries in a "Monocultural" Society

One of the key questions that animates public debates in Poland and intrigues social scientists alike, is what pluralism and secularism can mean in a "monocultural" society like Poland, which is approximately 95 percent ethnically Polish and (nominally) Catholic (cf. Waligórska 2008; Zubrzycki 2010, 2012). While the current ethnic and religious "homogeneity" is the by-product of relatively recent and violent historical events and political processes[6], it was successfully *naturalized* in the postwar period by both the state and the Catholic Church, institutions that built or boosted their legitimacy by emphasizing this new ethnonational and denominational homogeneity and suppressing even the *memory* of diversity. The Party-State represented itself as the protector of the primeval "Piast" Poland, while the Church could claim speaking in the name of the nation. The association between Polishness and Catholicism was further tightened as a result (Zubrzycki 2006, 60–76; Porter-Szűcs 2012).

If ideological pluralism was a politically sensitive issue under state socialism, systemic transformations after 1989 have not made it less so. In postsocialist and then EU Poland, the mere idea of pluralism has been vigorously

---

5   By "material erasure" I mean the building over Jewish ruins or the repurposing of Jewish buildings such as the conversion of synagogues into libraries or cinemas; yeshivas into cultural centers; and the like. On the neighborhood built over the ruins of the Warsaw ghetto, see Janicka (2011) and Chomątowska (2012); on the treatment of Jewish ruins more broadly in Poland, see Weizman (2022), on Poland and Germany, see Meng (2012). On Polish memory/amnesia of Jews, see Irwin-Zarecka (1989), Gitelman (2003), Steinlauf (1997), and Zubrzycki (2006, 2013, 2022).

6   The Holocaust, postwar pogroms, the forced relocation of ethnic minorities, and the 1968 anti-Semitic campaign that pushed some twenty thousand Jews to leave Poland.

contested. Intellectuals and politicians on the left and center as well as liberal Catholics typically stress the nation's ideological heterogeneity and argue that in a plural society, religion (and Catholicism more specifically) is only one among many competing or overlapping value systems. Therefore in the 1990s they demanded denominational neutrality of the state in order to protect the rights of minorities, atheists, or nonpracticing Catholics, and to ensure citizens' equality de jure and de facto. The Catholic right and the official hierarchy of the Catholic Church, on the other hand, emphasized the "objective" homogeneity of Poland's population, wielding Poland's demographic statistics ("95% ethnically Polish, 95% Catholic, 95% believers") to bolster claims of monolithic unity and legally enforce a narrow vision of Poland. Such statistics were used to support and justify the inclusion of an *invocatio Dei* in the 1997 Constitution (Zubrzycki 2001) and are often invoked to defend the state's policing of social movements that deviate from an imagined national norm. Such statistics were thrown around when gay pride parades were banned in Warsaw in the name of public morality, for example. On the occasion of Corpus Christi in 2013, the Archbishop of Kraków, Cardinal Stanisław Dziwisz, gave a new twist to that argument by recognizing that "there exists a plurality of opinions in Poland, [and that] in a democratic society the majority rules." "But," he added, "truth is not determined through voting," which is why "even the parliament cannot create a moral order other than the one deeply inscribed in the heart of man, in his conscience."[7] Religious discourse since 1989, then, has been used primarily to constrain individual rights and to *shrink* the boundaries of Polishness by symbolically excluding those considered "morally unworthy" for full membership: "Jews," secularists, "bad Catholics," masons (all code names for Jews), and, increasingly, feminists and sexual minorities.[8]

---

7   http://krakow.gazeta.pl/krakow/1,44425,14010318,Kard__Dziwisz__Prawdy_nie_ustala_sie_przez_glosowanie.html#ixzz2h3v23Lj0 (accessed May 31, 2013).

8   The use of the adjective "Polish-speaking" (instead of "Polish") is a common discursive strategy meant to delegitimize someone by implying that they are not "truly" Polish. That strategy serves to "reveal" the individual's alleged "passing" and unmask "impostors." The use of someone's alleged 'real (Jewish) name" is also common. For a discussion of this process of turning political opponents into symbolic Jews, with specific quotes, see Zubrzycki (2006, 208–212). For visual examples of that strategy, see Zubrzycki (2016, 75–78). On sexual minorities, see Graff's fascinating collection of essays (2008), in which she argues that gays are the "new Jews," noting also the ideological alliance between minority groups targeted by the Catholic right. This argument has also been made by feminist

This form of symbolic exclusion points to an interesting paradox. As we know from a rich literature on nationalism (cf. Brubaker 1992; Schnapper 1994; Yack 1996; Nielsen 1999; Zubrzycki 2001), ideological forms of exclusion are typical of places where the nation is understood in civic terms, and where, therefore, one's national identity—at least ideally—is determined by his or her adherence to the principles of the social contract—whatever its terms may be. The American case is a paradigmatic example of ideologically defined national identity, where "being" American means the support of a specific set of values and practices, and therefore where it is possible to be considered "un-American," say, for supporting communism during the McCarthy era, by criticizing the Bush administration in post 9/11 America, or supporting Obamacare. Ideological exclusion from the nation however ill-befits a place where the nation is primarily understood in *ethnic* terms, following the German Romantic model of nationhood. In line with this conception, national identity can neither be chosen nor escaped; it is transmitted through birth, "flowing through one's veins," constitutive of an imagined primordial self.

How is it possible, given the latter, to exclude ethnic nationals from the nation? How can the conservative Catholic right insist on an ethnic definition of Polishness while simultaneously symbolically excluding some ethnic members on the basis of their beliefs, political opinions, or sexual orientation? How is the tension between these two modes of social closure—one based on blood and culture, the other based on ideological orientations and political bonds—reconciled? In *The Crosses of Auschwitz* (2006) I showed how "ideological deviance" from the ethno-Catholic definition of Polishness is ethnicized such that individuals and groups who are *not* defending the prominent place of Catholicism and its symbols in the public sphere (advocating instead a civic-secular Poland) are turned into "Jews." This logic and the multiple examples of its application in the public sphere—in both verbal and nonverbal discourse—provide rich examples of a phenomenon analyzed long ago by Jean-Paul Sartre (1986 [1946]), who famously claimed that "If the Jew did not exist, the anti-Semite would invent him," or more recently by Enzo Traverso (1997) who explained how one can be Jewish merely by virtue of the Other's gaze. Polish

---

scholar and public intellectual Magdalena Środa in an editorial called "The New Jews," in which she analyzed the witchhunt against feminists and the Catholic Church's blaming "gender ideology" for all sorts of social ills, from broken families to pedophile priests ("Nowi Żydzi," *Wprost*, no. 4, 2014, accessed on January 22, 2014 at http://www.wprost.pl/ar/432887/Nowi-Zydzi/. On the use of Jewishness and homosexuality as tropes for symbolic exclusion to the national community see also Mosse (1985) and Bunzl (2004).

public intellectual Adam Michnik refers to this specific form of anti-Semitism as "magical antisemitism": "The logic of normal ... antisemitism is the following: 'Adam Michnik is a Jew, therefore he is a hooligan, a thief, a traitor, a bandit etc.' Magical antisemitism however works this way: 'Adam Michnik is a thief, therefore he is most probably a Jew" (Michnik 1999, 73).

But why Jews instead of Ukrainians or Germans, who are also significant Others in the Polish social imagination? A simple answer to this complex question might be that communism, Western-style capitalism, and cosmopolitanism are all specifically associated with Jewishness and that Jewishness is an ethno-religious category that many Poles on the right perceive as the polar opposite of the *Polak-katolik* (Krzemiński 1996, 2001; see also Porter-Szűcs, this volume). As Jewishness becomes a symbol standing for a liberal, plural, cosmopolitan, and secular Poland, the conservative Catholic right maintain that Poland is ruled by "Jews"—by symbolic Jews—who must be neutralized. Political opponents are indeed often accused of being Jewish. Recall how Lech Wałęsa had declared himself a "pure Pole" during the 1990 presidential election, when he ran against Catholic intellectual and former Solidarity ally Tadeusz Mazowiecki. Use of that expression implied that Mazowiecki had Jewish roots, a claim that Mazowiecki tried to dispel by providing the public genealogical information (see Grudzińska-Gross, this volume). Aleksander Kwaśniewski, former president of Poland (1995–2005), and even John Paul II were often accused of being Jewish in far-right milieux because these figures were not "Polish enough" in their politics or ecumenical teachings. This is why and how "antisemitism without Jews" can exist in Poland.

Although the diversity that characterized Poland for most of its history is unlikely to return, civic and cosmopolitan nationalists see the recognition of that legacy as a tool not only to build an open society but also to mark Poland as a polity that meets the standards of an internationally normative model of nationhood that values and encourages pluralism and multiculturalism.

Breaching Polishness

The very process of ethnicization of "deviation" from the ethno-Catholic model of Polishness is also at the source of *philo-Semitism*. For if ethno-religious nationalists contend that "Jews" are contaminating the nation with their civic ideals, building a pernicious postnational, cosmopolitan world and must therefore be politically marginalized, "Jews" must for the same reason be resurrected and Jewishness promoted, according to proponents of a civic and secular vision of the polity. Precisely because Jewishness carries specific significations and symbolic capital that other minorities in Poland (such as Ukrainians, Silesians, or the Vietnamese) do not possess, it is primarily through Jews and Jewishness that a modern multicultural Poland is articulated. Hence liberal, leftist youth wear T-shirts and brandish placards in protests against religious nationalists, subversively claiming that they are "Jews," mocking conspiracy theories of the right. "I'm a Jew" T-shirts were part of a campaign by the Foundation for Freedom that consisted in "spreading . . . slogans signaling the existence of some taboo topics . . . and discriminated social groups in Poland," including atheists and homosexuals,[9] while a hip clothing label in Warsaw launched a "Jewish" line called "Oy." Initially targeted at young Jews, Risk "Oy" produced relatively pricey t-shirts and hoodies with slogans such as "Thanks to My Mom," adorned with a variety of Star of David designs and Hebrew inscriptions. The owner of the brand told the *Times of Israel* that "what we really want . . . is to re-brand Jewish identity. We want to show the modern, positive aspects of it. What we are doing is showing that being Jewish is cool and sexy."[10] According to Kraków's Jewish Community Center (JCC) director Jonathan Ornstein, there might be no need to "rebrand" Jewish identity, as he's been insisting for years now, that "it's hip to be Jewish in today's Poland" (personal communications, March 2011, March 2012, and March 2013). Several non-Jewish volunteers at the JCC and non-Jewish members of a Kraków-based Israeli dance troupe made similar observations, commenting on the fact that "Jewishness is fashionable," one even adding that "just like in Warsaw it's fashionable to have a gay friend" (interviews, March 2012).

The important question, here, is why Jewishness (and gayness) is "fashionable" for some non-Jewish Poles. What does it signify for them? The president of the Joint Distribution Committee (JDC) in Warsaw, Karina Sokołowska, specified in *The Times of Israel* article on Risk's "Oy" clothing line, that "in general, Jews in Poland are looking for ways to express being Jewish, [but the clothing line] *is an attractive item for Poland's many philo-Semites* (emphasis mine)." One such non-Jew quoted in the story, a forty-year-old lawyer living in Warsaw,

---

9 Other t-shirts part of the 2004 campaign included "I don't go to church," "I don't want to have kids," or "I'm gay" (http://www.tiszertdlawolnosci.tiszert.com/ (accessed July 22, 2012). The Foundation for Freedom is dedicated to protecting ethnic, racial, religious, and gender and sexual minorities from discrimination.

10 http://www.timesofisrael.com/polish-fashion-entrepreneur-makes-being-jewish-sexy/?utm_source=Newsletter+subscribers&utm_campaign=0c5a586595-JTA_Daily_Briefing_1_31_2014&utm_medium=email&utm_term=0_2dce5bc6f8-0c5a586595-25416689 (accessed February 1, 2014).

explained that "Wearing [Risk "Oy"] is like taking part in a public discussion about Jews in Poland—that Jews live here and that Jews can live here." This is an important comment: that public discussion about Jews in Poland is actually about the very identity of Poland and a critique of the still-dominant vision of the nation as ethnically Polish and (nominally) Catholic.

Poking Holes in the Catholic Fortress

It is in that broader context of struggles to define Poland that many non-Jewish Poles' participation in and support for the revival of Jewish communities and Jewish culture take on their full significance. My interviews with key cultural entrepreneurs and numerous non-Jewish activists suggest that their promotion of Jewish culture is part of a broader attempt to expand what it means to be Polish; to counter the monopoly of the Catholic right over the definition of Polishness (Zubrzycki 2013a) and to build and promote a plural and secular society in a nation-state with an ethnically and religiously homogenous population. What is intriguing here, however, is that many of those who argue for a secular society in Poland do not object to the public display of Jewish religious symbols and often even support it. Aneta, a longtime JCC volunteer who is expressly anticlerical and declares herself an atheist, explained to me during a Shabbat dinner: "I think it's great to see all of that [Jewish religious activity]. I'm not religious but I think it's good to see that there's something else than what we already know—and frankly speaking—that we're sick of—processions, pilgrimages here and there, crosses everywhere."

Evangelical Christians repeatedly emphasized in our conversations that it was important for them to discover Judaism for theological reasons—"to go back to the source" and "get to know Jesus as a Jew"—but also to support the revival of Jewish communities in order to build a counterweight to the all-too-heavy presence of Catholicism in Poland. Moreover, most practicing Catholics among the JCC volunteers and members of the Israeli dance group I interviewed associated themselves with Catholic movements related to what is called in Poland "open Catholicism": this movement is known for being more "intellectual" than ritualistic, with close philosophical ties to the liberal Catholic weekly *Tygodnik Powszechny* and actively preaching John Paul II's call for ecumenism and respect for "our older brothers in faith."[11]

---

11 For a typology of Catholicisms within the Polish Catholic landscape, and different orientations' specific rapport to Jews and anti-Semitism, see Zubrzycki (2005). *Tygodnik Powszechny*, the most prominent "open" Catholic publication,

Some also articulate their support of the revival of Jewish culture partly in opposition to the conservative, reactionary Catholicism of Radio Maryja.[12] When, at one point in my conversation with Natalia, a Lutheran from Silesia who majored in Judaic studies and art history, I mention that the controversial right-wing Radio Maryja is organizing an antigovernment protest in the following days, the young woman responds:

> Argh, I forgot that they still exist . . . [But] let's leave these marginals in the margins! Radio Maryja, it's a bunch of old ladies—hopefully they don't have too many young followers. There's a chance, with Jewishness being fashionable, that it means that the young generation is more open [and] that there will be more openness in the future.[13]

---

with which John Paul II was associated before his papacy and that has long worked on Polish- and Christian-Jewish dialogue, is nicknamed "Żydownik powszechny" by people on the far right; the word "weekly" (tygodnik) is transformed into "Jewishy" (żydownik). For its sixty-fifth anniversary in 2010, the weekly published a special commemorative issue on Polish-Jewish relations and Christian-Jewish dialogue and changed its name on the first page to *Żydownik Powszechny*, an astute reversal. *Gazeta Wyborcza*, Poland's center-left daily founded by Adam Michnik, is also "Jewified" by those on the far-Right by being called "Gazeta Koszerna"—the Kosher newspaper, which both implies "Jewish ties and perspectives" but also liberal political correctness.

12 Founded in Toruń in 1991 by Father Tadeusz Rydzyk, Radio Maryja is the voice of anticommunism, anti-EU, and anti-Semitism. In recent years, it has also loudly promoted antirefugee, antifeminist and anti-LGBT opinions. Often accused by the left and by progressive Catholics with having created a sect that borders on heresy, its charismatic leader has managed to create a social movement around the Radio's right-wing politics (Krzemiński 2009, 2017; Sekerdej and Pasieka 2013, 61–65), consistently mobilizing followers devoted to the cause of protecting or restoring a "true Poland." While Radio Maryja is not the dominant face of Catholicism in Poland, it is the most vocal and occupies public space with immense semiotic force: through related publications such as *Nasz Dziennik* (Our daily) and *Nasza Polska* (Our Poland) it exerts a significant influence on the public face of Catholicism in Poland by affixing the terms and relative positions that bound public debate.

13 Natalia's dismissive comments about Radio Maryja's followers is common in liberal circles. They are frequently referred to as "mohair berets" (*mohery*) after a popular type of coif elderly Polish women wear. Radio Maryja and its supporters quickly and self-consciously adopted the derogatory moniker as a badge of pride in their beliefs and political goals. The mohair beret, ridiculed by the young and the liberals, has even become a symbol of the empowerment of older women,

Whether or not Natalia is right about generational change, what is significant for our purpose is that the hegemony of Catholicism and the Catholic Church is not combated via the promotion of other religious communities such as Protestants, Russian Orthodox, Muslims, or Jehovah's witnesses—who do exist in Poland but not in great numbers—but through Judaism and Jewishness more specifically because of the specific meanings Jewishness carries in contemporary Poland.

Expanding Polishness through Jewishness

Because in the eyes of ethno-Catholic nationalists only "objective facts" like ethnicity and religious affiliation matter, and since ethnonationality is the dominant mode of thinking the nation in Poland, many activists and state agencies create visible, countable, "objective" counterweights. They do so in two main ways: by supporting the institutional growth of Jewish communities and thereby introducing Jewish symbols into the public sphere, and by promoting knowledge about Poland's Jewish past and present through a multitude of cultural events, performances, and programs.

The multiple festivals of Jewish culture in the four corners of Poland seek to educate Poles (and tourists) about the culture of Jews who once lived in Poland and contributed to Polish culture. The claim is not merely about mutual influence: rather Jewish culture is *constitutive of* Polish culture. Polish culture, these activists insist, is not only about Catholic practices and folklore. It is about broad universalist values that have shaped a long tradition of "religious tolerance" and "civic openness" that led to the flourishing of Jewish religious and communal life, prosperous Jewish towns and peaceful shtetls, *and* Polish culture. As Janusz Makuch, the co-founder and director of Kraków's famous Festival of Jewish Culture, told me in one of our conversations:

> Whether people know it or not, it is a *fact* that Jews, for many many centuries..., made tremendous contributions to Polish culture. So when we're talking about Polish culture, we're equally talking about Jewish culture. Without the contribution of

---

who will not remain silent at home but instead come in the streets to fight for the kind of Poland they want. In 2009, Father Rydzyk encouraged his female followers to knit miniature berets to be distributed at a pilgrimage to Częstochowa, a practice the "Family of Radio Maryja" has now included in its repertoire of routine actions. Women followers knit and distribute approximately half a million mini berets every year (*Gazeta Wyborcza*, February 2, 2012).

Jews, true Polish culture couldn't exist. Forget it! Literature, architecture, sculptures, historians, intellectuals, music, economics, politics, food. So everything was intertwined and still is, thank God. What I'm trying to do . . . is to help Poles realize what is theirs (March 1, 2012. Original conversation in English).

The recognition of the Jewish past and the presence of Jewish symbols and markers in the public sphere therefore allows public figures, teachers, and activists to plausibly argue for a civic definition of Polishness. Because in the postwar period the communist regime co-opted (and corrupted) civic discourse, that vision of the national community is often perceived as "foreign." Most recently, it is also portrayed by the far-right as an ideological import from the European Union and its postnational agenda. Today's civic nationalists must therefore work harder to create a plausible and desirable civic project. To do so, they attempt to legitimize that model of nationhood by "Polonizing" it: they reach to the distant past and renarrativize Polish history to emphasize ethnic and religious diversity, political openness and tolerance, and political freedom. They point to the large number of Jews who settled in Poland as evidence of the historical roots of a Polish civic nation. Poland's historical religious tolerance also allows them to articulate a discourse that sets Poland apart from other European nations. As I heard so many times in various venues, "When Jews were being kicked out from Southern and Western Europe, King Kazimierz the Great was welcoming them in Poland." That narrative of Polish exceptionalism is significant, and I will return to some of its implications later, but here I want to emphasize the link that cultural entrepreneurs, public intellectuals, artists, and ordinary citizens make between Jews and Poland's Europeanness. For Mirka, a young woman in her early twenties who had been volunteering at the JCC for two years when I met her, the presence of Jews in Poland would allow Poles to feel more at ease in the new Europe: "I'm totally for Jews living here, as it was before, as it was before the war. Then it would be more comfortable for us in Europe because we'd be more open, more understanding toward differences in general." The promotion of Jewishness in festivals, memory projects and many other institutional projects are also thought to be bringing Poland back to her "true essence." In the words of Makuch:

> Kraków was always a multicultural place, where cultural pluralism was often very obvious. However, this national monotheism, religious monotheism, that was created after the Second World War is scorching me, hurting me. I really don't like this—so let's go back here to what is the basis of our spirituality, actually, since Jews were Polish citizens (Interview, March 19, 2011).

That discourse has been perfectly integrated by various groups involved in the Jewish revival. Ula, a woman in her late twenties who dances in the Israeli dance group as a hobby and is a practicing Catholic, explained to me that she wants to learn about Jews and Jewish culture to better know herself *as a Pole*:

> Well, basically, there's been a Jewish presence in our country (*u nas*) for 800 years, on our lands, here in Poland, so there's this influence that we don't remember anymore because there are almost no Jews left in Poland. There are very few. [But it's important to know that culture] so that we can better know ourselves. Our identity, who we are, what we have—... we owe [it] not only to ourselves, but also to other communities who lived here. And Jews lived here in great numbers. So we owe them for their contributions in the academic and scientific sphere where there were a lot of Jews, and in the administration here in Kraków. There were Jewish mayors, many well-known lawyers at Jagiellonian University, many architects, in music too. So they contributed a lot. In literature too! They were a big influence. Not long ago I was talking with friends about hospitality, how Poland and Poles are known for their hospitality (kind of), but that hospitality actually comes from Jewish culture! [14]

In this discourse and related practices, modernity, Europeanness, multiculturalism as well as cultural forms and national traits such as hospitality are achieved through, and thanks to, Jews.

"Our Jews." Otherness and Indigeneity

This still begs the question: why do those who wish to build pluralism focus on Jews instead of Ukrainians or Vietnamese? One explanation that I have already provided is that Jewishness carries a specific signification and symbolic capital: modernity, cosmopolitanism, urbanity. Another is that Jews are basically absent from the Polish landscape and are therefore both nonthreatening and easy objects of people's fantasies: dreams or nightmares depending on one's political orientation. Yet another reason is that Jewishness, unlike Ukrainianness, Silesianness, or Vietnamese-ness is at once exotic and somewhat "indigenous." It is different enough; yet as Kasia told me in a conversation in 2012, it "was nourished from the Polish soil and grew on these lands." Natalia explained:

---

[14] Ula was referring to the image of Polish hosts (mothers more specifically) preparing an abundance of food not only at special occasions but at casual social events as well, insisting that their guests eat to their hearts' content.

> On the one hand, [Jewish culture] is, let's say, "oriental." But on the other hand, because it developed in Poland, in spite of everything it's somehow very much tied with Poland, yes? It's kind of an exotic element in our environment. It's not something like ... Swahili somewhere far off in Africa, but [rather] something that is different from Polish culture yet at the same time related to it, inseparable [from it] even.

It is that duality—the exoticism and familiarity—that according to another JCC volunteer makes Jewishness so appealing for non-Jewish Poles:

> We could talk about [Jewish culture] as a foreign culture, different from Polish culture if we wanted ... to separate, but we're still aware that we're talking about a culture that was here for centuries. But it's still something exotic, right? And yet, totally close to us. So it's easy to become interested in [Jews and Jewish culture] and become fascinated. It becomes fashionable.

Jewishness is thus both Other and "ours," an observation made spontaneously by countless other interviewees. As another young woman who volunteers at the JCC told me, "Jewish culture is 'exotica' right here at home." It is the ideal *indigenous Other*. In that discourse, to revive Jewish culture allows Poles to become "authentically" multicultural. It allows the recovery of a truer national self and the reshaping of symbolic boundaries of the nation through the Other. Poland's monoethnic and monoreligious landscape is interpreted as a casualty of the Nazis and communists, a historical anomaly that should be corrected. Although the diversity that characterized Poland for most of its history is unlikely to return, civic and cosmopolitan nationalists see the recognition of that legacy as a tool not only to build an open society but also to mark Poland as a polity that meets the standards of an internationally normative model of nationhood that values and encourages pluralism and multiculturalism. Embracing Jewishness therefore gives Poland back her "true" shape and allows a rebranding of Poland as modern and European.

These discursive and performative strategies do not always and necessarily whitewash history to erase traces of anti-Semitism. For many of my (thirty-five and older) interviewees, "revelations" of violent crimes committed against Jews by ethnic Poles (e.g., Gross 2000, 2006; Gross and Grudzińska-Gross 2012) sparked their initial interest in Jewish history and culture, or of consciousness-raising efforts.[15] Nor are these discursive and performative strategies purely instrumental: I am not asserting that the non-Jewish Poles involved in the

---

15   "Millennials" in my interviews showed much less interest in Poles' participation in the Holocaust and even knowledge about the Jedwabne pogrom and the

Jewish turn are not genuinely interested in Jewish culture or Judaism, or that they do not care about the memory of those murdered in the Holocaust. But in their artistic creations, beliefs, discourses, and actions—and alongside and through their cultural investments in Judaism—they weave their individual identities and private life projects into a vision of Poland that is severed from that presented by the traditional motto *Polonia semper fidelis*.

Conclusion

The extermination of Jews and destruction of Jewish culture in Poland is presented (and increasingly experienced) in liberal intellectual, artistic, and ecumenical milieux as a tragic loss for Polish culture and identity: so it is in this sense that Jewish culture is seen as something that must be rescued, saved, or even resurrected. Many in these milieux argue that Poland is not homogeneous. But instead of emphasizing the ideological heterogeneity of its current population as a legitimate form of diversity, they emphasize its (ethno)cultural heterogeneity, the result of an ethnically and religiously diverse past.

The Jewish turn, of course, is also about other important projects and processes, led by and for Jews.[16] What I have argued in this chapter, however, is that there exists an elective affinity between non-Jewish Poles' support of, and participation in, the revival of Jewish culture and preservation of Jewish memory and their desire to build a Poland that is different from the one forcefully promoted by the Catholic Church and the political right. Resurrecting Jewish culture and actively supporting Jewish communities' renewal gives concrete shape to seemingly amorphous ideological pluralism in order to trump the "hard" demographic "facts" of Poland's ethno-religious homogeneity. By creating "objective," tangible, visible, countable—and growing—Jewish Others, social actors and cultural agents implicitly and often explicitly contest the claim of the nation's ethnic and religious homogeneity.

I have shown that the expansion of Polishness is attempted through three diachronic, overlapping processes of symbolic boundary making: *softening*, *stretching*, and *reshaping*. The symbolic boundaries of Polishness are softened discursively, through critiques of the Catholic Church and of the *Polak-katolik*

---

debates about Jan Gross's book *Neighbors* (2000). This is most likely because they were small children when those issues were most intensely debated.

16 I analyze those in chapter 6 of my *Resurrecting the Jew: Nationalism, Philosemitism, and Poland's Jewish Revival* (2022).

normative model of national identity. They are stretched by making the contemporary Jewish presence visible and by materializing traces of the Jewish past; the stretched boundaries of Polishness are then *reshaped* and legitimated by cultural work that indigenizes the Jew and Jewish culture, thereby naturalizing an alternative model to the dominant one that links Polishness to Catholicism.

Jewishness, then, can serve as a foil to construct not only an exclusive ethnic nation but also used to build an inclusive, civic, and secular nation. I have shown that in Poland the national self is being built not only *against* the Other (the Jew) but also *through* that indigenous Other in opposition to an alleged primordial self—the ethno-Catholic Pole. This is more than the simplistic story of philo-Semitism opposing anti-Semitism. Rather, Polish philo-Semitism is part of a larger process of redefining national identity. Jewish culture is but one thread woven into the dense tapestry of the civic national counter-narrative, yet it is an especially important motif given both the long history of Jews on Polish lands and the trauma of their eradication from the national landscape. It is also important because it helps the state to rebrand Poland on the international scene, a motivation that cannot be ignored.[17]

The Polish case shows just how complex the process of national redefinition can be. While it is by including Jews in the national narrative and conception of a new national self that the symbolic boundaries of Polish national identity are stretched and reshaped, it is so precisely because Jews are seen as different and Other. The inclusion of Jews within the symbolic perimeter of the nation in order to redefine Polishness does not—and cannot—de-otherize the Jew: for Poland to become plural and "inclusive," distinctions between citizens based on

---

17 To give a few examples of the Jewish motif: Israeli filmmaker Yael Bartana's Poland-based trilogy *And Europe Will be Stunned* was selected by the Civic Platform-led Polish ministry of Culture to represent Poland at the 2011 Venice's Biennale, making Bartana the first non-Pole to represent Poland at this prestigious event. A year later, in 2012, Kraków's Festival of Jewish Culture was invited by the Polish Embassy in Belgium to represent Polish cultural achievements. An exhibit about the festival was organized in the embassy's foyer, but the main event was a public conversation with Janusz Makuch and a concert by the Kraków klezmer band Bester Quartet. Since its opening in 2014, The POLIN Museum of the History of Polish Jews has become one of Poland's calling cards abroad and is widely used at home in cultural diplomacy; a visit to the museum is now standard fare for VIPs. Even Law and Justice's controversial "Holocaust Speech Law" was used by the government to rebrand Poland as a "protector of historical truth" and crusader against Holocaust denial. See https://www.youtube.com/watch?v=R9bS9z5OiWY&t=147s (accessed February 2, 2018).

ethnicity and religion must be retained. And these distinctions maintain more or less rigid hierarchies (e.g., Bourdieu 1984; Pasieka 2015).

This paradox is important for scholars and memory activists alike to ponder. How can Jews be given their history and legacy, their due place in Poland's past *and* present, without being Othered? How can Poles rediscover Jews and Jewish culture without exoticizing and fetishizing them and without reproducing so-called intrinsic differences between "Poles" and "Jews"? And how can this be achieved without making them disappear into a civic narrative of "Polish citizens" that erases them from the national landscape altogether (Irwin-Zarecka 1989; Zubrzycki 2006)?

Part of the answer is to work even more diligently at problematizing the Catholicity of Polishness. While there is a rich scholarship undertaking this agenda (e.g., Bjork 2008; Porter-Szűcs 2012; Pasieka 2015), much remains to be done on the ground—in school curricula, museums, and public spaces to question the default, taken-for-granted Catholicity of Polishness. In recent years, some have undergone the complex process of apostasy in order not to be included into statistics that legitimize the Catholic narrative of the nation (Centrum Badania Opinii Społecznej 2018, 2021; Zubrzycki 2020; Sadłoń 2021). Another strategy is to insist that ideological, political, and sexual diversity are legitimate forms of *national* pluralism. This is an area where the last few years have brought significant developments in the public sphere, with women's and LGBTQ rights movements gaining visibility and undermining the patriarchal model of society promoted by the Catholic Church. When Poles start thinking about Polishness in political terms, Jews will be Jews *as* Jews, instead of as proxies for diversity and multiculturalism.

Bibliography

A. Formal Interviews (public figures)

Horovitz, Itzchak (Rabbi and Kantor), Audio-recording, Kraków, February 29, 2012.
Makuch, Janusz (co-Founder and Director of Kraków's Festival of Jewish Culture), Audio-recordings, Kraków, March 19, 2011; March 1, 2012; March 27, 2013.
Ornstein, Jonathan (Director, Jewish Community Centre), Audio-recordings, Kraków, March 2011, 2012, 2013.
Pash, Boaz (Rabbi), Audio-recording, Kraków, March 6, 2012.
Schudrich, Michael (Chief Rabbi of Poland), Audio Recording, Warsaw, September 28, 2012.

Segal, Tanya (Rabbi, Beit Kraków), Audio-recording, Kraków, March 7, 2012.
Herberger, Tyson (Rabbi in Warsaw, 2010–13, Wrocław 2013–15), Warsaw, September 27, 2012.

B. Statistical Reports and Other Primary Sources

Centrum Badania Opinii Społecznej. 2018. *Religijność Polaków i ocena sytuacji Kościoła katolickiego*. Warsaw: Centrum Badania Opinii Społecznej.
Centrum Badania Opinii Społecznej. 2021. *Religijność młodych na tle ogółu społeczeństwa*. Warsaw: Centrum Badania Opinii Społecznej.
Gebert, Konstanty. 2008. *Living in the Land of Ashes*. Kraków: Austeria Publishing House.
Krajewski, Stanisław. 2005. *Poland and the Jews: Reflections of a Polish Jew*. Kraków: Austeria.
Kraków Festival of Jewish Culture (FKŻK), *Annual Reports*, 1991–2013.
Ostachowicz, Igor. 2012. *Noc żywych Żydów*. Warsaw: Wyd. WAB.
Penn, Shana, Konstanty Gebert and Anna Goldstein (eds). 2009. *The Fall of the Wall and the Rebirth of Jewish Life in Poland: 1989-2009*. Warsaw: The Taube Foundation.
Sadłoń, Wojciech. 2021. "Religijność Polaków" in *Kościół w Polsce. Raport*. 13–20. Warsaw: Katolicka agencja informacyjna.
Tuszyńska, Agata. 2005. *Rodzinna historia lęku*, Kraków: Wydawnictwo Literackie.
Zubryzcki, Geneviève. 2016. "Nationalism, 'Philosemitism' and Symbolic Boundary Making in Contemporary Poland" in *Comparative Studies in Society and History* 58:1.

C. Secondary Literature

Bourdieu, Pierre. 1991. *Language and Symbolic Power*. Cambridge, MA: Harvard University Press.
Bunzl, Matti. 2004. *Jews and Queers: Symptoms of Modernity in Late-Twentieth Century Vienna*. Berkeley: University of California Press.
Brubaker, Rogers. 1992. *Citizenship and Nationhood in France and Germany*. Cambridge, MA: Harvard University Press.
Chomątowska, Beata. 2012. *Stacja Muranów*. Sękowa: Wyd. Czarne.
Forecki, Piotr. 2010. *Od Shoah do Strachu: Spory o polsko-żydowską przeszłość i pamięć w debatach publicznych*. Poznań: Wydawnictwo Poznańskie.
Gitelman, Zvi. 2003. "Collective Memory and Contemporary Polish-Jewish Relations." *Contested Memories: Poles and Jews During the Holocaust and its Aftermath*, edited by Joshua D. Zimmerman, 271–290. New Brunswick, NJ: Rutgers University Press.
Graff, Agnieszka. 2008. *Rykoszetem. Rzecz o płci, seksualności i narodzie*. Warsaw: WAB.
Gross, Jan T. 2000. *Sąsiedzi*. Sejny: Pogranicze.

Gross, Jan T. 2006. *Fear: Anti-Semitism in Poland After the Holocaust*. New York: Random House.
Gross, Jan T., and Irena Grudzińska-Gross. 2011. *Złote żniwa*. Kraków: Znak.
Gruber, Ruth Ellen. 2002. *Virtually Jewish: Reinventing Jewish Culture in Europe*. Los Angeles: University of California Press.
Irwin-Zarecka, Iwona. 1989. *Neutralizing Memory: The Jew in Contemporary Poland*. New Brunswick: Transaction.
Janicka, Elżbieta. 2011. *Festung Warschau*. Warsaw: Wyd. Krytyki Politycznej.
Krzemiński, Ireneusz, ed. 1996. *Czy Polacy są antysemitami? Wyniki badania sondażowgo*. Warsaw: Oficyna Naukowa.
Krzemiński, Ireneusz. 2001. "Polacy i Żydzi: wizja wzajemnych stosunków, tożsamość narodowa i antysemityzm." In *Trudne sąsiedztwa. Z socjologii konfliktów narodowościowych*, edited by Aleksandra Kania, 171–200. Warsaw: Wydwanictwo narodowe Scholar.
Krzemiński, Ireneusz, ed. 2009. *Czego nas uczy Radio Maryja?* Warsaw: WAiP.
Krzemiński, Ireneusz, ed. 2015. *Żydzi—Problem prawdziwego Polaka: Antysemityzm, ksenofobia i stereotypy narodowe po raz trzeci*. Warsaw: Wydawnictwa Uniwersytetu Warszawskiego.
Krzemiński, Ireneusz. 2017. "Radio Maryja and Fr. Rydzyk as a Creator of the National-Catholic Ideology." In *Religion, Politics, and Values in Poland: Continuity and Change since 1989*, edited by Sabrina Ramet and Irena Borowik, 85–112. New York: Palgrave Macmillan.
Lehrer, Erica. 2003. "Repopulating Jewish Poland—In Wood." *Polin: Studies in Polish Jewry* 16: 335–55.
Lehrer, Erica. 2013. *Jewish Poland Revisited: Heritage Tourism in Unquiet Places*. Bloomington: Indiana University Press.
Lehrer, Erica, and Magdalena Waligórska. 2013. "Cur(at)ing History: New Genre Art Interventions and the Polish–Jewish Past." *East European Politics and Societies and Cultures*, 27, no. 3: 510–44.
Lehrer, Erica. 2014. *Na szczęście to Żyd / Lucky Jews: Poland's Jewish Figurines*. Kraków: Ha! Art Press.
Meng, Michael. 2012. *Shattered Spaces: Encountering Jewish Ruins in Postwar Germany and Poland*. Cambridge, MA: Harvard University Press.
Michnik, Adam. 1999. "Wystąpienie." In *Kościół polski wobec antysemityzmu, 1989–1999: Rachunek sumienia*, edited by B. Oppenheim, 69–76. Kraków: WAM.
Mosse, George L. 1985. *Nationalism and Sexuality: Respectability and Abnormal Sexuality in Modern Europe*. New York: Fertig.
Nielsen, Kai. 1999. "Cultural Nationalism, Neither Ethnic nor Civic." *The Philosophical Forum: A Quarterly* 28, no. 1–2: 42–52.
Porter-Szűcs, Brian. 2012. *Faith and Fatherland: Catholicism, Modernity, and Poland*. New York: Oxford University Press.

Reszke, Katka. 2013. *Return of the Jew: Identity Narratives of the Third Post-Holocaust Generations of Jews in Poland*. Brighton, MA: Academic Studies Press.
Sartre, Jean-Paul. 1986. *Anti-Semite and Jew*. New York: Schocken Books.
Schnapper, Dominique. 1994. *Sur l'idée moderne de la nation. La communauté des citoyens*. Paris: Gallimard.
Sekerdej, Kinga, and Agnieszka Pasieka. 2013. "Researching the Dominant Religion: Anthropology at Home and Methodological Catholicism." *Method and Theory in the Study of Religion* 25: 53–77.
Steinlauf, Michael. 1997. *Bondage to the Dead: Poland and the Memory of the Holocaust*. New York: Syracuse University Press.
Traverso, Enzo. 1997. *L'Histoire déchirée. Essai sur Auschwitz et les intellectuels*. Paris: Ed. Cerf.
Śpiewak, Paweł. 2012. *Żydokomuna*. Czerwone i Czarne.
Waligórska, Magdalena. 2008. "Fiddler as a Fig Leaf: the Politicization of Klezmer in Poland." In *Impulses for Europe. Tradition and Modernity in East European Jewry*, edited by Manfred Sapper, 227–38. Berlin: Osteuropa.
Waligórska, Magdalena. 2013. *Klezmer's Afterlife: An Ethnography of the Jewish Music Revival in Poland and Germany*. New York: Oxford University Press.
Weizman, Yechiel, 2022. *Unsettled Heritage: Living Next To Poland's Material Jewish Traces After the Holocaust*. Ithaca, NY: Cornell University Press.
Wodziński, Marcin. 2011. "Jewish Studies in Poland." *Journal of Modern Jewish Studies* 10, no. 1, 101–118.
Wodziński, Marcin. Forthcoming. "Prospects for Jewish Studies in Poland: An Update for a New Decade." *Studies in Contemporary Jewry* 32.
Yack, Bernard. 1996. "The Myth of the Civic Nation." *Critical Review* 10, no. 2: 193–211.
Zubrzycki, Geneviève. 2001. "We, the Polish Nation": Ethnic and Civic Visions of Nationhood in Post-Communist Constitutional Debates. *Theory and Society* 30, no. 5: 629–69.
Zubrzycki, Geneviève. 2005. " 'Poles-Catholics' and 'Symbolic Jews': Jewishness as Social Closure in Poland." *Studies in Contemporary Jewry* 21: 65–87.
Zubrzycki, Geneviève. 2006. *The Crosses of Auschwitz: Nationalism and Religion in Post-Communist Poland*. Chicago: University of Chicago Press.
Zubrzycki, Geneviève. 2010. "What is Pluralism in a 'Monocultural' Society? Considerations from Post-Communist Poland." In *After Pluralism: Re-imagining Models of Interreligious Engagement*, edited by Courtney Bender and Pamela Klassen, 277–95. New York: Columbia University Press.
Zubrzycki, Geneviève. 2013. "Narrative Shock and (Re)Making Polish Memory in the Twenty-First Century." In *Memory and Postwar Memorials: Confronting the Violence of the Past*, edited by Florence Vatan and Marc Silberman, 95–115. New York: Palgrave.
Zubrzycki, Geneviève. 2022. *Resurrecting the Jew: Nationalism, Philosemitism, and Poland's Jewish Revival*. Princeton, NJ: Princeton University Press.

Part Two
Identity in the Making

Chapter Six

Human Mobility and the Creation of a Transatlantic Polish Culture

Keely Stauter-Halsted

Polish social scientists have long portrayed migration as a net loss for the nation, a depletion of human resources needed for building an independent state. During much of the twentieth century, scholars working in the United States represented immigrants as dangerously "uprooted" from their communities of origin, while specialists in Poland lamented the depleted villages back home and miserable lives of countrymen abroad, themes that reflected ongoing concern about the loss of cultural capital via emigration.[1] But human mobility also helped define Polishness in important ways, especially during the great labor migration from the 1870s to 1914. This chapter suggests that far from weakening the nation, the process of migration and return fostered new conceptions of Polishness to include wider categories of populations both at home and abroad. The transatlantic movement abroad "for bread" (*za chlebem*) crystalized a sense of national belonging for millions of small farmers and other uneducated residents of the Polish lands. The influence of circular migrants in particular,

---

1   In many ways late twentieth-century scholars of Polish migration reflected the concerns of the experts who studied migration during the great labor migration of the late nineteenth and early twentieth centuries, including Caro, *Emigracya i polityka emigracyjna ze szczególnym uwzględnieniem stosunków polskich*. The shifting understanding in Poland of fortunes and promise of emigration is nicely summarized in Walaszek, "Wychodźcy, Emigrants or Poles?," 78–84. On the metaphor of "uprooted" immigrant families, see Handlin, *The Uprooted*.

sojourning abroad for months or years only to return to their birth communities, has been underappreciated in much of the scholarship on mobility. In the Polish case, over two million countrymen left partitioned Poland between 1870 and 1914, and some 40 percent of them returned.[2]

By considering this circular pattern of human movement to and from the Polish lands, I would like to challenge paradigms of migration studies that categorize transatlantic relocation as a disruption requiring a generation or more to stabilize. For Poles, I suggest, migration and return were the norm, especially for rural communities in Austrian Galicia and parts of the Russian-controlled Kingdom of Poland, where plot sizes were small, nonagricultural jobs scarce, and overpopulation prevalent. Far from harming the nation-building process, these sojourners remained connected through correspondence and remittances. Their contact with the growing *Polonia* community, which helped them navigate the difficult transition to life in North America, often reinforced their attachment to Polish customs and their sense of belonging to a broader transatlantic national entity. The resulting transformation of national subjectivity paved the way for a multiclass identity that found reflection in the newborn post–World War I Polish state.

Narrating Human Migration

A whole generation of anthropologists and sociologists working in the interwar Polish Second Republic turned to the legacy of prewar labor migrations, conducting extensive research on its long-term impact for Polish society. One of the communities that sent large numbers of residents abroad for work each year and to which a majority eventually returned was the village of Babica, near Rzeszów, in southern Poland. Thanks to the pioneering fieldwork of anthropologist Krystyna Duda-Dziewierz, we have a detailed understanding of the social effects of this migration pattern. Duda-Dziewierz surveyed the changing landholdings and social status of the 53 percent of labor migrants from Babica who ultimately resettled in the village. Among them was Józef Pokrywka, whose story highlights many characteristics of circular migration and its local impact. In the autumn of 1904, Pokrywka, then a thirty-two year-old agricultural laborer, left Babica to seek his fortune in America. He had previously worked as a seasonal laborer in Vienna, Budapest, and the fields of Saxony, but this was his first attempt to find work overseas. For the next seven years, Pokrywka

---

2   US Secretary of Labor, *Eleventh Annual Report*, 133.

would travel to and from the United States three times, spending a few months at home between each voyage. He worked first at an iron foundry in Elizabeth, New Jersey, then in a Pennsylvania coal mine. When the workers there went on strike, Józef secured a spot at a Ford plant in Detroit, where he remained a little over a year before returning home to Babica. Six months later, he was on his way back to America to a coalmining town near Pittsburgh, where several family members from Babica had already settled. From there he made his way again to Detroit and found work in his old Ford plant. After yet another six-month hiatus in Babica, Pokrywka returned to Detroit for his third and last time. In each location, he found accommodations in inexpensive rooming houses shared by extended family or compatriots from his native parish, carefully saving his wages to pay for the return passage while sending regular remittances home to his family.[3] Finally, according to letters and later interviews with Pokrywka, his wife insisted he remain in the village, so he paid off his debts, bought a few acres of land, spruced up his cottage, and settled into a life of farming, fishing, and various odd jobs.[4]

What difference did Józef Pokrywka's experience as a transatlantic migrant have in the construction of a nonterritorial sense of Polishness? In what ways did exposure to northern industrial cities like Detroit, Pittsburgh, New York, and the coal mines of Pennsylvania change him? And how did his return affect Babica itself? According to Duda-Dziewierz, the only concrete manifestations of Pokrywka's time in the States were some "urban" clothes, the stories he told his grandchildren, and a slightly larger landholding. Yet, as this chapter suggests, these trips abroad shaped the very consciousness of Józef Pokrywka and of Poland more broadly during the early years of the twentieth century. Contact abroad, exposure to urban life, familiarity with foreign business and political practices, along with the resourcefulness and ingenuity required to sustain migrants in these complex excursions helped prepare Poles for the challenges of independence, for democratic governance, and for the economic transformations they would face in the twentieth century. Rather than functioning as "disruptions" or sources of "disorganization" as scholars of migration would later maintain, this circular pattern from the Polish village to any number of destinations around the globe was actually integral to Polish community life, connecting migrants to the world beyond their small settlements and helping introduce

---

3   On the structure of émigré Polish communities in the United States and their mutual support systems, see the foundational work of Thomas and Znieniecki, *The Polish Peasant in Europe and America*, 29–33.

4   Duda-Dziewierz, *Wieś Małopolska a emigracja amerykańska*, 90–99.

an understanding of "Polishness" that was not limited to a particular territorial space.[5] My argument challenges the way scholars have approached migration from the Polish lands. It seeks to redefine the movement of people from Poland as a study of the concentric circles of seasonal, chain, and return migration that helped create a sense of transborder Polishness able to adapt to and incorporate shifting patterns of cultural practice. In the end, I argue, Polishness has never been rooted (merely) in physical space but rather is tied to a movable set of experiences and attitudes that are constantly evolving through lived experience. Just as Romantic thinkers proclaimed, the nation need not be bounded by its physical presence or the existence of an independent state. Rather, national values could be reflected in an extraterritorial spirit embodied in works of culture and in its exiled representatives. In short, migration and return have effectively kept *polskość* fresh, helping to affirm a sense of community far beyond the parish pump.

Migration scholars have begun to reconceptualize the relationship between communities of origin and those abroad. No longer treating migration as unidirectional or permanent, researchers on both sides of the Atlantic instead increasingly approach population movement in terms of migration systems that include networks of travelers often transplanting themselves repeatedly for relatively limited periods.[6] In the Polish case, tracing broader patterns of human movement, including concentric circles of mobility, has moved the discussion beyond the nineteenth-century notion of migration as a "loss" of human resources to the nation. Earlier migration specialists generally focused on the semipermanent relocation of people out of the Polish lands, stressing the desperation that drove the exodus and the manipulation of imperial states to impede their departure.[7] More recently, Polish scholars have explored the direct impact of return migration to Polish shores, especially during the period following World War I and the advent of Polish independence but have devoted

---

5   Thomas and Znaniecki's *The Polish Peasant in Europe and America* argued that rural families migrating to the industrialized United States experienced social disorganization, the collapse of moral authority, increased rates of juvenile delinquency, and declining respect for religious institutions.

6   The work of Dirk Hoerder has been especially instrumental in shifting to the "systems" approach to migration studies. See, especially, Hoerder, *Cultures in Contact*.

7   For a comprehensive assessment of migration out of the Polish lands in the modern period, see Pilch, *Emigracja z ziem polskich w czasach nowożytnych i najnowszych*. For a study of the range of elite attitudes about out migration in the pre–World War I period, see Murdzek, *Emigration in Polish social-political thought 1870–1914*.

little attention to the lasting influence of these sojourns abroad. What follows is a reassessment of the role human mobility has played in the evolution of Polishness over the past century and a half, and an appeal to a sense of Polish belonging that transcends the borders of any given state. Once we stop thinking about the nation as a physical place and acknowledge that residents of the Polish lands made some fifty million trips back and forth across the Atlantic in the era of "nation-building," we can begin to appreciate the influence of human mobility on the development of the nation itself. These two developments, population movement and nation building, I argue, are not distinct but rather mutually reinforcing.[8]

The remainder of this chapter looks first at the shifting approaches contemporary actors and scholars alike have taken to assessing the impact of mass labor migration on the development of Polish national consciousness. Attitudes toward movement from the Polish lands have ranged from panic at the loss of laborers to anxiety about the moral decay among migrant communities, but rarely have researchers considered the effect of ongoing contact between "Poles" in Europe and their countrymen abroad on the development of transborder national attitudes. I then look at evidence from ethnographic research conducted within Polish villages and migrant biographies to suggest ways in which travel abroad consistently colored cultural interactions back home. The chapter concludes with a reevaluation of the effects of transatlantic contact on small-town and village *polskość*, proposing a new understanding of national affiliation that extends beyond the physicality of the native community.

As I will show, Józef Pokrywka's story highlights a number of elements common to migration tales of all kinds: Pokrywka left home in the company of fellow villagers and was helped along the way by those who had gone before him. These countrymen would ease his transition to life abroad, helping him find jobs and offering him housing and companionship in the local saloon—creating a sort of cocoon of Polishness that would insulate him from some of the hardships of his new environment. More educated residents of rooming houses would even help temporary migrants pen letters back home. Józef was a lifelong illiterate and does not appear to have learned much English, so these reciprocal relationships from the village were crucial to his success. Typical also was the ever-widening pattern of migration and return characteristic of Polish laborers. Józef himself had left home countless times before he set foot on the steamer for America. Already at the age of twelve he had been put out to work on a

---

8   Dirk Hoerder has made this observation in support of a slightly different point in his "Historians and their Data," 85–86.

neighboring estate. At age twenty-one, he left for service in the Austrian army. Later, he made his way to Budapest where he worked laying bricks and then as a coachman for a horse trolley. Thereafter, he labored in the coal mines of Upper Silesia and then on an estate near Przemyśl digging fishponds. By the time Józef announced his plans to try his luck in America, he had spent more of his young life away from the village than at home. Nonetheless, after each stint abroad, the ties of family, farm, and custom drew him back, helping to sustain the integration of the outside world into small town Polish life.

Transatlantic Labor Migration in Historical Context

To be clear, the decades preceding the outbreak of the Great War when Pokrywka did most of his sojourning were by no means the only historical period when Poles left the homeland in large numbers. Migration scholars identify five major waves of exodus from Poland, beginning with the "Great Migration" of the mid-nineteenth century in response to failed national uprisings, and including those who fled Soviet-occupied Poland after the Second World War (or who refused to return from abroad), those who gave up on resistance to communism after the dream of Solidarity collapsed in 1981, and the cohort of young adults who left the country during the economic downturn following European Union accession in 2004 to work in the United Kingdom and elsewhere. Over the past two centuries, migration has been central to the development of Polish culture. It has conditioned how Poles look at the world and how the world looks at Poland. It is therefore essential that we treat this pattern of moving peoples as an integral part of Polish history and not an exception to it. This is particularly true for the most numerically significant and long-lasting phase of Polish migration history—the great labor migrations that rocked Polish society during the latter part of the nineteenth and early twentieth centuries and that colored the overall history of Poland.[9]

It is no revelation that the Polish lands were a source of enormous out-migration during the period leading up to the Great War. Tens of thousands of landless peasants and impoverished smallholders such as Pokrywka left their native villages each year in this period bound for the factories and farms of Western Europe, South America, Canada, and the United States. Between 1870 and 1914, over two million ethnic Poles left the lands of partitioned Poland at a

---

9   Kołodziej, "Emigracja z ziem polskich od końca XIX"; Walaszek, *Preserving Or Transforming Role?*

rate of roughly 100,000 to 200,000 annually by the end of the century. This overseas migration represented only a fraction of the people involved in short-term migrations both within the Polish territories and to locations elsewhere in Europe. By the last decade before World War I, between 300,000 and 600,000 laborers departed each year for seasonal trips to Western Europe. All told, between 1860 and 1914, these multidirectional European and transatlantic movements involved a total of about ten million people or roughly one-third of the interwar Polish population of twenty-nine million.[10]

This huge exodus did not go unnoticed among contemporary leaders. In America, the crush of new immigrants from Eastern Europe overwhelmed urban neighborhoods, creating slums full of crumbling tenement houses, smelly cesspools, and rowdy saloons. Turn of the century social workers worried about the hygienic conditions of immigrant ghettos. They fretted about juvenile delinquency, the high rates of truancy and the rising incidence of alcoholism.[11] Sociologists, including the founders of the University of Chicago School of Sociology, viewed this transplanting of human lives as a sociological "disruption," an extended crisis that bode ill for assimilating the newcomers into American culture. Chicago School scholars characterized migration as largely unidirectional, devastating for the family and the local community, and with very few positive consequences for Poland. The foundational work of Chicago School sociology was William Thomas and Florian Znaniecki's five-volume study *The Polish Peasant in Europe and America*, published between 1919 and 1921. Researchers of this school portrayed labor migration as portending a rupture in community authority, the decline of religion and morality, the rise of generational tensions, and a growth in criminality and family dysfunction. Although Thomas and Znaniecki's now-classic work addressed the reorganization of American migrant communities in response to waves of social disruption, it failed to consider the impact of circular and return migration (not to mention transatlantic correspondence and remittances) on communities of origin, thus presupposing a comparatively static social context back home. Florian Znaniecki himself, through his work with the Warsaw-based Society for the Care of Emigrants [Towarzystwo Opieki nad Wychodźcami] had previously expressed concern about Polish emigrants maintaining contact with their mother country. As he noted in the journal he edited, *Wychodźca Polski*, it

---

10 Morawska, "Labor Migrations of Poles in the Atlantic World Economy, 1880–1914," 238, 247–49.

11 For one reaction to the hardships suffered among immigrant communities, see Addams, *Twenty Years at Hull-House*.

was "necessary to do everything possible to ensure that the enormous wave of emigration did not lead to de-nationalization and did not become a loss for the country."[12] Yet he, along with others committed to shepherding Polish migrants abroad, focused more on the economic motivations of travelers and the financial well-being of Polish "colonies." Others, such as the young Roman Dmowski and entrepreneur Józef Okołowicz, sought ongoing ties to Polish settlements in Brazil and elsewhere in order to expand Poland's economic interests, but the cultural impact of the migration experience overseas did not fall under their purview.[13]

The framework established in *The Polish Peasant* informed migration scholarship for much of the twentieth century. Znaniecki, one of its authors, returned to Poland after the war and took up a position in Poznań, where he influenced a generation of cultural anthropologists, including Krystyna Duda-Dziewierz, author of the study on Babica. His students completed a series of case studies focused on migration from individual villages, most of which concluded that despite generations of migration and return, the social hierarchies of the Polish village remained largely unchanged. Those on the periphery of rural society continued to be marginal, agricultural practices were still primitive, and economic development was scarcely affected by the wages and experiences of the *Amerykanie*.[14] Instead, labor migrants who returned to Polish soil took up the same occupations they had left behind. Most, like Józef Pokrywka, simply lived out their days in exactly the same position they had occupied prior to their risky and exhausting departure.

This perspective is also reflected in much of the research published by sociologists and historians working today. Sociologist Ewa Morawska, for example, places Polish migrants in the context of transatlantic labor systems, arguing that despite all the millions of dollars in remittances sent home, the country maintained its "double dependency" throughout the partitioned period. The agricultural sector remained "dependent" on an under-industrialized domestic economy, and Poland as a whole continued to lag behind the rest of the Western world. In short, migration for work may have helped peasants sustain their way of life in the short run, but it did little to alleviate Eastern Europe's

---

12   Znaniecki, Redaktor "Wychodźcy Polskiego," 42.
13   On the "colonizing" efforts of the Polskie Towarzystwo Emigracyjne, see Okołowicz, *Wychodźtwo i osadnictwo polskie przed wojną światową*. For Roman Dmowski's attitudes toward Polish settlement overseas, see Koreywo-Rybczyńska, "Roman Dmowski o osadnictwie w Paranie."
14   Zawistowicz-Adamska demonstrates the static nature of the rural economy in the face of migration and return in her *Społeczność wiejska*.

historic economic "backwardness" vis a vis the developed West.[15] Peasant farmers poured money into village institutions such as the church, but their experience working in foreign factories did not lead to increased mechanization of agriculture or the growth of industry in the region. And yet, as Linda Reeder has argued for the Sicilian case, those left behind in communities dependent on migrants often experienced dramatic shifts in social status, patterns of consumption, and even political sensibilities.[16] Scholarship addressing migration outside of Poland thus suggests that individual attitudes and relationships to the wider world were transformed in important ways through the regular coming and going of villagers.

Back in Europe, contemporary governments and local officials were also concerned about the disruptive effects of the late nineteenth-century exodus. They worried about the demoralizing effects of migration, which was heavily weighted in favor of young male laborers from the countryside, many of whom left wives and families at home. Authorities feared depopulated villages, the loss of military conscripts, and a drop in fertility rates. For Polish nationalists, the migration of young workers represented a potential demographic rupture for the future Polish state. Leopold Caro, a Polish Galician lawyer and staunch opponent of emigration, helped popularize the view that migration contributed to a decline in overall morality as families resettled in communities lacking adequate leadership from organized religion. More concretely, Caro claimed that local economies were adversely affected by the depletion of manpower from native soil. Across the Galician countryside, Caro depicted "crops left in the field, potatoes rotting because of lack of working hands, a shortage of farmworkers and girls left to pasture cattle [all of which] leads to general misery." No matter how high the wages émigrés garnered abroad, Caro concluded, they could not possibly make up for "the loss that the national economy must bear through the absence of its most vigorous workers."[17] At the same time, the governments controlling Polish territory sought to stem the tide of migration by highlighting the unscrupulous practices employed by travel agents who assisted migrants in crossing international borders and gaining passage on transatlantic steamers. A series of high-profile legal cases, such as the Wadowice trial of 1889–1890, helped focus public attention on the ostensibly slavelike conditions laborers experienced in North America. Lawmakers referred to migration agents, many

---

15   Morawska, "Labor Migrations of Poles in the Atlantic World Economy."
16   Reeder, *Widows in White*. See also Brettell, *The Men who Migrate and the Women Who Wait* and Fitzgerald, *A Nation of Emigrants*.
17   Caro, *Emigracya i polityka emigracyjna*, 7, 67.

of whom were Jewish, as "hyenas" and described how they swindled migrants out of all of their money before sending them back home to the village as medically unqualified.[18] The persistence of such stories helped convince many upper-class members of Polish society that all forms of migration were potentially harmful.

Migrant Tales and the Development of Transatlantic Networks

The correspondence and memoirs of migrating peasants themselves reveal consistently positive portrayals of the relocation experience, a perspective that sets them apart from much of the contemporary newspaper coverage of those who left home. Marcin Kula's collection of several hundred letters written between Poles in Latin America and the United States to their compatriots in Russian Poland demonstrates a steady flow of advice about the care of crops, childrearing matters, the sale of livestock, and any number of other day-to-day concerns. The letters include detailed information about the journey abroad, the types of materials and documents loved ones would need if they followed, and expressions of respect for parents and village elders. In a sense, these letters reflect a continuation of day-to-day life in the village. They are considerably less preoccupied with the risks and dangers of migration and the failures of those who left the village than later scholarship suggests.[19]

Nonetheless, on both sides of the Atlantic, the contemporary press often stressed migration stories ending in failure. Those who returned after fulfilling their expected goals are represented as a minority, and instead the dominant motif became migrants who opted to leave because the American dream had eluded them. Under the pressure of imperial censorship, such reports depicted re-migrants as having wasted all their savings on a futile voyage and been "turned into beggars on the street." Polish-language newspapers in the early twentieth century were replete with stories of such failed migration odysseys. One group of Galician peasants reportedly was unable to find either jobs or land, and then was forced to beg and appeal to local authorities for return

---

18   Zahra, "Travel Agents on Trial," 161–93; Kowalski, *Przestępstwa emigracyjne w Galicji, 1897–1918*.

19   Kula and Assorodobraj-Kula, *Listy emigrantów z Brazylii i Stanów Zjednoczonych, 1890–1891*.

tickets.[20] Others complained of low wages and a shortage of jobs especially during the winter months.[21] A particularly tragic story was that of the emigrant who left his settlement of Wrześniak, outside of Warsaw, living for several years in poverty in America, only to return home to discover his wife and children had died in his absence.[22] A family from Mazuria lost most of their money along the road to America and was forced to sell their personal belongings to purchase return tickets.[23]

Even during the mass exodus back to the homeland in the early days of independent Poland, American newspapers often pronounced the decision to return as the result of "hard times" in America rather than personal sentiment or economic success.[24] In one particularly egregious case, a Polish father in Cleveland reportedly attempted to sell his twin children to earn the money to transport the rest of his family back to Poland.[25] American papers described ships leaving New York harbor filled with hundreds of forlorn return migrants. Such devastated returnees reportedly found themselves at Polish train stations without money, dependent on the kindness of neighbors or the goodwill of the local government.[26] Re-migrants faced persistent disappointment after returning to independent Poland, from rampant inflation that nullified their American savings to land swindles, haughty bureaucrats, unwelcoming neighbors, and the "backwardness" of rural society.[27] This paradigm of migration as an act of desperate people willing to risk social disruption to repair their economic fortunes and who returned "home" to Poland only after failing at their efforts abroad has maintained its traction in scholarly research. Rarely has circular migration received the attention of Polish scholars and still more infrequently are the lasting influences of the migration experience addressed. Instead, the narrative of uprootedness and the negative consequences of dislocation from family and

---

20 "Korespondencja Kuryera Poznańskiego," 1.
21 "Kroniki miejscowa, Prowincjonalna i zagraniczna," 5.
22 "Ofiary emigracji," 3.
23 "Polacy wracają zza oceanu bez dobytku i pieniędzy," 2.
24 "More Poles to Go Home," 11.
25 "Father Offers Twins for Sale," 9.
26 "Wiadomości miejscowe i potoczne," 3; "Wiadomości miejscowe i potoczne," 6; "Z różnych stron," 2; "Z różnych stron. Dola emigrantów," 3.
27 Walaszek, *Reemigracja ze Stanów Zjednoczonych do Polski po I wojnie Światowej (1919–1924)*; Niemyska, *Wychodźcy po powrocie do kraju*; *Wspólny Powrót*.

tradition continued to dominate research on population movement from the Polish lands.[28]

Migration and Return Migration: A Reevaluation

How then do we reposition migration to take better account of its long-term influence on Polish society? How can we best incorporate the experiences of Józef Pokrywka and others for whom travel abroad was almost a routine event? To begin with, we must recognize that relocation—especially temporary relocation—was hardwired into life for most villagers. Memoirs and local histories report that "one of the most characteristic traits of life among the village population is emigration for work."[29] Thousands of migrants left Polish territory each year, especially during the great labor migrations of 1880–1920, and a good portion of them returned. Second, we need to look past narrow questions of economic restructuring and consider the cultural impact of thousands of letters, remittances, and human beings coming and going across international boundaries. Migration to the States alone had touched almost every rural family by the end of the nineteenth century. Contemporary studies show that in the Galician countryside nearly one in three adult males had worked in the States for at least a year. A 1903 report revealed that over three thousand people from the Nowy Targ district alone were "across the ocean." "Literally hundreds of villages send over one hundred people at a time to America," the report concluded.[30]

This pattern of routine travel for work began even before the peasants were emancipated from serfdom. The pressure of growing families, severe land shortages and a limited growing season in the 1840s sent Polish highlanders across the border into Hungary and Slovakia to work harvest "down below." The delayed growing season in the mountains meant they could work on the flatlands and return home to collect their own meager crop. After emancipation in 1848, villagers left home to work as tinkers or petty salesmen. Each spring "whole villages set off on rafts" down the Dunajec River to sell products farther north. Others smuggled goods across the border with Russia or took part in building

---

28 The dominance of this narrative stems partly from the early influence of Thomas and Znaniecki's foundational study of Polish migration, *The Polish Peasant in Europe and America*, and partly from the mid-century dominance of the "uprooted" paradigm introduced by Oscar Handlin in his 1951 monograph.
29 Bujak, *Wybór pism*, 301–4.
30 Bujak, *Wybór pism*, 303.

projects sponsored by the Austrian government, including the construction of new roads and railways. Farther afield, villagers headed to mines and brickworks in Romania and Hungary. The village of Żmiąca in Western Galicia, for example, sent eight villagers to Hungary to work in the Koszyc brickyards in 1902. That same year, seven made their way to coal mines in America and four to Ostrawa, also to work in coal mines; two had been hired to build sewers in Vienna, and five more were performing agricultural labor in Prussia.[31] Thousands of Polish workers traveled to Germany (*na saksony*) each year to work the harvest, only to be sent home in the fall with their annual earnings. German imperial regulations acknowledged the need for agricultural labor on Junker estates but limited the influx to single migrants under the age of twenty-six in order to discourage Poles from settling permanently on German territory. Each November, work permits expired, and laborers were forced back home to Galicia or Russian Poland.[32]

What is important about these migration streams is the continuous connections most migrants maintained with their home villages. The vast majority of laborers who went abroad intended to return to Poland and many of them did. We know that in the period between 1908 (when the United States first started keeping records) and 1923, around 40 percent of all migrants to America came back to Poland for good.[33] In Babica, Pokrywka's native village, 53 percent of labor migrants returned home before World War I, many of them having crossed the Atlantic several times before making their final trip home.[34] During the interwar period after the reemergence of the independent Polish state, the numbers were still higher. In 1919, for example, the newly formed Polish Consul General in New York was besieged by applicants for Polish passports, receiving over one thousand new applications per day and predicting that over the next year and a half some two hundred thousand Polish Americans would leave the country.[35] This pace of return migration kept up for the bulk of the interwar period. All told, during the period from 1918 to 1938, some two million Polish citizens migrated to the United States, and over one million of them eventually returned to Poland.

---

31 Bujak, *Żmiąca*, 99–100.
32 Lucassen, *The Immigrant Threat*, 50–73; Murdzek, *Emigration in Polish Socio-Political Thought*, 3–32.
33 According to US Secretary of Labor, *Eleventh Annual Report*, a total of 788,957 Poles migrated to the US in this period, while 318, 210 returned to Europe (see p. 133).
34 Morawska, "Labor Migrations of Poles in the Atlantic World," 263–64.
35 "North Europe Now Sends Most of Immigrants," 11.

Even those who remained abroad leveraged considerable influence on their compatriots back in Europe. Polish settlers sent hundreds of dollars home each year, supporting the construction of new churches and homes and the acquisition of new landholdings. They formed migrant associations to help others navigate the path abroad. And they communicated their experiences (and their advice) to their families through steady correspondence. But those who physically returned to their birthplaces brought back more concrete influences. Some established small shops or taverns, elevating themselves into the stratum of local merchants. Returnees encouraged literacy and a respect for education, helping stimulate support for the new Polish government's policy of universal mandatory schooling. The "Amerykanie" were known for their love of newspapers, and their subscriptions brought the outside world into the village as never before. Some of the experiences and sentiments the returnees introduced into the village represented a challenge to existing social hierarchies. In particular, communal authority, patriarchy, and ecclesiastical power came under their critical eye. An account of how such challenges played out within a single village suggests some of the ways influences from outside Poland helped mold attitudes in the countryside.

The Democratizing Influence of Return

During the early twentieth century, peasants from the village of Skrzypne, in the Rzeszów district, began a steady migration to Chicago. By the eve of the Great War, there was hardly a household in the village that lacked a member working "over the water." Like other immigrant populations, Skrzypne natives soon established a foundation to stay connected with their parish back in Poland. Before too long, however, the activities of the association upset the balance of power within the village, challenging long-standing structures of patronage. Prior to World War I, the emigrants' sense of honor had been enhanced by the ability to donate significant sums to rebuilding the parish church and by receiving letters of gratitude from the local priest. Yet because correspondence was difficult between migrant communities and Central Europe during the war, many emigrants refocused their energies on their parish in America, to which they donated a significant portion of their earnings.[36]

---

36   Józef Chałasiński argues that the culture of money and the emigrant's commitment to building his parish in emigration were important parts of the assimilation process. Chałasiński, "Parafia i szkoła parafialna wśród emigracji polskiej we Ameryce."

Once the war ended, the dual identity of the worker migrant in Chicago and his peasant Galician self collided.

In 1926, the pastor of the parish church in Skrzypne turned to the Chicago Association for help in rebuilding two bells damaged during the war. Parishioners in Chicago formed a committee and encouraged their fellow émigrés to support the purchase of the bells. Over 150 members made contributions. They were driven by patriotism and a commitment to their families back home but also by their sense of honor and a desire for the respect of their countrymen. Importantly, they were promised that the names of every donor would be inscribed on the bells and would appear on a stone tablet inside the church. What's more, they were told they would be remembered during a mass. Very soon, however, the question of who should be lauded for charitable patronage arose among the émigrés themselves. Soon after the $1,200 in funds were forwarded through the Chicago Consulate to the village pastor, two separate members of the Chicago association wrote the priest, one requesting that *only* the names of the "leaders" of the committee be inscribed onto the bell and the plaque, the other insisting that *all names* be listed, thus demonstrating the "new concept of democratic patronage."[37]

The tension between a new democratic spirit and an older form of patronage based on social status in the community was not limited to the parishioners in emigration. Instead, the "spirit of democracy" was also making inroads back home. The peasants living in Skrzypne itself soon complained that although the *people* of the village and their families across the ocean had raised the money to repair the church and to buy the bells, the parish *priest* continued to make decisions on his own. Even after the funds for the bells were in place, the priest asked for more money to *ring* the bells on the occasion of the death of the mother of one of the committee members. As one local landless peasant (who had not been abroad) commented, today "a poor woman died here. [The priest] stood before the bell and did not allow it to be rung ... but that bell is not his ... it is our relatives in America who bought it."[38]

In this case and in many others, hierarchies of authority were disrupted through interactions with emigrants across the water. At the most obvious level, these shifts involved direct challenges to power structures in the village. Not only was the position of local clergy made more vulnerable, but the authority of gentry landholders was slipping as economic need forced them to sell off parcels to local peasants, many of whom wielded greater buying power after returning

---

37 Makarewicz, "Emigracja amerykańska a macierzysta grupa parafialna," 523–34.
38 Makarewicz, "Emigracja amerykańska a macierzysta grupa parafialna," 530.

from North America. Then, too, the *"Amerykanie"* claimed greater knowledge of the inner workings of democracy than their Polish cousins, a contrast that presented its own awkwardness when re-migrants insisted on returning to the States in time to vote in the 1920 presidential election.[39] Across the Polish countryside returnees and their correspondence prompted transitions in local attitudes. One long-time migrant from Babica routinely sent Polish-language books and newspapers back home during the twenty-nine years he spent working in the coal mines of Pennsylvania, even though he was never able to return to Babica himself. By the time he died in 1936, the migrant's nephew, who had never been abroad, had amassed a collection of seventy-two books including works on Polish history and culture, religious conflicts, and governance in both the United States and Poland. A clear anticlerical thread is reflected in the collection, which was accessed by villagers in all the surrounding communities. One particularly popular edition entitled *Księży Chleb* [The priest's bread] discussed various forms of corruption among the clergy. Some of the readers of the collection were reported to be active in the growing peasant political movement in Poland and often relied on American examples as a model for Polish political practices. As a researcher in the 1930s concluded, "Contact with America is still the most important source of authority in the village. Locals refer to American democracy as the most effective method of rule. They praise American newspapers and claim that if you want to learn the truth of what is going on in the world, including what is happening in Poland, it is necessary to read the American press."[40]

Admittedly, not all members of the village community welcomed input from beyond their borders. Religious authorities often feared the influence of the returnees, many of whom attended church only erratically and subscribed to newspapers perceived as anticlerical. And it is true that the volume discussing clerical indiscretions eventually fell victim to an overzealous neighbor who was so upset by its contents that he set the book on fire. Moreover, as Adam Walaszek has argued, some villagers were initially "repulsed by the return migrants . . . because of their different lifestyle, the innovations they were trying to introduce, and the aloofness with which they treated the local environment." Returnees were ridiculed for their Western dress and criticized for spending time in local bars while avoiding church services. But how far-reaching did this resentment go and what can we learn from its parameters? Even after the clergy banned the reading of American papers, returnees reported that their village

---

39   "Mayor of Sheeley Going to Poland," 13.
40   Duda-Dziewierz, *Wieś Małopolska a emigracja amerykańska*, 118–29.

neighbors continued to listen eagerly as they were read aloud. Moreover, returning males were wildly popular with village girls, partially for their perceived wealth but perhaps also because they appeared less ravaged by wartime deprivations than other eligible bachelors. Certainly economic improvements could shift the returnee's socioeconomic position in the village hierarchy, challenging the status quo in important ways.

To be clear, these shifts in the socioeconomic position of *individuals* within the village did not typically portend an *overall* transformation of rural conditions or the rural economy. As earlier researchers have demonstrated, American money did *not*, in fact, usher in the economic modernization of the Polish countryside. Plots remained small, agricultural processes under-mechanized, and little rural industry developed as a result of the adventures of Poles who crossed the Atlantic. But arguably the limited economic benefit gained through two centuries of nearly constant migration does not tell the whole story. What we learn when we look at wider patterns of transnational travel is that beyond connecting isolated, unchanging villages with the churn of big city life across the ocean, migration also created a constant two-way flow of cultural interaction that shaped and transformed Polish society. Travel abroad and return helped encourage critical thought on political developments, religious practice, and social policies. It helped stir up the village to participate in wider discussions of matters pertaining to the nation as a whole. It may even have helped reinforce the peasantry's attachment to the idea of Poland itself.

Moreover, it is no small thing that migration mattered in the lives of the individuals who participated in it, giving them a broader perspective on world affairs and allowing them to become authorities within their communities. This is why they continued to do it. But they also left the village for adventures in the wider world because such activities were considered natural and normal—an almost routine part of rural life—and not as a disruption or the source of social disorganization as many sociologists have suggested. The habit of leaving the village for a time and returning is one of the many factors that brought change—however incremental—to the Polish countryside. These experiences included not only travel to the States and back, but all the other forms of short and long-term, local, and regional migration that figure into the Polish past. Once we take account of the kinds of influences migration and return have introduced to the Polish countryside, we can begin to appreciate the impact human mobility has had in wider processes of modernization and integration across the Polish landscape. While the pace of change and cross-border assimilation necessarily accelerated after the founding of the Second Republic in 1918, the genesis of these transformations lay in a century or more of prior population movements.

In the end, these scenarios remind us that Poland is in many ways a nation of migrants. Though scholarly literature on Polishness often emphasizes the centrality of local and regional attachments, the value of inherited farmland, or the continuity of particular cultural practices, it is also important to recognize that mobility—both forced and voluntary—has played its role. Migration has spread and often solidified many of the "regional" habits foundational to Polish identity, effectively preserving through them a *Polskość* that transcends the borders of the country. In the past century alone, Poles have been repatriated from Austria, Czechoslovakia, Italy, Siberia, the *kresy*, Iran, France, and most recently from the United Kingdom, in addition to the massive waves of return migrants who headed back from North America. Alongside these resettlers, Polish citizens have moved from country to city and sometimes back again. Polishness has been transplanted and redefined with each of these movements, a pattern that may have helped make it both more adaptable and more durable. Even as individual travelers made decisions independently about their own economic fortunes, each transported local, regional, and national cultural traits that found reinforcement in Polish communities constructed abroad. The process of migration and return has both cemented certain essential components of Polishness (famously preserving conservative elements in many Polonia settlements) and also served to link remote villages across the Polish landscape in a nearly constant exchange with the wider world. This web of interconnectedness represents a key element of modern Polish national belonging and one that is worthy of continued research.

Bibliography

Addams, Jane. *Twenty Years at Hull-House*. Champaign: University of Illinois Press, 1990.
Brettell, Caroline. *The Men who Migrate and the Women Who Wait: Population and History in a Portuguese Parish*. Princeton, NJ: Princeton University Press, 1986.
Bujak, Franciszek. *Wybór pism*. Vol. II: *Z dziejów społecznych i gospodarczych Polski X-XX w.*, edited by Helena Madurowicz-Urbańska. Warsaw: Wydawnictwo PWN, 1976.
Bujak, Franciszek. *Żmiąca: Wieś powiatu Limanowskiego. Stosunki gospodarcze i społeczne*. Cracow: Gebethner i Spółka, 1903.
Caro, Leopold. *Emigracya i polityka emigracyjna ze szczególnym uwzględnieniem stosunków polskich*. Trans. Karol Englisch. Poznań: Drukarnia św. Wojciecha, 1914.
Chałasiński, Józef. "Parafia i szkoła parafialna wśród emigracji polskiej we Ameryce." *Przegląd Socjologiczny* 3, no. 3–4 (1935).

Dulczewski, Zygmunt, ed. *Florian Znaniecki, Redaktor "Wychodźcy Polskiego*. Warsaw: Ludowa Spółdzielnia Wydawnicza, 1982.
Duda-Dziewierz, Krystyna. *Wieś Małopolska a emigracja amerykańska: studium wsi Babica powiatu rzeszowskiego*. Warsaw, Poznań: Polski Instytut Socjologiczny, 1938.
"Father Offers Twins for Sale," *Bradford Era (PA)*, October 22, 1924.
Fitzgerald, David. *A Nation of Emigrants: How Mexico Manages its Migration*. Berkeley: University of California Press, 2008.
Handlin, Oscar. *The Uprooted, the Epic Story of the Great Migrations that Made the American People*. Boston: Little, Brown and Co., 1951.
Hoerder, Dirk. *Cultures in Contact: World Migrations in the Second Millennium*. Durham, NC: Duke University Press, 2002.
Hoerder, Dirk. "Historians and their Data: The Complex Shift from Nation-State Approaches to the Study of People's Transcultural Lives," *Journal of American Ethnic History* 25, no. 4 (2006).
Kołodziej, Edward. "Emigracja z ziem polskich od końca XIX wieku do czasów współczesnych i tworzenie się skupisk polonijnych". In *Emigracja z ziem polskich w XX wieku. Drogi awansu emigrantów*, ed. Adam Koseski. Pułtusk, Poland: Wyższa Szkoła Humanistyczna, 1998.
"Korespondencja Kuryera Poznańskiego," *Kurier Poznański*, November 22, 1872.
Koreywo-Rybczyńska, Maria T. "Roman Dmowski o osadnictwie w Paranie," *Przegląd Polonijny* 10, no. 1 (1984).
Kowalski, Grzegorz Maria. *Przestępstwa emigracyjne w Galicji, 1897–1918: z badań nad dziejami polskiego wychodźstwa*. Kraków: Wydawnictwo Uniwersytetu Jagiellońskiego, 2003.
"Kroniki miejscowa, Prowincjonalna i zagraniczna," *Kurier Poznański*, May 26, 1881.
Kula, Witold, Assorodobraj-Kula, Nina, eds. *Listy emigrantów z Brazylii i Stanów Zjednoczonych, 1890–1891*. Warsaw: Ludowa Spółdzielnia Wydawnicza, 1973.
Lucassen, Leo. *The Immigrant Threat*. Urbana: University of Illinois Press, 2005.
Makarewicz, Tadeusz. "Emigracja amerykańska a macierzysta grupa parafialna." *Przegląd Socjologiczny* 4, no. 2 (1936): 523–34.
"Mayor of Sheeley Going to Poland." *Evening World-Herald* (July 14, 1920), 13.
Morawska, Ewa. "Labor Migrations of Poles in the Atlantic World Economy, 1880-1914," *Comparative Studies in Society and History*, 31, no. 2 (April 1989).
"More Poles to Go Home." *The Springfield Daily Republican* (April 27, 1921), 11.
Murdzek, Benjamin P. *Emigration in Polish social-political thought 1870-1914*. Boulder, CO: East European Monographs, 1977.
Niemyska, Marja. *Wychodźcy po powrocie do kraju. Remigranci w województwie białostockiem w świetle ankiety 1934 roku*. Warsaw: Instytut Gospodarstwa Społecznego, 1936.
"North Europe Now Sends Most of Immigrants." *Chicago Daily Tribune*, May 28, 1920.
Okołowicz, Józef. *Wychodźtwo i osadnictwo polskie przed wojną światową*. Warsaw: Gebethner i Wolff, 1920.

CHAPTER SIX

"Ofiary emigracji," *Dziennik Poznański*, April 29, 1886.
"Polacy wracają zza oceanu bez dobytku i pieniędzy." *Dziennik Poznański*, April 13, 1873.
Pilch, Andrzej, ed. *Emigracja z ziem polskich w czasach nowożytnych i najnowszych (XVIII-XX w.)*. Warsaw: Państwowe Wydawnictwo Naukowe, 1984.
Reeder, Linda. *Widows in White: Migration and the Transformation of Rural Italian Women: Sicily, 1880–1920*. Toronto: University of Toronto Press, 2003.
Thomas, William, Znaniecki, Florian. *The Polish Peasant in Europe and America: Monograph of an Immigrant Group*. 5 vols. Boston: Gorham Press, 1918–1920.
US Secretary of Labor. *Eleventh Annual Report*. Washington, DC, 1923.
Walaszek, Adam. *Preserving Or Transforming Role? Migrants and Polish Territories in the Era of Mass Migrations*. Warsaw: German Historical Institute, 1995.
Walaszek, Adam. *Reemigracja ze Stanów Zjednoczonych do Polski po I wojnie światowej (1919-1924)*. Cracow: Uniwersytet Jagielloński, 1983.
Walaszek, Adam. "Wychodźcy, Emigrants or Poles? Fears and Hopes about Migration in Poland 1870–1939," *Association of European Migration Institutions Journal* 1 (2002): 78–84.
"Wiadomości miejscowe i potoczne." *Dziennik Poznański*, December 8, 1882.
"Wiadomości miejscowe i potoczne." *Dzienik Poznański*, January 10, 1908.
Wspólny Powrót. Chicago: Towarzystwo Skup, n.d.
"Z różnych stron." *Dziennik Poznański*, August 23, 1904.
"Z różnych stron. Dola emigrantów." *Dziennik Poznański*, August 11, 1912.
Zahra, Tara "Travel Agents on Trial: Policing Mobility in East-Central Europe, 1889–1989." *Past and Present* 223, no. 1 (2014): 161–93.
Zawistowicz-Adamska, Kazimiera. *Społeczność wiejska: wspomnienia i Materiały z badań terenowych Zaborów, 1937–38*. Warsaw: Ludowa Spółdzielnia wydawnicza, 1958.

Chapter Seven

"Good Americans" and Polish Modern Identity Construction after World War I

Krystyna Lipińska Illakowicz

> Something new and unknown engulfed me. A powerful deep breath, huge territories, big money resources, colossal technology—to make it short—Americanism.[1]
>
> —*Kurier Poranny* 1928

Polish daily newspapers from the 1920s and the 1930s were inundated with information about the United States.[2] On a daily basis they published articles, short and longer notes, stories, and pictures presenting all areas of American life to the Polish public: politics, economy, education, culture, and sports. It seems that a "slice" of American daily life was a necessary component of a Polish breakfast and that a modern Polish engineer, accountant, or office worker could not go to work without knowing what was happening in his or her "neighbor's"

---

1   In Polish: Wionęło na mnie czymś nowem, nieznanem. Jakaś potęga szerokiego tchnienia, wielkich obszarów, dużych środków pieniężnych, kolosalnej techniki—jednym słowem: amerykanizm. All translations from Polish in this text are the author's.
2   In the title, I am paraphrasing a variety of qualifiers that Polish newspapers ascribed to Americans. They referred to them as brave, optimistic, generous, loving, as in this quote: "Nobody can work the way they do. Optimism, belief in life—this is the American religion." *Kurier Poranny* 4.

home on the other side of the Atlantic. Reading all these papers we often have an impression that New York or Chicago was just next door to Warsaw or Poznań.

Why was that so? Why was the information about America so vital for the generation of Poles after World War I? Why did the United States come to be such a frequent point of reference and to some extent a cultural qualifier in the Polish popular press? What was the reason for the fascination with that country? In the present volume the question of Polish identity is investigated from a variety of historical and cultural perspectives highlighting specific models subtending Polish identity formation such as Christianity/religion, gentry-oriented values, peasant culture, colonialism in the form of partitions (i.e., the lack of sovereignty for 123 years), cultural belatedness, geographical position and east-or-west orientation, and many others. The present chapter highlights one important perspective that shows how constructing the modern image of Poland resulted from the ways the Poles viewed the United States and how that country became the often-overlooked point of reference for the construction of modern Polish identity. This chapter points to how the United States functioned not only as a traditional democratic ideal but also how almost every aspect of life including sports, home life, architecture, education, and jazz became in Polish eyes a denomination of modernity modeled on the American example.

Referring to the newspaper coverage of everyday American life, this chapter shows how the media narrowed the divide between Poland and the United States and more or less presented the Poles as America's close neighbors and friends, brothers and sisters, and members of the same family. My examples and observations come from popular daily newspapers such as *Kurier Poranny* (Morning courier), *Kurier Warszawski* (Warsaw courier), *Gazeta Polska* (Polish gazette), *Tygodnik Ilustrowany* (Illustrated weekly), weekly literary journals *Wiadomości Literacke* (Literary news) or *Pion* (Plumb), women-specific publications, such as *Kobieta Współczesna* (Modern woman) and *Świat Kobiecy* (Women's world), or specialized publications such as *Życie Teatru* (Theatre life), *Scena Polska* (Polish stage), and *Teatr i Kino* (Theater and cinema). I also discuss the business journal *Ameryka*, founded in 1923 by the American-Polish Chamber of Commerce, which played a prominent role in disseminating information about the United States in the early 1920s and was foundational for constructing America's image in Poland. All these publications attracted a broad spectrum of readers. Thus, they all contributed to creating as well as reflecting the general perceptions and interests of Polish popular readership in the interwar period.

A Bit of History

In the 1920s and 1930s, Polish authorities energetically set to work in order to rebuild the foundations of the state, including its political institutions, socioeconomic infrastructure, culture, education, and all other systems governing social and political life. The new political and historical context not only influenced the way Poles came to shape their own identity, but as members of a newly sovereign country they also shaped the images of other countries with which they began to establish regular and normalized political, cultural, and economic relations. At the same time, it is important to remember that the United States also entered a new phase and, in spite of its traditional isolationist policy, was on its way to becoming a world power: the image of America was disseminated all over the world, mainly through print media and cinema. In a way, both countries, Poland and the United States, connected on a similar identity-related ground: after nearly 123 years of colonial oppression Poland reconstructed its identity along with the challenges of modernity (often taking the United States as its model) and America forcefully consolidated its image as a world power.

Poland aspired to develop strong political, economic, and cultural ties with the United States, partly due to the perception of the country as a former war ally. The articles about the United States that appeared in the most popular Polish daily papers offered a variety of perspectives: as a rule they covered daily political and business contacts but also harked back to the traditional Polish American historical narratives from the American Revolutionary War (often relating to famous personalities such as Tadeusz Kosciuszko and Kazimierz Pulaski) and presented various slices of American reality reaching a broad readership and therefore playing a major role as opinion-forming channels of communication.

Articles, advertisements, editorials, film, and theater programs point to a vivid American presence on the Polish cultural scene by the early 1920s. How did it happen that at the beginning of the 1920s American culture was so pervasive in Polish everyday life? The influence of Ignacy Jan Paderewski, the first prime minister (*premier*) of independent Poland, a famous, charismatic pianist whose personal connection to the American establishment was incomparable, immediately comes to mind. Paderewski was premier of Poland from January 16 to December 10, 1919, and in large part due to his acceptance of that position, America recognized the Polish government (on January 30) before France,

Great Britain, and Italy.[3] Thanks to Paderewski's artistic mien, charisma, and personal charm he was on friendly terms with the most influential people of his era including presidents, ministers, and artists. Apart from being a celebrity pianist and composer, he was also known and revered as a great philanthropist supporting all sorts of actions all over the world. It is also important to note that Paderewski was extremely active in the circles of American *Polonia*[4] as an artist and politician when he advocated in 1915–1918 for the Polish cause. He was able to connect with elites as well as with regular people. Many initiatives of the Polish authorities in the interwar period—including the celebrations of the anniversary of American Independence in 1926, the *Emblem of Good Will Project* (1926), or funding and unveiling Woodrow Wilson's monument in Poznań in 1931—would not have been possible without Paderewski's generous help and financial support.[5]

Another important venue that promoted Polish American contacts was the Polish American Society (*Towarzystwo Polsko-Amerykańskie*) and the American-Polish Chamber of Commerce and Industry (*Amerykańsko-Polska Izba Handlowo-Przemysłowa*). In fact, Paderewski was also behind these organizations. In 1919, the Polish American Society was founded and in turn set up the American-Polish Chamber of Commerce and Industry in 1921.[6] In 1923 the Chamber began publishing a monthly magazine, *Ameryka* (after 1925 known as *Ameryka-Polska*) a major vehicle to disseminate information about America and to promote American culture in Poland.

The activity of Paderewski, as important as it was, was only part of the long tradition that Polish American contacts and their representations shared in both countries. In Poland, most influential in this regard was Henryk Sienkiewicz's *Listy z podróży do Ameryki* (translated as *Portrait of America: Letters of Henry Sienkiewicz*) written in 1876–1878 and modeled on Alexis de Tocqueville's *De*

---

3 See Zamoyski, *Paderewski*. See also Wandycz, *The United States and Poland*, 128–129, and Paderewska, *Memoirs, 1910—1920*.
4 Polish immigrants living in the United States and in other places outside of Poland are referred to as *Polonia*. The United States has the largest Polonia, which amounts to about 9.5 million people.
5 I discuss all these events in more detail in the book I am working on about the American image in Poland in the 1920s and 1930s.
6 The American-Polish Chamber of Commerce and Industry was registered by the Minister of the Interior by W. Z. Kuczyński on June 11, 1921. A brother organization, The American-Polish Chamber of Commerce and Industry in the USA, was earlier funded in New York in 1920. Both chambers were energetically expanding American Polish trade relations.

la démocratie en Amérique (*Democracy in America*), and his American short stories.[7] The Polish imagination was also fed by popular literature for young people such as James Fenimore Cooper's *Last of the Mohicans* or Harriet Beecher Stowe's *Uncle Tom's Cabin*.

By the end of the 1930s, the image of America was already deeply rooted in the Polish imaginary and evident, for instance, in Witold Gombrowicz's famous novel *Ferdydurke* (1937). On the surface it shows no traces or connections to American culture, yet deeper reading discloses how early twentieth-century images from the popular press and other media penetrated the texture of Gombrowicz's prose, subtending the main *topos* of his work in which the ideas of immaturity and modernity inseparably intertwine. Zuta, a modern schoolgirl (*nowoczesna pensjonarka*) and Kopyrda—a modern boy (*nowoczesny chłopak*) are the two main protagonists. They play sports, are open and straightforward, wear tennis shoes (today they would be called "sneakers") and shorts, and they exhibit no provincial phobias. We can easily imagine Zuta in a short skirt and tennis shoes as an American student athlete—the photographs of such beautiful, slim girls breaking records in sports, driving cars, or flying planes, like Amelia Earhart, and displaying curiosities from American life were beloved by the Polish daily press. Kopyrda—the male counterpart of Zuta—is drafted in Gombrowicz's text with a similar dose of Americanness. This type of modern tone characterizes the homelife of Zuta's parents, Mr. and Mrs. Youngblood (*Młodziakowie*). When the novel's main protagonist, Joey (*Józio*), is introduced by his professor (*Profesor Pimko*) to the Youngbloods, he immediately equates their lifestyle with America: "No respect, no reverence for the past, just dancing, canoeing, America, impulse of the moment, *carpe diem*, oh, you young ones" (108). And he rebukes the new Americanized generation that prefers an active everyday life to tedious work and the ethos of patriotism. This is how Joey recalls Pimko's grumbling:

> "Legs," he egged me on to modernity, "legs, I know you, I know your athletics, I know the ways of the new Americanized generation, you prefer legs to hands, legs are the most important thing to you, the calves of your legs." (110)

---

7   The so-called American stories are: *Komedia z pomyłek/ A Comedy of Errors/* (1878), *Przez stepy / /Across the Plains/* (1879), *Orso* (1879), *W krainie złota / In Gold Country* (1880), *Za chlebem / In Search of Bread/* (1880), *Latarnik /The Lighthouse Keeper/* (1881), *Wspomnienia z Mariposy / A Memory from Mariposa/* (1882), *Sachem* (1883).

Modern cultural behavior modes return in Gombrowicz's text as references to American film culture—Fred Astaire and Ginger Rogers photographs pinned to the walls in Zuta's room. In *Ferdydurke* (published in 1937 and written in the mid-1930s) as well as in his next popular novel *Opętani (Possessed)* (1939), we see the modern identity paradigm as a proposition and possibility not yet fully accepted and embedded in the texture of the modern Polish mind. By resorting to the images of young people modelled on sports or film, Gombrowicz was able to stir the reader's imagination, thus indicating that the construction of modern Polish identity was still in process. Newspapers from the 1920s and early 1930s allow us to follow this process and trace how American paradigms were slowly assimilated into Polish culture as the desired set of values and social norms.

The image of the United States as presented by the Polish popular press in the 1920s and 1930s is definitely exaggerated and sugar-coated for propaganda purposes and lacks a deeper, broader, and critical perspective (offered by de Tocqueville or Sienkiewicz). However, they greatly contributed to creating the image of a modern country.

Visions of Prosperity and Success

When reading the monthlies *Ameryka, Kurier Poranny,* and other popular papers, we can see how quickly and on how many levels Polish-American contacts began to flourish.[8] Advertisements of the transatlantic ocean liners were the first visible sign of the growing contacts between the two countries. On January 1, 1921, *Kurier Poranny*[9] announced the opening of a regular passenger and freight connection by Linia Bałtycko-Amerykańska (Baltic-American Line)

---

8   I am focusing here on the perception and presentation of these contacts. The enthusiastic tone of the newspaper coverage differed from the matter-of-fact approach of the diplomatic notes Halina Parafianowicz writes about in her essay about Hugh S. Gibson, the first American envoy to Poland: "Hugh S. Gibson's Diplomatic Service in Poland After the First World War"; see Parafianowicz, *Białostockie Teki Historyczne,* 159–174. On the complicated Polish American diplomatic relations see also Winid *W cieniu Kapitolu* and Wandycz, *The United States and Poland.* Also, sometimes business publications like *Ameryka* introduced a sober tone. For example, when they complained about insufficient Polish exports to the United States.

9   KP 1921, 1:1. From now on I will be referring to *Kurier Poranny* as KP, then I give the year, edition, and page number.

between Gdańsk and New York on the big comfortable ships *Polonia, Lithuania,* and *Estonia* sailing from Gdańsk every other week. By mid-February four other ocean-liner companies offered their services to Polish citizens willing to travel or transport goods to or from the United States.

At the very beginning of that same year, Packard and Chevrolet started advertising made-in-America modern auto technology to the newly reborn republic. On February 15, a huge advertisement in *Kurier Poranny* announced the arrival of "Chevrolet cars that have full warranty, service, low prices and are, of course, the best in the world." American business entered the scene (as the Polish American Syndicate of the Rebuilding of Polish Industry) offering financial help to rebuild Polish national industry. The huge announcement on the first page of *Kurier Poranny* (March 4, 1921) was signed by the representatives of the Union Liberty Bank, Spółka Akcyjna POMOC (selling agricultural equipment), Union Liberty Company, "Wolność," Furniture Company in Mszana Dolna, and Polish American Foundry in Warsaw. The number of various business connections also grew rapidly, indicating a heightened interest in Poland beginning in Polonia[10] circles but moving also to other business-related groups, students, humanitarian workers, and others. In 1921–1922 *Kurier Poranny* often advertised American office equipment (mostly typewriters and billing machines) and even products like rubber boots and foodstuffs such as lard, flour, and beans.

So, despite Poland's disastrous economic situation caused by the First World War and the post-partition devastation,[11] during the first years of independence newspapers reported a lot of activity in Polish-American trade. There was little capital flowing to Poland, yet the creation of the American-Polish Chamber of Commerce and Industry facilitated contacts between Polish and American entrepreneurs. One of the earliest and largest Polish transactions with the United States was the purchase of 170 locomotives from the Baldwin Locomotives Company of Philadelphia in 1922–1923. That operation must have been also significant for the American company since it was heralded by all major newspapers.

---

10 Polonia was a term relating to the Poles living in the United States.
11 After the end of World War I the situation in three formerly partitioned areas differed substantially. One hundred and twenty-three years of foreign domination (Russian, Prussian, and Austrian), comparable only to colonization, left a deep imprint on all areas of life in postpartition Poland. The three formerly colonized parts (known as *zabory*) had different languages, economies, and legal systems. And their approaches to education, culture, and social life varied substantially in all these parts, which after 1918 were supposed to function as one political body.

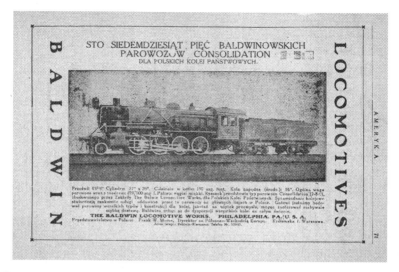

Figure 7.1. Announcement about the purchase of Baldwin Locomotives. *Ameryka*, no. 11, 1923.

Even though the real trade balance was not in Poland's favor, popular papers like *Kurier Poranny*, *Tygodnik Ilustrowany (Illustrated Weekly)*[12], and business-oriented magazines such as *Ameryka* emphasized substantial growth and the potential for further development in Polish-American business relations. Their advertisements suggest that following America's approach to business was the only solution for Poland.

Car advertisements (for Ford, Packard, Chevrolet, and Buick) that inundated Polish papers with their offers of comfortable, high-quality, and inexpensive cars not only offered their products but, more importantly, were selling a new lifestyle. The Ford ad from *Kurier Poranny* (December 1928) presents a picnicking family with all its members in a splendid mood, smiling and enjoying their time thanks to the machine parked in the back. The text informs readers in a matter-of-fact way about the car's capabilities, but the jubilant atmosphere emanating from the picture is more important than the written message. Buick advertised its cars without even showing a single automobile; we see elegantly dressed men walking somewhere and talking about "the newest Buick model." The text gives no details, apart from mentioning a low price ("this is the most

---

12 *Tygodnik Ilustrowany* was a very popular weekly newspaper offering news via photojournalism.

POLISH MODERN IDENTITY CONSTRUCTION   141

Figure 7.2. Ford advertisement from 1928. *Kurier Poranny*, December 1928.

affordable high-class car") and encourages the reader to compare prices. Both advertisements appeal to emotion rather than to reason, stirring desires for a better, carefree, and high-class lifestyle. There were many advertisements like the ones above presenting all sorts of modern appliances—such as typewriters (Royal, Remington), radios, telephones, railway cars—that not only created a vision of a modern life but made people believe that such a high standard of living was possible. They empowered people with the sheer potential of attaining a bit of the wealth, ease, and elegance emanating from the image of Buick or Ford.

By imagining themselves as possible car owners, the readers could believe that they were able to work and produce such products as effectively as Americans. Such messages evidently responded to the need in Polish society for constructive, positive, pragmatic approaches to reality.

Thus in the 1920s, the traditional Polish ethos of martyrdom and sacrifice (resulting from the partitions) that was at the core of Polish nineteenth-century identity started fading. This idea, developed by Polish Romanticism, maintained that the only way of regaining freedom was through endless sacrifice for the country. Even in the second half of the nineteenth century during the time of the so-called Positivist movement that propagated the ethos of constructive work, ideas of progress, modernization, as well as pragmatic worldviews, there was little space for the daily pursuit of happiness. As long as Poland was partitioned, every Pole's daily life and work had to be subordinated to the ethos of the fight for freedom. Positivism, like Romanticism before it, still propagated patriotic ideals that called for subordinating individual goals and ambitions to a higher cause. But such an attitude no longer satisfied the Poles who, for the first time after years of struggle, saw the possibility of shedding this constraining ideology and evolving into a modern, success-oriented nation. Advertisements such as Ford's and Buick's addressed mostly the middle-class or modern Poles who were ready to move forward adopting new ways of life and stop from constantly invoking the past[13] in striving to attain their future vision.[14]

New Gender Roles

Daily contact with American culture through advertising in the papers was one of the most powerful channels exposing the Polish public to a modern syndrome. But there was another equally powerful medium: film. In the early silent film era *Kurier Poranny* was already publishing listings of all Warsaw movie theaters showing many American and European productions.

Toward the 1930s, in the sound film era, more and more films featured famous early Hollywood film stars such as Charlie Chaplin or Joan Crawford. On July 22, 1928, the first page of *Kurier Poranny* announced that United Artists would be promoting movie stars like Gloria Swanson, Dolores Del Rio,

---

13   Poles, even nowadays, love to constantly relate to their difficult history and the partitions.
14   The ethos of hard work relates to the so-called positivistic worldview from the second half of the nineteenth century, which called for rejection of high Romantic ideals and instead focused on work and gradual bettering of the situation in Poland.

Douglas Fairbanks, Charlie Chaplin, Buster Keaton, Lionel Barrymore, Norma Talmadge, Alice Terry, Lillian Gish, and many others. It's no wonder then that Zuta, from Gombrowicz's *Ferdydurke*, pins photographs of Ginger Rogers and Fred Astaire to the walls of her room while Kopyrda, her boyfriend, assumes a modern American pose keeping his hands in his pockets. The scene between the narrator (Joey) and Zuta (the schoolgirl) is reminiscent of a set from an American movie. The passage is sprinkled with references to modern American girls dressed in tennis pants who dangle their legs of the side of boats.[15] The paradigm of modernity manifests itself in Gombrowicz's world through the film-proliferated cult of the body—always agile, supple, ready for action. Zuta and Kopyrda are built like athletes and models from car advertisements. Sports such as tennis, even more strongly than in *Ferdydurke*, saturates the world of *Possessed*. The young, supple, modern bodies of Walczak and Maja (the main protagonists), are in sharp contrast to the outdated, old, bent, and shrunken figure of the count, who represents the old world and old values.

As the cinematographic examples show, the paradigm of modernity was often personified as a modern American woman. This image was especially prominent in women's magazines such as *Kobieta Współczesna* (*A Modern Woman*), *Świat Kobiecy* (*Woman's World*), *Bluszcz* (*Ivy*) but also in popular daily papers like *Kurier Poranny*, *Tygodnik Ilustrowany*, and others. In 1928, *Kurier Poranny* started a new column titled "From the Women's World." It was mostly devoted to presenting interesting pieces about American women who in the Polish popular imagination existed as educated young people often occupying typically male professions (at that time) such as a lawyer or a policewoman. Sometimes they were pilots, automobile drivers, or female athletes. But they had to be young, pretty, elegant, enthusiastic, optimistic, and athletic, so they were fit, energetic, and always ready to act. This is how Winifred Richmond describes modern American women in *Kobieta Współczesna*:

> They go alone to the theatres, restaurants, and cafes ... they wear clothes that do not restrict their movements, they drive cars ... and in many cases they live their lives as they wish. ... Two basic factors contribute to such a radical change of American girls: our school system and the fact that women entered almost all work spaces. America brings up the generation of women who will look their life straight in the face and who will be able to find their place in society."[16]

---

15 See Witold Gombrowicz, *Ferdydurke*. New Haven; Yale University Press, 2000, pp. 123–124.

16 *Kobieta Współczesna*, no. 4, p.17, 1927. *Kobieta Współczesna* printed this article by Winifred Richmond from Washington as a reprint from the London *Child*

Thus, an American woman is presented as an embodiment of modernity, energetic, fast-moving, independent, professional, and boldly facing the future.

The papers loved to include information about famous American women such as Amelia Earhart, a celebrity pilot who flew across the Atlantic in 1928, or Emilia Napieralska, the president of the Polish Women of America organization who visited Poland many times and organized relief help and nursing programs. Short and longer articles and photographs of American actresses were a must. Women represented professionalism, power, effectiveness, and the ability to perform in traditionally male roles: in other words, they represented progress clad in youth, feminine grace, and beauty. Very often the articles and photographs focused on young women, often of Polish descent, who represented the potential of the young generation of American women. Emilia Napieralska, in an interview for *Kobieta Współczesna*, described such women as "very practical, very realistic in everyday life, but in their souls [they] carry strong feelings towards Poland. Many of them graduate from American universities. They are devoted to medicine, law, or teaching" (1928, April, 13).

But the most revered place was the traditional kitchen. And here women reigned as real queens of advanced technology and as authentic professionals combining traditional roles with modern requirements.

In the first issue of *Kobieta współczesna* (1927) the publishers focused on the organization of work in the kitchen and state that "American women rarely have a house servant, hence they manage their house wisely and frugally. . . . They save time, money, and energy (. . .) the American economy is based on three basic elements representing advancement of modern culture. These are: radio, telephone, and electricity." How then, we can ask, do these women manage their household so effectively? The answer is: "The American woman first listens to information about prices on the radio, then she orders the products by phone, and the store delivers them by car. This way, in a couple of minutes, all shopping is done" [17]. Then the author describes how efficiently she cleans the house/apartment with an electric vacuum cleaner and later cooks on an electric stove, not a coal one, even knowing the time of day when electricity is the cheapest.

The popular perception was that American women save money, time, and work because they "respect housework and treat it in an intelligent way [using their] . . . qualifications, capabilities, intelligence, and organizational abilities."[18] Figure 7.4 illustrates the kitchen application of an organizational practice

---

magazine (my translation into English). The article's title in Polish is "Młoda amerykańska dziewczyna" (A young American woman).

17   *Kobieta współczesna* no. 4, p.13, 1927.

18   *Kobieta współczesna* no. 4, p.14, 1927

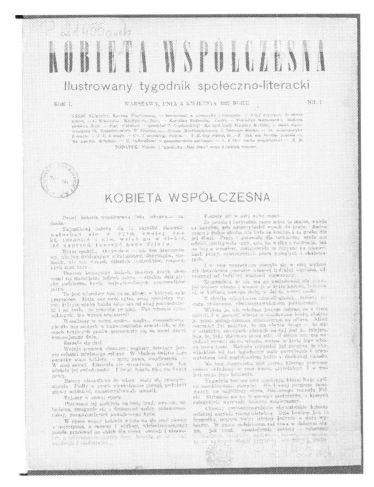

Figure 7.3. *Kobieta Współczesna*. Page one of the first issue, 1927.

known as Taylorism. Invented by Frederick W. Taylor it presupposed that in order to achieve maximum efficiency the worker needed to use a minimal number of movements.[19] Taylorism in the kitchen is the best example of women's

---

19   Taylorism is a system of scientific production management invented by Frederick Winslow Taylor and theorized in *The Principles of the Scientific Management* (1911). Taylor's approach, based on his observations of factory work, focused on inventing the most efficient tools and the control of the worker's movements so that no movement is wasted. This approach was implemented in the United

Figure 7.4. Organization of the efficient kitchen. *Kobieta współczesna*, no. 2, 1928.

professionalism manifested through the intelligent organization of the household, including all activities as well as the kitchen setup and the use of appliances. Thus, the American woman represented everything modernity offered. Magazines such as *Kobieta współczesna* often point to how professionalization of

---

States at the beginning of the twentieth century and often led to the exploitation of workers.

kitchen work through good organization and the use of modern appliances such as electric stoves or kitchen aid products is synonymous with women's professionalization in other areas. "House work demands no less, but even more qualifications, capabilities, intelligence, and organizational abilities than any other work" (1927, 14:4).

Poland as America's Diligent Student

Since the Polish media was dedicated to presenting America as a model modern country, we often find articles in which we witness the element of "learning" from American technology, work organization, the structure of democratic institutions, and education. For instance, many articles in *Ameryka* show almost every aspect of American culture and, in a sense, invite the Poles to learn how to build a similar efficient and free country.

In the first year of its existence in 1923, *Ameryka* began publishing a series of articles about work efficiency and organization in American companies, encouraging Poles to adopt these methods. In issue no. 8 could be found an article entitled "How Do They Work in America?," while issue no. 10 stressed "The Need to Americanize Polish Companies" or "Cooperation Between America and Poland." These discussions mainly highlighted the efficiency of work through good organization and management. Others often presented modern technological wonders such as radio, electricity, cars, sewing machines, typewriters, or modern agricultural machines and "taught" the readers, for example, "what the radio station looks like,"[20] "about electricity,"[21] or inquires like "Why does the car move?" (*Dlaczego samochód sam chodzi?*).[22] Often they gave more specific "lectures" about "the role of feet when driving" (*Rola nóg przy kierowaniu samochodem*).[23] Apart from technology, the papers invited their readers to learn modern banking or marketing practices from articles like "A Secret of a Sold Hat: Poles Learn How to Sell" (*Tajemnica sprzedanego kapelusza. Naucz się Polaku sprzedawać*) or "What Does the Buyer Need?" (*Czego potrzebuje kupujący*).[24] In a similar way, other publications I have been discussing encouraged Poles to follow the American example in almost every other sphere of life:

---

20   *Ameryka*, no. 11, 1923.
21   *Ameryka*, no. 2, 1924.
22   *Ameryka*, no. 4, 1925.
23   *Ameryka*, no. 2, 1925.
24   *Ameryka-Polska*, no. 1, 1921.

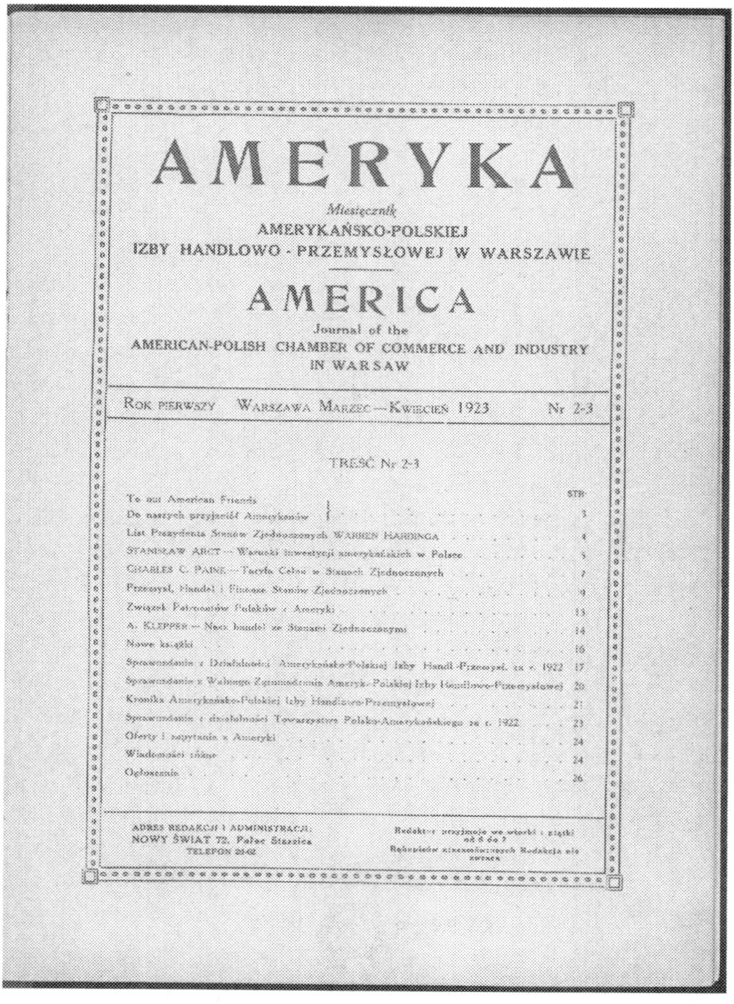

AMERYKA

Miesięcznik

AMERYKAŃSKO-POLSKIEJ

IZBY HANDLOWO - PRZEMYSŁOWEJ W WARSZAWIE

AMERICA

Journal of the

AMERICAN-POLISH CHAMBER OF COMMERCE AND INDUSTRY

IN WARSAW

ROK PIERWSZY WARSZAWA MARZEC—KWIECIEŃ 1923 Nr 2-3

TREŚĆ Nr 2-3

ADRES REDAKCJI I ADMINISTRACJI:
NOWY ŚWIAT 72. Pałac Staszica
TELEFON 21-62

Figure 7.5. The first issue of *Ameryka*. It is listed as no. 2-3, but there was no number 1. March–April, 1923.

starting from the grand democratic ideals of the US Constitution and democratic government[25] through education, sports, architecture, and the organization of the kitchen and cleanliness at the farm.

25 "Za przykładem Ameryki," *Ameryka*, no. 2, 1925.

In the late 1920s and 1930s, however, we can observe a tendency to present Poland more as America's business partner since more and more Polish-American ventures, such as the General Motors plant, ocean liners, and banks had already been established in Poland. Poles' self-esteem was definitely boosted when GM and other companies started opening branches in Poland. The newspaper articles with a "let's learn from America" approach[26] compare both countries by placing them on more less equal footing. The articles in a special American edition of *Kurier Poranny* from December 1928 prominently display this tendency. In this issue, Supreme Court Justice Robert Moschitzker from Pennsylvania delves into Polish and US constitutions in "The U.S. Constitution and the Polish Constitution," showing the constitutions' similarities and differences. Another article "Poland and America" by Louis E. Van Norman compares the historical predicaments of Poland and America. Dr. Julius Klein focuses on Polish economic growth, America's confidence in Poland, and the question of growing trade balances between both countries in his text "Rebuilding of the Polish Economy from an American Business Perspective" (*Odbudowa Gospodarcza Polski z punktu Widzenia Interesow Amerykanskich*).

Such approaches consolidated the image of Poland as America's equal, not just its diligent student. Polish willingness to shape its identity in reference to the significance of power, progress, and technological advancement (as American attributes) came to be synonymous with the rejection of the traditional historical references grounded in martyrdom and postcolonial (or postpartition) inferiority complexes (or "second-classness") resulting from the predicament of lagging behind the so-called first-class cultures.[27] In order to strengthen their modern image, the Poles began to promote themselves through their economic ventures such as the construction of the Gdynia port and shipyard (such promotion was often practiced by the journal *Poland* in the United States—the sisterly publication to *Ameryka*). We can also read many articles presenting traditionally backward sectors of the economy like farming as blossoming thanks to new technologies and new forms of organization.

At the same time, to support that trend, the press disseminated statements by representatives of business and politics commenting on Polish economic growth and industrial development. We find American officials' statements such

---

26 "Uczmy się od Ameryki," KP, December 1928.
27 Witold Gombrowicz's concepts of "second-class cultures"/ "kultury wtórne, drugorzędne" and "the countries of weak form"/ "Kraje ... formy osłabionej" belong to that category. (*Testament*, 26–27). About belatedness see Jusdanis, *Belated Modernity and Aesthetic Culture*. See also Illakowicz, *European Peripheries*.

as Francois de St. Phalles's (vice president of Am-PL Chamber of Commerce) remark about the increase in Polish contacts with the United States or observations by American bankers, politicians, and industrialists relating to Polish efficiency and technological development. The American edition of *Kurier Poranny* (December 1928) quotes short statements by Walter Chrysler from Chrysler Dodge Corporation, George E. Vincent from the Rockefeller Foundation, US vice president Charles G. Dawes, US treasurer Andrew Mellon, and others expressing their admiration for Poland's success, economic progress, cooperation, and dedication. Such demonstrations of mutual friendship and the American appreciation of Polish efforts and willingness to continue in the spirit of partnership were seminal for solidifying the image of a modern Poland.

America as a Model Modernity: Space, Speed, and Skyscrapers

For the generation of Poles living in the 1920s, the beauty Sienkiewicz and de Tocqueville extolled in the lakes and forests manifested itself in American cars, skyscrapers, and fast-growing industry. One of the Ford slogans from 1928 states that their car is "brave and fast . . . does not require expensive service and is ready to hit the road . . . any day," and Chrysler "rushes forward as an arrow."[28] In fact, the whole American world rushes forward. Progress and speed dominate the image of America in the twentieth century. But there is one more element to it—not a horizontal but a vertical embodiment of speed and progress: skyscrapers.

Due to the popularity of photography at the end of the 1920s, papers began publishing more photographic news coverage and illustrations. For instance, *Tygodnik Ilustrowany* (Illustrated weekly) devoted a whole section to such photographic coverage, and the Polish reader could experience with their own eyes the wonders of modern America. One of the most spectacular domains was architecture. *Tygodnik Ilustrowany* began to publish pages with photographs of "always the tallest" skyscrapers, the most efficient railway stations, and the most technologically advanced bridges. Even though some authors complained about the ugliness of skyscrapers, most articles about modern American architecture extolled its technological advancement and beauty—skyscrapers symbolized all the positive values stemming from the conflation of practicality, imagination, and modern science. We must remember that by the late 1920s Poland started implementing Eugeniusz Kwiatkowski's project of modernizing Polish

---

28   KP, January 12, 1928.

Figure 7.6. Skyscrapers and architecture became a recurring photographic topic. *Ameryka –Polska*. September 1924.

industry including building the transatlantic port in Gdynia, chemical plants in Mościce, and Centralny Okręg Przemysłowy (COP) /Central Industrial Area COP. References to American technology enhanced the project's viability and highlighted Poland's dedication to modernization.

Among raptures over new architecture there appeared some interesting opinions showing tensions between the desire to implement modern inventions and the attachment to traditional norms and values. In that vein, T. Bagniecki, in the article "New Architecture," approaches modern American architecture as a hybrid and a conflation of the old and the new, thus revalorizing (a bit negatively) the traditional idea of American practicality. "Americans, not restrained by traditional aesthetic considerations, as the first in the world, started building *practical*[29] skyscrapers," he states "[whereas] in Europe, these aesthetic considerations play a more significant role."[30] His comment expresses a characteristic ambivalent approach to the project of modernity characterizing all belated cultures[31]—

---

29 Emphasis mine.
30 *Tygodnik Ilustrowany*, 1931, no. 5, 88. Later in the text I use TI for this publication.
31 I am using the term "belated cultures" in reference to the cultures that (like Poland or Greece) joined the project of modernization later than other countries

fascination with a hint of jealousy and European superiority.[32] *Practicality,* so appreciated in reference to Herbert Hoover's humanitarian mission and other early 1920s American ventures, implies lower aesthetic quality and some kind of necessary lesser evil. Modernity in Poland, as elsewhere, has never been accepted without friction.

Not all authors writing about America had doubts similar to Bagniecki's. Wacław Sieroszewski, for instance, in a series of articles from his American journey for *Kurier Poranny* in December 1929 and January 1930, is impressed with the skyscrapers and approaches them as an embodiment of American beauty. His entire discussion about American modern aesthetics (his article is titled "Beauty in America") is in fact inspired by skyscrapers. Even though Sieroszewski notices the ugliness of some American cities—he states that "American cities are ugly and without style" —he stresses that it is "in the skyscrapers . . . Americans found the architectonic expression of their soul." [33]. He experiences America through its modern energy—observing the country from the plane, listening to jazz, reading literature. Still in his reflection we can find a familiar Romantic spirit (and also pathos) but in a modern, technological form. His writing elevates modern American reality to unreachable heights where technology reigns and becomes synonymous with nature. Thus, he promotes the myth of modern America, which like all myths is a projection of desires and goals characteristic for a given community in a specific time and space. As such, myth encapsulates the discursive systems circulating in a given time and space. Sieroszewski captures all the elements of the modern America myth in his descriptions.

> A flight over the Atlantic, the defeat of sub-zero temperatures and polar snowstorms, a victory over space and time, bringing to the world new tones and hues. . . . Applause for Lindbergh, Edison, and honor to Skłodowska-Curie, interest in television, and the rocket-plane—these are powerful [modern] manifestations incomparable to any other in the world. [34]

---

such as England, France, Germany, and of course the United States. See also n. 25 (Gombrowicz).

32   The first Polish skyscraper, and the only one until the Palace of Culture, was the Prudential Building in Warsaw finished in 1934. The construction started in 1931. The designer was Marcin Weinfeld; the reinforced concrete frame was designed by Stefan Bryła and Wenczeslaw Poniż.

33   KP, December 1, 1929.

34   Ibid.

But modern America in Sieroszewski's perception undergoes a process of hybridization (it becomes a cluster of two seemingly exclusionary components—old and new) and comes to be mythologized anew. The country appears to him as a new Prometheus who, acquiring energy from Niagara Falls "uses the power of nature to serve humanity"[35] and this work produces beauty. Even though Sieroszewski cannot avoid romanticizing, and his aesthetics ring a familiar lofty tone, modern references and connotations still dominate his linguistic topography.

Indeed, modernity in its American form spread into almost all domains of life. The papers wrote about the previously unheard-of increase in industrial production thanks to new organization methods of Fordism and Taylorism, automatization, new telecommunication technologies (radio and telephone), jazz music, film, fashion, sports, and the amusement park at Coney Island. The photographs showed mighty skyscrapers, various machines, modern kitchens, and even modern cow-milking methods. The possibility to talk via telephone with distant places fascinated everybody, and *Kurier Poranny* happily showed a picture of the radio-telephone station in Rocky Point near New York enabling "conversation at the distance of 6000 km." The same note also announced that "the American council in Berlin has just inaugurated a transoceanic radiotelephone connection" and "soon they will open the radiotelephone line between America and Poland"[36].

Similarly, the modern American lifestyle captured the Polish imagination. The papers often linked modern technology with liberal moral values and all kinds of scandals and schemes, describing them as "loose manners" or "divorce American style."[37] But since America was featured as a country of diversity, the ethos of liberated morals coexisted with the image of good family. Many articles extolled successful, hard-working men and women representing all kinds of professions: lawyers, teachers, businesswomen, and policewomen. For women, professionalism did not coincide with being a good mother and wife. And of course, "typical" modern, fast-rising careers like that of Patrick Hurley who "from cowboy ... became a minister" fascinated *Kurier's* journalists.[38] All these careers and scandals evolved rapidly and "as everything happening on the other side of the Atlantic" they assumed unheard-of forms and an "enormous,

---

35   KP, 1, XII, 1929.

36   KP, February 16, 1928.

37   For instance, the gossip section of *Kobieta współczesna* "Czy wiecie, że" (Do you know that) states that "in America every seventh couple divorces" (*W Ameryce na każde siedem małżeństw jedno się rozwodzi*).

38   KP, January 9, 1930.

niem. Już w kilka godzin po otwarciu zapisów subskrybowano przeszło $250,000,000.

W Nowym Jorku prasa przygotowuje banki i społeczeństwo do nowej pożyczki w sumie $20,000,000, którą zamierza zaciągnąć rząd szwedzki dla ustabilizowania kursu korony. Zapisy na pożyczkę tę rozpoczną się w maju lub czerwcu r. b.

Również rząd węgierski pragnie w Ameryce zaciągnąć pożyczkę w sumie $15,000,000. Dowiadujemy się z pewnego źródła, że sfery bankowe amerykańskie przyrzekły już poprzeć te zamiary Węgier.

Węgiel i nafta. W roku 1923 wydobyto w Stanach Zjednoczonych 545,300,000 tonn węgla kamiennego (w r. 1922 422,268,000 ton), antracytu zaś 95,197,000 ton (w r. 1922 54,683,000 ton). Produkcja koksu w r. 1913 wynosiła 17,919,000 ton, t. j. dwa razy więcej aniżeli w r. 1922. Ceny węgla kamiennego i koksu znacznie spadły w porównaniu z rokiem 1922. Natomiast cena antracytu znacznie się podniosła.

Produkcja ropy w roku 1923 pobiła wszystkie poprzednie rekordy. Wydobyto 753,000,000 baryłek, to jest o 30%/o więcej niż w r. 1922.

Domowy aparat radjotelefoniczny do rozmów i słuchania koncertów. Setki tysięcy takich aparatów jest dzisiaj w użyciu w Ameryce.

Oferty i zapytania z Ameryki

600/24 Firma nowojorska oferuje kasetki oszczędnościowe, żelazne, typu wypożyczanego przez Kasy Oszczędności i banki.

433/24 Firma w Chicago pragnie nawiązać stosunki z firmami polskiemi, handlującemi kanarkami, klatkami i karmą dla ptaków.

71/24 Amerykański dom handlowo-importowy nawiąże stosunki z przemysłowcami polskimi, pragnącymi eksportować swoje wyroby. Towar kupują na rachunek własny lub przyjmą przedstawicielstwo.

357/24 Poważna firma amerykańska pragnie importować z Polski przybory piśmienne etc., np.: artykuły z ebonitu, małe przybory szklane i metalowe, wyroby skórzane, kałamarze, obsadki, ołówki, małe zabawki automatyczne, scyzoryki, nożyczki oraz rozmaite nowości w podobnych dziedzinach.

3982/23 Firma w St. Louis pragnie nawiązać stosunki z firmami eksportującemi kawior w puszkach.

34/24 Firma nowojorska oferuje większe ilości koszulek spodnich, typu używanego przez armję amerykańską. Próbki koszulek obejrzeć można w biurze Izby.

306/24 Firma nowojorska nawiąże stosunki z polskimi fabrykantami lub eksporterami ręcznych i ustnych harmonji, zegarków, maszynek do strzyżenia włosów i brzytew.

171/24 Fabryka w Chicago produkująca maszyny do wyrobu puszek blaszanych i automatycznego pakowania konserw odda przedstawicielstwo na Polskę.

352/24 Firma w Brooklinie, handlująca używanemi maszynami do pisania nawiąże stosunki z takimiż firmami polskiemi.

4228/23 Firma nowojorska reflektuje na kupno w Polsce większej ilości octanu amylowego i oleju fuzlowego.

Figure 7.7. Radio at home. One of the first radios at home. Ameryka, no. 2, 1924.

American size." [39]. American modernity for the Polish mind had to be manifested by grandeur, unusual proportions, and might no matter whether it was associated with spectacular careers, fast-growing businesses and luminous cities, or scandalous behaviour.

Exceptionalism Turned Upside Down

Descriptions of big scandals, big careers, and the super achievements of athletes and pilots crossing the Atlantic in lonely flights not only contributed to the "everything is bigger in America" category but stressed the unique, unusual nature of these events. Thus, the language of these descriptions was reminiscent of the old concept of American exceptionalism.[40] Through Polish eyes, America, in both positive and negative ways, was full of strange phenomena, odd habits, and other surprises.

The category of strangeness at the beginning of the twentieth century often conflates with the syndrome of modernity. It is modernity that is clad in strangeness; it often shocks and evades classifications (like in Bagniecki's reaction to skyscrapers) while inducing unprecedented emotional responses—even though modernity per se usually functions as a domain of reason, not emotion. Many articles highlight the element of unusualness in their descriptions of modern city lights, throngs of cars moving along the streets, glistening railway cars, railway stations, and railroads.

They extol "the richness of public buildings" and the fact that "in rich homes almost every servant has his automobile." [41] From little notes here and there the reader can learn that Chicago already has a streetcar without a human driver, operated from a distance by radio;[42] they can find out about a wedding of two

---

39 KP, January 3, 1929.
40 The concept of exceptionalism consists of the perception of America and Americans as unique and singular, and it subtends all constructs of American identity. For the discussion of American exceptionalism see Greene, *The Intellectual Construction of America*, 1–3. G. Hodgson, *The Myth of American Exceptionalism*, 1–29; Saito, *Meeting the Enemy*, 54–66; Madsen, *American Exceptionalism*, 2. See also left-wing historians such as Noam Chomsky and Howard Zinn who are critical of this concept. For the discussion of exceptionalism in the Polish context see also Parafianowicz, "Exceptionalism of America: Some Reflections," 213–24.
41 KP, November 27, 1922.
42 KP, October 7, 1928.

pilots in parachutes—but, alas the parachutes did not open.[43] "America Is an Astonishing Country"—*Tygodnik Ilustrowany* titles one of its articles—about a fashion show for children. In fact, American children are often the objects of that "astonishment" as in the case of a four-year-old boy smoking two cigars at once, or a children's orchestra with a six-year-old boy conductor.[44]

Strangeness, as an attribute of the modern paradigm, was creating something comparable to exceptionalism *à rebours*, that is, mythologizing not in relation to high values, grandeur, and unusual greatness but to a more familiar, folksier context. When earlier exceptionalism stemmed from presumed cultural superiority—descriptions of unusual heroism, moral values, beauty of the landscape—modern oddities eventually came to embody what was "exceptional" about America: quotidian, sometimes funny, sometimes even frivolous incidents (flops such as the aforementioned unfortunate parachute wedding), and other events or scenes carnivalesque in tone but lacking pathos. Carnival always brings reality closer to home. And this is how that modern "low" exceptionalism worked. Friendly shots of cars and smiling people (no longer monumental models of humanitarianism, might, and just government), children in various strange situations, made America more accessible for everybody. All these pieces of information and seemingly insignificant details from American life had a very important function. They shortened the distance[45] between America and Poland and, at the same time, balanced power relations between both countries, making American reality attainable. In this way all the quirky stories and oddities, even if not 100 percent true, domesticated the modern American myth and helped it become deeply encoded in the common Polish imaginary.

In the nineteenth and early twentieth centuries, America represented for the Poles a fulfillment of their identity-related goals and desires. Therefore, at that time the perception of the United States most strongly accentuated the ideas of freedom, national sovereignty, and equality of its citizens. In the late 1920s and 1930s these issues moved to the background; while creation of successful modern economic and ideological structures, securing a strong position for Poland among other European and world countries, moved to the foreground. The image of modern America served that end. Even though Gombrowicz's

---

43 KP, January 1, 1930.
44 *Tygodnik Ilustrowany*, no. 48, 1931, p. 903.
45 In all travel/colonial narratives aiming at foregrounding the civilizational advancement of the traveler/viewer (and his power over the object of observation), as McClintock observes, we notice a reverse maneuver of expanding distance. See McClintock, *Imperial Leather*, 40.

references to America in *Ferdydurke* and *Possessed* are idiosyncratic and parodic—and he already perceived the murky sides of modernity in the fascist and Nazi disguise—like many others he was seduced by the image of American modernity synonymous with the power of youthful immaturity and the seductive green of the dollar.[46]

At this point another Polish writer, Stefan Żeromski, and his infatuation with American technological myth comes to mind, especially considering that in 1925 the journal *Ameryka* published a short article titled "A Letter to Cezary Baryka"[47] capturing all the main elements of the fascination with the American syndrome during the period of Poland's modernist awakening. The title recalls the protagonist of Żeromski's 1925 novel *Przedwiośnie* (The coming spring), one of the most emblematic Polish texts bridging the old and new world orders and proposing the idea of glass houses as a metaphor for the future. Interestingly, the author of the *Ameryka* article, A. Mikulski, juxtaposes Bolshevism (*Przedwiośnie* starts during the Russian Revolution in the city of Baku) to Americanism.

> In our time the history of mankind all over the globe produced two new powers: Bolshevism and Americanism. Between these two poles dwell all other civilizations. [After the description of Bolshevism the author moves to Americanism].... There is the second pole of human reality—Americanism. If you knew it, Cezary, you would have found what you lacked in your life. You would not see there [in America] a Warsaw café, nor Nalewki, nor Nawłoć. There you would have gotten involved in an incredible whirlwind of work and you would not even have noticed how all your youthful "Weltschmertz" evaporates from your soul. You would become a new citizen. An American. You would be brave, useful for everybody and appreciated by yourself. You would be the biggest individualist in the world. You would create such a social order and organize work in such a way that no communist (no matter how fantastic or devoted) could do it better. America in the shortest time and most perfect way has realized the ideals of mankind's happiness and no other country can match it. If it starts building glass houses it will find much better resources than the ones your father talked about.[48]

---

46 About Gombrowicz's attitude toward the United States also see his *diary*, his correspondence with Jerzy Wittlin, Jerzy Giedroyc, Kot Jeleński, Litka de Barcza, and *Kronos*. For the discussion of Gombrowicz and his American connections see Iłakowicz, "Gombrowicz i Ameryka: boje wydawnicze" (Gombrowicz and America: Publication Struggles). This is a chapter in *Witold Gombrowicz—nasz współczesny*.

47 In Polish, "List do Cezarego Baryki," 8–10.

48 *Ameryka*, no. 6, 1925, 910.

Przedwiośnie was a seminal and representative text for its time for its focus on 1914–1925 and comments on the transition from the old, traditional ethos to the modern one. Żeromski was one of the most influential voices of his time, considered as the so-called conscience of Poland, and every statement of his really mattered. In *Przedwiośnie* he showed the collapse of the old gentry (*szlachta*) culture with its obsolete ideals and unsustainable lifestyles. But he also pointed out how difficult it was to lose these old habits and patriotic ideals and adopt new, modern ways of thinking. But modern, dynamic people, unrestricted by the old prejudices, were necessary to restructure and resurrect the country. Thus, Żeromski promoted modern Polish identity but also highlighted the frictions accompanying the transition. He showed that the old ideals representative of the gentry culture hinging on patriotism and the fight for freedom lost their relevance in the country that had been rebuilding and strengthening its sovereignty. His narrative stops at that moment of transition, on the bridge, so to speak. Since his book was very popular in his time, it is significant that the journal *Ameryka* that was disseminated among representatives of business circles (coming often from the gentry) in 1925 (the year of Żeromski's death) continued the discussion initiated by the writer pointing to the necessity to move on and adopt the new modern paradigms based on the American experience.

Of course, the traditional bond solidified by historic events—exemplified by Tadeusz Kościuszko and Kazimierz Pulaski's participation in the Revolutionary War as well as by American humanitarian help after World War I—constituted points of reference in Polish-American relations for the interwar audience. One such exemplifying occasion was the 1931 unveiling of Woodrow Wilson's monument in Poznan (financed by Paderewski). Yet, in the late 1920s and early 1930s America was perceived not only as Poland's friend and a model modern country but more so as Poland's partner. In 1928, *Kurier Poranny* reported that the president of the Bankers Trust Company stated, "There is no country in the world whose economy would heal as fast [as Poland]."[49] The same year the paper commented on American companies' interest and trust in Polish investments and *Kurier Poranny* (September 21, 1928) commented on General Motors opening its first assembly plant in Warsaw.

The fact that America stopped being perceived only as a permanent rescuer, guardian of liberty, and the proverbial friend of all oppressed nations of the world and eventually treated as Poland's economic partner marks a shift in the consolidation process of modern Polish identity. Unfortunately, that process was interrupted by World War II and the era of communism that pushed the Polish

---

49   KP, April 17, 1928.

imagination back into its old ways when the fight for freedom and independence again came to the fore and reinstated the traditional connotations of the American image as a guardian of liberty and democracy.

Bibliography

Journals

Ameryka (192, 1924, 1925)
Ameryka-Polska (1921)
Kurier Poranny (1921, 1922, 1928, 1930)
Tygodnik Ilustrowany (1931)
Kobieta Współczesna (1928)
Gombrowicz, Witold. *Diary*. Translated by Lillian Vallee. New Haven, CT: Yale University Press, 2012.
Gombrowicz, Witold. *Ferdydurke*. Paris: Instytut Literacki, 1969.
Gombrowicz, Witold. *Kronos*. Edited and annotated by Rita Gombrowicz, Jerzy Jarzębski, and Klementyna Suchanow. Cracow: Wydawnictwo Literackie, 2013.
Gombrowicz, Witold. *Opętani*. Warszawa: Res Publica, 1990.
Gombrowicz, Witold. *Testament*. Warsaw: Res Publika, 1990.
Greene, Jack P. *The Intellectual Construction of America: Exceptionalism and Identity from 1492 to 1800*. Chapel Hill: University of North Carolina Press, 1993.
Hodgson, Godfrey. *The Myth of American Exceptionalism*. New Haven, CT: Yale University Press, 2009.
Illakowicz, Krystyna. "European Peripheries: Poetics and Politics of Eastern Europe." PhD diss., New York University, 1998.
Iłłakowicz, Krystyna. "Gombrowicz i Ameryka: boje wydawnicze". In *Witold Gombrowicz – nasz współczesny*, ed. Jerzy Jarzebski, Cracow: Universitas, 2011.
Jusdanis, Gregory. *Belated Modernity and Aesthetic Culture: Inventing National Literature*. Minneapolis: University of Minnesota Press, 1991.
Madsen Deborah L. *American Exceptionalism*. Edinburgh: Edinburgh University Press, 1998.
McClintock, Ann. *Imperial Leather: Race, Gender and Sexuality in the Colonial Contest*. New York: Routledge, 1995.
Parafianowicz, Halina. "Exceptionalism of America: Some Reflections," *Białostockie Teki Historyczne*, no. 9 (2011).
Paderewska, Helena. *Memoirs, 1910–1920*, edited by Maciej Siekierski. Foreword Norman Davies. Stanford, California: Hoover Institution Press, 2015.
Parafianowicz, Halina. "Hugh S. Gibson's Diplomatic Service in Poland After the First World War." *Białostockie Teki Historyczne* 12 (2014): 159–74.

Taylor Saito, Natsu. *Meeting the Enemy: American Exceptionalism and International Law.* New York: New York University Press, 2010.
Wandycz, Piotr. *The United States and Poland.* Cambridge, MA: Harvard University Press, 1980.
Winid, Bogusław W. *W cieniu Kapitolu. Dyplomacja Polska wobec Stanów Zjednoczonych Ameryki 1919–1939.* Warsaw: POMOST, 1991.
Winslow Taylor, Frederick. *The Principles of the Scientific Management.* New York, London: Harper & Brothers, 1911.
Zamoyski, Adam. *Paderewski.* London: Collins, 1982.

Chapter Eight

From "True Believers" to "Cultural Feminists"

Polish Identity and Women's Emancipation in Post-1945 and Post-1989 Poland

Magdalena Grabowska

As theoretical tradition and a set of activist practices, feminism in Poland often formulates and reformulates its subjectivity in reference to (and often as a critique of) what is recognized as dominant intellectual, cultural, and social traditions. Similar to other movements around the world—particularly in locations that dealt with impositions of foreign totalitarian powers—in Poland emancipatory struggles are seen as being formed in the broader context of the fight for national independence and against foreign domination. Consequently, issues related to sovereignty and the existence of Polish national identity constituted important points of reference for narratives of women's subjectivity in the nineteenth and twentieth centuries. Feminist historiography in Poland has historically (and sometimes still is) centered on how women fought for independence, freedom, and democracy, and how over the past centuries they have been mobilizing against various hegemonic discourses that have emerged or reemerged during national and global upheavals or transitions.[1] More recently, various approaches to the feminist identity formation process have emerged in response to changes brought about by the systemic transformation of 1989.[2]

---

1   Penn, "The National Secret," 55–71.
2   Walczewska, *Damy, rycerze, feministki*.

As a plural formation feminism developed a number of strategies to work around i national identity, both as a concept and as a set of required criteria of belonging (language, geography, literature). This chapter focuses on the ways in which Polish national identity was tackled by the emancipation struggles after 1945 and explores how the connection between Polishness and emancipation continued to be constructed and deconstructed after 1989. I first examine discursive spaces—such as the women's departments of the Polish Workers Party and Polish United Workers Party, women's press and international organizations—which, after 1945 were major venues where debates, negotiations, and conflicts over women's emancipation, representation, and identity of women's movement in Poland took place. My aim is to illuminate the constraints faced by political actors able and willing to imagine women free from the bounds of Polish nationalism and political Catholicism and to examine the motivations of those who propagated the vision of emancipation that reached beyond the entanglement with local political forces: patriotism and Catholicism.[3]

The second part of the chapter traces transformations of the Polish emancipation project after 1956 and 1989. Following the historian Małgorzata Fidelis, I argue that the masculine woman on the tractor from the Stalinist period was, from 1956 on, represented as a symbol of the (failed) communist emancipation, a symbol of the foreign nature of communist projects in Poland, and the exemplification of the Soviet imposition on Polish national identity.[4] The fear of masculinization of women seen as a threat to the "order of nature," and Polish family, then became part of Polish political discourses: it was also effectively used to divide society into "us" and "them" after 1989. While in the 1990s the woman on the tractor was once again used as a symbol of imposed communist emancipation, new women's organizations founded after 1989 joined forces with all political actors that aimed to erase the communist past, as a breach in the march toward modernized Poland. Feminist appropriation of anticommunist discourses became, however, a double-edged sword. While on the one hand it helped legitimize gender equality discourse as part of the public debate after 1989—mainly through the appropriation of Western-style cultural

---

3   In this chapter I use a data collected between 2011 and 2014 as a part of European Commission's Marie Curie Fellowship as well as a research project "Bits of Freedom" funded by National Science Centre in Poland (6731/B/H03/2011/40). I draw on archival research of the Communist Party in Poland, press analysis and individual in-depth interviews conducted with 60 women's activists in Poland and Georgia, that were part of this project.
4   Fidelis, *Women, Communism, and Industrialization in Postwar Poland*, 265.

feminism—on the other it contributed to the reinforcement of the representation of women's equality as "foreign" to Poland. From the 1990s onward, "catching up" with Western-style feminism became a hallmark of Polish emancipation; and while it helped to reintroduce emancipation ideas to the mainstream liberal discourses, it also failed various groups of women in Poland, including working and rural ones who remained by default alienated from the middle-class emancipation efforts.

In the past and present feminism in in Poland is generally represented (and represents itself) as oppositional and critical of the identity narratives that center on nationhood. By definition the emancipatory feminists theories and practices challenge the vision of women's subjectivity as subservient to family and nation, and in particular oppose the idea of womanhood as confined to the figure of Mother-Pole (*Matka Polka*)—a symbol of a caring mother for the soldier sons fighting for national independence and a mother of the suffering nation. Critical assessments of traditional Polishness often led feminism to be seen as an outsider of the national community, a foreign import. Most recently the attacks on "gender ideology" claimed feminism to be a form of neocolonization from the west, "Ebola from Brussels."[5] At the same time, for various reasons, over past decades—during communism, during the democratic transformation period, and even during the recent "black protests"—female political leaders, feminist scholars, and activists surrendered to the pressures of mainstream political narratives, which center on presumed homogeneity of Polish society. Assuming the sameness of all women, politics of appropriating national rhetoric and symbols, and feminist patriotism are repeatedly assumed to be the only ways in which feminism can articulate itself in Poland.[6] As a strategy of conformity may seem successful in gaining popularity in Poland, it also hinders the movement's objective of achieving social justice for various groups of people. In this article I argue that only recently feminism was able to free itself from the politics of national homogeneity. It was during the 2020–2021 protest against further restrictions of the abortion law that the patriotic narrative was visibly marginalized, giving way to ideas of diversity understood as solidarity between various intersecting struggles (e.g., against economic oppression, for climate justice, for LGBTQI+ rights), bringing a shift from reactionary positions—which aimed at adjusting feminist projects to dominant political narratives—to proactive approaches enabling feminism to reach the new language foreground of emancipatory struggles in Poland.

---

5   Graff and Korolczuk, "Gender as 'Ebola from Brussels,'" 797–821.
6   Ramme, "Framing Solidarity," 469–84; Zawadzka, "Polityka mimikry," 56–62.

Postwar Women's Activism: Toward Communist State Emancipation

In narratives on the history of women's activism and emancipation there is usually no mention of the ways in which state socialism contributed to the advancement of their rights and empowerment or how emancipatory actions during the period of communism challenged and/or complied with dominant discourses on Polish women's identities, and, more broadly, aspects of Polish identity in general. Routinized narratives about postwar women's emancipation in Poland not only claimed that communism was (and still is) "by nature" foreign to Poland and Polish national identity but also represent postwar policies promoting women's equality as "imported" from the Soviet Union and enforced on the Polish female masses.[7]

While traditional feminist historiography renders the decades between 1945 and 1989 as a period of "stagnation" or decline of feminism, recent studies note that unraveling the complex connections and connectivities between the post-1945 and post-1989 women's mobilizations may produce new and fascinating, if controversial, knowledge on genealogies of modern feminism in Poland.[8] These newer works aim to represent communism as well as communist ideas of emancipation as phenomenon not entirely alien to Poland and locate it within the continuing efforts to improve the position of women in society.[9] They claim that in terms of issues and strategies there is a continuity between the state socialist period and contemporary women's struggles, especially where national identity and patriotism are concerned.[10] Feminist historians, sociologists, and literary critics explore how generations of women, including Izolda Kowalska, Edwarda Orłowska, Eugenia Pragierowa, Irena Sztachelska, and Zofia Wasilkowska, participated in building the new system after 1945. They evidence that these women were often active in prewar socialist and communist movements and worked toward the emancipation of the working class (especially women) while simultaneously negotiating their ideas within existing social and cultural contexts.

Within these newly emergent scholarship there is still a debate whether female communist activists instrumentally used patriotic, nationalist discourse

---

7 Fuszara, "New Gender Relationships in Poland in 1990s," 259–78.
8 Graff and Sutowski, *Jestem stąd*; Titkow, "Poland, New Gender Contract in Formation."
9 Fidelis, *Women, Communism, and Industrialization in Postwar Poland*.
10 Grabowska, *Zerwana genealogia*.

to legitimize the changes they implemented or were they forced to strategically utilize references to nationalism and the national imaginary as the only effective tool for mobilizing women (even in the context of radical social change after 1945). In 1945, when the new regime came into existence, attracting women to communism and encouraging them to enter the workforce and reproduce became the primary and most profound tasks of the women's departments of the Polish Socialist Party (PSP) and Polish Workers' Party (PWP). Their agendas correlated with the broader aims of the new socialist state, which focused on fighting the devastating effects of World War II in Poland. They also fit into an overall representation of the "new democracies" as progressing in the area of women's equality and endorsing world peace that was promoted at the international level, including within the Women's International Democratic Federation (WIDF). As in many Eastern European countries, in postwar Poland the state, not civil society, became a major agent for enforcing women's equality. State regulated mass incorporation of women into the labor force[11] was supplemented by state-funded childcare, socialization of housework, and the promotion of equality "at home."

In Poland, which after World War II and due to the Holocaust and postwar resettlements became almost uniformly Catholic and ethnically homogenous, "radical" measures for women's equality were introduced only briefly between 1945 and 1948. Still, immediate postwar communist emancipation projects represented the plurality of intersecting (often seemingly contradictory) identities of women who participated in its implementation. Diverse paths and origins impacted the ways in which various groups perceived the role and objectives of the new women's movement. While prewar communists viewed the state as an agent to implement the international project of communist emancipation, others cautioned against distancing new emancipation policies from the historically rooted emancipation processes in Poland.

In general, postwar female activists aimed to transform the prewar social gender structure by broadening emancipation efforts to include working-class and rural women and to extend it into the sphere of social reproduction. Their project was discussed, negotiated, and constantly reformulated to fit local social and cultural contexts. Within the Polish Wokers' Party itself, debates about the specificity of the Polish cultural and social context were often reduced to questions about the possibility of attracting women to the communist emancipation model, given the cultural dominance of the traditional model of patriarchal

---

11 Jarska, *Kobiety z marmuru. Robotnice w Polsce w latach*; Ghodsee, "Rethinking State Socialist Mass Women's Organizations," 49.

family and prevalence of the Catholic Church. Jewish communists (including female communists) were at the forefront of struggles to bring about the "new language" of emancipation based on the empowerment of working-class women and the secular state. Activists such as Edwarda Orłowska, Żanna Kormanowa, and others opposed the narrow model of cultural belonging centering on *Polak-Katolik* (Pole-Catholic) by attempting to directly (or indirectly) extend the boundaries of citizenship in Poland. Their visions of society and their political biographies were uniquely shaped by "dimensions of difference" related to ethnic and cultural backgrounds, religion, and class. Their loyalties lay with the international communist movement rather than with the Polish national cause. Many, one may presume, shared Rosa Luxemburg's belief about the primacy of class over nation in political priorities.

Communists' attempts to introduce radical social changes were tempered by the postwar political and cultural landscape, characteristic of which was not only ethnic and religious homogeneity but also callousness about violence, including anti-Semitic violence. Actions of Jewish communists, including Edwarda Orłowska, head of Women's Department of PPW and the key figure of postwar emancipation, were mistrusted and the Polish Wokers' Party employed various measures to prevent accusations of suspicious origin. As they cared about the image of the Polish Wokers' Party in Poland and wanted to seem more authentic to society, many Jewish communists subdued their origins, agreed to convert names and customs,[12] and decided not to fight openly with traditional vision of Polishness.

New ideas of equality were promoted differently in various political and social spaces, with more open critique of the traditional social order within the Polish Wokers' Party and a less confrontational approach in women's press. Women active in the Women's Department (WD), founded in 1946, envisioned transformation of female lives as an intersectional effort—focused on class and gender struggle. In 1946, Orłowska argued:

> Our goal is to wrest women from the influence of the reaction ["reactionary forces" of the Catholic Church and Western Europe and US sympathizers], to create a powerful women's organization. The women's party apparatus has to be strong. Women's departments in the provinces should consist of five to seven women representing the League of Women, Trade Unions, Rural Self-Help.[13]

---

12 Schatz, *Pokolenie*.
13 Archives of New Record, 11.

Recruiting women to the party proved to be a daunting task. Activists faced patriarchal bias in their own party; many local party leaders defied the very existence of "women's instructors" (paid representatives of the Women's Department in the field) and forced them to work as a secretaries or assistants. The success of circulars on "women's work" issued by the Central Committee also proved to be limited—by and large they were ignored by the local secretaries.

During the postwar period communist women activists followed the official party line of not fighting the church openly,[14] yet members of Women's Department were divided about the strategies of approaching ideological tensions between Catholicism and communism. In postwar Poland women's emancipation was legally introduced through various bills that were in direct opposition to Catholic visions of society and gender order. The 1945 Civil Marriage Decree and 1946 Family Law brought up a separation of church and state, civil marriage, divorce, and recognition of children born out of wedlock. These laws, paired with mass introduction of women into the labor force, resulted in (possibly of) almost complete female independence from family, marriage, and men. Many women activists signaled conflict of loyalties that individual women may experience in the new social reality. "In practice," one of the WD delegates said, "Even when some of the activists denounce the role of religion and the Church in society, their daughters still receive confirmation."[15] They warned that spreading the idea that the party opposes religion will eventually hurt communists. Others described the church as a reactionary force keeping women from the party and needed to be invigilated. These activists believed that providing useful services for women (health care, education, and childcare services during harvests) along with "food for thought" (Soviet cinema and political education) would be an effective way of pulling even the most conservative rural women away from the church.[16]

From the point of view of identity struggles faced by the new regime in postwar Poland, winning support for women's organizations was a must. After 1945, the League of Women was the sole representative of the independent women's movement in Poland. The organization claimed continuity with the prewar formation of the same name (founded in 1913), and its leadership was initially separated from the party—only in 1951 was Irena Sztachelska replaced by the

---

14 Fidelis, *Women, Communism, and Industrialization in Postwar Poland*.
15 Archives of New Record, 3–29.
16 Archives of New Record, 3–29.

Workers' Party representative, Alicja Musiałowa.[17] The league, unlike the Polish Wokers' Party, was popular among women "in the field," and some party officials wanted to keep it that way, hoping to introduce communist influence into the movement quietly. "The work in the field is spoiled by the party officials, we are called 'communists' said one of the local representatives at a WD meeting in 1946[18]. "We should influence women through the League of Women, but without the label of the Polish Workers Party." The head of the department, Edwarda Orłowska, however, wanted the battle for women's support for communism to be clear. She hoped that the work of her comrades would help overcome a cultural resistance to communism. "The fear of the Polish Workers Party will be deafened when we are able to solve women's problems appropriately," she said. "If our comrades work properly within the League, they will be able to gain trust, and the women will understand that this is a party that defends their interests and stands behind them."[19]

The New Polish State and the Needs of Working Mothers: Women's Press

After 1945, the women's press was an important propaganda tool—between 1945 and 1948 the League of Women published ten titles, including the *Kobieta* [Woman] weekly, headed by Janina Broniewska, a well-known editor, communist, and close friend of Wanda Wasilewska. The magazine's first goal was to convince women to support the new regime and to urge them to become active, mostly as workers. *Kobieta* was a mouthpiece of the League of Women and Women's Department. The social and systemic changes introduced by the "new Poland" were represented as progressive and transformative, constitutive of women's subjectivity as workers, citizens, and family partners: "Far behind us are the times when a woman swore her obedience to her husband, the gesture

---

17   Until 1966, the League of Women also had workplace units that were abolished, presumably as a reaction to its involvement against massive layoffs of women in 1958, which resulted in a significant drop in its membership from two million to seventy thousand. The League of Women returned to the workplace in 1981 after the announcement of martial law, as its leaders proclaimed full support for the actions of the Military Council of the National Salvation, the institution that represented an authoritarian socialist state.
18   Archives of New Record, 14.
19   Archives of New Record, 16.

which was a symbol of her unconditional subordination to the 'head of the family' stated one of the articles. Today marriage is a union of two free, independent people, who make a decision about mutual duties and the duties towards their potential children."[20] The editors of the magazine were, however, aware that in the 1940s Polish familial versions of patriotism and nationalism were still a dominant form of creating cultural-symbolic belonging. They were thus cautious not to attack existing social practices: the magazine intertwined politically engaging articles with pieces about fashion and cooking and respected the Catholic calendar of holidays: including Easter and All Saints' Day.

In the majority of articles equality at home was represented by a precondition for women's equality at work and many authors argued that as much as wage work had no gender, the same was true with housework. In the weekly, discussions about a woman's place at work was accompanied by a debate on the status of housework, in which communist ideas about women's work were discussed along with two models that were promoted by the state: one that assumed more engagement of men in housework and the other that called for socialization of domestic work. In 1948 Wanda Melcer wrote: "We can only agree (that young girls should be trained for housework) if we consider housework of young people regardless of sex, as we assume that everybody works at home, and everybody has the same responsibilities. There is nothing in housework that should be considered the work of a man or woman, a boy or girl."[21] Socialization of housework was also seen as complementary to the idea of shared responsibility for house chores. Irena Gumowska, the director of the Household Institute, argued:

> Today's women must and want to work. It is in the state's interest.... Working 7-8 hours, as much as a man does, a woman has no possibility or energy for good housekeeping.... Today, as we could not modernize individual households, we created the most rational thing in postwar Poland: various forms of socialized households. These include, in the first place, cafeterias, childcare facilities, and kindergartens. Then: mother and children homes,[22] socialized launderettes, social bakeries in the country side, and service cooperatives.[23]

Kobieta was geared toward envisioning the diversity of women's concerns, mostly across the social classes—struggles of working-class women were

---

20   Staniszkis, "Równość kobiet w miejscu pracy," 7.
21   Melcer, "Instytut Gospdarstwa Domowego," 8.
22   Domy matki i dziecka.
23   Gumowska, "Institute of Household Affairs," 4.

presented in conflict with bourgeois women's interests. Issues of nationalism remained untouched and female ethnic homogeneity in Poland was assumed in the majority of articles. Moreover, the idea of shared Polishness was strategically used in several texts. For example, postwar Polish regulations related to homemaking were seen as having far-reaching consequences, and *Kobieta* editors were not afraid to present them as a national issue. "The fate of the nation lies in food" read the title of one article in which the author argued: "Women who work like men do not have time to take care of the kitchen alone.... From the point of view of the state and science, new possibilities are now opening up, we have new opportunities for intervening in the process of food consumption, a biological matter of the individuals of whom the nation consists."[24]

Regardless of the hopes and beliefs of many prewar communists, national rhetoric proved to be most attractive when talking about the emancipation provisions introduced after 1945. In spring 1948, Edwarda Orłowska discussed the new regulation regarding protection of pregnant women in the following way:

> 28 April 1948 will forever be a day written in gold in Polish legislation. On this day Polish working women received the most progressive legislation in the world, one that ensures that a woman-mother receives the most sufficient care.... Until today the law did not protect pregnant women from the possibility of losing their job during their most vulnerable time.... In pre-September [prewar] Poland the employer had the right, and often tried to get rid of the female employee when she was pregnant.... The new law was based upon the burning wishes of hundreds of thousands of Polish working women. It responds to the very crucial demographic needs of our nation. It demonstrates our Democratic People's Republic's full commitment to care for the human being: mother and child.[25]

While the "new Polish state" was represented as promoting working-class women, prewar Poland was painted as oppressive to workers. This criticism constituted a context for condemning the work of prewar women's movements. "Since the last World War [since 1918] women in Poland have been passive in organizational life, they had no impact on the social and political life and the content of the legislation," one editor of *Kobieta* weekly wrote in 1948: "Interwar women's organizations cared more about official balls and representation than the rights of working women. It was only the new Poland that radically changed women's rights."[26]

---

24   "The Fate of the Nation Lies in the Family," 22.
25   Orłowska, Where a Woman," 5.
26   Staniszkis, "Równość kobiet, 3

During the early postwar period developments in Poland were often discussed in the context of the situation of women in other countries. Systemic solutions regarding housework were not accounted for as specific to Poland or even as trademarks of socialist emancipation but as global economic issues. Given the growing number of working women worldwide, the editors argued, solving an issue of domestic work required moving away from the traditional gender division of labor "at home." Showing communist emancipation in a broader international context played an important role in promoting the communist visions of equality and legitimizing it in generally anticommunist society. In the late 1940s modern emancipation was represented as a model passed on from the Soviet Union, and the provisions introduced in Poland were claimed to be coherent with development, both behind Poland's eastern border and in western world. For example, the modernization of households and socialization of some chores by moving them to the public domain were seen as part of a process of converging with more civilized and advanced countries in the world. In 1948 Irena Gumowska wrote: "Women are unable to take care of households not only because they are tired, but also because they do not have the time [...] We have not managed to modernize our homes, make them more 'technically advanced', as other countries have [...] In our conditions and today's technical advancement, preparing dinner for three people takes two to three hours. In France it is 10–30 minutes. In America 10–15 minutes."[27]

While presenting the examples of advancement in other countries, the magazine fed into the desire to "catch-up with the west": a cultural narrative omnipresent in Polish culture since the nineteenth century. Yet the magazine also attempted to dislocate the West as a leader in women's emancipation, and evidence that progress in the area of women's emancipation takes place in socialist Poland as well. In 1948 one of the editors wrote: "I think that it is nice to hear how people live in America, or Australia, but we do not have to go to Sydney to find examples of men who help housewives in their duties. Far closer, on Puławska Street [in Warsaw], I know of a young father, a clerk, who at nights helps his wife, and in Żoliborz [a Warsaw district] I know of a happy father of four who shares his duties evenly with his wife and takes care of his children day and night, feeding his several-month-old babies."[28]

---

27 "Gospodarstwo domowe," 10.
28 Łempicka, "Praca domowa dziewcząt," 8.

From Local to Global and Back: Polish Women and International Activism after 1945

The archives of the Polish Workers' Party and Polish United Workers' Party suggest that during the immediate postwar period, women's equality was to a large extent conceptualized as a political issue at both the international and local levels. International women's activists and politicians, both communists and socialists, emphasized the role of women as peace fighters. The Women's International Democratic Federation (founded in 1945) became a major venue for antiwar, antifascist, and anticapitalist activism of women from East and West.[29] The agenda of the international women's movement after World War II correlated with the broader aims of the new socialist state, which focused on fighting the devastating effects of war on Poland and working toward representing "new democracies" at the international level, including within the Women's International Democratic Federation (WIDF)—a beacon of women's emancipation. Consequently, in narratives of Polish WIDF representatives, fighting the capitalist and imperialist "reactionaries" was concurrent with an overall international agenda for peacemaking and progression in women's rights. References to the specificity of the Polish context and national identity permeated public appearances of communist delegates to transnational women's gatherings organized by the Women's International Democratic Federation. In the international sphere the specificity of the "Polish experience" rested on the assumed homogeneity of Poles while the cultural-ethnic diversity of victims, in particular Jews, of the war was not mentioned. During the Second WIDF Congress in 1948, Edwarda Orłowska, a Polish-Jewish communist stated:

> I speak here in the name of women from one of the countries most devastated by Hitler's fascism. We still mourn and weep for 6 million Polish men, women, and children killed during the war. One must see the ruins of our capital, Warsaw, in order to understand the full meaning of the word "war": "war," a word so lightly played with by those who know how to profit from it, how to turn blood into gold. It is not astonishing that Polish women are fighting with all their strength to safeguard peace and freedom.[30]

Delegates from Poland present at WIDF conferences conformed to the general massage asserting that progress in the area of women's rights is possible only under state socialism. Their speeches emphasized the dedication to the idea that

---

29   De Haan,"Ten Years After: Communism and Feminism Revisited," 102–29.
30   WIDF, *Second Women's International Congress*, 169.

elimination of reactionary forces—imperialism, capitalism, and religious fundamentalism active both locally and globally—was crucial to achieving such progress. During the Second Women's Congress in 1948, Izolda Kowalska, a representative of the League of Polish Women, declared:

> We promise to tighten our ranks of Polish women around our Federation even more to fight actively with it against the menace of imperialist war, against the forces of international reaction, against the forces of imperialism.[31]

Internationally, references to Polish identity intensified after the 1956 "thaw." During that period the idea of the "Polish road to socialism" aimed at building a political order while referring to old "gender contract"; the socialist state's emancipation projects was reformulated as resting on the traditional family, to which the figure of "Mother Pole" remained crucial. Added emphasis on national motherhood as a profound role for women was noticeable in the ways in which the Polish representative, Wanda Piemiczna, spoke at the Fourth Congress on "defense of life" in Vienna in June 1958:

> We, Polish women, who suffered particularly thoughout the war, want to continue to work in peace as we have done in the past 13 years.... In our country there is no one family that was not directly affected by the horrors of war. We lost 6 million people and that means that in our country there is no woman who has not lost either her husband, son, brother or daughter. I personally lost my husband, my only son, and one of my daughters, and I myself made the terrible acquaintance of concentration camps.... As a mother and grandmother, as a Pole, as a Catholic, as Deputy of the Polish Provincial Parliament, I am conscious of this.[32]

Emancipation through "Practical Activism": Discrimination and Women's Agencies under State Socialism (1956–1989)

The Women's Departments of the PSP and PWP merged in 1948 and continued their work to facilitate women's participation in the workforce, including provisions for working mothers like maternity leave, childcare (such as factory daycare centers, seasonal childcare in rural areas), the liberalization of divorce and parental laws, health care for pregnant women and infants, nursing breaks, and breastmilk banks.[33] While the depoliticization of women's issues progressed

---

31   WIDF, *Second Women's International Congress*, 68–69.
32   WIDF, Fourth Congress of the Women's International Democratic Federation, 71.
33   Jarska, *Kobiety z marmuru*.

from late 1940, the time after Stalin's death brought about major effects on women's rights. In her 2012 book *Women, Communism, and Industrialization in Postwar Poland*, Małgorzata Fidelis characterized these changes as follows:

> On the one hand, coercion in the workplace decreased. Women could voice their views more freely, including those on persistent discrimination in the workplace and at home. Some were able to leave full-time employment, often in horrid conditions, and devote themselves to full-time homemaking, if they so wished. And the state liberalized its anti-abortion law, making the procedure more readily available.[34]

On the other hand, however, the "Polish road to socialism" proposed as a new political paradigm after 1956 sought to reconstitute the prewar gender contract; the new gender order was therefore inspired by traditional values and gender roles. In short from 1956 on, provisions introduced by the state were directed not at radical reconstitution of gender hierarchies at home and in the public sphere, but rather at maintaining the high percentage of women who worked while simultaneously assisting them in fulfilling traditional gender roles in the household.

The state remained the main locus of debates about equal rights and the crucial agent of implementation for emancipation policies, yet the year 1956 initiated a period of "practical activism."[35] In the 1950s, 1960s, and 1970s, women's emancipation was based on the idea of steady yet limited work toward improving the status of working women, and provisions on behalf of women's equality in the workplace were embedded in processes of modernization and the rationalization of the labor force and household.[36] While the immediate postwar political engagement of communist women can be seen as aiming at "bringing about effects and (re)constituting the world," 1950s women's activism was rule governed and occurred within the context of limited autonomy. After the dissolution of the Women's Department in 1952, the Polish United Workers' Party no longer had institutional tools that could lead to the steady advancement of women in politics. After 1956, Poland followed its own path to socialism, comprising socialist values mixed with traditional nationalism and a special place for the Catholic Church in the public sphere. The new version of women's

---

34   Fidelis, Małgorzata. *Women, Communism, and Industrialization in Postwar Poland*, 170.

35   The term "practical activism" was coined by historian Barbara Nowak in reference to the League of Polish Women's activism after 1945; see Nowak, "Where Do You Think I Learned How to Style My Own Hair?," 185–99.

36   Katarzyna, Stańczak-Wiślicz, "Household as a Battleground," 123.

emancipation was accompanied by the removal of the "old" communist activists—and Jewish women's activists, like Orłowska—from power. The traces of internationalism were ultimately eliminated from the Polish model of emancipation in 1968, when Polish politics became officially ethnically homogenous, and all Jewish women were relegated from the official positions at the League of Women.[37]

From the 1950s onward, the emancipatory measures undertaken by the state were more sympathetic to traditional perceptions of women's skills and features. For example, the need to promote women to higher positions was rationalized from the perspective of women's new roles, which were modified to fit presocialist beliefs about the characteristics of women (for example collectivism, responsibility, and submissiveness). Wiesława, a longtime director of a textile factory in Łódź, recalled a conversation she had with a party official: "In the textile industry there were a lot of women in higher positions, so I asked him once, 'How come you have promoted so many women?' And he replied, 'because I don't have to worry, I'm at peace with them. I can trust them and I don't have to supervise them. They don't fight with each other and they don't fight with me.'"[38]

The Committee for Household Economics, established in 1957, was an organization—quite elaborate in structure—that combined the promotion of women's economic emancipation with maintaining traditional gender roles. Unlike during the previous period, the activities of this new institution did not include challenging the gender division of labor at home. In the 1960s and 1970s in particular, the Committee for Household Economics and the League of Women focused on educating women for traditional gender roles that were to be combined with new roles in the labor market. In this sense, these institutions carried out the party's orders among women to facilitate the so-called double burden of life at work and in the home.

Although the concept of Mother Pole was widely utilized to connect state socialist emancipation with the older legacies of traditionalism and patriotism, during the post-1956 period it also acquired new meaning. Making motherhood a matter of public interest shaped women's sense of validity and provided some measure of agency through the roles related to motherhood. One of the female directors of a large institution recalled: "Employees were saying to me, one after another, first child, second child, pregnancy and maternity leave and parental leave, every time.... They said to me, 'I'm not giving birth for myself, I'm doing

---

37   Grabowska, *Zerwana genealogia*.
38   Interview by author with the deputy director of women's organisation.

it for society.' So they had a certain attitude.... Having children was not an individual choice for women, but the expression of a certain attitude, the recognition of motherhood as a social role that requires the support of society."[39]

After 1956, women also remained active in the public and political sphere and were able to bring about political changes crucial to women's equality, including the right to legal abortions. In 1956, during a heated debate about the new law in Polish parliament, women activists, and politicians, including Maria Jaszczukowa, Wanda Gościmińska, and Zofia Tomczyk, brought up important arguments on behalf of women's equality and well-being. Within the debate, references to women's freedom of choice and autonomy appeared alongside the socialist claim for the liberalization of the abortion law for health and social reasons. Zofia Tomczyk, a representative of a rural party (Polish Peasants' Party), stated for example: "The people's state gave women equal rights, created conditions for the implementation of these rights which are now being deepened.... It must be allowed that issues as important as bringing a new person into the world are decided by society, parents, and most of all the mother, with a strong sense of the responsibilities which are related to that."[40] In 1966, the government created a new body to promote women's political participation. The Women's Council consisted of Communist Party members and League of Women activists who were loyal to the authoritarian regime. In the view of some of its members, however, the council had some impact on the situation of women. "As a representative of the Women's League, I evaluated all the legislative initiatives, all the proposed legal changes. Then they were passed to the Sejm. So yes, we had an impact." During the crisis years of the early 1980s, the League of Women uniformly supported martial law. In 1981, the units of the league were brought back to workplaces, and the organization changed its name to the League of Polish Women. Supporting women economically, as well as mobilizing them for economic activity, became their unofficial focus.

"Catching Up with the West": Anticommunism and Post-1989 Women's Activism in Poland

Feminist activists during the transformation period served their communist foremothers with a harsh judgment, rendering the work of previous generations of women as ideological, superficial, and inauthentic. After 1989, the experience

---

39   Interview by author with the former head of the local branch of League of Women.
40   Sejm PRL, Kadencja I.

of communism was mostly seen as an obstacle to modernization, and overcoming the limitations created by a communist past was presented as a condition for the transition's success. The political and scholarly imperative of anticommunism became a hallmark of late twentieth-century Eastern European emancipation studies in the region and beyond. It helped to legitimize narratives of lack and delay and to construct the stereotypical image of the postsocialist woman as failing to enter the process of modernization or as delayed in the process of emancipation in comparison to the "Western world." Within such a vision, the Soviet style and socialist state women's organizations and policies were generally considered relics of a shameful past, representative of a Soviet mentality (passive, conformist, submissive) that was contradictory to the Western model of feminism: self-confident, progress oriented, and liberal. Communist emancipation was seen as not "native" to Poland, not Polish, but imposed from above by the imperialist Soviet Union. In the 1990s, in Poland and elsewhere around the world, researchers of history, sociology, cultural studies, and political theory seemed to be in agreement that Poland had not advanced far enough with regard to the right to legal abortion, maternal provisions, extended childcare, and the prominent presence of women in the labor market, all of which had been introduced in socialist states before the West. Rather, they considered the period of communism to be a move backward in the history of the Polish women's movement—one responsible both for the lack of feminism after state socialism and Eastern Europe's slow progress in women's rights and emancipation.[41]

The "narrative of lack" that dominated the postcommunist debate on feminism depended on a more fundamental argument about the impossibility of feminism after communism: a system that, it was claimed, hampered civic activities in Eastern Europe, including those on behalf of women's emancipation.[42] The inability (and unwillingness) of the socialist state to challenge Eastern European traditionalism and conservatism along with a strong collectivist orientation among these societies were listed as reasons why feminism remained "homeless" in the postsocialist states and remained "allergic" to the ideas of women's emancipation that centered on individual rights.[43] The discourse of delay complemented that of absence, while representing the development of Eastern European feminism simply as a variation of global Western movements. It portrayed the Eastern European transformations as conservative processes

---

41   Rosner, "Czy istnieje w Polsce ruch feministyczny?," 34; Walczewska, "Liga Kobiet: Jedyna organizacja kobieca w PRL," 4.
42   Goldfarb, "Why Is There No Feminism after Communism?," 236.
43   Marody, *"Why I Am Not a Feminist,"* 853; Snitow, *"Feminist Futures in the Former East Bloc,"* 39.

directed mostly at catching up with the West in the march toward modernity. Within mainstream political discourse, Poland's integration with the West was articulated as a leading objective for the transformation from an authoritarian regime to democracy. The desire to reach the West was seen as a historical necessity and an opportunity for societies previously belonging to the Eastern Bloc to erase the consequences of the failed communist experiment in the area of women's rights and social emancipation.

After 1989, some aspects of transformation in Poland—such as the reinforcement of the Catholic Church as a critical political actor (resulting in the introduction of religious education in school and a ban on abortion), the reemergence of ethnic nationalism (including the reinstatement of a number of openly nationalistic political parties and organizations), political conservatism, and a decrease in social welfare were problematic from the point of view of women's emancipation.[44] Yet, the concept of returning to or catching up with the West resonated (and still does) with many people, some of whom are feminists. From the 1990s onward, scholars, researchers, and activists broadly appropriated the experience and language of the "second wave" of Western feminism as their own. They used Western concepts and genealogies to construct individual and collective feminist subjectivities at various registers. At the individual level, identification with one of the streams of the Western emancipation movement was part of the formation of feminist subjectivity. In 2004, a feminist scholar declared in an interview: "My feminism is a liberal feminism. I mean it is a feminism of equality rather than difference. I'm closer to Betty Friedan."[45] At the collective register, scholars and activists widely used the metaphor of waves to assess the development of women's mobilization in Poland (or lack thereof) through the lens of American feminist history and without much attention to the local genealogies of the women's movement. Such appropriations posed fundamental methodological and chronological challenges (for example, the fact that women in Poland had a right to legal abortion from 1956, far earlier than women in most Western countries, did not fit the convergence narrative), yet the general idea that the West was the only logical point of reference for Eastern European feminisms persisted throughout the decades.[46]

---

44 Limanowska, "Pytania zadawane w cieniu pomnika," 43–46; Walczewska, "Jaki feminizm, czyli dokąd idzie Marianna?," 53–55.
45 Interview with feminist activists for author's doctoral thesis; Grabowska, "Between East and West."
46 Graff, "Lost between the Waves?," 100; Limanowska, "Zagubione w metodologii," 32.

At the institutional level in the mid-1990s, Western-style women's nongovernmental organizations replaced the initial service-organizing and consciousness-raising activism characteristic of the late 1980s.[47] While the former focused mostly on reacting to particular women's needs (for example, sexual and gender-based violence, economic inequalities), the latter centered on education (workshops, training for women), evaluation of government policies, and politics.[48] The objectives of post-1989 nongovernmental women's activism were often delineated by Western donors and represented what Kristen Ghodsee called "feminism by design": a women's movement shaped according to Western experience, expertise, and advice transmitted to Eastern Europe.[49] Cultural liberal feminism imported from Western Europe and the United States, highlighted the common oppression of all women and disregarded important differences between the experiences of women from Eastern Europe and the West, including the distinct paths of women's emancipation in the area of economics and sexual autonomy, as well as disparities between various female emancipation experiences from diverse economic backgrounds: for example, working-class and rural women.

While many women in Poland benefited from pre-1989 gender equality, communist emancipation was still strongly stigmatized as imposed by a foreign imperial power (Soviet Union). Older historical sentiments (looking down upon Russia) interfered with the possibility of more nuanced assessments of post-1945 history. At the normative register after 1989 "chasing the West" required symbolic separation from the "East"—Russia and its heir the Soviet Union—even if such a separation went against the past experience of a common history. One of the leaders of the women's movement said in a 2006 interview that "[w]e are in the sphere of Russia's influence. And if feminism in Russia were developed, if Russia were any kind of an intellectual centre, as America is, then [the dialogue with other post-state socialist feminisms] would make sense.... At this point, however, we think about Russians as barbarians."[50] Another activist argued that "Polish women, with our history and contemporary problems, are much closer to the West than to Russia or Ukraine."[51]

---

47 Grabowska, "Bringing Second World In," 385.
48 Hrycak, "From Mothers' Rights to Equal Rights," 66; Popa, "Translating Equality between Women and Men across Cold War Divides," 59.
49 Ghodsee, "Feminism-by-Design," 727–53.
50 Interview by author with feminist activists.
51 Interview by author.

Narratives of lack and convergence represented Polish women and entire Polish society as conservative, unwilling to change, passive, and unable to act; in short, as opposed to an active and dynamic West. Polish anthropologist Michał Buchowski examined the process of self-orientalization—a process of creating "the other" and producing symbolic divisions within Polish society—as characteristic of the 1989 transformation.[52] He argued that in the 1990s the subjective production of the winners of the transformation—a civilized "us" who were able to conform to the values of individualism and liberalism—was accompanied by the production of "others": incompetent and anti-intellectual masses unable to join the Polish march toward the West. Passivity and the inability to change and achieve progress were important features of *Homo Sovieticus*, which became the embodiment of the transformation's other.

During the transformation anticommunism played an important role in dividing groups of people into "good" and "bad" citizens. This division permeated feminist movement as well. Some groups of feminist activists were able to establish new ways of doing feminism, according to Western standards, while others fell into the category of the unwanted legacy of the communist past (e.g., the League of Women). In the 1990s a turn to a "foreign" but Western genealogy was seen as a strategy that allowed feminism to become an important part of mainstream political debates. The common criticism against feminism has been, and continues to be, that it is unpatriotic or "un-Polish" because its politics are fed by foreign ideas: in the present by Western liberal feminism and in the past by a Soviet-style emancipation narrative and practices. To avoid such a label, some feminists have publicly evoked their commitment to the national community while denying any relations with the communist past. Sławomira Walczewska explained this approach as follows: "On the one hand, there was a need to articulate oneself; on the other, we had to separate ourselves from the representation of feminism as a regrowing head of [the] Hydra of Marxism."[53] The objective of incorporating feminism into the Polish public sphere required an appropriation of Western-style feminist knowledge production and activism as the template of any feminist mobilizing and progress in women's rights. The exclusion of the more local legacies of socialist-style emancipation was the byproduct of this shift. What started as a survival strategy during the transition had, after decades, become a mainstay of feminism in Poland.

Until today, the depiction of communist activists as foremothers of the women's movement in Poland seems to be an aberration. Anticommunism prevailed as a powerful tool that set the horizon of Polish contentions for subjectivity,

---

52   Buchowski, "The Specter of Orientalism in Europe," 463.
53   Walczewska, "Jaki feminizm, czyli dokąd idzie Marianna?," 53–55.

marking the boundaries of the feminist archives, understood broadly as preserving, documenting, and producing and collecting history of the feminist movements, at the individual and collective level. In 2014, Agnieszka Graff, a prominent Polish feminist scholar, activist, and author of a number of canonical texts about Polish feminism and the nation, argued: "For me this [current interest in communist women's activism in Eastern Europe] is interesting, as a piece of Poland's history, as a piece of women's history. But it is absolutely not convincing to me as my own history. These are not my roots.... The idea that the people who created the women's units within the [Communist] Party are my foremothers is absolutely not convincing to me. They are not my foremothers!"[54]

In recent years, scholars in the humanities, social sciences, and arts have made significant efforts to reclaim the voices and experiences of communist women as part of the trajectories of Polish emancipation movements. Literary critics and art historians are making biographical attempts—based on literature and memoirs[55] as well as artworks created by communist women[56]—to recover firsthand accounts of experiences. These works are most often concerned with the evolution of the communist consciousness and the experiences of actively contributing to the systemic transformation brought by the communists to postwar Poland. Historians' and anthropologists' work with press and media accounts, specialist literature,[57] and institutional archives[58] is set in the realm of "historical facts" and social processes that may (or may not) be indicative of women's emancipation after 1945. The ongoing research goes against silencing, discounting, and ignoring state socialism as part of emancipatory genealogy, which remains the cornerstone of feminist subjectivity. They break the symbolic boundary between "us" and "them," calling for transgression of the symbolic boundary of feminist archives. As such they also propose new ways of conceptualizing feminist history, not in terms of synchronic "waves" (or generations) but rather through the delineation of vertical, diachronic connectivities between various groups and individuals engaged in feminist struggles.[59] Such an approach shifts an emphasis from the (collective) identity and focuses on the

---

54 Graff and Sutowski, *Jestem stąd*.
55 Artwińska and Mrozik, *Gender, Generation, and Communism*.
56 Talarczyk-Gubała and Jakubowska, Warszawa: Wydawnictwo Krytyki Politycznej.
57 Klich-Kluczewska, *Rodzina, tabu i komunizm w Polsce 1956–1989*; Kościańska, *Płeć, przyjemność i przemoc*.
58 Nowakowska-Wierzchoś, "Społeczno-Obywatelska Liga Kobiet 1945–1949."
59 Weigel, *Generation*.

inherited, transgenerational memory and transmission of experiences within the movement.[60]

What seems to be obvious from recent accounts of the feminist past and the presence of feminism in Poland is that the 1945–1989 period brought about a "gender revolution" that the majority of the Polish society perhaps "slept through."[61] The immense diversity of female experiences under communism and state socialism warns us against broad generalizations that were characteristic of the past approaches to the history of postwar women's emancipation in Poland. Neglecting the "forgotten gender revolution" could be argued as one of the reasons for the current identity issues experienced by the Polish women's movement. As long as these fundamental changes introduced in the postwar period are not recognized as part of emancipatory genealogy in Poland and part of the feminist archive, the narratives of patriotism and liberalism that often ignore histories of local struggles for social justice will permeate the women's movement with the effect of alienation and misunderstanding of its own emancipation trajectories.

Between Past and Present: New Challenges for the Contemporary Emancipation Movement in Poland

While in the mid-1990s activism on behalf of gender equality in the region was driven by two transnational tendencies, institutionalization and professionalization, in the first decades of the 2000s the movement experimented with ideas of "feminist patriotism." Transnational shifts were strongly related to global transformations; broader processes of political, social, and economic dislocation; and transition from a bipolar to a unipolar world dominated by the supranational market economy. In Eastern Europe accession and then membership in the European Union meant more interaction with Western-developed ideas

---

60 Artwińska and Mrozik, *Gender, Generation and Communism.*
61 In *Sleepwalking through a Revolution* (2014) Andrzej Leder argues that in Poland the period between 1939 and 1956 can be seen as an "unconscious revolution" that the majority of the country "slept through." Postwar upward mobility of the rural and working classes benefited Polish society to an extent but because it was the result of violence in which Poles participated in, this revolution was accompanied by an unconscious feeling of moral guilt. Consequently, radical changes that transformed Polish society during the war and immediate postwar period are by and large experienced passively, as something that happened to them rather than something they had an active hand in. See Leder, *Prześniona rewolucja..*

and strategies influencing the agendas of local NGOs. Locally European Union's gender mainstreaming policy helped to incorporate progressive policies on gender equality into nation-state agendas.[62]

In the last two decades in Poland, marked by dominance of nationalism and right-wing populism, Polish feminism was weighed down with a sense of failure when it came to attracting many women to the ideas of Western-style feminism. Many scholars and activists publicly criticized earlier feminist entanglements with (neo)liberal policies, claiming that the alliance between feminism and liberalism might have been responsible for further distancing the movement from "women's masses." They saw "feminist patriotism" as a way of reconnecting the movement to local emancipatory struggles (e.g., the Solidarity movement) and mainstream Polish history.[63] It was hoped that subversive usages of national symbols would make feminism more visible and relevant to wider female audiences. The examples from the Congress of Women (where the national anthem is sung at the opening sessions), equality parades (whose participants hold Polish national flags alongside rainbow ones and begin the march with the national anthem), 2016 Black Protest (with national flags and patriotic symbols such as those related to World War II), and 2018 feminist celebrations of one hundred years of women having the right to vote (which focused on "Polish women," but did not acknowledge how independence and the right to vote affected various groups of women-citizens living in Poland at that time) demonstrated that utilizing the national imaginary can be a successful strategy to attract women to the feminist cause(s). The turn toward patriotic narratives and feminist engagement with mainstream governmental politics brought the long-awaited recognition of feminism as a local legacy (as opposed to being represented as a "Western import" or "Soviet ideology"). Using patriotic narratives helped feminism become visible and relevant to wider female audiences and allowed feminist thought to free itself from exclusion and marginalization—as well as helping to represent it as part of the national tradition.

Yet "feminist patriotism" has fewer desirable consequences within the movement itself. Excluding certain groups of people (non-Polish women, Polish non-women, and trans women) from the struggle is one of them. Inability to address "marginal" or "controversial" problems such as rights of immigrant women, trans people, and also the right to abortion is another. At the symbolic register "patriotic feminism" represented a gesture of "bending a knee" to the dominant "historical politics" that center on Polish exceptionalism, ideas of national

---

62 Rawłuszko, "Gender Mainstreaming Revisited," 70–84.
63 Graff, "Polskość nie jest Własnością Endeków."

interest, and assumed homogeneity of Polish society. With this act feminism lost its critical edge, relevance, and ability go beyond what it set out to be—an acceptable horizon of Polishness. It became a reactionary movement rather than one able to create the new language of politics.[64]

Interestingly, while they were still very much present in 2016, black protests, women's strikes (mass street demonstrations organized against a threat of further restrictions of the abortion law in Poland), and references to patriotism were marginal during October 2020 (mass demonstrations organized after the abortion law was restricted by Constitutional Tribunal) and the later mobilizations against further restrictions of abortion rights.[65] This new wave of protests attracted by far the most people in the history of the Polish emancipation movement. They were quite different from previous protests. Significantly intersectionality and inclusion, solidarity, and empathy became the trademark of recent protests that combined struggles against gender, racial, ethnic, class discrimination, building strong alliances with LGBTQ, youth climate strike, and social and economic rights movements. They were unique in many other ways too. First, it was an overwhelming collective sense of women's fury that drove these protests (think of today's #MeToo movement. Anger and outright rage were well manifested in the protest slogans, among them: "Get the fuck out" ("wypierdalać"), and "fuck PiS" (***** ***) (PiS being the ruling party). The vulgar language did not, as some feared, diminish the struggle's purpose. To the contrary, it helped move from a position of passive recipient of mainstream politics to that of an active agent impacting what is acceptable. As the writer and academic Inga Iwasiów put it: "The moment we started being vulgar, the other side started to listen."

Indeed, almost overnight the political debate in Poland shifted, and feminism was able to move from a reactionary position to a proactive place. Women's groups, such as All Poland Women's Strike (co-organizer of protests demanding full abortion rights), and Abortion Dream Team (referral collective that helps women mange abortions at home), previously deemed "to radical" even for some feminists became a proper partner in mainstream political debates and drew attention from major media outlets. They were no longer framed as

---

64   Ramme, "Framing Solidarity," 469–84; Zawadzka, "Polityka mimikry," 56–62.
65   The most immediate reason for this mobilization was the ruling of the Constitutional Tribunal, the political body that, according to many observers, is no longer independent from the ruling right-wing party, Law and Justice. In simple terms, on October 22, the Tribunal, led by a woman judge, ruled that abortion for fetal defects is unconstitutional, Graff "Gdzie się podziały?"

a "radical minority" and extremists that have to be silenced for the sake of the balanced middle.

The extent of engagement among young people, mostly women—often deemed to be apolitical and ignored by politicians and feminists—was very telling as well. Their generation grew up in a social reality of consecutive governments (both "liberal" and conservative) depending on the church's political support, militarization, and nationalism; it was the moment to articulate their political subjectivity. The possible impact that "minority" groups can have on Poland's future was signaled through the rhetoric of threat and fear expressed by the ruling party as a reaction to protests. The head of Law and Justice Party Jarosław Kaczyński called for the "defense of Poland, and the Catholic Churches," and warned that the new movements are "intended to destroy Poland," aiming at "the end of . . . the Polish nation as we know it."

Conclusion

This chapter focused on examining ways in which the political subjectiveness of Polish emancipation movements has been constructed over the last century, in reference to various dominant identity narratives. My analysis suggests that emancipation political projects after 1945 and after 1989 were rooted in the challenging attempts at Polish uniformity. Their practices were, no less than other identity formations, conditioned by the structures of political and discursive power and domination.

Explorations of the post-1945 and post-1989 past may seem unimportant in light of current affairs related to Polish emancipation. However, paying attention to the communist period and facing its failures and successes provide a means to break from the cycle of retribution and appropriation that adversely affect feminist identities and practices in the region. It helps to overcome their quandary of being confined to a choice between liberal cultural feminism "imported" from the West, and "patriotic feminism" imposed by traditionalist, and conservative, social and cultural context. Examining the postwar Polish women's emancipation project exemplifies the plurality of voices and experiences that coexisted within this endeavor. Yet it also illuminates the extent to which normative ideas about "Polish society" and "Polish women" impacted even the most politically progressive and egalitarian political projects. Seeing post-1945 and post-1989 emancipation struggles in the context of continuity rather than the "broken genealogy" illustrates that questions and strategic choices faced by the contemporary feminist movement in Poland are not "new." They are also not the same as the issues faced by postwar women's activists. Rather, they are part of the same genealogy of women's emancipation and the ongoing debate about the Polish feminist identity, a debate that engages various actors, some of which do not meet a narrow definition of "feminism" and/or "Polishness."

Bibliography

Archives of New Record. Protocols of Women's Department of Polish United Workers Party (Protokół z zebrania aktywu warszawskiego (odbitka), 27 maja 1946 r., in Wydział Kobiecy PPR, sytuacja i zatrudnienie kobiet w Polsce—protokoły, sprawozdania, okólniki, instrukcje, uchwały, opracowania, korespondencja, sygn. 295/XVI, (1946), 14–16.

Archives of New Record. Protocols of Women's Department of Polish United Workers Party (Protokół z Krajowej Odprawy Kierowniczek Wojewódzkich Wydziałów Kobiecych odbytej dnia 19 maja 1949 r., in Archiwum Akt Nowych (1949–1951). Polska Zjednoczona Partia Robotnicza, Komitet Centralny, Wydział Kobiecy), 237/XV-1 (1949), 3–29.

Artwińska, Anna. "Transfer międzypokoleniowy, epigenetyka i "więzy krwi." O Małej Zagładzie Anny Janko i Granicy zapomnienia Siergieja Lebiediwewa, in Teksty Drugie 1 (2016), 13.

Buchowski, Michał. "The Specter of Orientalism in Europe: From Exotic Other to Stigmatized Brother." *Anthropological Quarterly* 79, no. 3 (2006): 463.

Cerwonka, Allaine. "Traveling Feminist Thought: Difference and Transculturation in Central and Eastern European Feminism." *Signs: Journal of Women in Culture and Society* 33, no. 4 (2008): 809.

De Haan, Francisca, ed. "Gendering the Cold War in the Region. An Email Conversation Between Malgorzata (Gosia) Fidelis, Renata Jambrešić Kirin, Jill Massino, and Libora Oates-Indruchova". *Aspasia The International Yearbook of Central, Eastern, and Southeastern European Women's and Gender History* 8 (2014): 162.

De Haan, Francisca, ed. "Ten Years After: Communism and Feminism Revisited." I*Aspasia: The International Yearbook of Central, Eastern, and Southeastern European Women's and Gender History* 10 (2016): 102.

Evans Clements, Barbara. "Bolshevik Feminist: The Life of Aleksandra Kollontai." Bloomington: University of Indiana Press, 1979.

Evans Clements, Barbara. *Daughters of Revolution: A History of Women in the U.S.S.R.* Wheeling, IL: Harlan Davidson 1994.

Fidelis, Małgorzata. *Women, Communism, and Industrialization in Postwar Poland.* New York: Cambridge University Press, 2010.

Foucault, Michel. *Discipline and Punish: The Birth of the Prison*, trans. Alan Sheridan. New York: Pantheon, 1977.

Funk, Nanette. "Feminist Critiques of Liberalism: Can They Travel East? Their Relevance in Eastern and Central Europe and the Former Soviet Union." *Signs Journal of Women in Culture and Society* 29, no. 3 (2004): 695.

Fuszara, Małgorzata. "New Gender Relationships in Poland in 1990s." In *Reproducing Gender: Politics, Publics, and Everyday Life after Socialism* edited by Gal and Kligman, 259. Princeton, NJ: Princeton University Press, 2000.

Ghodsee, Kristen. "Rethinking State Socialist Mass Women's Organizations: The Committee of the Bulgarian Women's Movement and the United Nations Decade for Women, 1975–1985." *Journal of Women's History* 24, no. 4 (2012): 49.

Goldfarb, Jeffrey. "Why Is There No Feminism after Communism?" *Social Research* 64, no. 2 (1997): 236.

Grabowska, Magdalena. "*Polish Feminism between East and West: The Formation of the Polish Women's Movement Identity.*" PhD diss., Rutgers University, 2019.

Grabowska, Magdalena. "Bringing Second World In: Conservative Revolution(s), Socialist Legacies and Transnational Silences in the Trajectories of Polish Feminism." *Signs: Journal of Women in Culture and Society* 37, no. 2 (2012): 385.

Górnicka-Boratyńska, Aneta *Chcemy całego życia* (Warszawa: Fundacja Res Publica, 1999).

Grabowska, Magdalena, *Between East and West: The Formation of Polish Women's Movement Identity*. PhD diss., Rutgers University, 2009. https://rucore.libraries.rutgers.edu/rutgers-lib/26287/.

Graff, Agnieszka. *Świat bez kobiet. Płeć w polskim życiu publicznym*. Warsaw: WAB, 2001.

Graff, Agnieszka "Lost between the Waves? The Paradoxes of Feminist Chronology and Activism in Contemporary Poland." *Journal of International Women's Studies* 4, no. 2 (April 2003): 100.

Graff, Agnieszka. *Rykoszetem. Rzecz o płci, seksualności i narodzie*. Warszawa: WAB, 2008.

Graff, Agnieszka, and Michal Sutowski. *Jestem stąd*. Warsaw: Krytyka Polityczna 2014.

Graff, Agnieszka. Gdzie jesteś, polski feminizmie? Pochwała sporu i niejasności [Where are you Polish feminism?] speech at the Heinrich Böll Foundation Conference, 2 June 2014. https://pl.boell.org/sites/default/files/uploads/2014/05/graff_referat_kobiety_solidarnosci.pdf (access: 25 November 2017).

Graff, Agnieszka, Gdzie się podziały „macice wyklęte?" In *Język rewolucji*, Warsaw: Fundacja Batorego 2021: 23.

Grzebalska, Weronika. *Płeć powstania warszawskiego*. Warsaw: IBL PAN 2014.

Gumowska, Irena. "Institute of Household Affairs." *Kobieta*, 1948.

Hrycak, Aleksandra. "From Mothers' Rights to Equal Rights: Post-Soviet Grassroots Women's Associations." In *Women's Activism and Globalization. Linking Local Struggles and Transnational Politics,* edited by N. A. Naples, M. Desai, 66. New York: Routledge 2002.

Ilić, Melanie. "Soviet Women, Cultural Exchange and the Women's International Democratic Federation. In *Reassessing Cold War Europe*, Routledge Studies in the History of Russia and Eastern Europe, edited by S. Autio and K. Miklóssy, 157. Abingdon, Oxon: Routledge 2011.

Jarska, Natalia. Kobiety z marmuru. Robotnice w Polsce w latach 1945–1960, Warsaw: Instytut Pamięci Narodowej, 2015.

Jarska. Natalia. "Rural Women, Gender Ideologies, and Industrialization in State Socialism: The Case of a Polish Factory in the 1950s." *Aspasia. International Yearbook of Central, Eastern, and Southeastern European Women's and Gender History* 9 (2015): 65–86.

Jacobsson, Kristen, Korolczuk, Elżbieta, eds. *Civil Society Revisited: Lessons from Poland.* New York: Berghahn Books, 2017.

Janion, Maria. *Niesamowita Słowiańszczyzna.* Warsaw: Wydawnictwo Literackie, 2006.

Jarska, Natalia. "Rural Women, Gender Ideologies, and Industrialization in State Socialism: The Case of a Polish Factory in the 1950s." *Aspasia: The International Yearbook of Central, Eastern, and Southeastern European Women's and Gender History* 9 (2015): 65.

Kałwa, Dobrohna. "Przemoc i zapomnienie. Druga wojna światowa z perspektywy płci kulturowej." In *Kobieta i historia. Od niewidzialności do sprawczości,* edited by K. Bałżewska, A. Korczyńska-Partyka. A. Wódkowska, 27. Gdańsk: Wydawnictwo Uniwersytetu Gdańskiego, 2015.

Klich-Kulczewska, Katarzyna "Making up for the losses of war: Reproduction politics in Postwar Poland." In *Women and Men at War: A Gender Perspective on World War II and its Aftermath in Central and Eastern Europe,* edited by R. Leiserowitz and M. Röger, 307. Osnabrück: fibre Verlag, 2012.

Kondratowicz, Ewa. *Szminka na Sztandarze.* Warsaw: Sic! 2001.

Korolczuk, Elżbieta. "Explaining 'Black Protests' Against Abortion Ban in Poland. Poland for Beginners", at: Krytyka Polityczna 2016. http://krytykapolityczna.pl/wydarzenia/explaining-black-protests-against-abortion-ban-in-poland-poland-for-beginners/. Accessed January 31, 2018.

Korolczuk, Elżbieta. "Promoting Civil Society in Contemporary Poland: Gendered Results of Institutional Changes." *International Journal of Voluntary and Nonprofit Organizations,* 25, no. 4 (2014): 949.

Korolczuk, Elżbieta, and Renata Hryciuk. "At the Intersection of Gender and Class: Social Mobilization around Mothers' Rights in Poland." In *Beyond NGO-ization? The Development of Social Movements in Central and Eastern Europe,* edited by K. Jacobsson and S. Saxonberg, 49. Farnham, UK: Ashgate, 2013.

Kościańska, Agnieszka. Płeć, *przyjemność i przemoc.* Kształtowanie wiedzy eksperckiej o seksualności w Polsce. Warsaw: Wydawnictwa Uniwersytetu Warszawskiego 2014.

Kubik, Jan, and Amy Lynch, eds. Postcommunism from Within: Social Justice, Mobilization, and Hegemony. New York: New York University Press, 2013.

Leder, Andrzej. Prześniona rewolucja. Ćwiczenia z logiki historycznej. Warsaw: Wydawnictwo Krytyki Politycznej, 2014.

Łempicka, Wanda, „Praca domowa dziewcząt". *Kobieta* 3 (1947): 6.

Limanowska, Barbara. "Zagubione w metodologii." Zadra 3–4 (2007): 32.

Mazowiecki, Tadeusz. "Przemówienie Tadeusza Mazowieckiego przed Zgromadzeniem Parlamentarnym Rady Europy w Strasburgu." *Więź* 4 (1990). http://laboratorium.wiez.pl/2016/11/21/odradzanie-sie-europy/. Accessed November 14, 2017.

Melcer, Wanda. "Instytut Gospodarstwa Domowego." *Kobieta* 4 (1948): 7.

Mrozik, Agnieszka. "Dziadek (nie) był komunistą". Między/transgeneracyjna pamięć o komunizmie w polskich (auto)biografiach rodzinnych po 1989 roku," *Teksty Drugie* 1 (2016): 46.

Mrozik, Agnieszka. "Nieobecne, ale użyteczne. O pożytkach z komunistek w polskim dyskursie publicznym po 1989 roku." *Sporne postaci polskiej krytyki feministycznej*, edited by Monika Świerkosz, 171. Gdańsk: Wydawnictwo Naukowe Katedra, 2016.

Marody, Mira. "Why I Am Not a Feminist." *Social Research* 4 (1993): 853.

Nowak, Barbara. "Serving Women and the State: The League of Women in Communist State." PhD diss., Ohio State University, 2004.

Nowak, Basia. "'Where Do You Think I Learned How to Style My Own Hair?' Gender and Everyday Lives of Women Activists in Poland's League of Women." In. *Gender Politics and Everyday Life in State Socialist Eastern and Central Europe*, edited by Shana Penn and Jill Massino. New York: Palgrave Macmillan, 2009.

Nowakowska-Wierzchoś, Anna. "Związałyśmy się z siłami demokratycznymi w Polsce: program polityczny i wizja roli kobiet w 'nowej Polsce' Związku Kobiet Polskich im. Marii Konopnickiej we Francji 1944–1950." In *Kobiety "na zakręcie" 1933–1989*, edited by E. Chabros and A. Klarman. Wrocław: Instytut Pamięci Narodowej, 2014.

Orłowska, Edwarda. Protocol of the Meeting of the Warsaw's Women's Cadres, May 27, 1946 (speech), Archive of New Records, Warsaw.

Orłowska, Edwarda. WIDF (Women's International Democratic Federation) (1948) (speech). Second Women's International Congress, Budapest, Hungary, December 1–6, 1948. Paris: Women International Democratic Federation.

Orłowska, Edwarda. "Po co owijać w bawełnę?" *Kobieta* 48 (1948): 5.

Orłowska, Edwarda. "Tam gdzie kobieta jest dyrektorem." *Kobieta* 47 (1948): 4.

Penn, Shana. *Solidarity's Secret. The Women Who Defeated Communism in Poland*. Ann Arbor: University of Michigan Press, 2005.

Penn, Shana. "The National Secret." *Journal of Women's History* 5, no. 3 (1994): 55.

Piemiczna, Wanda. WIDF, IV Congress of the Women's International Democratic Federation (speech) Vienna 1–3 June 1958, conference on "Defense of Life." Paris: Women International Democratic Federation (1958), 77.

Popa, Raluca Maria. "Translating Equality between Women and Men across Cold War Divides: Women Activists from Hungary and Romania and the Creation of International Women's Year." In *Gender Politics and Everyday Life in State Socialist Eastern and Central Europe*, edited by Shana Penn and Jill Massino, 59. New York: Palgrave Macmillan, 2005.

Protocol of the Meeting of the Regional Representatives of Women's Departments, June 4, 1946, Archive of New Records, Warsaw.

Regulska, Joanna, and Magda Grabowska. "New Geographies of Women's Subjectivities in Poland." In *Global Babel: Questions of Communication in a Time of Globalization*, edited by S. Dayal and M. Murphy, 108. Newcastle, UK: Cambridge Scholars, 2007.

Rosenberg, Dorothy. "The Emancipation of Women in Fact and Fiction: Changing Roles in GDR Society and Literature." In *Women, State, and Party in Eastern Europe*, edited by S. Wolchik and A. Meyer, 344. Durham, NC: Duke University Press, 1985.

Rosner, Katarzyna. "Czy istnieje w Polsce ruch feministyczny?" *Pełnym Głosem* 5 (1997): 34.

Second Women's International Congress, Budapest, Hungary, December 1–6, 1948. Women's International Democratic Federation 1948, 297.

Sharp, Ingrid. "Seksualne zjednoczenie Niemiec." In *Antropologia seksualności: Etnografia, teoria, zastosowanie*, edited by A. Kościańska, 95. Translated by Michał Petryk. Warsaw: Wydawnictwa Uniwersytetu Warszawskiego, 2012.

Snitow, Ann. "Feminist Futures in the Former East Bloc." *Peace and Democracy News* 7, no. 1 (1993): 39.

Snitow Ann. "Women's Anniversaries. Snapshots of Polish Feminism since 1989." *Dissent*, Fall 2009, 61.

Staniszkis, Maria. "Równość kobiet w miejscu pracy." *Kobieta* 4 (1948): 7.

Stańczak-Wiślicz, Katarzyna. "Household as a Battleground of Modernity: Activities of the Home Economics Committee Affiliated to the League of Women (1957–80)." *Acta Poloniae Historica* 115 (2017): 123.

Talarczyk-Gubała, Monika. *Wanda Jakubowska: Od nowa*. Warsaw: Wydawnictwo Krytyki Politycznej, 2015.

Titkow, Anna. "Poland, New Gender Contract in Formation." *Polish Sociological Review* 3:127 (1999): 377.

Todorova, Maria. *Imagining the Balkans*. Oxford: Oxford University Press, 1997.

Voronina, Olga. "Soviet Patriarchy: Past and Present." *Hypatia* 8, no. 4 (1997): 112.

Walczewska, Sławomira. "Liga Kobiet: Jedyna organizacja kobieca w PRL." *Pełnym Głosem*, 1 (1993): 4.

Walczewska, Sławomira. "Jaki feminizm, czyli dokąd idzie Marianna?" *Pełnym Głosem* 5 (1997): 53.

World Congress of Women. *Reports, Speeches (Extracts) Documents*. Berlin: Women's International Democratic Federation, 1953.

Chapter Nine

Labor, Gender, and Interethnic Relations among Polish American Communities in Rural Massachusetts

Agnieszka Pasieka

Walking between two rows of benches in the modern Catholic church, the bride looked radiant and sparkling with happiness. "Janet looks stunning," the groom's aunt, Judy, told me with pride before leaning closer to add: "But above all she loves Kevin so much. She even converted for him!" When I asked about Janet's religion before embracing Catholicism, Judy responded: "I don't know exactly. But I guess she must have been Jewish?" Janet's family was not Jewish, as I learned later; yet who was a more likely candidate for a "stranger" and "convert" in the Polish American community's eyes? This conviction grew in me the more oral histories on the local Polish American community I got to know and the more I talked with its youngest generation.

The priest concurred with Judy's observation, devoting a good deal of his sermon to the bride's engagement in the new church and the mature relationship she developed with the new creed. After the mass was over, the wedding guests dashed to the wedding venue, a rural winery. The groom's best man (Kevin's closest friend and the leader of the local polka band) gave a touching speech in a mixture of English and Polish, recalling Kevin's deceased parents. Then, adopting a more humorous tone, he spoke about why Janet would be a perfect wife, this time focusing not on her religious devotion but on her farming skills. Among the guests were many of Kevin's relatives and other local Polish Americans, who today are the biggest ethnic community in Hatfield and Hadley, Massachusetts, the two towns I am focusing on in this chapter.[1] Talk of Polish wedding and culinary traditions dominated the event, leaving Janet's family somewhat in the background. The presence of a Polish anthropologist—"a real Pole," as the hosts proudly presented me—slightly unsettled these discussions, as not only did I turn out to be incapable of dancing polka, but my lack of knowledge of certain "Polish" dishes and my vegetarianism put my ethnic identity in question. If any other ethnic community was visible, it came in the form of several Mexican families—described to me as Kevin's "best employees"—who were invited to the wedding and prepared a folk music performance.[2]

Although my chapter focuses primarily on developments in the first decades of the twentieth century, I decided to open it with an anecdote from a 2014 wedding. There are two reasons for this. First, the wedding story encapsulates a series of issues that are crucial for understanding the trajectory of Polish immigrants from minority to part of the majority: views on gender, ideas about ethnicity and religious background, and statements on Mexican workers' reliability are all important elements of this trajectory. Second, my opening story is supposed to constitute a methodological argument, demonstrating the importance of both a "historical anthropology" and a "history *and* anthropology," meaning not only a study aimed at integrating archival research with anthropological sensitivity to the complexities of cross-cultural relationships but also a "joint" exploration of past and present developments. For although a good deal of my research meant studying different sorts of "past" narratives of and about the Polish American community inhabiting the two western Massachusetts towns, I could make sense—or rather make *better* sense—of them only thanks to the observation of what this community is like today.

In this chapter, I thus intertwine interviews with a few Polish American families and observations from my fieldwork in rural Massachusetts with archival

---

[1] Hadley (pop. 5250) and Hatfield (pop. 3300) are neighboring towns, separated by the Connecticut River. I am focusing on these two towns, but it is important to mention that Poles were also present in several adjacent localities, such as Sunderland, Deerfield, and Northampton. Since the US census no longer collects data on ethnic ancestry, the data are only an estimation. Local people provided me with very different numbers, ranging from 20 percent to 80 percent. According to the statistics, 22 percent of Hadley and 30 percent of Hatfield inhabitants claim Polish ancestry. http://statisticalatlas.com/place/Massachusetts. This area has been underrepresented in the scholarship on Polish Americans, and I hope that my work will begin to fill the existing gap.

[2] Based on fieldnotes, April 26, 2014.

materials, mostly articles from journals, newspapers, and magazines.[3] I first present a short history of the Polish presence in the Connecticut River Valley and then proceed with an analysis of Polish identity in a broader, multiethnic context. Although in my historical account I refer to "Polish immigrants" and "Poles," this usage is meant neither to underestimate the internal diversity of the category of Polishness nor to assume that the people who migrated to New England were nationally "conscious" Poles. In using these terms, I simply refer to the descriptions found in archival materials and secondary sources and/or use emic (people's own) terms used by my interlocutors, who unanimously described their (great-)grandparents as Polish/Poles. Similarly, I speak of Polish Americans (rather than of "Americans of Polish descent") due to the fact that my interlocutors usually presented themselves to me in this manner.[4]

Historical Background

Polish immigrants began arriving in New England in increasing numbers via labor brokers, family, and village networks in the last decades of the nineteenth century, in direct response to an increasing demand for labor. Most of them came from small villages in the Austrian-Hungarian and Russian empires via Hamburg and Bremen. According to some accounts,[5] Poles were first brought into Hatfield and Hadley via Boston as laborers for Irish farmers who owned land in the area. Others mention that, having recognized the value of cheap and reliable Polish workers, two enterprising Yankees would regularly go to New York to recruit new laborers.[6] The fee for the travel was equivalent to the first month's pay of the immigrants working on the farm. Contrary to the majority of "Polish peasants in America," who opted for factory work, Poles settling in the towns in question would become farm laborers, which, at least in the initial

---

[3] This chapter is based on materials found in the following archives and libraries: Hatfield Historical Museum, the Polish Center of Discovery and Learning in Chicopee, the Holyoke History Room, Chicopee Historical Society, University of Massachusetts in Amherst, Elihu Burritt Library at the Central Connecticut State University in New Britain.

[4] They would also say: "When I am in the US, I say I am Polish; when I am outside the US, I say I am American."

[5] For example, Copithorne, "The Role of Slovak Immigration in the Development of a Second Protestant Church in Hatfield, MA," 10.

[6] Abel, "Sunderland: A Study of Changes in the Group Life of Poles in a New England Farming Community."

stage of their stay, meant extremely hard and shamefully low-paid work, compared in some accounts to slavery.[7] The choice of farm employment constitutes an important trope in the oral histories I have collected: notwithstanding the labor hardship, Polish farmers would discuss their grandparents' and great-grandparents' choices in terms of "freedom," "real work," and as something "they had always done and known."[8] In turn, they would describe factory work as like a "prison" and complain of a "lack of fulfilment." Using a quasi-Marxian language of alienation, they would go on in detail about the importance of one's relation to the product. The following quotations illustrate this approach well: "No matter how many times you have participated in the harvest, you feel like crying when you see and touch healthy crops"; "Because when you are farming, you kind of control your own destiny."

The approach to farming and a perception of what "real" work entails is essential for understanding the rapid success of Poles in the area. Polish settlement occurred according to the following pattern: male immigrants would work for a few years at a local farm, earning around $20 to $25 per week (in the period 1905–1910), on average $5 less than Americans did.[9] As soon as they learned basic English, became acquainted with the basics of the local institutional systems, and collected enough money, they bought a small piece of land and brought their families to the United States or married a local Polish girl who had most likely worked as a servant before getting married. Women were often in charge of money and took in boarders to contribute to the family budget. Entire families would work on the farms, which astonished New Englanders.[10]

These aspects are frequently emphasized in discussions on Polish immigrants in rural areas. John Bukowczyk refers to "underconsumption and thrift" as

---

7   Ibid.
8   Similar comparisons between farmers and factory workers are also reported by John Radziłowski in his book on Polish immigrants in Minnesota (Radziłowski, *Poles in Minnesota*). However, older works suggest that the decision to work on the farm was extremely difficult as the city jobs were better paid (e.g., Kryszka, *Historya polska w Ameryce*, 111). Such contrasting views may suggest that the idealization of farm work is present mostly among successful farmers, but they also point to the fact that the New England context was quite distinctive in terms of the availability of cheap and fertile lands (cf. Hardin, *Poles and Puritans in Hadley*).
9   Balch, *Our Slavic Fellow Citizens*, 327.
10 These accounts on the beginnings of settlement resemble accounts about other Polish immigrants, also from industrial centers. See, for example, Lopata, *Polish Americans*, 42–43.

factors enabling Poles to become first renters and then land owners.[11] Theodor Abel explains the relatively rapid success of Polish immigrants with "cheap labor offered by a numerous family," a "willingness to do hard work," and a "low standard of living."[12] Helena Znaniecki Lopata adds that new immigrants did not compare themselves to non-Polish neighbors, but they would depend on the status symbols they knew from back home[13]—and that related precisely to the question of house and land ownership.

Yet, the money Poles managed to save or borrow from relatives was usually enough only for a cheap piece of land and abandoned farms nobody else wanted. Kevin's ancestors' story is exemplary in this regard. Two brothers, Peter/Piotr and James/Jakub, bought a piece of land back in 1899. In order to facilitate their proceedings with the local administration, they Americanized their surname.[14] The field they bought was full of stones and overrun by bushes. The brothers worked hard to clear it and soon discovered that the fertile soil was perfect for growing tobacco (which is still cultivated on the farm). Due to a quarrel in 1918, they split their business, bought two adjacent fields, and began living on two separate farms with their families. Kevin's great-grandfather, Peter, had six children—four sons and two daughters. He decided that only one of them would remain on the farm and invested in the education of the others, choosing professions for them that were supposed to serve the farm. As a result, Kevin's grandfather stayed on the farm while one of his brothers became a judge, another a banker, and another an insurance salesman; the two sisters married other farmers. Kevin and his brother Paul have the following to say about their grandfather's siblings:

> *Kevin*: They always came back to help with the tobacco, whenever they could. Like they would come on the weekends and help harvest tobacco, help stripping in the fall time when you gotta strip the leaves of the stock so that the tobacco dries down. They would always ... still come and help out just ... just to keep their hands on.

---

11   Bukowczyk, *A History of the Polish Americans*, 20.
12   Abel, "Sunderland," 216.
13   Lopata, *Polish Americans*, 45.
14   The strategy of Americanizing one's surname is commonly referred to in literature, also in references to later periods (see e.g., Bukowczyk, *A History*, 106). I heard an anecdote about a man named Obrycht whose name was difficult to pronounce and therefore was changed to O'Brien. My interlocutor laughed at Obrycht/O'Brien, who by mistake switched one ethnic identity for a different one (O'Brien being a typical Irish surname).

Paul: Yeah, they didn't forget their roots. And again, with the two big families, there were still kids like ... our grandfather didn't graduate from high school, because he was... someone had to stay on the farm (...) The girls obviously married and were housewives. You know, that's what they did back then in the day.

(...) *Kevin*: They made a lot of money on the tobacco, so ... they had the means to send their kids off to college.

Kevin's grandfather had three sons and continued the pattern: one of the sons stayed on the farm and the other two graduated in engineering and law). Kevin's father then left the farm to Kevin and his brother Paul, who took it over after attending college, while two older brothers chose different professional pathways and left the area.

Kevin's ancestors' successful case was talked about a lot in the area, making a local newspaper in 1924. In an article entitled "How Poles Get Rich on N.E. Farms Where Yankees Fail," the journalist admires farmers' thrift and the work of entire families in the field.[15] Generally, the picture painted by the local press is favorable, albeit not free of dubious remarks. Polish immigrants come across as extremely industrious, healthy, and ready to accept even the most humiliating conditions to succeed; they also eat a lot (some men even ten to fifteen potatoes!).[16] Apparently, the harsh experiences of the old country and "Russian steppes" (the term used to convey the remoteness and wilderness) prepared them for hard work. Observers praise their neat houses and farms and thrift, as evidenced by the amount of money Poles send home and the ability to live cheaply in order to save and acquire properties, and, last but not least, the fact that once they get a farm, immigrants are likely to stay.[17] They also praise Poles' ethnic solidarity,[18] and although they mention their quarrelsome character, they state that, luckily, Poles argued mostly among themselves.

The quoted press articles were also concerned with the issue of women's participation. Not only did the reporters stress that entire families are devoted to the farm and write in astonishment (mixed with admiration) about women carrying their newborns on their backs or sporadically peeking at the napping kids

---

15 *The Sunday Herald Boston*, May 4, 1924.
16 *Daily Globe*, June 29, 1902.
17 *Daily Hampshire Gazette*, May 18, 1915.
18 The importance of helping other Polish immigrants is also reflected in the minutes of the Polish club in Hatfield. Reports from the club's meetings include information about money collection for widowers, sick people, those who lost their property, and other Poles in need.

while doing farm work, but they also emphasize women's roles as farm accountants. The fact that thrifty and resourceful women were in charge of money—apart from helping on the farm, raising children, taking care of their own as well as (often) boarders—supposedly contributed to the farms' growing success. As accountants, women were responsible for the family savings and also contributed the money collected from boarders and lodgers to the family budget.[19] Consequently, the role of women in the families, conceived of as "economic units," grew significantly.[20] This is not to say that exercising authority in households significantly altered gender hierarchies; even if strategically important, work (or rather various tasks) at home was not supposed to affect traditional family relations, tantamount to the "Old World" family values.[21]

Other press reports were more concerned with the idea of Poles as candidates for citizenship. Some authors expressed doubts about whether Poles—"hard working" and "attached to tradition"—could also understand "the institutions of free government" and become real citizens; they wondered to what extent the new "invasion" would be detrimental for Yankee culture.[22] Discussing the possibilities of cultural assimilation, they also complained about unpronounceable names and the excess of consonants characteristic of Polish (and other Slavic) languages. Yet, they also began to contrast Poles with "decadent Yankees" who were too lazy to take care of farms, while Poles would transform even idle fields into successful enterprises. Such opinions are also widespread among Polish farmers. Bernie, a representative of the third generation of farmers, recalls his grandfather's stories on how

> the Polish would start working for them [Yankees], but for some reason, you know, whether lazy or not . . . They [Poles] went and bought farms up in the hills, you know, where it's rocky, stony soil, dairy farms, apple, fruit tree farms, but there is hardly any English town here now. It's all Polish that owned all this land. So, you know then, you know we just got to know, you know the Polish farmers, you know, doin' business with one another, rotating land, meeting at meetings, fertilizer, chemical meetings, you know, just socializing at, you know, polka dances and places like that.

---

19 This was quite common among immigrant families. For evidence on Italian and Jewish families, see: Foner, "Immigrant Women and Work in New York City, Then and Now," 95–113.

20 Cf. Bukowczyk, *A History*, 25.

21 Again, comparative insights shed light on the Polish case: Yans-McLaughlin, *Family and Community*.

22 Article: "Coming of the Poles," newspaper name illegible (copy owned by the author). See also: Brewer, *The Conquest of New England by the Immigrant*.

Not only are such accounts very common, but they became a sort of foundational story of the Polish American community living in the valley. Its first component is precisely the distinction between lazy and incapable Yankees and hardworking, frugal Poles. The second, no less important, component relates to the presence of other ethnic communities.

Polishness in the Multiethnic Context

"Yankees" were not the only group Poles were compared with. Even though other Slavic people came to the area, due to the dominant position of the Poles, Ruthenians and Slovaks were often identified as "Polanders"—adopting the neologism created—or indeed wished to identify themselves as such due to the relatively "prestigious" position of Polish immigrants.[23] Therefore, the main ethnic groups Poles would refer to were Irish and French-Canadians who, by the time Poles arrived in the Connecticut River Valley, were relatively well established. The Irish who owned the farms initially welcomed newcomers, but once whole Polish families began migrating their number far exceeded what the Irish businessmen wished for. As for the less wealthy French and Irish, the fact that Poles accepted the lowest possible wages simply meant that they were perceived as a threat and competition (the data shows that wages indeed dropped).[24] Even later on, once Poles become proprietors of farms, interethnic competition rather than cooperation remained the norm. This aspect constitutes one of the important differences between the rural and the industrial settings: in the latter one, the struggle for better work conditions in the factories and experiences as union members often led to strengthening the common class background of the immigrant laborers.[25]

Besides, the French and Irish considered the Slavs wild and backward, which was probably similar to how Yankees perceived the French and Irish a few decades earlier, an issue well illustrated by accounts of the immigrants' religious lives. Even if all three ethnic communities practiced Roman Catholicism, having a joint service was inconceivable and not just because parts of the services were performed in the respective ethnic languages. Rather, the communities

---

23   Abel, "Sunderland," 230.
24   Balch, *Our Slavic Fellows*, 327.
25   However, in industrial settings employers also initially used the newcomers to break the power of the unions. See, for example, Mink, *Old Labor and New Immigrants in American Political Development*.

carefully guarded their ethnic parishes, which constituted the sociocultural centers of immigrants' lives.[26] Irish inhabitants from Hadley eventually allowed Poles to use their church (until the Polish community built their own in 1919) but claimed they had to air out the building for hours after the "stinky" Poles had left. Generally, present-day inhabitants claim that local Irish politicians and board members were much more hostile toward Poles than Yankees were. They also recall violent, often alcohol-fueled fights between Poles and Irish. Given that the French community diminished and the number of Irish and Poles evened up, the latter two groups became the biggest competitors.[27]

Consequently, ethnic communities were insular and did not socialize much across ethnic borders. They called each other derogatory names, and intermarriage was perceived as treason. One of the farmers, ninety-five-year-old Stanley, told me about the first Franco-Polish couple he remembered from the late 1920s. The couple went around Hadley with invitations for the wedding and stopped by Stanley's house. "I am so sorry but we are busy that Saturday," his mother answered politely. After the couple had left, she sighed, "Such a nice Polish girl marrying a French man" and rushed to the neighbors to discuss the shocking news. Most Polish inhabitants turned out to be busy that Saturday. It was only in the 1950s, people recalled, that the idea of intermarriage became easier to swallow. In our discussion, Stanley strongly empathized with young people who were not able to marry the person they loved, as he himself was forced by his parents to abandon his beloved girlfriend and marry a Polish neighbor's daughter. The arranged marriage enabled the two families to merge their fields and establish a larger farm enterprise.

Yet, it was not only due to community-oriented practices and attachment to one's tradition that ethnic solidarity thrived. Polish people also relied on each other because, being "latecomers," they lacked representation among the authorities and experienced discrimination with regard to property acquisition and bank loans. In order to facilitate their socioeconomic integration, the Hatfield Poles established a Polish club (in 1923) that promoted the idea of naturalization and organized evening school for adults. It numbered around sixty members who,

---

26 Much literature exists on ethnic parishes. Here, it is useful to recall a classic conception of ethnic churches as providers of "3 R—refuge, respect, and resources." See Hirschman, "The Role of Religion in the Origins and Adaptation of Immigrant Groups in the United States," 1206–33.

27 Irish-Polish competition is often interpreted in the context of Irish clergy dominance in the Catholic Church. This aspect, however, was not referred to in my conversations.

through the club's activities, managed to become part of a local board. Minutes from the club's meetings reflect a spirit of ethnic solidarity, expressed in the collection of money for less successful farmers or widowed Poles. Another relevant initiative came from the Massachusetts agricultural college, which invited (for several years from 1911) all Polish farmers to come in for lectures and learn how to modernize their farms, prevent tobacco diseases, and raise healthy dairy. The college organized a special program for both men and women and hired a translator even though, as reporters noted, many people were able to understand basic English at the time.[28]

In short, in the first decades of the twentieth century the Polish community was increasingly established due to a mix of factors, from state-supported initiatives to grassroots mobilization (often intended to counter those state officials who were perceived as hostile). Interethnic relations played a big role in shaping identities, and accounts of the following decades demonstrate that they have continued to be important to this day.

Climbing the Ladder

By the late 1920s it was evident that not being the main clients of local banks would be beneficial for the Polish community: the economic depression did not hit them as hard as it did other inhabitants. As a result, in the 1920s Poles broke into their home-kept savings and began buying up properties from their fellow inhabitants. The second considerable source of wealth at the time was illicit alcohol, an activity Poles reportedly specialized in.[29] Consequently, Poles' socioeconomic importance grew substantially. Although the number of Polish people in rural settlements was not high compared with neighboring factory towns (such as the heavily Polish Chicopee), what made their case important was the proportion of the Polish landowners to the native born. In 1906, in Hadley, two-thirds of the foreign-born population were Poles: they made up about 20 percent of the town's total population and owned roughly 5 to 10

---

28   *The Springfield Daily Republican*, April 1, 1911.
29   Many of the people interviewed recall illicit alcohol production. Newspapers from the era include information about burnt barns, and my informants associated some of these incidents with making moonshine.

percent of lands.[30] By 1929, they constituted 60 percent of the population and owned 40 percent of the land.[31]

The economic success enabled their social mobility. As the school records show, the number of Polish schoolchildren—boys and girls alike—grew steadily. Not only did Poles learn to appreciate the value of education, but they were rich enough that their children did not have to work full time on the farm. Still, the school calendar was strictly connected with the farming one, and the school guaranteed parents a week of spring break for onion harvest (a practice that continued for many decades).

Onions and potatoes were among the most important local farm products, along with asparagus and tobacco, which grew easily in the fertile soil of the Connecticut River Valley. Producing tobacco also meant the need to sell it, and it is here that Jews come into the picture. In local stories, they are depicted as cunning, calculating, and business-oriented people. Having done my earlier fieldwork in the Polish countryside in the early 2000s,[32] I was struck by the language used in descriptions of Jews. Although Poles were most likely meeting and interacting with the French and Irish in Massachusetts for the first time, Jews had long featured in the Polish immigrants' imagination. No doubt supplemented by new experiences, the image of Jews was marked by prejudices against peasant-exploiting Jews brought from the old country. In my interlocutors' view, Jews owned a lot of property and spoke Polish better than any Polish farmer did. They were both despised for their business mentality and admired as the people who knew how to get ahead. In the local accounts, however, "the worst of all" were several local Poles who abandoned Polish-sounding surnames (ending in "-ski" for instance) to sound more Jewish and to trade with Jews in New York, as the following quote suggests:

> All that tobacco that was sorted, cigar buyers would buy it. And they were all Jewish. So he would be dealing with them, see? So in order to be on their level, he changed his name to sound as if he was Jewish too. See?

In contrasting themselves with Jews, local Poles painted a picture of their own community as "honest" and "hard-working" (i.e., performing *physical* labor) people, but at the same time they would be proud when able to "get a deal." The view of physical labor as real labor relates to the importance of farmwork,

---

30 In 1905, Hadley had 1895 inhabitants, among them 372 Poles, 110 Irish, 33 French-Canadian. See Balch, *Our Slavic Fellows*, 329.

31 Lucey, *The Immigration of Slavic Farmers to Hadley*, 37.

32 Pasieka, *Hierarchy and Pluralism*.

strongly contrasted with both "Jewish" people and with those Poles who took over "Jewish professions." Speaking about one of them, a Polish American who sold insurance, one of the farmers told me: "What does he know about farming and real work? His shoes are always so clean [i.e., not dirtied by soil]!"

The idea of what constitutes true labor has persisted even though post–World War II decades brought about a variety of new developments. As farms grew bigger, more modern, and more prosperous, their owners slowly joined the ranks of the middle class. Farms would rely less on family members' help: an increasing number of children would be sent to college, and women started looking for jobs outside of the farms, in the service sector, schools, and administration. Middle-class status, education, and nonagricultural forms of employment facilitated assimilation, foregrounding the American mainstream lifestyle. During vacations and at weekends, family members would still be involved in various farm chores, but this aspect no longer distinguished Polish Americans from other Americans. Nonetheless, the presence of the Polish American community in the area would be noticed by the press, which would write about Polish Americans' unpronounceable words—those few Polish expressions that were still in use[33]—and comment on their hard work, thereby contributing to the self-congratulatory narrative of the second and third generations.

Interestingly, however, the postwar years do not feature prominently either in local archival collections (which document in detail the developments in the late nineteenth and early twentieth centuries) or in local inhabitants' narratives. The latter seem eager to talk only about their grandparents' "epic" journeys to the United States, the hardships of the first year, and about present-day farming. In so doing, they tend to compare people employed at their farms to their grandfathers:

> Oh it's interesting because you can . . . if you watched those Mexicans for a week, if you understood them, if you worked with them for a year, it's just like the way it was a hundred years ago with the Polish, because . . . you know, they all came to this country, they find the community to live in where there is a big population of them . . . um, you know, they shared housing, um . . . and . . . the other thing is our guys that worked for us, they have friends and family that worked for other farms and so . . . there is this big network between like Mexicans and between farms.

My interlocutors thus respect Mexican workers due to the fact that the latter organize their work and social relations similarly to Polish Americans' ancestors.

---

33 None of my interlocutors (third and fourth generation) knew Polish, and their parents rarely spoke Polish to them.

In our conversations, they frequently emphasized how much they detest supposedly "lazy" Puerto Ricans but value "hard-working" Mexicans who work *nearly as hard* as Polish people did when they came to the Connecticut River Valley and who share similar values—attachment to family, mutual support, the importance of ethnic solidarity.

One more aspect of the discussions on climbing the ladder is the previously mentioned conviction about the importance of being proprietors. My interlocutors would proudly emphasize that most farms in Hatfield and Hadley have owners of Polish descent. "Polish people don't sell land" was a motto repeated in both stories about the 1930s and those in the present day. Its importance became clearer to me thanks to an event I attended in the autumn of 2014. On a warm September day, I had a tour with the guide from the Hatfield farm museum, who recounted to me in detail the history of the Polish community and persistently emphasized Poles' reluctance to sell land ("Don't you know? Polish people don't sell land!"). The guide had lots of information to share with me, and his tour could have lasted for hours if not for the fact that I had to attend the one hundredth anniversary of the introduction of the first agricultural classes for Polish farmers, held at the University of Massachusetts in Amherst. The event gathered big crowds, among them lots of Polish American farmers I knew already. They were proud to present me to their colleagues and friends, some of whom came for the event from far away.

One such person was Bernie's friend James, who no longer lived in Massachusetts. Bernie had been pestering him for a long time, begging him to sell him a piece of land that bordered with Bernie's farm and that he desperately needed given his farm's success. James did not need the land but refused to sell. He would answer curtly: "I was taught you should not sell your father's land." I have no means to judge if he was simply waiting for a better offer or expressing a genuine attachment to the family property (or both), yet the recurring question of ownership is no doubt a very important aspect of the Polish (American) identity question. Owning land, a house, and a farm was a way of "making it" in American society, but at the same time it was interpreted as a realization of a specifically Polish inspiration.

This self-image of hardworking and ambitious Poles prompts us to ask: What was decisive in the—undeniable—success of Polish immigrants in the area? Or, to put it differently, how can we explain this phenomenon beyond the self-congratulatory notion of "Polish work ethic" that local Polish Americans were keen to employ? Since the locals' answer to this question is "because we are Polish," let us summarize the earlier observations by identifying key facets of their idea of "being Polish."

Redefining Polishness, Rethinking Identities

Living far from big centers (such as Chicago or New York), Polish Americans in the Connecticut River Valley did not participate in politics and seldom expressed interest in the international situation. Contrary to the protagonists of Stauter-Halsted's chapter (this volume), to the best of my knowledge few people maintained regular contacts with relatives living in Europe. Consequently, their idea of Poland remained mostly unchanged. Construed on the basis of their grandparents' stories, their idea of Poland conveys the image of a rural, poor, and backward country but also a place of dear traditions, such as a particular celebration on Christmas Eve (*Wigilia*, referred to as *Vilia*) and family anniversaries celebrated with Polish-style dishes and vodka. Henceforth, my interlocutors' references to Polishness tended to be very emotional, which was no doubt reflected in the fact that the only references to the Polish language were present in either swear words or sentimental stories about *babcias* and *dziadzias* (grandmas and grandpas). Equally emotional were the expressions of attachment to the farm and land, insistently presented as a "typically" Polish attachment.

Generally speaking, more than one hundred years after the settlement of the first Polish immigrants in the area, Polish American farms thrive thanks to a number of factors that may be said to intertwine some ethnic customs and stereotypes with simple calculation. Firstly, a turn toward organic farming and *local* food, which middle-class inhabitants of Massachusetts are very fond of, has brought new sources of income to the farms. Many owners set up vegetable stands, which attract many visitors on weekends. Kevin and Janet are considering setting one up as well, as Janet could easily take care of it while looking after the children. As one of their fellow Polish American farmers jokingly said, it must be a (nice, friendly) woman to take care of the stand, as people will be less likely to try to bargain with her aggressively or cheat her—and here he used an ethnic slur categorizing this practice as a Jewish one. Clearly, negative attitudes toward Jews, especially with regard to their supposed business practices, have proved resistant to change among some members of the Polish American community in this region.

Secondly, and relatedly, the ethnic revival that has characterized recent decades has created a growing interest in ethnic food, and Polish American farmers are increasingly mobilizing ethnicity as a marketing tool. Nothing exemplifies this better than Bernie's plan to launch the production of—an inherently Polish—*potato* vodka. This trend is by no means specific to a particular group or area; rather, it represents a broader phenomenon of "*ethno*preneurship."[34]

---

34   Comaroff and Comaroff, *Ethnicity, Inc.*

A variety of commodities and consumables—from Polish pottery to Polish food—is increasingly marketed for a non–Polish American audience. At the same time, it should be noted that the possibility of being proud of Polish origins is a relatively recent phenomenon, long limited by derogatory stereotypes and jokes directed at Poles. Being "fresh," Polish ethnic roots appear more interesting than the overdone St. Patrick's Day and overeaten crepes.

Thirdly, the transmission of farms from generation to generation is one of the keys to success, and the strong emphasis placed on the family's responsibility for and dependency on the farm is equally crucial. I was surprised to find out that two of Kevin's brothers, a lawyer and a doctor, spend a good chunk of their family vacation collecting tobacco (as their grandfather's brothers did). When I inquired about this during Kevin's wedding, they replied that they would not have been where they are now—which is in a comfortable position—if it had not been for the farm ("It was the farm that made our education possible"). Such comments also suggest a continuous emphasis placed on *physical* labor and its primacy. Numerous other farms employ entire families throughout the year—as stated earlier, not by necessity but by choice. Bernie's enterprise is run by four brothers. Another farmer, locally known as the "king of potatoes," employs, in addition to around one hundred Mexicans, all possible family members (representing five generations), including wives, daughters, and daughters-in-law who are "traditionally" in charge of accounting and marketing.

As a matter of fact, gender relations within the Polish community perfectly reflect a successful adaption to actual needs. At the outset of the twentieth century, Polish women worked hard in the fields and took care of boarders and farm finances. In the postwar period, they accepted the middle-class housewife role. Today, many of them either work on the farm in accounting or actually find employment outside of the farm and are able to support the farm *through* that employment, namely by providing good health insurance and stable income. As such, gender relations also illustrate the transformation of the models brought from the home country in accordance with patterns set by new contexts, both cultural and economic ones.

But such an adaptation/assimilation to the mainstream American model is rarely recognized by locals. In recounting how they succeeded without abandoning their ethnic identity, Polish Americans persistently claim that they got ahead due to certain "Polish" characteristics, such as frugality, hard work, sturdiness, and an emphasis placed on education. They emphasize how much they owe to their Polish ancestors and that their "Polishness" is the key to their success. Even if intermarriage is absolutely normal nowadays, and even if rather than talking about other inhabitants of the town as "French" or "Irish" people refer to them simply as "Americans," having a Polish ethnic background is emphasized, to the extent that non-Polish wives of Polish farmers come to be in charge of spreading the gospel of Polish success and preparing traditional Polish dishes.

Equally important is an emphasis on the fact that Poles *made it* themselves, not receiving any welfare or help from the state, simply because they were "dreamers" and because "America is a land of opportunities" that they managed to exploit. Politically conservative now,[35] they adopt a peculiar attitude toward new immigrants; in praising industrious Mexicans and Guatemalans they predict that the new immigrants will surely climb the social ladder thanks to their *own* hard work and initiative. Again, then, what they call a maintenance of a distinctively Polish identity perfectly corresponds with the broader American ideology of the self-made man.

I believe these are precisely the broader implications of the herein discussed "identity issue" that matter most here. The story of Polish farmers in Massachusetts illustrates key issues in the study of ethnic identities—the importance of "ethnic boundaries" and "ethnic others" for a group's self-definition, the growing importance of the "Ethnicity, inc." phenomenon,[36] the power and the durability of ethnic stereotypes, as well as the continuous sociopolitical valence of white ethnicity.[37] It demonstrates the complex interrelation between ethnic, class, and gender identities. And it shows that studying the ways in which an idea of Polishness has been constructed, defined, and redefined by the Massachusetts community sheds light on two seemingly contradictory aspects. It makes evident, on the one hand, the malleability of ethnic and national identities, and on the other, the fact that social actors are so willing to deploy ethnic identity precisely because to them it appears far from malleable but rather as a durable framework of experiences and attachments.

Bibliography

Abel, Theodor. "Sunderland. A Study of Changes in the Group Life of Poles in a New England Farming Community." In *Immigrant Farmers and their Children*, edited by E. Brunner. Garden City, NY: Doubleday, Doran & Co, 1929.

Anagnostou, Yiorgos. "A Critique of Symbolic Ethnicity: The Ideology of Choice?" *Ethnicities* 9, no. 1 (2009): 94–122.

---

35   The majority of the farmers I talked to vote for Republicans.
36   See Comaroff and Comaroff, *Ethnicity, Inc.*
37   See, for example, a critique on the color-blindness of discussions of "ethnicity as choice" in the United States: Anagnostou, *A Critique of Symbolic Ethnicity*.

Balch, Emily. *Our Slavic Fellow Citizens,* New York: Charities Publication Committee, 1910.
Brewer, Charles D. *The Conquest of New England by the Immigrant*, New York: G. P. Putnam's Sons, 1926.
Bukowczyk, John. *A History of the Polish Americans*, New Brunswick, NJ: Transaction, 2009.
Comaroff, Jean, and John Comaroff, *Ethnicity, Inc.* Chicago: University of Chicago Press, 2009.
Copithorne, Alan C. "The Role of Slovak Immigration in the Development of a Second Protestant Church in Hatfield, MA." Hartford Seminary Foundation, 1971.
Foner, Nancy. "Immigrant Women and Work in New York City, Then and Now." *Journal of American Ethnic History* 18, no. 3 (1999): 95–113.
Hardin, Peter. *Poles and Puritans in Hadley: Massachusetts: An Historical Study of Hadley's Polish Population*. MA thesis, Hampshire College, 1975.
Hirschman, Charles. "The Role of Religion in the Origins and Adaptation of Immigrant Groups in the United States." *International Migration Review* 38, no. 3 (2004): 1206–33.
Kruszka, Wacław. *Historya polska w Ameryce*. Milwaukee: Drukiem Spółki Wydawniczej Kuryera, 1905.
Lucey, Edward. *The Immigration of Slavic Farmers to Hadley*. MA thesis, Massachusetts State College, 1936.
Mink, Gwendolyn. *Old Labor and New Immigrants in American Political Development: Union, Party, and State, 1875–1920*. Ithaca, NY: Cornell University Press, 1986.
Pasieka, Agnieszka. *Hierarchy and Pluralism. Living Religious Difference in Catholic Poland,* New York: Palgrave, 2015.
Radziłowski, John. *Poles in Minnesota*, St: Paul: Minnesota Historical Society Press, 2005.
Yans-McLaughlin, Virginia. *Family and Community: Italian Immigrants in Buffalo, 1880–1930,* Ithaca, NY: Cornell University Press, 1977.
Znaniecki Lopata, Helena. *Polish Americans. Status Competition in an Ethnic Community.* New York: Prentice Hall, 1976.

Chapter Ten

Being European in Poland and Polish in Europe

Transnational Constructions of National Identity

Marysia Galbraith

What does it mean to be Polish within the context of European integration? The chapter examines Poles' everyday conceptions of themselves in relation to their nation and in relation to Europe, and explains how national identity is shaped by personal experiences with transnational ideas, people, and goods. When seeking answers to the question, "What does it mean to be Polish?" it can be easy to reproduce stereotypes, paint unidimensional portraits of a fixed and unchanging "national character," or especially during this time of political polarization, inscribe separate camps with deeply divided views of Polishness and Poland's place within Europe. However, careful attention to people's self-characterizations and perceptions reveals more complex, nuanced, and sometimes idiosyncratic views, wherein opposing perspectives often come into play *within* an individual's viewpoints. Understanding the ambivalences and tensions at the heart of Poles' responses to questions about Polishness in relation European integration can help to make sense of overwhelming support for membership in the European Union even in the face of growing nativist, pronational sentiments.

The study draws from a person-centered ethnographic study that began with high school students in 1992 and continued for twenty years as they established their adult lives.¹ Initially, participants attended high school in either the city of Krakow or the rural southeastern Bieszczady region, but I followed them as they matured and some relocated to other towns, cities, or countries. Their personal reflections, documented periodically as Poland solidified democratic institutions, embraced the neoliberal market, and entered the European Union, help to reveal the long roots of "transnational Polishness": namely, a sense of national identity embedded in relations with broader geographic, political, and cultural spheres. Of particular relevance for this chapter, between 2005 and 2012 participants in my study described the connection between Poles and Europe as long-term, self-evident, and (for the most part) positive. They identified no conflict between "being European" and "being Polish," and indeed most said they value membership in the European Union as a signal of Poland's return to its rightful place at the "heart of Europe."² Nevertheless, the recent rise of populist nationalism in Poland in the years since I completed this longitudinal study compels me to revisit my ethnographic data and take another look at some of the concerns

---

1   This chapter analyzes some of the ethnographic material included in my book *Being and Becoming European in Poland: European Integration and Self-Identity*. I refer to the people I interviewed as "participants" to emphasize the way they engaged as active agents in the study, sometimes providing essential information, sometimes critiquing the questions I asked them, sometimes suggesting I approach matters from a different angle.

2   Imagining Poland as the vital, emotional, sacred "heart" of Europe has occurred at least since poet Juliusz Słowacki wrote in 1836: Jeśli Europa jest nimfą—Neapol / Jest nimfy okiem błękitnem—*Warszawa / Sercem*—cierniami w nodze: Sewastopol / Azow, Odessa, Petersburg, Mitawa— / Paryż jej głową—a Londyn kołnierzem / Nakrochmalonym—a zaś Rzym . . . szkaplerzem. "If Europe is a Nymph, then Naples is the nymph's bright-blue eye—Warsaw is her heart, whilst Sevastopol, Azov, Odessa, Petersburg, and Mitau are the sharp points of her feet. Paris is her head—London her starched collar—and Rome her bony shoulder." Słowacki, "Podróż na Wschód," ll. 85–90, cited and translated in Davies, *Heart of Europe*, x–xi. Davies adopted this metaphor as the title of his short history of Poland, written from the perspective of the Solidarity movement of 1980–81. He notes that the metaphor gained renewed relevance as a symbol of protesters' longing for Poland to be freed from the forces that separated it from the rest of (Western) Europe. Davies concludes his book, "For Poland is the point where the rival cultures and philosophies of our continent confront each other in the most acute form, where the tensions of the European drama are played out on the flesh and nerves of a large nation. Poland [. . .] is the *heart* of Europe" (463).

they also expressed about European integration, including the potential threats to national autonomy, local economies, and traditional values. Poles' personal narratives display the diverse, and sometimes idiosyncratic, ways in which identity is negotiated, while also exposing common themes that shape the broader social discourse on national and European identity. They offer important background for understanding contemporary debates in Poland about national identity in the context of European integration.

Personal narratives reveal different ways of conceptualizing the relationship between Polish and European identities. Put simply, being European in Poland is easy, while being Polish in Europe can be more problematic. Regarding the former, the Poles I spoke with tend to regard "European" as an inherent component of "Polishness." They explained this both geographically and culturally: Poland is on the European continent and culturally part of the grand European cultural tradition. However, being Polish in Europe is complicated by political and socioeconomic hierarchies that diminish Poland's status relative to other European nations. Politically, the key challenge emerges with regard to membership in the European Union and the degree to which integration requires the forfeiture of national autonomy. It is within this realm that Polish and European interests might be seen as oppositional rather than complementary. Similarly, to the extent that European integration contributes to social advancement in an imagined hierarchy of nations,[3] being Polish in Europe tends to be viewed as beneficial and desirable. To the extent, however, that social and economic inequalities persist between member states, some participants fear the EU just institutionalizes Poland's weaker position relative to the leading nations within a global hierarchy. I suggest that the swirling discourses and associated sentiments about being European in Poland and Polish in Europe provide some hints about the ambivalences that may contribute to support for European integration, and at the same time reactivate nationalist and nativist sentiments. Participants' narratives contain both viewpoints, existing in uneasy tension with each other. One

---

3   In *International Migration*, Pajo seeks to understand Albanians' motivation to migrate to Greece even when they experience social demotion in their adopted country, closed off from higher-status positions by language barriers and negative bias. In "Media, Markets, and Modernization," Mark Liechty discusses the "self-peripheralizing" consciousness of Nepali youths in Kathmandu who aspire to achieve what they see as modern middle-class lives based on an international standard that is far from the Nepali norm. In both of these cases, as in the Polish case, people seem to make choices based on an imagined global hierarchy of nations, in which often their native place is seen as marginalized relative to nations with greater economic and political power on the world stage.

need not look for opposing social or political factions, each pitted against each other with opposing perspectives, as is commonly portrayed in contemporary politics. I focus on the ambivalences at the heart of cultural debates about the Polish nation and its place within and in relation to Europe.

The study interrogates responses to the kinds of transnational comparisons made possible by globalization. New technologies of communication and transportation and increasing long-distance interconnectedness across national borders[4] and space-time compression[5] all in effect shrink the distance between places and accelerate the pace of information that moves between them. More than ever, people around the world are exposed to different lives and lifestyles. Within this context of globalization, I am particularly interested in the criteria by which people rank their nation in relation to what they consider to be leading world powers and how this perceived hierarchy influences their self-perception. As Erind Pajo emphasizes, global hierarchy is imagined, in the sense that it is a social construct: it is a particular reading of objective reality that lends priority to certain ways of being over others and measures the worth of nations by specific, often hegemonic criteria.[6] In Poland, transnational distinctions have often been characterized geographically and culturally, where the developed West is contrasted with the backward East, and Poland is situated uneasily between them.[7] According to Leszek Koczanowicz, Poles have usually characterized themselves as freer, more imaginative, less orderly, and more anarchic than the Germans and more Western than the Russians.[8] Such comparisons and perceived rankings within an imagined global hierarchy can be expressed explicitly in personal narratives and public discourse, though often they operate under the surface as an implicit component of culture, fueling personal and collective aspirations to gain a more central position on the world stage.

The chapter is divided into two main sections. The first considers general patterns in the way participants in my study talked about "European" as a characteristic of being "Polish." The other discusses what they say it means to be Polish within Europe and in particular within the European Union. I conclude with some thoughts about the ambivalences expressed by participants and suggest they help to explain widespread support for European integration

---

4   Hannerz, *Transnational Connections.*
5   Harvey, *The Condition of Postmodernity.*
6   Pajo, *International Migration.*
7   Galbraith, "Between East and West." Horolets, *Obrazy Europy w Polskim Dyskursie Publicznym*; Kostrzewa, *Between East and West.*
8   Fischer, "Working through the Other."

even as nationalist and nativist inclinations have gained a foothold in contemporary political debates. But first, I introduce the person-centered methodology upon which the study is based and provide general information about the participants in the study. I also introduce the concept of "constellations of debate," the discursive arena in which participants grapple with their ambivalence about Poland's place within Europe.

Person-Centered Ethnography

From my earliest ethnographic fieldwork in 1992, participants have pondered the relationship between Poland and Europe, a topic whose salience has grown alongside the intensifying process of European integration.[9] Most of the quotations cited in this chapter were collected between 2005 and 2012, after Poland's entry into the European Union in 2004. Over the years, I have spoken with hundreds of Poles about these and related issues, but the core of my study comprises person-centered ethnography with thirty-two Poles, nine originally from Krakow and twenty-three originally from the Bieszczady region.[10] Starting from their years in high school, participants shared their life stories with me in semistructured and open-ended interviews and conversations. I added a longitudinal dimension to person-centered ethnography, returning to participants periodically to ask many of the same questions, with the addition of questions relevant to their place in the life course and related to contemporary events in Poland. Even though the formal interviews have stopped, I still remain in regular contact with many participants. During the later phases of the study emphasized here, I increased the number of participants in one-on-one interviews from twenty to thirty-two, adding participants from Bieszczady known to me through earlier

---

9   Galbraith, "Between East and West"; Galbraith, *Being and Becoming European*.
10 Initial contacts with participants occurred through the schools they attended. In an effort to ensure some diversity of class backgrounds and educational aspirations, I conducted group interviews in both urban and rural settings with students at college-track high schools as well as those attending technical high schools or trade schools. I met informally with students outside of school and did multiple person-centered interviews with a subsection of students who also seemed best able to articulate opinions about the transition in Poland and issues related to national identity. I also interviewed teachers, school principals, and local community leaders, and engaged in participant-observation of school and community events.

group interviews or other school activities.[11] Because participants were in high school when the study began, I didn't know where their lives would take them. In the ensuing years, a number of them had moved; I took into account their current place of residence so that roughly equal numbers of participants live in villages, towns, and cities. Additionally, most participants have had some experience abroad including three who have settled in other European countries. I spoke with equal numbers of males and females, as well as people with varying professions and levels of education.

Over the course of multiple in-depth interviews, participants in person-centered ethnography reflect upon their lives in relation to broader cultural frames, revealing their personal processes of meaning-making. According to Robert Levy, by attending to "personally organized statements," one can "investigate, in a fine-grained way, the complex interrelationships between individuals and their social, material, and symbolic contexts."[12] In person-centered ethnography, interview participants are not only "informants" who provide culturally salient information about a domain of inquiry but also the "object of systematic study and observation in him- or herself."[13] At issue is not just what people say but also how they say it, the emotional resonance of certain topics, and the impact associated meanings may or may not have on their lives. Thus, taking a person-centered approach, this study emphasizes individuals' experiences of, and reactions to, the profound transformation of social life in Poland since the fall of state socialism and the expansion of the European Union. It explores the personal meanings Poles attach to the collective categories "Poland" and "Europe," and identifies more generalized cultural patterns within their responses. This longitudinal, qualitative approach helps to illuminate individuals' long-standing perspectives on personal and national identity and how those perspectives are reinscribed, revised, and invented in response to shifting social conditions within the transnational context of Europe.

A person-centered approach is particularly important when considering issues like identity, which are formed and reformed at the juncture between

---

11 Because of the intensive nature of person-centered ethnography, such studies typically involve ten to twenty participants. More generally, qualitative research tends to add subjects until the point of saturation, when little new material is added by additional interviews. The longitudinal nature of my study allowed me to increase the number of participants to capture a greater variety of experiences while still having in-depth knowledge of peoples' lives over time.

12 Levy, *Tahitians*, xxii; Levy and Hollan, "Person-Centered Interviewing and Observation," 313. Hollan, "Setting a New Standard," 465.

13 Levy and Hollan, "Person-centered Interviewing and Observation," 316.

subjective experience and collective institutions and categories. In a sense, I explore the relationship between what Ulf Hannerz calls "agency" and "habitats of meaning."[14] Agency, the choices individuals make, is shaped by the cultural setting (habitats of meaning) but can also in some ways produce those settings. Habitats of meaning are thus akin to Pierre Bourdieu's concept of habitus,[15] but Hannerz emphasizes the complexity, diversity, and flexibility of meanings produced and reproduced within these relationships. Bourdieu defines habitus as

> a system of lasting, transposable dispositions which, integrating past experiences, functions at every moment as *a matrix of perceptions, appreciations, and actions* [emphasis in the original] and makes possible the achievement of infinitively diversified tasks, thanks to analogical transfers of schemes permitting the solution of similarly shaped problems, and thanks to the unceasing corrections of the results obtained, dialectically produced by those results.[16]

In other words, culture isn't just "out there" in the public sphere; it is also internalized in the form of dispositions that orient people toward certain forms of practice. Applying this framework to the concerns of this chapter, orientations toward nation and Europe are not just dictated by habitats of meaning or generated by political power and institutions of the state. It is important to account for the multiple ways people interact within habitats of meaning to decide who they are, what groups they belong to, and what kinds of associated rights and responsibilities they have.

Close attention to individuals' perspectives shows that their views are rarely unitary or consistent. Nevertheless, it is possible to identify common channels of inquiry and shared processes by which people weigh different options. I use the term "constellations of debate" to describe the varied perspectives that swirl around central issues and the common ways in which people talk about them as they try to figure out where they stand personally or attempt to reach a collective

---

14   Hannerz, *Transnational Connections*, 22. Hannerz adapts Zygmunt Bauman's discussion of the relationship between agency and "habitat," where habitat is both the setting in which agency operates and also produced by agents: "Habitat neither determines the conduct of the agents nor defines its meaning; it is not more (but not less either) than the setting in which both action and meaning-assignment are possible." See *Intimations of Postmodernity*, 191. Neither Hannerz nor Bauman apply an explicitly psychological understanding of "agents" like I do. They tend to focus on social groups and institutional actors.
15   Bourdieu, *Outline of a Theory of Practice*.
16   Ibid., 82–83.

agreement. Similarly, Theodore Schwartz calls such shared debates the "litigation of culture," while Daniel Linger suggests that identity be reconceived "in terms of a congeries of problems rather than a set of assumed attributes or a prototype."[17] Constellations of debate take shape in personal as well as public discourse. A key dimension I emphasize here is the ambivalence aroused by some issues, wherein individuals wrestle to reconcile polarized opinions they encounter within their habitats of meaning, rarely ever reaching an unambiguous, undisputed resolution.

In what follows, I discuss patterns in the ways participants in my study talked about Poland, Europe, and the relationship between them. I highlight the constellations of debate orbiting two central points: what it means to be European in Poland and what it means to be Polish in Europe. Ambivalence entails holding alternate viewpoints simultaneously, allowing, for instance, supporters of EU integration to also push for legislation that goes against EU standards, or Eurosceptics to nevertheless celebrate Poland's place within European culture.

Being European in Poland

"Europe" usually evokes positive associations for participants in my study, even among those critical of the European Union. However, what exactly Europe stands for is variously understood by different people and in different situations. This lack of a fixed meaning makes "Europe" what Mummendery and Waldzus call an "empty" category.[18] People tend to attach whatever significance they believe is relevant to the given circumstances. I do want to stress, however, that such mutability does not diminish a cultural category's symbolic importance. On the contrary, the most powerful symbols tend to be the ones that encompass variable and sometimes even contradictory meanings.[19]

For most of the Poles I interviewed, being European in Poland is a simple matter. It does not require them to do anything or change anything because, as I was told on numerous occasions, "Poland has always been in Europe." Despite only vague agreement about what Europe is, participants express favorable views of Europe. Participants in my study regard Poland's place within Europe

---

17 Schwartz, "Where is the Culture?"; Linger, "Has Culture Theory Lost Its Minds?," 304.

18 Mummendery and Waldzus, "National Differences and European Plurality." See also Risse, "European Institutions and Change."

19 Turner, *Forest of Symbols*.

as long-standing and undisputed. They explain it in both geographic and cultural terms: geographically, Poland is located within the European continent; and culturally, Poland shares the same religious and intellectual heritage that forms the foundation of European culture. Responses reflecting this taken-for-granted sense of "being European" include:

- I am a Pole, and Poland is in Europe, so I am also a European. I am in two groups.
- If we talk about geographic borders, we are a part of Europe.
- I feel like a Pole, therefore I feel European ... I'm a European because I'm Polish.

Furthermore, participants commonly associate "Europe" with cultural elements, such as Roman Catholicism and the value of freedom. They also root transnational Polishness in history, referring to Poland's historical presence in multiethnic states and empires, cultural influences from both the West and the East, and flows of migrants spanning generations.

Of all the participants in my study, Wojtek probably has the most developed views about Poland's transnational cultural connections with Europe. Nevertheless, he opposes European integration. Born in a rural mountain village in southeast Poland, he grew up in one of the few places that remained ethnically heterogeneous after World War II, with both ethnic Poles who were predominantly Roman Catholic and ethnic Ukrainians who were Greek Catholic or Eastern Orthodox. The region's prewar Jewish population was decimated during the Nazi occupation, leaving behind little more than an overgrown cemetery. Wojtek's father told him all about the history of his native place, including the fact that various ethnicities are represented within their own family. This awareness of cultural differences also made Wojtek realize that one's ethnic affiliation is on some level something one must choose. Wojtek chose to be Polish and to embrace conservative forms of Roman Catholicism, patriotism, and nationalist politics. Wojtek went to university in Krakow, where he became a professor. He has settled down in the city with his wife and children, but he maintains a romanticized connection with Bieszczady, a region he associates with a multicultural vision of Poland. Although Wojtek voted against Poland's accession to the European Union, he nevertheless celebrates Poland's many cultural and historical connections with Europe, ranging from the centrality of Christianity at the foundation of European society, the common use of the Roman alphabet (as opposed to Cyrillic), and European styles of architecture. Wojtek positions Poland as a part of Europe, but he does not believe the nation should cede autonomy to the EU.

Frequently, participants imagine Europe positively, as a global center of culture, power, and economic development. Their views correspond with the broader discourse documented by Anna Horolets in her study of portrayals of Europe in the Polish press.[20] Horolets notes that Europe is often equated with "civilization," and the "return to Europe" tends to be regarded as a way of gaining higher social and political status. Additionally, some of my participants emphasized Poland's peripheral position within such a global imaginary. This sense of being far from the center of Europe is particularly strong in the Bieszczady region, which is sometimes called Poland's "Wild East" because its remote mountains and villages are mythologized as a refuge for artists, criminals, or anyone who wants to escape the watchful eye of society. Darek, a lifelong resident, explained, "I think we can be proud because Europe is the cradle of knowledge and culture. But Poland is on the edge of Europe, and we live on the edge of Poland."

Nevertheless, participants commonly expressed annoyance with discourse that characterizes Poland's accession to the European Union as "joining Europe," exclaiming "where else has Poland ever been?" They defiantly reject the inferiority implied by the idea that Poland is not already and always in the heart of Europe.

- I have always felt like a European. It didn't require entrance into the EU.
- I don't know what it means to "feel like a European" because I believe that much earlier, before we found ourselves in the EU, we were "in Europe."
- What does it mean that Poland "entered Europe"? Does that mean that we were in Asia before?
- I find it very disturbing when people come to Poland and act as if some miracle happened and we suddenly became civilized when we entered the EU on the 1st of May [2004].

All of these comments reflect the opinion that Poland cannot "join Europe" because it is already in Europe, both geographically and culturally. They push back against the Cold War division that situated Poland with the "backward" East, held back by decades of communism, asserting instead the nation's rightful place among countries of the "civilized" West.

The question remains just what "being European" entails, and the influence it might have on "being Polish." Are cosmopolitan, deterritorialized identities emerging in response to increasing interconnectedness across national boundaries? Are they replacing geographically and historically bounded attachments

---

20   Horolets, *Obrazy Europy w Polskim Dyskursie Publicznym*.

to particular places and people? These questions are at the heart of the most fundamental debates about European integration and about globalization generally.[21] Participants' responses suggest that, even as some sense of being European is growing, it is not replacing national and regional identities, which tend to remain stronger. This is reflected in terms used to describe the relationship between Poland and Europe.

I asked participants if they feel connected to their region, country, and Europe. I also asked how their feelings of connection at these various geographic levels influence each other and whether they ever conflicted. These questions are quite abstract, so sometimes I had to explain further, usually by asking more specifically, for example, if feeling European might get in the way of feeling Polish. The power of person-centered ethnography is that interviews occur as part of a long-term relationship with participants. This helps to establish trust and makes participants more willing to explore deeper levels of self-understanding. Even when they misunderstand research questions, the way they respond can nevertheless reveal important information about their particular perspective on their cultural setting. *How* are these questions misinterpreted, and what do these misunderstandings suggest about the way Poland is conceptualized in relation to Europe? Often, even if answers are idiosyncratic, they fit into constellations of debate; participants engage with shared areas of concern about which there is no general consensus and that tend to be common subjects of discussion.

Participants talked about attachment to local region and to nation in similar ways, but they tended to describe connections to Europe quite differently. In contrast to the multilayered and intimate connections they feel toward their native region and country, sentiments expressed toward Europe tend to be cooler, more distant, and even more rational. This is not a particularly surprising observation; a wide range of interdisciplinary scholarship documents similar patterns both before and after the 2004 EU expansion, in both EU member states and candidate states.[22] Nevertheless, person-centered ethnography

---

21 About European integration, see in particular Shore and Black's "Citizen's Europe" for an early anthropological look at institutional attempts to forge a European unity and the limited degree to which these efforts have been successful even among the EU's bureaucratic elite. Herrmann, et al., *Transnational Identities* explores the issue from an interdisciplinary perspective. Regarding the more general question about the relationship between global and local, see Appadurai, *Disjuncture and Difference*, and Hannerz, *Transnational Connections*.

22 Studies that focus on Poland include McManus-Czubińska et al., *Understanding Dual Identities in Poland* and Roguska, "Polska Droga do Unii Europejski." Studies that examine multiple countries include Citrin and Sides, "More than Nationals;"

provides added insight into the various ways that Poles integrate national and European affiliations into their self-identity. It reveals the specific language used, as well as connections individuals make to lived experiences and emotional responses.

All participants found it easy to discuss their attachment to region and to Poland, but some struggled when asked about their attachment to Europe. Only about half said they feel they have anything like "European identity." A few who said they don't know if they feel any attachment to Europe, nevertheless emphasized that Poland has "always been in Europe." The difficulties some participants had with questions about European identity are instructive. Marta and Zosia, who live in rural Bieszczady, simply did not understand the question. Even when I repeated it or used different words, they seemed unable to grasp that it is possible to feel attachment to something as abstract as Europe. Notably, it is not just a matter of limited experience beyond the local or national sphere because both have lived and worked in other European countries. The responses of Dorota and Paulina are even more curious. Both grew up in Bieszczady, went abroad to work, and ended up staying. One is a college graduate, while the other completed technical high school. When asked about their attachment to Europe, they instead described their feelings of attachment to two national-level scales—to Poland and to their country of destination. Their responses indicate how conceptually challenging it can be to think about the term "European" as a distinct identity that might evoke loyalty, intimacy, or familiarity.

For other residents of rural Bieszczady, the particularities of this remote region help explain why they have never thought about "being European." Darek, a nurse who has rarely traveled outside of Poland said:

> Life is more down to earth here. Consciousness about being European already goes beyond the normal life of the people in Bieszczady. Here, you think about what the winter will be like, whether there will be enough hot weather until the fall, whether there will be work, whether you'll be healthy. Such thoughts about "being" are a luxury for people who are economically well off.

His response attributes the lack of European identity in Bieszczady to the relative poverty and ruralness of the region. Notably, Darek himself is not poor and lives in one of the largest towns in Bieszczady, so he is projecting here a romanticized vision of his native place.

It is also instructive to examine the particular words participants use to characterize the relationship between Poland and Europe. When asked whether they

---

McLaren, *Identity, Interests and Attitudes to European Integration*; and Robyn, *The Changing Face of European Identity*.

experience any sense of conflict between a broader European connection and smaller-scale national or regional identities, all of them responded that feelings of identity at local, national, and European levels do not preclude each other (*nie wykluczają się*). On the contrary, these loyalties were most often considered complementary, as in for instance:

- Bieszczady is contained [*się zawiera*] within Poland; Poland is contained within the European continent. Even if we've been told otherwise, that's how it is.
- It's like this: Bieszczady is in Poland, and so is a part [*część*] of Poland; at the same time, Poland lies within Europe, and so is a part of Europe. So it is possible to be connected with all of them—with Europe, and with Poland, and with Bieszczady.

The specific language participants used helps to illustrate the unmarked, taken-for-granted ways Poles conceptualize the relationship among scales of territorial identity. The assertion "We are European because we are Polish" is a way of saying that "being European" is a fundamental characteristic of "being Polish." Comments such as "they can all be reconciled" (*wszystko się da pogodzić*), and "you can connect them all" (*wszystko można połączyć*) emphasize connections, integration, and indivisibility of territorial identities. Further, assertions like "that's how it is" point to the way such viewpoints are seen as self-evident.

Commonly, participants talked about territorial identities in ways that suggest they are "nested." This is evident in the language quoted above: each territorial scale is "a part" (*część*) of the other or "contained within" (*zawiera się*) each other. Others used related terms like "they overlap" (*zazębiają się*), and they "lie within" (*leży w*) each other. Piotr, a salesman in Krakow, said, "I see it like this: the bigger circle is Europe, the smaller circle is Poland. Smaller still is Małopolska [the province], and smaller still is the heart, in the middle, which is Krakow. It's all together. They don't preclude each other." Piotr's characterization captures the way many associate smaller scales with intimacy and emotion, while wider scales are progressively farther from that "heart."

Participants agreed that being European does not require giving up or losing regional or national identity:

- You don't have to renounce your nationality to feel good in Europe.
- You can be connected to every one of these structures.

Participants associate their regional (and in many regards national) identity with their essence. By contrast, participants' responses show how "European" is more often understood as a characteristic of "Polish" than as a separate supranational scale of identification. This makes Europe familiar, but it remains conceptually undeveloped, even for many who have had frequent encounters beyond the national sphere. Although participants claim to feel much more intensely connected to their region and/or nation, most nevertheless express some degree of allegiance to Europe, and many say their sense of European identity has grown since Poland became a member of the EU.

Being Polish in Europe

Being European in Poland tends to be defined in clichéd geographic and cultural terms, but being Polish in Europe involves more fraught political and socioeconomic distinctions. Within the structure of the European Union, membership entails relationships not only with "Europe" as an empty category with vague (though positive) associations. It also requires figuring out what it means to be Polish in relation to transnational structures of the European Union, and in relation to the other EU-member states. Being Polish in Europe foregrounds Poland's position as one of many nations within Europe, subject to the same EU laws within shared governance structures but whose interests may conflict with those of other member states. In this section, I explore the ambivalence revealed in constellations of debate about the overall effects of EU membership on Poland, particularly with regard to questions of national autonomy and socioeconomic benefits. In the context of these concerns, it is perhaps surprising that public opinion research shows sustained and overwhelming support for Poland's membership in the EU.

The Center for Public Opinion Research (CBOS) has been tracking popular perceptions of the European Union since the early 1990s (see figure 10.1). Before 1997, when membership remained an abstract goal, 70 to 80 percent of those surveyed supported integration. Enthusiasm waned during what Milada Vachudova calls the period of "active leverage," when the EU laid out clear conditions for membership and candidate countries began the work to meet those conditions in earnest.[23] Support rose after the passage of the referendum on membership in 2003, and it has been above 80 percent since 2007, except for a brief dip in 2013 when the Polish economy finally felt some negative effects of the European economic crisis. In April 2017, support reached 88 percent of those surveyed, and it remains at that level even though the ruling party defies EU standards and the European Parliament threatens to sanction Poland for

---

23 Vachudova, *Europe Undivided*, 105–37.

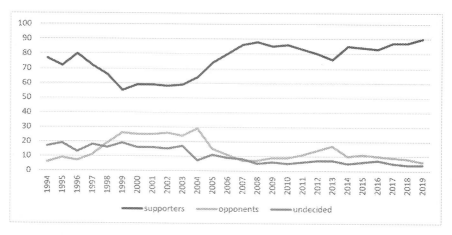

Figure 10.1. Levels of support for and opposition to European integration 1994–2019. Data from surveys conducted by CBOS.

new legislation it deems antidemocratic.[24] Polish levels of support for the EU are remarkably high, and in fact, higher than in neighboring Hungary (82 percent), Slovakia (74 percent), and Czechia (56 percent).[25]

These overwhelming numbers can obscure important patterns of variation across occupational and other demographic categories. When disaggregated, support for EU membership tends to be highest among professionals and business owners, urban residents, and those with higher levels of education. Farmers tend to be the occupational group reporting the lowest level of support. The most recent surveys reveal some notable trends. For one, membership is supported by 86 percent of those who align with the ruling Law and Justice Party, even though their party has pushed a nationalist agenda.[26] A second notable trend involves the decline of support for the EU and for further integration among the youngest Poles. Twenty-two percent of eighteen- to twenty-four-year-olds said they oppose EU membership, in contrast to just 9 percent

---

[24] Roguska, *Jakiej Unii Chcą Polacy?* and Roguska, *Po Rezolucji PE: Opinii i Obawy*, 6–7.

[25] CBOS Report, *Polacy, Czesi, Słowacy i Węgrzy o Członkostwie w Unii Europejskiej*, 6. Notably, 52 percent of Poles express strong support, compared with just 30 percent of Hungarians and Slovaks, and 18 percent of Czechs.

[26] Roguska, *Jakiej Unii Chcą Polacy?*, 4–5 and Roguska, *Po Rezolucji PE: Opinii i Obawy*, 7.

in all age groups combined.[27] One arena in which some young Poles, mostly men, have expressed their commitment to an ethnically homogeneous nation has been through November 11 Polish Independence Day Marches in Warsaw, which in recent years have attracted tens of thousands of participants from around the country. The theme of the march in 2015 was "Poland for Poles, Poles for Poland" and in 2016, "Poland, the Bastion of Europe." In 2017, marchers carried placards asserting WHITE EUROPE. Notably, these slogans reassert Poland's place within Europe, while also promoting ideals of racial and ethnic purity.[28]

Clearly, the general trend in favor of EU membership does not tell the whole story. This trend has not always translated into corresponding support for specific EU policies, for multiculturalism, or for other member nations. Comments by participants in my study reveal the grounds for ambivalence about the relationship between Poland and Europe. Specifically, participants weighed whether the EU promotes order and equality or is just a new form of imperialism challenging Polish autonomy. They also questioned whether membership brings opportunity to Poland or serves the interests of more established member states.

Ambivalence about the overall effect of EU membership on Poland's sovereignty, advancement, and stability emerges most clearly in participants' reflections about governance. They alternated between praise for the order and equality promoted by EU standards and criticism of the rigidity of those same standards. Nevertheless, they expressed respect for a system that actually makes it possible to get things done. This must be understood against the backdrop of the inefficiencies of state socialism, when government reports of economic progress were contradicted by daily struggles to accommodate systemic shortages, followed by the uncertain 1990s when official channels continued to provide unreliable or poorly defined pathways to opportunities.[29] By contrast, the EU delivers a clear and stable structure for individual and national social advancement, even though outcomes remain uncertain. Information about subsidies may be readily available for those who know where to look, but there are no guarantees that funds will be granted. Open borders provide the freedom to travel and seek employment abroad, but they do not guarantee good pay, or

---

27 Roguska, *Jakiej Unii Chcą Polacy?*, 2.
28 Galbraith, "Independence Day."
29 About general trends during and after state socialism, see Verdery, *What Was Socialism?* About Poland, see Dunn, *Privatizing Poland*, Galbraith, "Between East and West," and Wedel, *The Private Poland*.

even decent working conditions.[30] Participants explain their growing sense of security in terms of stable EU-supported structures. Nevertheless, they remain subject to the uncertainties emerging from what Beck calls "the privatization of risk." Within "risk societies," states abdicate responsibility for citizens' social welfare, shifting the costs onto workers themselves, who must fashion their own economic security via private insurance, retirement pensions, and the like.[31] Within postsocialist Poland, as Buchowski notes, "The privatization of socialist property also means that the state partially abandoned its liability toward those who worked on it; privatization of land means also privatization of 'social security.'"[32]

Recent scholarship has focused on the related consequences of neoliberalism in both Eastern and Western Europe, where socioeconomic inequalities have deepened within a neoliberal economic framework defined by market liberalization, deregulation, and privatization.[33] Elizabeth Dunn, Don Kalb, Michał Buchowski, and others have traced similar effects of neoliberal restructuring in Poland that has left whole classes of citizens disenfranchised.[34] Buchowski asks why, for a certain segment of the population, objective criteria of economic development have not translated into subjectively felt satisfaction. He argues that the key to understanding this lies in the idea of social exclusion, where some social groups feel left out of the prosperity that others have realized since the fall of communism and opening of national borders.[35] This explanation is consistent with the idea that an imagined global hierarchy has real effects on people's self-perception, but Buchowski also emphasizes the importance of deconstructing common distinctions between supposed "winners" and "losers" in the "transition" from socialism and capitalism. Certainly, dynamics of class hierarchies and social relations matter but not necessarily in the ways a neoliberal model of progress dictates. For instance, the supposedly new "middle class" of private entrepreneurs, regarded as the engines of capitalism within the neoliberal model, are in fact an extremely diverse group with different ties to the socialist past and with different prospects within the capitalist economy.[36] Kalb

---

30   Galbraith, *Being and Becoming European*.
31   Beck, *Risk Society*, 143.
32   Buchowski, "Anthropology in Postsocialist Europe," 73.
33   Ther, *Europe Since 1989, A History*.
34   Buchowski, *Czyściec*; Dunn, *Privatizing Poland*; Kalb, "Conversations with a Polish Populist."
35   Buchowski, *Czyściec*, 12.
36   Buchowski, "Anthropology in Postsocialist Europe," 74–75.

also argues for renewed attention to the dynamics of class and (borrowing from Eric Wolf) "structural power" associated with capitalist globalization.[37] He says, "Populism refers to the moods and sensibilities of the disenfranchised as they face the disjunctures between everyday lives that seem to become increasingly chaotic and uncontrollable and the wider public power projects that are out of their reach and suspected of serving their ongoing disenfranchisement."[38] Both Buchowski and Kalb point to structural constraints that have constricted opportunities for certain social classes and call into question the neoliberal emphasis on individual personal traits as the determinant of success or failure within global capitalism.

Person-centered interviews help to reveal how participants make sense of their day-to-day experiences within habitats of meaning increasingly shaped by European integration. Not all think ceding some national autonomy to the EU is a negative development. As Zbysiek, who runs his own business in Lesko, said:

> It would be foolish to not enter such a structure, which is a kind of insurance of stability of certain processes. Few can afford to be completely independent states (...) However, I believe that all of the effort, the transformation so to speak, the changed regulations that were forced on us so that Poland could enter the EU, made it possible to fix many things that lay fallow, were not done at all, or were done poorly over those 50 years in the Eastern Bloc. That's why I think it was the only way, a reasonable solution; it was a "marriage of convenience." But it wasn't an accident, or blind reverie. We always wanted to be in the West.

Zbysiek described the necessity of integration, and even the benefits of harmonization, the optimistic-sounding term that refers to the establishment of common standards, rules, and policies in all member states. In public opinion surveys, business owners are generally supportive of EU integration, but person-centered ethnography shows that even supporters can feel ambivalence about what Poland may be losing in the process. Zbysiek's lack of enthusiasm for these changes derives from a sense of being forced into the EU and the corresponding loss of national autonomy. Despite his ambivalence, Zbysiek suggested that, on balance, trading some national sovereignty for greater stability and social advancement is worth it; the EU promises to finally repair the infrastructural neglect that characterized governance during late socialism.

---

37 Wolf, "Distinguished Lecture: Facing Power"; Kalb, "Introduction: Headlines of Nation."
38 Kalb, "Introduction: Headlines of Nation," 14.

Some participants expressed ambivalence about European integration by comparing the EU with Soviet influence before 1989. In both instances, a stronger external power sets the rules. They pointed out uncomfortable similarities between European Union and Soviet Union management styles, and they complained about the lack of sovereignty in the EU because member states are compelled to follow the dictates of Brussels without any effective voice in the European parliament. Wojtek, a professor, argued, "The EU is just like a centralized economy. Because they decide: how many tons of grain to produce, how many liters of milk. After all, we already had that [under communism]. I don't believe that kind of system has a chance of surviving." These critics associate the EU with loss of autonomy. Nevertheless, most participants view EU membership more favorably than Soviet control because Poles chose this allegiance, as opposed being forced into it. They also associate integration with social advancement. Basia, who works for a multinational corporation, explained, "If we hadn't [voted for EU membership] where would we find ourselves? Would we be in the same bag as Russia? . . . For me, it was natural that we're going in a certain direction." Her comment illustrates how Russia is seen as less advanced within the global hierarchy of nations and naturalizes the inclination to aspire to a more powerful position among nations.

Another source of ambivalence about EU governance stems from uncertainty regarding the long-term viability of the EU itself:

- The EU is not entirely stable, and I'm not entirely convinced it will continue in the form it has now.
- Honestly, I don't trust it. For now I'm suspending judgment. I believe it's difficult to support so many countries, to handle policy, to distribute funding to everyone, to more or less stabilize the legal system so it will be more or less the same everywhere. It's too much. How can they succeed?
- Sooner or later, it will all fall apart. You can already see divisions in the EU. There isn't that cohesion anymore.

Some participants suggested that Poland entered the EU too late, and much like a pyramid scheme, only the countries that joined early stand to profit before the whole thing crumbles. This skepticism has proved prescient considering the vulnerability of the EU exposed by Britain's exit and by the EU's delayed rollout of Covid vaccinations.

The ambivalence with which participants regard centralized governance within the EU provides an important counterpoint to the overwhelming support shown to the European Union in public opinion surveys. It shows some of the challenges of being Polish in Europe, and in particular Poles' divided opinions about ceding some national autonomy to the supranational level.

While they talked about governance, participants also described EU integration in terms of socioeconomic factors. They associate the EU with "prospects for a better life": opportunities for mobility—particularly to work legally in other EU countries—and direct subsidies for economic development *within* Poland.

- Poland isn't such a rich country, and we get a good amount of money from their till. So it's to our benefit.
- It's a chance for Poland to move forward in those areas where we can't manage financially.

Hopes for "a better life" in the EU extend beyond pure economic factors. In many ways economic prosperity stands as a marker for something less tangible but nevertheless of deep value: Poland's social advancement within an imagined hierarchy of world nations. Participants express the position that Poles want respect on the world stage, and more specifically they want to gain a more prominent position at the "heart of Europe." They also debated whether EU membership would fulfill that promise.

A common concern participants raised was that the established EU countries were really just looking out for their own economic welfare. Some said, "They would not admit us if it were not in their interest." Several expressed concern that Poland would just become a consumer market (*rynek zbytu*) for Western Europe's surplus merchandise. About EU subsidies, Paweł said, "Nothing is for free." Despite economic benefits coming from EU integration, participants emphasized that Poland is the weaker partner in the union. *Rynek zbytu* can be translated simply as "market," as in an arena for the sale of products, but it more commonly carries a negative connotation, as for example:

- The EU wanted to connect more countries to themselves because it opened a *rynek zbytu*. Because they have already saturated their own. And this is the next problem (with EU integration). There are many (Polish) firms that lacked the proper infrastructure or finances to improve their company so it would meet EU requirements. And essentially this squeezed our workplaces, squeezed our industry.
- Germany, Brussels, France, and Spain, too, have taken advantage of our *rynek zbytu*. They dumped old lines of production. The ones who benefited were the first ones to form the EU. There is no equality. The rich always look out for themselves. After all, no one will give one hundred million unless they were going to get two hundred million back.

Serving as the *rynek zbytu* of established EU countries implies a weaker position in the balance of trade, and correspondingly, in a global imaginary in which nations are hierarchically organized around powerful centers that dictate the criteria for participation within the global sphere. Despite their overwhelming support for Poland's membership, participants expressed a deep and widespread ambivalence about the benefits they will gain from the EU, as indicated by their expression of concern about Poland being taken advantage of and being used by stronger partners for their own enrichment.

Nationalism in Transnationalism

To summarize, participants in my study voice a number of ambivalences about the European Union's likely impact on Polish autonomy and Poland's position in a global hierarchy of nations. They cited economic benefits from increased public and private investment in Polish infrastructure and commerce and benefits for individuals who find more lucrative and legal employment in other member states. They also noted possible downsides of these same factors. They feared Poland might become a consumer market enriching foreign companies, with Poland's best talent leaving the country for good. Concerns about governance were more multifaceted. With regard to national autonomy, the EU was alternately viewed as a source of protection against potential threats and as a compromise of sovereignty uncomfortably similar to Soviet control. Some worried that the EU had become a new gatekeeper, with the power to set the conditions for prosperity and to decide who measures up to those standards. And finally, not everyone was convinced that the EU experiment would succeed. Constellations of debate about what it means to be Polish in the context of European integration encompass contradictory and contrasting opinions.

How might a person-centered approach help to explain the recent rise of nativist and nationalist politics? Perhaps the answer lies within the ambivalences I have discussed; shifting from support to skepticism toward Poland's membership in the EU is not a matter of radical changes in perceptions so much as a matter of shifting salience among opposing orientations.

Since gaining power in 2015, the Law and Justice Party (PiS) has instituted a number of political changes that suggest a turn toward a narrower form of nationalism. These include weakening the independence of the judiciary, changing the exhibits in the World War II Museum in Gdansk to express the "Polish point of view," opposing refugee resettlement, and criminalizing statements that falsely claim the Polish state or nation was complicit in Nazi atrocities.[39] They assert a nativist perspective and push back against perceived threats from foreign ideas, values, and people. The orientation of these reforms resonates with some areas of sustained concern raised by participants in my study. Within constellations of debate about European integration, there are elements of dissent and discomfort: ambivalences. In his discussion of transnational connections, Hannerz points out that "in the meeting of the alien and familiar . . . it seems that the familiar wins out in the end."[40] Perhaps this is what we are seeing in the turn toward stronger nationalist sentiments. However, Hannerz also argues that in such comparisons between alien and familiar/ global and local, "The local has to be brought up to the surface, to be demystified," so therefore, "socially organized meanings . . . must come up and present themselves to the senses. And whenever they do so, they are also at risk: ready to be interpreted, reorganized, even rejected."[41] Correspondingly in Poland, the nationalist turn of the current government is hotly contested by many citizens who favor a more open and inclusive understanding of the Polish nation. We have yet to see if connections to Europe will be rejected in favor of more immediate and intimate connections with nation and region. The way participants in my study talked about being European in Poland and Polish in Europe shows some of the constellations of debate within which these decisions are being made.

Person-centered ethnography helps to show the taken-for-granted nature of Poles' cultural and geographic connections with Europe, but it also reveals debates about the political and socioeconomic effects of being Polish in Europe. Participants in my study articulated ambivalence about two particular dimensions of European integration: whether EU membership contributes to Poland's power on the world stage or compromises national autonomy and, similarly, whether Poland gains socioeconomic influence or has its status reinscribed at some distance from the top of the global hierarchy of nations. This ambivalence is worth studying because it does important psychological work, helping individuals cope with (and even sometimes reconcile) contradictory impulses. Personal narratives reveal that polarized perspectives are not just relegated to opposing sectors of Polish society, although in recent years polarization has been amplified by rivalries between political parties.

---

39   Lyman, "The Polish Parliament Reshapes Courts;" Stawikowska, "Muzeum II Wojny Zmienia Wystawę;" Beylin, "PiS Straszy Polaków Uchodźcami;" Santora, "Poland's President Supports Making Some Holocaust Statements a Crime."
40   Hannerz, *Transnational Connections*, 25.
41   Hannerz, *Transnational Connections*, 28.

I suggest that ambivalence creates a particularly active site for the production of lasting ties with Europe, but, significantly, ones that do not result in (nor require) severing emotional or material ties with one's nation or region of origin. Participants responded with ambivalence because they are unsure of the best course of action. This might be because they do not know enough, or there is so much uncertainty that it is difficult to anticipate the likely outcomes of any choices. Ambivalence might also reflect their difficulty accepting the trade-offs necessary no matter which direction the country goes. In cases of ambivalence, the choices relating to Poland's future exist in uneasy tension with each other, each promising different benefits and sacrifices. As such, personal perspectives provide an important view into broader cultural and political transformations. In the case of current debates about Poland's place within Europe, they show the roots of dissent that lurk near the surface, even among supporters of European integration.

My research suggests that consistently high levels of support for the European Union can be explained by the institutional validity EU structures and practices add to Poles' sense of already being part of Europe. Being European is seen as a characteristic of being Polish—Poland has always been a part of Europe. EU membership is consistent with cultural understandings about Poland's place as a key player on the world stage. Nevertheless, uncertainty and ambivalence expressed in constellations of debate all point to a shifting field of meanings and evaluations, wherein there can be simultaneous movement toward transnational integration and the reassertion of a narrow notion of Polish nationalism that leaves little room for cultural diversity or transnational compromises.

Bibliography

Appadurai, Arjun. "Disjuncture and Difference in the Global Cultural Economy." *Theory, Culture & Society* 7, no. 2–3 (1990): 295–310.

Bauman, Zygmunt. *Intimations of Postmodernity*. New York: Routledge, 1992.

Beck, Ulrich. *Risk Society: Towards a New Modernity*. Translated by Mark Ritter. Newbury Park, CA: SAGE, 1992.

Beylin, Marek. "PiS Straszy Polaków Uchodźcami, Teraz Sprawa Uchodźców Zaczęła Straszyć PiS." *Gazeta Wyborcza*, December 30, 2017. http://wyborcza.pl/7,75968,22840997,pis-straszy-polakow-uchodzcami-teraz-sprawa-uchodzcow-zaczela.html.

Bourdieu, Pierre. *Outline of a Theory of Practice*. Translated by Richard Nice. Cambridge: Cambridge University Press, 1977.

Buchowski, Michał. "Anthropology in Postsocialist Europe." In *A Companion to the Anthropology of Europe*, edited by Ullrich Kockel, Máiréad Nic Craith, and Jonas Frykman, 68–87. Malden, MA: Wiley-Blackwell, 2012.

Buchowski, Michał. *Czyściec: Antropologia Neoliberalnego Postsocjalizmu*. Poznan: Wydawnictwo Naukowe UAM, 2017.

Citrin, Jack and John. Sides. "More than Nationals: How Identity Choice Matters in the New Europe." In *Transnational Identities: Becoming European in the EU*, edited by Richard K. Herrmann, Thomas Risse, and Marilynn Brewer, 161–85. New York: Rowman and Littlefield, 2004.

CBOS Report. *Polacy, Czesi, Słowacy i Węgrzy o Członkostwie w Unii Europejskiej*. Center for Public Opinion Research Report 103, 2017.

Davies, Norman. *Heart of Europe: A Short History of Poland*. Oxford: Oxford University Press, 1986.

Dunn, Elizabeth. *Privatizing Poland: Baby Food, Big Business, and the Remaking of Labor*. Ithaca, NY: Cornell University Press, 2004.

Fischer, Michael M. J. "Working through the Other: The Jewish, Spanish, Turkish, Iranian, Ukrainian, Lithuanian, and German Unconscious of Polish Culture or One Hand Clapping: Dialogue, Silences, and the Mourning of Polish Romanticism [Interview with Leszek Koczanowicz]." In *Perilous States: Conversations on Culture, Politics, and Nation*, edited by George Marcus, 187–234. Chicago: University of Chicago Press, 1993.

Galbraith, Marysia. "Between East and West: Geographic Metaphors of Identity in Poland." *Ethos* 33, no.1 (2004): 51–81.

Galbraith, Marysia. *Being and Becoming European: Self-Identity and European Integration in Poland*. London: Anthem Press, 2014.

Galbraith, Marysia. Independence Day: The Emotional Tenor of Populism in Poland. In *Cycles of Hatred and Rage: What Right-Wing Extremists in Europe and Their Parties Tell Us about the U.S*, edited by Katherine Donahue and Patricia Heck, 143–68. London: Palgrave Macmillan, 2019.

Hannerz, Ulf. *Transnational Connections: Culture, People, Places*. London: Routledge, 1996.

Harvey, David. *The Condition of Postmodernity: An Enquiry into the Origins of Cultural Change*. Cambridge, MA: Blackwell, 1990.

Herrmann, Richard K., Thomas Risse, and Marilynn Brewer, ed. *Transnational Identities: Becoming European in the EU, 247–71*. Lanham, MD: Rowman and Littlefield, 2006.

Horolets, Anna. *Obrazy Europy w Polskim Dyskursie Publicznym*. Krakow: Universitas, 2006.

Kalb, Don. "Conversations with a Polish Populist: Tracing Hidden Histories of Globalization, Class, and Dispossession in Postsocialism (and Beyond)." *American Ethnologist*, 36, no. 2 (2009): 207–23.

Kalb, Don. "Introduction: Headlines of Nation, Subtexts of Class: Working-Class Populism and the Return of the Repressed in Neoliberal Europe." In *Headlines of Nation, Subtexts of Class: Working-Class Populism and the Return of the Repressed in Neoliberal Europe*, edited by Don Kalb and Gábor Halmai, 1–36. New York: Berghahn Books, 2011.

Levy, Robert. *Tahitians: Mind and Experience in the Society Islands*. Chicago: University of Chicago Press, 1973.

Levy, Robert and Douglas Hollan. "Person-centered Interviewing and Observation." In *Handbook of Methods in Cultural Anthropology*, 2nd edition, edited by. H. R. Bernard, 313–42. Walnut Creek: Altamira Press, 2015.

Linger, Daniel T. "Has Culture Theory Lost Its Minds?" *Ethos* 22, no. 3 (1994): 284–315.

Lyman, Rick. "The Polish Parliament Reshapes Courts, Drawing Criticism." *New York Times*, December 8, 2017. https://www.nytimes.com/2017/12/08/world/europe/poland-laws-courts.html.

McLaren, Lauren M. *Identity, Interests and Attitudes to European Integration*. New York: Palgrave Macmillan, 2006.

McManus-Czubińska, Clare, William L. Miller, Radosław Markowski, and Jacek Wasilewski. "Understanding Dual Identities in Poland." *Political Studies* 51 no. 1 (2003): 121–43.

Mummendey, Amélie and Sven Waldzus. "National Differences and European Plurality: Discrimination or Tolerance between European Countries." In *Transnational Identities: Becoming European in the EU*, edited by Richard K. Herrmann, Thomas Risse, and Marilynn Brewer, 59–72. Lanham, MD: Rowman and Littlefield, 2004.

Pajo, Erind. *International Migration, Social Demotion, and Imagined Advancement: An Ethnography of Socioglobal Mobility*. New York: Springer, 2008.

Risse, Thomas. "European Institutions and Identity Change: What Have We Learned?" In *Transnational Identities: Becoming European in the EU*, edited by Richard K. Herrmann, Thomas Risse, and Marilynn Brewer, 247–71. Lanham, MD: Rowman and Littlefield, 2004.

Robyn, Richard. *The Changing Face of European Identity: A Seven-Nation Study of (Supra) National Attachments*. London: Routledge, 2005.

Roguska, Beata. "Polska Droga do Unii Europejskiej." In *Polska, Europa, Świat: Opinia Publiczna w Okresie Integracji*, edited by Krzysztof Zagórski and Michał Strzeszewski, 16–57. Warsaw: Scholar Academic, 2005.

Roguska, Beata. *Jakiej Unii Chcą Polacy?* Center for Public Opinion Research Report 50/2017.

Roguska, Beata. *Po Rezolucji PE: Opinii i Obawy*. Center for Public Opinion Research Report 171/2017.

Santora, Marc. "Poland's President Supports Making Some Holocaust Statements a Crime." *New York Times*, February 6, 2018. https://www.nytimes.com/2018/02/06/world/europe/poland-holocaust-law.html.

Schwartz, Theodore. "Where Is the Culture? Personality as the Distributive Locus of Culture." In *The Making of Psychological Anthropology*, edited by George D. Spindler, 419–41. Berkeley: University of California Press, 1978.

Shore, Cris, and Annabel Black. "Citizens' Europe and the Construction of European Identity." In *The Anthropology of Europe: Identities and Boundaries in Conflict*, edited by Cris Shore, Victoria Goddard, and Josep Llobera, 275–98. Oxford: Berg, 1994.

Stawikowska, Emilia. "Muzeum II Wojny Zmienia Wystawę, Ma Pokazywać Polski Punkt Widzenia." *Gazeta Wyborcza, Trójmiasto*, November 1, 2017. http://trojmiasto.wyborcza.pl/trojmiasto/7,35612,22592037,muzeum-ii-wojny-zmienia-wystawe.html.

Ther, Philipp. *Europe since 1989: A History*. Princeton, NJ: Princeton University Press, 2016.

Turner, Victor. *Forest of Symbols: Aspects of Ndembu Ritual*. Ithaca, NY: Cornell University Press, 1967.

Vachudova, Milada. A. *Europe Undivided: Democracy, Leverage, and Integration after Communism*. Oxford: Oxford University Press, 2005.

Verdery, Katherine. *What Was Socialism and What Comes Next?* Princeton, NJ: Princeton University Press, 1996.

Wedel, Janine. *The Private Poland*. New York: Facts on File, 1986.

Wolf, Eric. R. "Distinguished Lecture: Facing Power—Old Insights, New Questions." *American Anthropologist* 92 no. 3 (1990): 586–96

Part Three
Portraits and Performances

Chapter Eleven

Views of Polishness

Style and Representation in Local and National Exhibitions

Małgorzata Litwinowicz

> The exhibition should, on the other hand, be so arranged as to make sure that from the beautiful *statue* to the *burial urn*, the platter, the exquisite glass, the finely woven basket, the whole circulation of the idea of *beauty* is clearly manifested. That from a tapestry representing the Raphaelian brush with silk thread to the simplest little canvas the whole gamut of the idea of *the beautiful* present in the work is visualized—then exhibitions will be useful and will do justice to the way the work is esteemed and assessed.
>
> —Cyprian Kamil Norwid

The nineteenth century was marked by great exhibitions. The list of phenomena and processes that revealed themselves in this context is extensive. The world expositions were clear manifestations of imperial clout. Their declared universality was always in service to the great national idea and the utopia of the universal accord that nations of the world would achieve by working together for civilization and progress held in check by a reality of ruthless political and economic competition, territorial disputes, and military tensions that intensified from the mid-nineteenth century onward. Exhibition buildings and entire complexes designed for the purpose were inserted into modernized urban space, sometimes radically redefining it, like the architecture of the 1851 Crystal Palace, the Vienna Prater (which hosted a world fair in 1873), or the Eiffel Tower built for the 1889 Exposition Universelle. Despite the universalizing aspiration, exhibition practice and national identity always proved to be connected. Such connections manifested themselves in various ways and on various levels. The question I would like to focus on here is whether—and, if so, to what extent—the themed exhibitions organized in partitioned Poland served to visualize Polishness. Was it possible, in the reality of a nonexistent nation state, to see the *nation* manifesting itself apolitically and indifferently at the same time through seemingly incompatible objects: historical artefacts and achievements of contemporary inventors and engineers?

The first line of thought leads to those nineteenth-century Polish exhibitions that were specifically meant to present forms of memory. Here I mean the various "antiquity" shows informed by Romantic narratives, inspired by the philosophy of Johann Herder about national roots and their possible legitimations. Searching for or actually producing material traces of national antiquity was a frequent practice in the nineteenth century; put on public display, the mementos became visible evidence of antiquity, legitimating the national community as existing in time, possessing a history, and, consequently, the right to tell it.

Permanent public collections of semiophores, or objects devoid of practical function but charged with sociocultural meanings (i.e., museums), legitimated the antiquity of the national community and its rootedness in history, emphasizing the continuity of nation-state traditions and linking it to a specific territory. In the nineteenth century they also served as testimonies of the universal role of national cultures, for example, as depositaries of the Mediterranean tradition, heirs to the Roman Empire, or, without going too much into redundant and controversial detail, simply as guardians of civilization (to mention such cases as the Altes Museum in Berlin or the British Museum). The notion of the semiophore, though crucial for understanding all forms of collecting and exhibiting (i.e., those of the museum or exhibition)[1] is limited. In principle, it does not refer in any way to actual practices and does not reveal the various tensions occurring at the contact of collection and collecting, exhibition and exhibiting, image and viewing. This tension between a thing and the practice of dealing with it, which always redefines the exhibit, is one that I believe merits a separate discussion.

What is equally interesting, however, is how, during the nascent era of modern nationalism, the national spirit materialized in things that had no relic status, that were not obviously myth-making or history-making: in everyday objects, mechanisms, machines, and architecture (e.g., that of exhibition pavilions). At

---

[1]   Cf. Pomian, *Historia*. See chapter "History of Culture, History of Semiophores."

this point, I believe we should broaden the definition of semiophore. The condition that an object has to lack function and practical purpose to become a medium of meaning—as Krzysztof Pomian would have it—seems controversial to me and I aim to demonstrate how utilitarian objects too were used in exhibition practices to convey specific meanings related to the construction/reconstruction of national identity. Pomian's sharp defunctionalization of the semiophore limits the concept and its applicability to exhibitions. The items presented in industrial or farming expositions were supposed to be practical (many had actually been or were supposed to be used). At the same time, the mowers, harvesters, and computing machines also represented the invisible (if somehow always discernible) meanings of progress, labour, and national identity.

In the history of Polish culture, the centres that I write about have been associated with the notion of the "provincial". This notion is heavily encumbered: provincial not only means distant from urban centres (Warsaw, Lviv, Kraków, or Poznań, for such is the orbit of actual or symbolic metropolises that we remain within), but also denotes backwardness, boredom, disgust, ridiculousness, and necessity for no one in their right mind would choose to live in a nineteenth-century provincial Polish town. The entire Polish literature of the period solemnly seeks to convince us that no worse fate exists, especially for an intellectual. And yet, irrespective of symbolic notations, with their focus on (untrue) metropolitan areas and (sentimentalized) villages, it is the small town that is the principal theatre of Polish modernity.

Antiquities, Collections, and Views

A report in the periodical *Tydzień* named the two goals of an exhibition of national antiquities held in Piotrków in 1881. These were to "bring to light locally owned artworks and historical artefacts" and to raise funds for the volunteer fire brigade and for a scholarship for talented students. Among the exhibits were Franciszek Krukowski's *Return from Golgotha*, Anthony van Dyck's *Head of an Old Man*, Fra Bartolomeo's *Savonarola*, and Henryk Siemiradzki's *Roman Orgy in the Time of Caesars*. Furthermore, it includes works by Marcello Bacciarelli, copies, oleographs; diplomas, stamps, old manuscripts and prints, drawings, medallions, and old coins; items from the collection of Kazimierz Stronczyński (including a royal diploma issued by King Władysław I the Short, a stamp of King Casimir the Great, a *Chronica hungarorum*, Roman coins, and letters of Tadeusz Kościuszko); Asian and ancient Egyptian figurines; and finally several gentleman's sashes, embroideries, a mammoth bone, two huge horns of the auroch ... collections of minerals, birds, insects. A beautifully preserved collection of hummingbirds. *In short, a lot of diversity that intrigues the spectator and awakens in him a yearning for consciousness and learning, which everywhere, and especially in the provinces, is not without benefit and significance.*[2]

The story behind an exhibition of antiquities and art that took place a decade later (1891) in Radom was described as such by a correspondent of *Głos*:

> Given a hard year for paupers and bad crops in the guberniya, with member fees falling behind, the economic council of the Charitable Society had to think about organizing some kind of public event to raise funds for its projects: the sanatorium, the community kitchen, the old people's home etc. ... the annual "flower fête" did not take place due to lack of interest, and there were discussions of a concert by the Lutnia choir, first the Warsaw branch, then the Radom one ... but nothing came of that.[3]

Such events mattered, therefore, as attempts by civic self-organization; in slightly different circumstances an antiquities exhibition could be replaced by the annual flower fête or "some kind of public event." Reports stress the fact that exhibitions are organized on a local level by "people of goodwill" and praise their grandeur (even if at least some of the shows seem to be rather random compilations) as well as social benefits: they not only educate but also help to raise funds for various noble purposes.

To what order did these local-scale national expositions belong? It's not clear whether they should be considered as forebears of modern memory-producing cultural institutions, such as national museums, or as possessing a spirit that would pair them with exhibitions of craft, that is, all manifestations of creativity and enterprise not identified as fine art. But perhaps they are closer to being collections of the keepsakes and curios that were a standard feature of the manor house or palace and firmly belonged to the constellation of Old Polish practices.

But if we examine, for example, an illustration[4] featured in *Tygodnik Ilustrowany* in connection with another exhibition of antiquities in Radom (1884), we begin to have doubts. The exhibition space brings to mind the interior of an antiquarian shop or warehouse; there are countless objects arranged

---

2   *Tydzień*, 2–3 (emphasis added). The exhibition was also covered or mentioned in the issues no. 10, 17, and 21–26 (1881).
3   Radom, "Wystawa starożytności i sztuki" [emphasis added].
4   Illustration by Kędzierski, *Tygodnik Ilustrowany*.

in a way that makes it virtually impossible to behold them. In fact, seemingly quite unusually, there is not a single spectator in view (and "images of viewing" happen to be pretty frequent in *Tygodnik*, whether it is an exhibition, the newly opened zoo in Warsaw, or a high-end retail outlet for Żyrardów textiles).

Ideas and thoughts of James Clifford on children's collections can be used here for more general purposes and understanding practices of provincial exhibitions:

> In these small rituals we observe the channelling of obsession, an exercise in how to make the world one's own, to gather things around oneself tastefully, appropriately. The inclusions of all collections reflect wider cultural rules—of rational taxonomy, of gender, of aesthetics. An excessive, sometimes even rapacious need to *have* is transformed into rule-governed, meaningful desire. Thus the self that must possess but cannot have it all learns to select, order, classify in hierarchies—to make "good" collections.[5]

Clifford also reminds us of the characteristics of good collecting, which is subject to certain rigors: it should be taxonomically and aesthetically structured and should make objects in a way equal—indeed, any "private fixation on single objects is negatively marked as fetishism."[6] One may add that the result of such a sound approach to collecting is an organized collection that may become an *exposition* but certainly is not an *assortment*; randomness (of things and the meanings produced by their encounters) is eliminated, and the ability to see the collection as a whole and to consistently fill its gaps is considered a value (ecstatic collecting is out of the question). A good collection—in the sense that Clifford uses the word—would begin by defining its scope as well as its intended meanings and messages. Its shape would be dictated by the order of ideas that the exhibition is supposed to correspond with (or reflect and embody) rather than by the order of events—random finds that mean something but whose meanings often remain indeterminate. I would say that in an exhibition (whether it is a local antiquities show or a "great" national exposition such as the Universal Domestic Exhibition in Lviv in 1894, the Exhibition of Industry and Farming in Częstochowa in 1909, or the Universal Domestic Exhibition in Poznań in 1929), things should speak according to a predetermined script, as if following a specific scenario; the "random communication" of objects should be minimized—and this, it seems to me, can be seen in the whole effort of cataloguing, fragmenting, separating. "Proper" collecting is the

---

5   Clifford, "On Collecting Art and Culture," 218.
6   Ibid., 219.

antithesis of "savage" collecting; practices of the former include classification and display, while the latter implies accumulation and secrecy. Clifford adds:

> The *making* of meaning in museum classification and display is mystified as adequate *representation*. The time and order of the collection erase the concrete social labor of its making.[7]

As a genre, the exhibition catalogue had already developed its own tradition by the late nineteenth century, with such publications as the *Catalogue of the Antiquities and Artworks Exhibition in 1856 at Count Potocki's Palace* in Warsaw and Karol Beyer's *Photographic Album of the Antiquities and Artworks Exhibition in Kraków* (1858–1859). From the perspective of the 1890s or the later decades, the effort of good—classifying and organizing—collecting had been in place for a long time.

The problem is that sometimes (in the case of small local antiquities exhibitions) the "social labour of their making" is as important as the show itself. Reading reviews of provincial exhibitions in places such as Piotrków Trybunalski or Radom, one may get the impression that they were above all occasions of self-organization and social mobilization, offering the initiators and organizers a sense of agency as well as serving as an opportunity to inventory local resources since the exhibits were ultimately on loan from private owners. Warsaw-based periodicals were harsh on the provincial shows for their inability to produce catalogues and proper captions; something that was sure to lead to confusion, they said, as spectators were forced to rely solely on the judgment of their own senses. This lack of exhibition-making professionalism (as one could evaluate the whole thing from contemporary perspective) was insignificant, however, in light of the social integrating power of the exhibitions as they visualized and materialized a glorious past, becoming a history lesson devoid of all the inconveniences of the cognitive effort.

Antiquities and Geography: Contemporary Space, Bygone Time

If we look at the idea of the exhibitions as a factor conducive to the emergence of a modern nation—an Andersonian imagined community—it may turn out that the diversity of exhibition practices is to some extent a reflection of the

---

7   Ibid., 220.

ambiguity and multidirectionality of the process. We may see antiquities exhibitions as a means of constituting a selective national memory, limited or aspiring, to the memory of the gentry, which was a small social group (never more than 10 percent of Polish society), but definitely the most influential in creating and controlling patterns of national identity (cf. Rodak, this volume). This is a kind of identity *decoupage*—composing a new picture from different elements, which after a particular process look older than they really are—as well as elaborating on (or more often reproducing) a genealogy, a process that could be referred to as the "impersonation of objects." This is the production of such collective memory that tallies with the narrative of the exhibits belonging to the world of the nobility. We can say that exhibitions of antiquities were sometimes a petty and bogus theater of history—theoretically universal/national, practically very local and class-conscious—in which the exhibits themselves mattered as much as the knowledge of whom has loaned them. They need, however, to be seen as an element that comprises the sense of what we call national identity.

The relationship between these antiquities and national history is rather obvious. Exhibited in Kraków or Warsaw, items previously owned by or related in some way to recognizable figures such as John III Sobieski, Bona Sforza, Józef Poniatowski, Wincenty Krasiński, or Tadeusz Kościuszko arranged themselves into an accessible, evident, and easily assimilable narrative about Polish history.[8] But the exhibitions had other consequences as well. The comprehensive, meticulously edited catalogues of major shows (Kraków, Warsaw, Lviv, Częstochowa) provided information not only about exhibits but also about their owners. They were coauthored by private owners (aristocrats loaning their family relics) and by collectors who could afford to treat national memory as an attractive product. Among the places of origin of some of the exhibits featured in the Lviv (1894) and Kraków (1904) shows, their catalogues mention, for example, the National Museum in Kraków, Kraków Museum of Technology and Industry, the Diocese Museum in Tarnów, and a number of other museums.[9]

---

[8] I am only signaling the theme, which is the subject of numerous general and monographic studies. On the mechanisms of identity and tradition construction, cf. for example: Hobsbawm and Ranger, *The Invention of Tradition*. On narratives concerning specific figures, cf. for example: Stefanowska and Tazbir, *Życiorysy historyczne, literackie i legendarne*; Oleksowicz, *Legenda Kościuszki*. On the circulation of objects that become national relics see, for example: Rosiek, *Zwłoki Mickiewicza*; idem, *Mickiewicz (po śmierci)*. On the performatics of memory, cf. Jurkowska, *Pamięć sentymentalna*. I discuss the relationship between collection and narration in "Teodor Narbutt: History and Collection."

[9] *Katalog wystawy zabytków*; *Katalog Powszechnej Wystawy Krajowej*.

This is an important institutional map. At the end of the nineteenth century it turned out that national relics could be owned not only by aristocrats who put them on public display through personal generosity or by collectors aspiring to the social elite but also by museums, which are without a doubt Polish public institutions (representing Polish collective identity). However, in the context of exhibitions the term most frequently used is "domestic"—which is not an obvious notion: we will try to explain its possible meaning and usages later in the chapter.

Domestic—But from What Country?

Are antiquities defined in the nineteenth century as "domestic" connected with "domestic production?" The question seems important to me since the answer may justify combining reflections on exhibitions openly aimed at shaping the space of national identity (antiquities exhibitions) with that of shows meant to popularize technological thought and progress, a theme not necessarily directly related to the rise of modern nationalism. Of course, the Great Exhibition in London in 1851 was a display of Britishness, and the successive expos in Paris were meant to prove France's supremacy in Europe and the world. It so happens, however, that by the end of the nineteenth century, products of the iron-and-steel industry like weaving looms or steam distillers had not yet entered the collective imagination as icons of the nation. While in Britain we see William Titcomb's *The Wealth of England—the Bessemer Process of Making Steel* (1895) or William Turner's famous *Rain, Steam and Speed* (1844), similar examples are nowhere to be found in nineteenth-century Polish art. Technological progress, discoveries, or inventions obviously were not popular themes among artists.

Still, the ideas of progress and the nation definitely seem connected—the two developed at virtually the same time—yet in the Polish context the connection remains unclear. The national pantheon never included an inventor, and isolated "cults" (like that of Ignacy Łukasiewicz, constructor of the first modern oil well) never grew beyond a local scale.

During the partitions period, all exhibitions larger than small-town ones were called "domestic."[10] What particular country is meant in the context of

---

10   Translator's note: The Polish term is *krajowy*, from *kraj*, "country." If we follow the "Polishness in oppression" trope, the regaining of independence should change significantly, yet the 1929 expo in Poznań, Powszechna Wystawa Krajowa, is "domestic" again.

"domesticity"? The Act of May 30, 1818, very closely regulated the organization of exhibitions in the Kingdom of Poland. The first expo was to take place on June 1–15, 1819, and biannually thereafter. These were to be "public exhibitions of outstanding works of domestic industry" (industry meaning here all kinds of production, including art, handicrafts etc.), and participation was limited to "domestic residents": "Before the objects are put on display, specially appointed commissioners will ascertain whether they are truly products of domestic industry and submit lists of applicants to the appropriate Government Committees."[11]

After the November Uprising of 1830–31, things changed radically. In 1840, the Kingdom's Administrative Council issued, on behalf of Nikolai I, a new regulation that legalized exhibitors from other provinces of the Russian Empire. Another "semantic shift" occurred in 1848 when a bill drafted in Saint Petersburg introduced cyclical industrial exhibitions for the Russian Empire as a whole, with the Kingdom of Poland's status reduced to that of one of its provinces, and so the idea of the domestic was absorbed by the idea of the imperial.

As far as the industrial production of the Kingdom of Poland is concerned, an important aspect needs to be mentioned here. Poland's economy before the partitions was weak. The country produced virtually nothing, imported everything, and the sole export was grain. There were no sectors that could be described as "domestic industry" or "domestic production." The Enlightenment modernizers warned that Poles are buying everything from abroad—silk, canvas, cloth, dishware, paper, even horn products—and the importation was always of goods, never of the technologies that actually made these products.[12] Such was the point of departure: no products or inventions that could be defined as "domestic." The grain stubbornly exported to Western Europe was not "domestic" but simply "Polish," and similarly the mineral resources, deposited deep within the earth, mysteriously preserved the national idea, which proved to be somewhat bizarre: no longer natural, but mineral.[13] The "Martin furnace" (*piec martenowski*) and "Jacquard" textiles (*żakard*) could not have been native inventions, as their foreign names clearly indicate.

---

11   Act of May 10, 1818, quoted in Drexlerowa, *Wystawy wytwórczości Królestwa Polskiego*, 168.
12   Cf. the writings of Nax (*Wybór pism*) and Staszic (e.g., "Rzut myśli o polepszeniu stanu krajowego przez zakładanie fabryk i rękodzielni," 334, 338, 339, 345); quoted in Drexlerowa, *Wystawy wytwórczości*, 97.
13   Those links are discussed by Jurkowska in *Pamięć sentymentalna*.

But the *country* is not just the Kingdom of Poland. The 1894 Universal Exhibition in Lviv also carries the adjective "domestic." One of the accompanying publications reads:

> A conference of exhibitors in 1877 passed a resolution that domestic exhibitions should take place in Galicia every 10 years to verify the results achieved on the path of the country's cultural development.... However, an exhibition like the one currently on show at Stryj Hill could not have been executed without the willing, unanimous, and generous cooperation of the *whole country*, all strata of society.[14]

The *Illustrated Guide to Lviv*, which the above quotation comes from, mentions "the country" on numerous occasions. Doubtless that country is Galicia, yet the collective subject inhabiting the unnamed country and speaking on its behalf seems to encompass a larger community: "The *love of our country* begot this work, and the *country's honour and benefit* will serve as motto of the work on its successful completion."[15] The exhibition is meant as a "measure of our progress and vitality,"[16] the country is to acquire a "rational self-consciousness," "all classes and professions are summoned to offer active help," to prove that "we comprise an organism with a future."[17] Sure, the country diet is the diet of Galicia. But all those uses where progress, vitality, or public benefit are so vocally mentioned by no means refer to a reality from which the Kingdom of Poland or Greater Poland (Wielkopolska) have been excluded as "non-domestic." So perhaps the *country* that presents and contemplates its achievements is a hinted alternative to *Polishness*, which can only be realized in the "kingdom of the spirit" (a concept developed in the Polish Romantic literature and philosophy during partitions) and to the political narrative of an independent *nation state*, the restitution of which in 1894 seemed but a chimera.

A feeling of a cross-partition bond is discernible in enunciations connected with another important show, the Exhibition of Industry and Farming held in Częstochowa in 1909. Its organizers noted with the utmost disappointment a lack of interest from Galician exhibitors and with equally strong glee the presence of Galician guests among the visitors.[18] On August 25, 1909, the exhibi-

---

14   *Ilustrowany przewodnik po Lwowie i Powszechnej Wystawie Krajowej*, 154.
15   Ibid., 156.
16   Ibid., 155.
17   Ibid., 156, passim.
18   Another aspect of the Exhibition of Industry and Farming in Częstochowa was its anti-German and pro-pan-Slavic profile. There were no German companies, nor any from Wielkopolska, among the six hundred exhibitors (no invitations

tion was visited by the country marshal for Galicia, Count Stanisław Badeni, who, according to press reports, made the following comments about the show: "In circumstances so unfavourable and in relatively such a short time, an exhibition has been created whose diversity and competent selection are worthy of the capital city."[19] He attributed the *désintéressement* of local business circles to the "lack of initiative from Galician industrialists and the exhibition's incompetent and unconvincing marketing in Galicia."[20] In fact, by "capital city" Badeni seems to have meant not Warsaw but rather Kraków or Lviv; cross-partition unity was also founded on tensions, among which the issue of the metropolitan capital must have mattered a lot, being crucial for the definition of the center-peripheries hierarchy.

From the View to the National Style

Among the visitors to the Częstochowa expo was a delegation of artists from the Kraków-based Polish Applied Art Society. This fact is of twofold significance. First, their presence, warmly welcomed in press comments, can be considered a momentary gesture of cross-partition unity. Second, and more importantly, it is tied to a broader issue—the search for visible forms of the "domestic," which is becoming increasingly tantamount with "national." The Częstochowa exhibition becomes an opportunity to clearly formulate the task of defining a national style: not only through antiquities or historical painting and not necessarily one reflected in mass-market industrial production. As more insightful commentators noted, the 1909 expo was ignored by major companies and factories: "From the height of their aspirations to mega-profit, they looked down at the planned exhibition as little more than a pilgrimage fair, something of no interest to major industry."[21] As a result, despite the original pitch presenting farming *and* industry, and despite the efforts of organizers who prepared an impressive Machine Hall, the exhibition remained a representation of a basically

---

    had been sent out to Germany), while the Czech representation, for example, was ample, both among exhibitors and among visitors. Detailed exhibitor lists can be found at www.wystawa1909.pl.

19 "Wystawa przemysłu i rolnictwa," 2, quoted in Złotkowski, *Wystawa Przemysłu*, 294.

20 Ibid.

21 Kempner, "Wystawa przemysłu i rolnictwa," 2, quoted in Złotkowski, *Wystawa Przemysłu i Rolnictwa*, 295.

precapitalist farming-and-handicraft reality. This was enhanced by the specific context of the place. A visit to the expo was an extra attraction for pilgrims to Jasna Góra, the Częstochowa Catholic sanctuary, and their movement was actually synchronized with the schedule of the exhibition:

> This year's pilgrimages had been put on hold to resume when the exhibition had launched. Our clergy had told the folk about the show that had been set up this year at the foot of the Pauline monastery, and the folk had sensibly realized that this year's pilgrimage would be an extraordinary one, combining benefits for the heart and the mind.[22]

Periodicals paternalistically enthused about hundreds of thousands of peasants who would view the exhibition, listen to lectures on hygiene, and understand that they should practice handicrafts in the winter and thus contribute to national welfare. Even though various peasant associations were in existence, not a single representative of those associations participated in the organization of the exhibition or even its opening.

The Częstochowa expo spurred frequent discussions on a national style, which was supposed to be conveyed no longer by single objects but by whole pavilions dedicated to specific historical and folkloristic movements. Properly inscribed in the landscape, they were meant to constitute a new version of a quintessentially Polish *view*. Reviewers of the 1909 exhibition emphasized the national style of the model farmstead, arguing that it was informed by architectural traditions dating from the time of King Casimir the Great. One can only guess what this was supposed to mean, but it was more likely a symbolic inspiration than a genuine reference to the material reality of the fourteenth century.

It was one of the manifestations of a broader movement—Stanisław Witkiewicz was but one of its proponents—choosing Zakopane and highlander folk style as possible inspiration for the national style. The early twentieth-century search for a national style in architecture and the applied arts was centered in Kraków, and among its main driving forces were the Polish Applied Art Society (TPSS, founded 1901), later the Kraków Workshops (1913–1926), and the Warsaw-based Spółdzielnia Ład cooperative (founded 1926). The first exhibition organized by the TPSS at the Kraków Art Palace in 1902 consisted of three sections—"Historical," "Folklore," and "Contemporary." This triad aptly reflects the philosophy behind the search for a national style, inspired by the ideas of

---

22 Kosiakiewicz, "Wystawa w Częstochowie" quoted in Kapsa, *Stulecie Wystawy*, 116.

John Ruskin and William Morris[23] as well as alluding to Norwid's *Promethidion*. Contemporary efforts meant to draw on the historical and folklore. The latter inherently connected to the landscape, utilizing local resources and techniques, its products addressing material, aesthetic, and spiritual needs. Also in 1902, the TPSS staged an exhibition of Polish applied art in Warsaw, at the Society for the Encouragement of the Fine Arts. The presentations were meant to prove that both "low-brow" (i.e., folk or folk-inspired) art and applied art were worthy of being called "art" and exhibited in "art palaces." Yet the idea meandered, and, for example, the Garden Exhibition of Architecture and Interiors, held at the Jordan Park in Kraków in 1912, was aimed principally at members of the middle and upper middle class who could afford to spend time at spas and sanatoriums, combining health care and leisure with patriotic duties. Seeking to promote Polish spa towns—Krynica, Zakopane, Szczawnica, Niemirów, Iwonicz-Zdrój, and Swoszowice—the Garden Exhibition presented them as rich in natural healing resources and, at the same time, sources of national identity. As part of that show, the Union of Societies for the Beautification of the Country and the Society for the Protection of the Beauty of Kraków staged their own show. According to a poster designed by Aureliusz Pruszyński, this was meant to "promote an effective struggle in defence of the beauty of our country." If the TPSS stands for an effort to equate the languages of folk art and fine art (we could imagine a reality where folk art belongs to the national museum rather than the ethnographic one), then it should be considered an important phenomenon in the history of Polish design—one whose social consequences were short-lived.

Yet another meaning for the framing of a national landscape is aptly reflected in much later texts, published after Poland's rebirth as an independent nation state, in the mid-1920s:

> When the eastern provinces received a larger number of eye-pleasing and rationally designed homes for the civil service, the time will naturally come for buildings for public institutions as well. Relating the style of both the former and the latter to the tradition of Polish architecture, we will carry on the work of our ancestors, bringing Polish culture to the East, and free the local populace from the untenable, and alas quite widespread, sense of the temporary character of Polish rule in the eastern provinces of the Republic.[24]

---

23 On the reception of these ideas in Poland, cf. Szczerski, *Wzorce tożsamości*.

24 *Budowa domów dla urzędników państwowych w województwach wschodnich*, 12. The brochure was edited and designed by the Wydawnictwo Artystyczne Południe fine press. Housing schemes for civil servants, sometimes referred to as

Authority becomes inscribed in the familiar landscape and finely designed, modest-yet-tasteful housing schemes for the civil service that were devoid of monumentality, yet very distinct, in part through contrast with the usually mediocre local development. The history of the search for a national style, particularly intense at the turn of the twentieth century and in the interwar period, can, I believe, be read as a history of nondoing and repression. This was a style that largely ignored social reality rather than, as its manifestos pledged, engaging or simply acknowledging it.[25] This ultimately meant that the national style—even if already developed as an aesthetic trend—was never commonly adopted.

There is much that distinguishes the International Exhibition of Modern Decorative and Industrial Arts in Paris (1925) from the domestic industry shows in the Kingdom of Poland and large open-air expos in Lviv and Częstochowa: themes of time, scope, significance. All, however, share the presence of an effort to pursue and define the Polish visual idiom. The latter was meant to fulfill the (not always explicitly stated) postulate of historicity, that is, stress the territorial continuity of ethnic Polish presence, relating it to folk culture but also making the impression of something naturally inscribed in the landscape. In Paris in 1925, domesticity/Polishness made an emphatic appearance as an export product, a brand whose values (not only aesthetic ones) should be clear and recognizable. "In the Paris expo, Poland must show a distinct face. With the selection of exhibited works, the most strenuous effort of Polish art and technology, it has to win its rightful place among the nations as they finally join in peaceful work after the war,"[26] wrote Jerzy Warchałowski in a proclamation published on the occasion of the start of preparations for the exhibition.

"government districts" (in otherwise very small towns), were to be developed in the Nowogródek, Polesie, Volhynia, and Vilnius voivodeships.

25 It seems that the process of endowing the cultural landscape with a national style in the late nineteenth century and in the interwar period is yet to be exhaustively described. The subject is discussed, for example, by Szczerski, *Cztery nowoczesności*. Writing about the 1899 construction of a railway station building designed by Stanisław Witkiewicz in the Zakopane style in Saldutiškis/Syłgudyszki (Lithuania), he refuses to see it as an example of domestic colonialism and a token of Polish cultural domination in an ethnically diverse borderland province. "For Witkiewicz, the Syłgudyszki railway station was primarily a Romantic attempt to save the civilizational community of the lands of the Polish-Lithuanian Commonwealth.... His use of the idea of a national style for building cultural community between different nations can be considered a unique achievement"; ibid., 32.

26 Warchałowski, "Wystawa Międzynarodowa w Paryżu 1924 r.," 368.

The Polish presentation at the Paris expo was very well received and the exhibits—pavilion, works of applied art, even education curricula in this field—won nearly two hundred medals and honorary mentions. A substantial body of specialist literature exists on the subject.[27] Jerzy Warchałowski's study *Polish Decorative Art*[28] occupies a special place. The author writes about the potential present in Polish art, recognizing a particularly creative source in the combination of artistic individuality, talent, uniqueness, and originality—with folklore. Folklore is an alphabet and inspiration, one used by artists with respect but also with a great deal of latitude. It should be stressed, however, that Polish applied art—as defined by the TPSS, the Kraków Workshops, or Ład—never took firm root in Poland. It remained a showcase created for the purpose of a world expo as well as an example of official/state art (Polish Art Deco, not always the most favorably viewed *jastrzębowszczyzna* style of the interbellum period). It was also the subject of intellectual reflection. Warchałowski wrote that "our creative power is great, but the productive one is weak."[29] Seeking to identify the causes of failure, which began precisely with the great success in Paris, Warchałowski stressed that in the West of the 1920s there existed an exchange between major capital (private and state-owned manufacturers) and applied art. Outstanding artists worked for upmarket department stores such as the Grands Magasins du Louvre, Galleries Lafayette, or Printemps, and their designs entered common circulation "artistic-industrial workshops." In other words, any *domesticity* as a brand was generated not only by individual talents but also by the economic flows of modern capitalism. Warchałowski also writes that the introduction of new styles, crafts, and technologies at the beginning of the nineteenth century did not work precisely because it was a wholly imported modernization project. Decorative art, he argues, has to be a creative reworking of a native idiom. But could folk/peasant art be considered *native* in late-nineteenth or early-twentieth century Poland at all?

---

27 Huml, *Sztuka przedmiotu, przedmiot sztuki*; Dłutek and Kostrzyńska-Miłosz, *W kręgu sztuki przedmiotu*; Rogoyska, "Paryskie Zwycięstwo Sztuki Polskiej w roku 1925," 21–25. The successful Polish presentation in Paris is discussed in detail by Drexlerowa and Olszewski, *Polska i Polacy na powszechnych wystawach światowych 1851–2000* (there is also an extensive discussion of the comments and reviews published in the international press). The Polish presentation was reviewed in *Wiadomości Literackie* (Husarski, "Triumf Polski na wystawie sztuki dekoracyjnej w Paryżu," 4; Iwaszkiewicz, "Polska na Wystawie Sztuki Dekoracyjnej w Paryżu," 2.
28 Warchałowski, *Polska sztuka dekoracyjna*.
29 Ibid., 37.

252 & CHAPTER ELEVEN

In this attempt to produce the *domestic style/domestic idiom*, informed by a notion of culture present in the *Promethidion* or in the aesthetic philosophy of Stanisław Wyspiański, it is impossible to see the same senile paternalism that resounds in the narratives of both domestic expos. What do I mean? For example, in Wincenty Kosiakiewicz's review of the Częstochowa show, the model farmstead consists of a number of diminutives: "wee hallway," "wee porch," "wee barn," "wee stable," and "wee pigpen." Only the manure pit, which is actually located in the very center of the farmyard, is not designated as "wee." But the overall tone of the review suggests that it just might have been. "All this is unfussy, simple, decorated in the easiest and most modest manner—very comfortable, reliable, and highly practical. Such a little manor house can well stand as the retired civil servant's ideal."[30] What a few lines earlier was still a "cottage" with two rooms now becomes a "little manor house." In fact, it is more of a *dacha* for the urban professional than a design for the peasant class. As the catalogue of the Universal Domestic Exhibition in Lviv in 1894 informs us,[31] exhibit no. 2648 was a specimen of a Galician peasant cottage, arranged by the organizers. Even considering the fact that the ethnographic exhibits—peasant cottages from Sokal and the Tatra Mountains, a Hutsul Orthodox church—had been made by local craftsmen rather than by artists better versed in the pure forms of traditional craft[32] bespeaks a certain emancipation of the peasant, the Galician cottage, an image of misery and backwardness, remained an example of internal colonialism. The cottage's inhabitants ("In the living room, Vasyl Shkriblak and Mikhailo Shkriblak carve their own designs in wood, while Vasilina Stolashchuk embroiders and weaves aprons") must have appeared to the viewers not as a materialization of domesticity and civilizational achievement but as a representation of the other; the cottage hardly belonged to the repertoire of national *views*. Peasant groups visiting the Universal Domestic Exhibition in Poznań in 1929 were urged to observe the following rules:

a) strictly follow the guide's instructions;
b) don't leave your group;
c) don't drink alcoholic beverages, e.g., vodka, wine, or mead, during the tour;

---

30   Kosiakiewicz, *Wystawa w Częstochowie*, 117.
31   *Katalog Powszechnej Wystawy Krajowej we Lwowie*, 238.
32   The "professionalization" of the Orient to adapt it to Western expectations is discussed by Mitchell, *Colonising Egypt*. The reference seems justified to me: the way the folk (and/or folk culture) were represented in the domestic exhibitions reveals numerous characteristics that would suggest an internal Orientalization of the peasant class and its portrayal as attractively exotic and fascinatingly alien.

d) *don't drink unboiled water, but soda or tea;*
e) *don't discuss political or party subjects.*[33]

Source texts dealing with domestic exhibitions—press reports and reviews, catalogues, regulations—are replete with similar paradoxical statements. Representatives of traditional cultures, villagers, peasants (various terms are used here), with their craft and costumes, traditions, and language are recognized as important for national identity, its true source and treasure. And the same group is permanently treated as socially adolescent, requiring guidance and control. A strange puppet dance is done around the peasant cottage; the latter turns out to be standing in the middle of the Polish landscape, the new view from which ruins of castles disappear. The history of the pursuit of representing domesticity (and exhibitions offer ample research material in this regard) suggests a rather obvious thing: that an aesthetic movement will not solve long-standing social issues. Reflecting on domesticity and the domestic, at some point we inevitably bump into the unresolved peasant question—infantilized, palliated, muted in all kinds of ways. Even if the peasant cottage, inhabited by Galician or other paupers silent in their kindheartedness, is a Polish paradise in narratives endlessly reconstituting social hierarchies, we should bear in mind that paradise, as Walter Benjamin says, is where a "storm is blowing from." In its face, every effort to stabilize the domestic view proves futile.

Bibliography

Journals

Tydzień (1881)
Tygodnik Ilustrowany (1884)
Głos (1891)
Gazeta Częstochowska (1909)
Świat (1909)
Przemysł i Rzemiosło (1921)
Wiadomości Literackie (1925, 1926)
Budowa domów dla urzędników państwowych w województwach wschodnich. Warszawa: Wydawnictwo Ministerstwa Robót Publicznych, 1925.
Clifford, James. "On Collecting Art and Culture". In: idem, *The Predicament of Culture. Twentieth-Century Ethnography, Literature, and Art*. Cambridge, MA: Harvard University Press, 1988.

---

33   Emphasis added.

Dłutek, Maria, Kostrzyńska-Miłosz, Anna eds. *W kręgu sztuki przedmiotu. Studia ofiarowane Profesor Irenie Huml przez przyjaciół, kolegów i uczniów*. Warszawa-Płock: Instytut Sztuki PAN, Muzeum Mazowieckie, 2011.

Dziedzic, Maria, ed. *Warsztaty Krakowskie 1913–1926*. Kraków: Wydawnictwo Akademii Sztuk Pięknych, 2009.

Drexlerowa, Anna M. *Wystawy wytwórczości Królestwa Polskiego*. Warszawa: Oficyna Naukowa, 1999.

Drexlerowa, Anna M., Olszewski Andrzej K. *Polska i Polacy na powszechnych wystawach światowych 1851–2000*. Warszawa: Instytut Sztuki PAN, 2005.

Hobsbawm, Eric, Ranger, Terence, eds. *The Invention of Tradition*. Cambridge: Cambridge University Press, 1983.

Huml, Irena. *Sztuka przedmiotu, przedmiot sztuki*. Warszawa: Instytut Sztuki PAN, 2003.

Husarski, Wacław. "Triumf Polski na wystawie sztuki dekoracyjnej w Paryżu," *Wiadomości Literackie*, no. 11 (1926).

Ilustrowany przewodnik po Lwowie i Powszechnej Wystawie Krajowej. Lwów: Towarzystwo dla Rozwoju i Upiększania Miasta, 1894.

Iwaszkiewicz, Jarosław. "Polska na Wystawie Sztuki Dekoracyjnej w Paryżu," *Wiadomości Literackie*, no. 25 (1925).

Jurkowska, Hanna. *Pamięć sentymentalna. Praktyki pamięci w kręgu Towarzystwa Warszawskiego Przyjaciół Nauk i w Puławach Izabeli Czartoryskiej*. Warszawa: Wydawnictwa Uniwersytetu Warszawskiego, 2014.

Kapsa, Jarosław ed. *Stulecie Wystawy Przemysłu i Rolnictwa w Częstochowie 1909*. Częstochowa: Muzeum Częstochowskie, 2009.

Katalog wystawy zabytków metalowych w połączeniu z zabytkami cechów krakowskich otwartej w miesiącu wrześniu 1904 roku. Kraków, 1904.

Katalog Powszechnej Wystawy Krajowej we Lwowie w roku 1894 pod protektoratem najmiłościwszego cesarza i króla Franciszka Józefa I, 2nd edition. Lwów, 1894.

Kempner, Stanisław A. "Wystawa przemysłu i rolnictwa," *Gazeta Częstochowska*, vol. 1, no. 60 (3 October 1909).

Litwinowicz-Droździel, Małgorzata. *O starożytnościach litewskich. Mitologizacja historii w XIX-wiecznym piśmiennictwie byłego Wielkiego Księstwa Litewskiego*. Kraków: Universitas, 2008.

Mitchell, Timothy. *Colonising Egypt*. Berkeley, Los Angeles, Oxford: University of California Press, 1991.

Nax, Jan Ferdynand. *Wybór pism*, Warszawa: Państwowe Wydawnictwo Naukowe, 1956.

Norwid, Cyprian Kamil. "Promethidion. Rzecz w dwóch dialogach z epilogiem" (1851). In *Pisma wybrane: Poematy*. Vol. 2. Warsaw: PIW, 1968.

Oleksowicz, Bolesław. *Legenda Kościuszki: narodziny*. Gdańsk: Słowo/Obraz Terytoria, 2000.

Pomian, Krzysztof. *Historia. Nauka wobec pamięci.* Trans. Hanna Abramowicz, Joanna Pietrzak-Thebault. Lublin: Wydawnictwo UMCS, 2006.

Rogoyska, Maria. "Paryskie Zwycięstwo Sztuki Polskiej w roku 1925." In Juliusz Starzyński, edited by *Z zagadnień plastyki polskiej w latach 1918–1939.* Wrocław: Ossolineum, Wydawnictwo PAN, 1963.

Rosiek, Stanisław. *Mickiewicz (po śmierci). Studia i szkice nekrograficzne.* Gdańsk: Słowo/Obraz Terytoria, Fundacja Terytoria Książki, 2013.

Rosiek, Stanisław. *Zwłoki Mickiewicza. Próba nekrografii poety.* Gdańsk: Słowo/Obraz Terytoria, 1997.

Stefanowska, Zofia, Tazbir Janusz, eds. *Życiorysy historyczne, literackie i legendarne.* Series 1–2. Warszawa: Państwowe Wydawnictwo Naukowe, 1984–1990.

Szczerski, Andrzej. *Cztery nowoczesności. Teksty o sztuce i architekturze polskiej XX wieku.* Kraków: Studio Wydawnicze DodoEditor, 2015.

Szczerski, Andrzej. *Wzorce tożsamości. Recepcja sztuki brytyjskiej w Europie Środkowej około roku 1900.* Kraków: Universitas, 2002.

Warchałowski, Jerzy. "Wystawa Międzynarodowa w Paryżu 1924 r." *Przemysł i Rzemiosło,* no. 2 (1921).

Warchałowski, Jerzy. *Polska sztuka dekoracyjna.* Warsaw-Kraków: J. Mortkowicz, Towarzystwo Wydawnicze w Warszawie, 1928.

Złotkowski, Dariusz. *Wystawa Przemysłu i Rolnictwa w Częstochowie 1909 roku w świetle prasy polskiej.* Częstochowa: Muzeum Częstochowskie, Częstochowskie Towarzystwo Naukowe, 2009. http://www.wystawa1909.pl.

Chapter Twelve

Plebeian, Populist, Post-Enlightenment

Mass Sarmatism and Its Political Forms

Przemysław Czapliński

This essay is based on two propositions. The first holds that in Polish culture, since the mid-twentieth century, there have been fewer contradictions between Sarmatism and modernity. The second is that Sarmatism remains a powerful cultural foundation for a political movement. Both these points might be met with indifference by someone who regards Sarmatism as a bygone (i.e., departed and nonviable) element of Polish cultural heritage. Such a view maintains that Sarmatism was no opponent of modernity even during the modernization of a reborn Poland after World War I or, even less so, in the case of the socialist Polish state. For this reason, it could certainly not be contradictory to today's phase of capitalist acceleration. It is precisely the holders of such views that I would like to convince. The situation was—and still is—quite different indeed.[1]

Let me begin by discussing obstacles that Sarmatism posed for modernization. Conflicts between the Sarmatian tradition and late modernity form crystal-clear pairs of opposites. Sarmatism was a class-based, colonial,[2] xenophobic,[3] antidemocratic,[4] and conservative ideology. It held that the nobil-

---

1 This article draws on my findings presented in Czapliński, *The Remnants of Modernity*.
2 Cf. Beauvois, *Trójkąt ukraiński. Szlachta*; Sowa, *Fantomowe ciało króla*.
3 Cf. Tazbir, "Początki polskiej ksenofobii," 367–406.
4 Cf. Beauvois, "Nowoczesne manipulowanie sarmatyzmem," 121–40.

ity was the only true "nation" living in the Commonwealth and that Sarmatian origin entitled nobles to superior status—confirmed by political and economic privileges—over other classes (bourgeoisie and peasantry). As it developed through history, it increasingly identified Polishness with Catholicism, limiting the access of other denominations and national groups to privileges. It also validated the nobility's eastward expansion, effected through colonial conquest and exploitation of the territories of Belarus, Ukraine, and, since the eighteenth century, Lithuania. Finally, it led to the establishment of regulations that blocked bourgeoisie and peasant development, assigning to the lower classes the status of serfdom or half-serfdom.

The meeting between Sarmatism—again, a class-based, colonial, xenophobic, antidemocratic, and conservative ideology—and late modernity appears as a clash of radical opposites since late modernity in Poland was a process powered by ideas of equality, internationalism, cooperation, antidiscrimination, and progress. The stronger side (i.e., modernity) is regarded as a challenge to Sarmatism and its derivatives. Within the framework of such a dictate, any form of heritage must be tested, so to speak, to prove its compliance with the rules imposed by modernity. Let us begin with class orientation, which must be associated with the "noble republic of Poland" and could not pass over in any form to a society going through subsequent stages of modernization and the processes that it entails: democratization, empowerment of oppressed groups, and their political subjectification. How then could modernity allow for the existence of an ideology of decreed inequality?

Plebeian Sarmatism

In order to answer this question, we must look back to the 1960s—a time when the authorities of the People's Republic of Poland (PRL) permitted film adaptations of Henryk Sienkiewicz's novels. Sienkiewicz (1846–1916), the first Polish recipient of the Nobel Prize for literature (1905) awarded for his novel *Quo Vadis* (1896), in terms of talent was like a combination of Sir Walter Scott, Karl May, and Alexandre Dumas (père): he wrote historical, adventure and love novels, confronting his protagonists with dilemmas that reflected the most important problems of Polish collective life. His fiction trilogy—*With Fire and Sword* (*Ogniem i mieczem*, 1884), *Deluge* (*Potop*, 1886), and *Colonel Wołodyjowski* (also known as *Fire in the Steppe*; *Pan Wołodyjowski*, 1888)—became, for better or worse, one of the most important forms of cultural production to shape the national and historical imagination of Poles at the time. In 1968, a film adaptation of *Colonel Wolodyjowski* was made, followed in 1974 by *The Deluge*. The former was seen by almost eleven million viewers, the latter by over twenty-seven million.[5] With these two films, the dispute over noble culture was opened to the masses.[6]

This gave enormous momentum to the process initiated when Sienkiewicz was put on the reading list in Polish schools after 1956, that is, after the Stalinist period: the formation of plebeian Sarmatism. The very expression "plebeian Sarmatism" is a contradiction in and of itself. Yet this oxymoron was incorporated into Polish twentieth-century culture, seemingly obvious at times but also having deeply enigmatic characteristics.

In trying to explain it one should take note of the position that films had in disseminating the image of Sarmatism vis-à-vis the development of Polish mass culture. In this respect, the 1960s and early 1970s witnessed a shift in the dominant medium: the radio and press, which had enjoyed a hegemonic status in communication were overtaken by television, which was the most expansive means of communication and the most powerful vehicle of mass culture. Development of television in Poland—as had been the case elsewhere in Europe a decade previously—resembled an avalanche. In 1953, Poland had eighty TV sets; by 1955, their number had reached ten thousand, and by 1963 there were a million. Toward the end of the 1960s, there were already 3.5 million registered TV users. The average viewership of programs in the early 1960s was around four million; in the mid-1960s the most important daily news service, *Dziennik Telewizyjny*, was watched by six million viewers.[7] In the late 1950s and early 1960s, regional broadcast centers were established in the largest cities, with the result that the TV signal reached almost 90 percent of households across the country. In 1970, a new television channel was launched, devoted mainly to culture, and in the case of especially spectacular broadcasts (for example, the 1974

---

5   Exact box office figures: *Colonel Wolodyjowski*—10,934,145; *The Deluge*—27,615,921. Source: http://pl.wikipedia.org/wiki/Lista_filmów_z_największą_liczbą_widzów_w_Polsce. Added to this must be the (unmeasurable) TV audience; a thirteen-episode TV series, *Przygody pana Michała* [The adventures of Sir Michael], was first broadcast in 1969, and *The Deluge* has been shown by TVP (Polish public broadcaster) at least once a year to this day.

6   Cf. Kłoskowska's pioneering study *Kultura masowa*. The author argued that the "massification" of culture was an irreversible process, impervious to any criticism, albeit susceptible (perhaps) to some modest attempts at improvement. At the same time, she saw the development of mass culture as a decisive factor influencing the broader social consciousness.

7   Source: *Polska telewizja w latach 1952–1989*.

soccer World Cup), audiences exceeded twelve million. The growing cultural industry was capable of producing the desired identity images with greater efficacy than ever.[8]

Television unites and unifies. It unites by producing a community. It unifies by operating signs that can be read correctly only in the context of a homogenous identity. Sarmatism gave Polish society three things: a long genealogy, unmitigated pride in belonging to a community, and ready-made cultural forms. Constructed by the defenders of tradition, seekers of "positive protagonists", and reclaimers of the right to national glory, the Sarmatism of the late 1960s was compensatory in nature. Compensation was inscribed in the very fact of adapting Sienkiewicz[9] and in the mode of reception of the films based on his fiction.

By permitting film adaptations of novels depicting Polish noble culture, the socialist authorities made a substantial concession as this meant introducing the image of a class-based, devout and belligerent Poland into television and cinemas. The propaganda of the 1960s presented precisely the opposite image—that of a Poland inhabited by equals who are indifferent to religion and find the meaning of life in work. This concession resulted from the inability to create an image of the past that could match the impact of Sienkiewicz's novels. However, it turned out to be a pragmatically good step as it served to pass on the nobility narrative in terms desirable for the authorities. Unity suggested in the films was illusory and the aspirations that stemmed from it led to an only seemingly ennobling culture. Noble fiction equated sociability with socialization, so that the films, while satisfying patriotic needs, successfully diverted people's attention from unjust law and lack of solidarity in the Polish People's Republic. The protagonists of Sienkiewicz's trilogy could not serve as social role models because their tribulations took Poles into the realms of existential adventure, which never even made contact with modernity in the people's republic. On the whole, the film adaptations of *The Trilogy* muffled reflection and activity, and the Polishness built on an identification with Sarmatism passed into a state of exalted passivity.[10]

---

[8] The cultural industry subjects culture to market competition and accelerates the processes of social standardization. Cf. Adorno, "Culture Industry Reconsidered," 98–107.

[9] Asked why he chose *Colonel Wolodyjowski*, the director Jerzy Hoffman said, "There is a huge demand for a positive protagonist"; see *Kultura* (Warszawa) 1967, issue 34.

[10] In the Polish culture of the nineteenth century, the Sarmatians and their heirs were very often depicted in an aura of powerlessness, as people incapable

But this was already mass Sarmatism. Its function was to dissect a new tradition from the old Polish heritage—a tradition stripped of real conflicts but full of illusory ones, which can be easily overcome by love of the homeland and male friendship. Sarmatism was to produce cross-society concord among Poles. It was to make them accept—regardless of their different views, attitudes, and historical roots—the common cultural capital, which comprised patriotism manifested in recognizing the PRL as an heir to the Polish noble republic; religiousness based on cult and ritual; and social traditionalism, entailing a patriarchal family model, a patronizing approach to women, and a strong emphasis on sociability. Such a vision of collective identity encouraged the audience to draw satisfaction from an ahistorical and bloody pastoral.[11]

Populist Sarmatism

Let us now turn to the political potential of plebeianism. From the point of view of Polish history, plebeian Sarmatism resembled payment of a debt incurred by the nobility from the rest of society delivered three hundred years late. Or rather, to be more precise: an execution of a debt enforced by the masses. But the old master-debtor relationship no longer existed, so the demand had to be directed elsewhere.

In order to determine the addressee of the demand, one needs to reveal the political aspect of the development of mass Sarmatism. I will elaborate this aspect by referring to the concept of populist reason, as formulated by Ernesto Laclau.[12] According to this theory, society exists in three states of matter: plebs, people, and authority. As a hegemon, authority not only decides on the distribution of privileges but, above all, exerts political control over communication. For Laclau, society exists only thanks to communication: for it is only within this framework of practices that people can formulate demands and situate

---

of taking action. Cf. Tischner, "Chochoł sarmackiej melancholii," 1243–54; reprinted in: idem, *Świat ludzkiej nadziei. Wybór szkiców filozoficznych 1966–1976*, 11–23.

11   K. T. Toeplitz: "Our audience saw in *The Deluge* an image compensating in some way the need for national success. They saw it, because this was what they wanted to see, but in fact this is not a film about success, but rather about a horrible—and, as it would turn out a hundred years later—deadly bleed-out," [*"Potop" czyli o rzetelności*] 89.

12   This concept was first used with reference to Polish nobility culture by Jan Sowa (see, in particular, 291–96).

themselves with respect to authority. As long as they do it as individuals, without coming together in a shared demand, they remain plebs (i.e., a multitude of individual persons devoid of political subjectivity). However, when they decide that a demand formulated by some individual coincides with their own expectations, plebs are transformed into people. A particular demand begins to represent social universality, and an act of articulation triggers a chain of equivalence. Hence, plebeianism means a state of dispersion and prepoliticalness, while populism means consolidation and politicization.

The kind of Sarmatism that developed in Poland in the 1970s was plebeian precisely in the sense characterized above: it was social rather than political Sarmatism. It was created by individual consumers of patriotic films, loosely and noncommittally united by emotions triggered from the adventure storyline. Although by watching films the plebeians did articulate a demand—connected with the possibility of practicing a different sort of patriotism—the authorities could satisfy this imprecise and uncrystallized demand by combining patriotism with an increased dose of entertainment.

In the 1960s and 1970s, when the cultural managers of the PRL injected the masses with archetypes of noble culture, they believed—and they were not wrong—that this was a dose of national Valium, an extremely powerful sedative. Making tradition available to the masses in essence led to a traditionalization of the masses, that is, to embed collective identity within the framework of the chivalrous struggle for woman, faith and homeland against nonexistent outsiders.

Sarmatism, understood as opium for Poles and an instrument for channeling collective desires, directed social energy toward an undefined higher model, yet at the same time inscribed this effort upward into nationwide peace. Toward the end of the 1970s, however, plebeian Sarmatism, at least for a short while, became populist Sarmatism. This transformation was possible because feudal cultural models were transformed into people's models.[13] Sarmatism was therefore semantically emptied of its class-based, elitist, and exclusive culture and immediately refilled with a demand for common participation in the making of political order. With this act, Sarmatism as a political attitude ceased to be

---

13   Błoński, "Polak jaki jest każdy widzi," 1505–8; reprinted in: idem, *Kilka myśli co nie nowe*: "In the olden days, the Pole saw himself—and was seen—as a nobleman (or a member of the intelligentsia, that is a nobleman's heir). All usual characteristics of the Pole—of course I do not mean here any real-life Polish person, but rather the image of the Pole, successfully used at home and abroad to excuse or encourage—were of a feudal origin: both among the nobility or the rich, and the peasantry or the poor" (56).

associated with social background because it was taken over by the mass political subject, which adopted the noble heritage.

Resemantization of the Sarmatian stereotype took place with the birth of Solidarity. Almost all analyses of this movement emphasize its hybrid cultural make-up. Solidarity was democratic, much like the workers' rallies and local parliaments (*sejmiks*) of the nobility. It was sensitive to political inequalities but also androcentric, misogynistic yet imbued with a most powerful Marian cult, ready to transform the political sphere but based on a negation of politics,[14] progressive in its demand for justice yet traditionalist,[15] and revolutionary yet conservative. Picking from the tradition of freedom, equality, and dignity Solidarity established an alliance between modernity and Sarmatism.[16]

I therefore believe that—paradoxical as this will sound—it was the PRL film adaptations of Sienkiewicz's fiction that helped turn workers into Sarmatians. When the noblemen of the proletariat defeated their communist opponent, i.e., accomplished the signing of the Gdańsk Agreement and the legalization of the first independent trade union in the Soviet bloc, society produced signs of Sarmatian culture on its own accord, becoming its rightful owner. The process of Sarmatian enfranchisement of the masses (potentially present in the reception of Sienkiewicz's novels) was accelerated by film adaptations, since they satisfied, in an illusory manner, the craving for emotional recognition. In 1980, a new demand followed: the collective subject called for legalization of the right of rebellion and for inclusion of all Poles under new rules of state-managed social security. Thus, it demanded being recognized by the law[17] and admitted—as a potential opponent—into the spheres of decision-making.

Like all previous forms, this new, altered type of Sarmatism did not have an original model. What it had at its disposal was collective experience, which allowed it to invoke the original. Unexpectedly, then, the PRL ghost of

---

14 Cf. Kowalski, *Krytyka solidarnościowego rozumu*, 135–36; Ost, *Solidarity and the Politics of Anti-Politics*.

15 Cf. Kowalski, "Recreating tradition is necessary for rebuilding the social bond, i.e., forming a true society" (84).

16 See, for example, Ash, *The Polish Revolution*: "Solidarity's approach to education and culture can perhaps best be characterised as conservative-restorationist (229). The Polish edition reads: "In fact, the Poles created an original combination of ideas drawn from various traditions. In politics, they were faithful to fundamental principles of liberal democracy, which they combined, however, with proposals of radical decentralization, social control, and local self-government, which do not exist in the West" (219).

17 Cf. Honneth, *The Struggle for Recognition*.

Sarmatism, accepted by the authorities with a view to pacifying society with an ideology of concord, was settled by a population of many million inhabitants who saw workers' demand for trade unions and the right to strike as an equivalent of their own claims against the authorities. Sarmatism was therefore cleansed of its previous meanings and infused with new ones. With this act, society took on the character of a political subject and was situated in a position similar to that of the nobility with respect to the king: as an opponent who can checkmate their hegemon.

The discovery of this potential of modern politicalness in Sarmatism came at a price: it revealed the fact that Sarmatism was an empty form. Ever since then, using the Sarmatian populist subjectivity requires a radical rejection of previous semantics and filling the empty framework with a new sign. At the same time, modern mass Sarmatism is threatened by its own plebeianism, that is, a return to prepolitical existence.

War for Culture

It is in this context that one should place the numerous, relentless, and diverse references to Sarmatism made in the 1990s. They should be perceived as efforts to arm or, on the contrary, to disarm the political potential of Sarmatism.

In 1990, the prominent theater director Mikołaj Grabowski staged a play at STU Theatre in Kraków based on Jędrzej Kitowicz's book *Opis obyczajów* (A description of customs). The book is a precise description of customs—rituals, festivities, dress, behavior—and cuisine prevalent in Polish society in the second half of the eighteenth century. Grabowski showed this as Sarmatian in character and the current face of Polish culture.[18]

In 1994, young conservative critics known as the "Frondists" commenced a long debate over Sarmatism. In the periodicals *Fronda*, *Arcana*, and *Nowożytny POSTtygodnik*, they presented a new vision of war as an all-out struggle between Polish collective identity based on Sarmatian culture[19] and liberal, secular late

---

18 Nyczek has called this the "Sarmatian avant-garde," 4–7.
19 I summarize in this way a number of different texts: Koehler, "Gdzie Jest Polska?"; "W rytmie 'Godzinek', na rosyjskim trupie"; "Monitor"; "Świetliści w środku, czyli notatki po oświeceniu"; "Sarmatia defensa"; and "Piotr Skarga, czyli witajcie w naszych czasach"; Bartyzel, "Pułapki progresywizmu"; "Pesymizm, konserwatyzm i postawy chrześcijaństwa"; and "Taniec na rozbitym szkle"; Wencel, "Granice rozumu."

modernity.[20] Their conceptual framework was in clear, antagonistic opposition to the Enlightenment. Seen from this perspective, the Enlightenment was not only foreign, imported from France and Germany, but also hostile, and even destructive, in a very literal sense, to Polish traditions. According to the Frondists, modernization had supplanted Sarmatism, threatening the loss of all things Polish. Meanwhile, the most important development in humanist thought in 1990s Poland, a theme in dozens of books and articles that began to appear in the 1980s,[21] was the rise of a radically transformed image of seventeenth- and eighteenth-century culture.

While this new narrative depicted a discursive conflict, it also featured mutual concessions, borrowings, and inspirations. Although Sarmatism and the Enlightenment were mutually opposed, they were not impervious to change. The consequences of abandoning the view of history as a treacherous destruction of Polish culture by foreign influences were significant. First, academic studies showed both Sarmatism and Enlightenment stances to be multifaceted and internally diverse, rather than monolithic. Second, within this newly revealed stratified culture, inclinations toward modernization could be observed within Sarmatism, and Sarmatian trends could be discerned in the Enlightenment. In place of what had seemed to be two mutually exclusive cultures, traditionalism, and modernization, there now arose the notions of "Enlightened Sarmatism"[22] and "Sarmatian Enlightenment."[23] Researchers described how the Enlightenment's diversity made Sarmatism susceptible to its influence. Moreover, Sarmatism expressed its own modernizing concepts. The Enlightenment, in turn, incorporated certain elements of Sarmatism and used them to temper European cultural projects. Instead of a portrayal of the

---

20   "Enlightenment culture destroyed everything, and nowhere outside the Catholic Church [...] can a source of renewal be found" (Smoczyński, "Pesymizm, konserwatyzm i podstawy chrześcijaństwa."

21   Among these were: Grześkowiak-Krwawicz, *O formę rządu czy o rząd dusz?*; Grzybowski, *Sarmatyzm*; Kostkiewiczowa, *Oświecenie—próg naszej współczesności*; Maciejewski, *Dylematy wolności*; Michalski, *Sarmacki republikanizm w oczach Francuza*; Roszak, *Środowisko intelektualne i artystyczne Warszawy w połowie XVIII wieku*; Staszewski, "Sarmatyzm a Oświecenie (uwagi historyka"; Stasiewicz, "Zapisy: Pytania o sarmatyzm."

22   Klimowicz, "Sarmatyzm Oświecony," 195. Klimowicz also used this term and related examples in his textbook *Oświecenie*. Similar terminology can be found in Karpowicz's *Sztuka oświeconego sarmatyzmu*.

23   This concept was formulated and well argued by Parkitny in his article "Oświecenie Sarmackie—próg nowoczesności w Polsce?," 531.

Enlightenment as a struggle against Sarmatism, in the 1990s we were presented with a clash between two opponents that changed over the course of their confrontation.[24]

At the end of the twentieth century, two great film directors, Jerzy Hoffman and Andrzej Wajda, made films that portrayed Sarmatism in both its heyday and its decline. In 1999, Hoffman directed *With Sword and Fire*, the last installment of Sienkiewicz's trilogy, thus closing his Sarmatian cycle. In the film—watched by seven million viewers—the director removed colonialism and the associated contempt for Ukraine from seventeenth-century Polish culture. All that remained was the mere cruelty of war between two nations. Wajda, meanwhile, filmed the national poem *Pan Tadeusz* (1999, over six million viewers), in which he combined old Sarmatian customs with decency and inclination to order. The Sarmatians remained explosive, fiery, and angry people but also honest and straightforward. These were the features that the director deemed necessary for the habitus of the Polish middle class at the turn of the twenty-first century.[25]

Post-Enlightenment Sarmatism

At the turn of the twenty-first century, historical and political reflection concerned itself with ends rather than beginnings.[26] The year 1989, a breakthrough year for Europe and the world, was dominated by a debate on Francis Fukuyama's essay "The End of History?" The American political scientist argued that with the disintegration of the USSR, we entered a new, posthistorical time characterized by an exhaustion of viable alternatives to liberal democracy. Although critics and polemicists accused Fukuyama of triumphalism, in fact he cooled rather than inflamed emotions by not claiming that liberal democracy had won but rather that its adversaries had failed. Nationalism, communism, and the theocratic state imploded, falling under the weight of their own policies,

---

24   "*Monitor* did not question Polish national values. On the contrary, even in times of the most intense national reforms and the reshaping of the mentality of the conservative Polish gentry, far from undermining national heritage, the newspaper rather praised it, urging the general public to defend and foster national traditions." Kostkiewiczowa, *Polski wiek świateł*, 44.

25   In an interview given after the premiere, Wajda stated that he had gone back to the past because he wanted to "create a pedigree" for the contemporary Polish middle class (quoted in Majmurek, *Dlaczego Wajda?*, 33.

26   The perspective of the end of modernity was first adopted by Lyotard, *The Postmodern Condition*.

which produced internal enemies, economic ineptitude, and too much energy spent on controlling society. Liberal democracy remained on the battlefield because it managed to create the least conflict-inducing way of solving crucial problems: society's participation in power, sexual liberty, and the scope of economic freedom.

The end of history as understood by Fukuyama results from the success of a system that owes its vitality to the ability to include all social groups facing discrimination—the proletariat; women; ethnic, religious, and sexual minorities—in the legal order and to grant them political subjectivity. If earlier history was fueled by the fight for equal rights, the inclusiveness of liberal democracy disarms this fight. If the dynamics of history resulted from a fight for recognition, liberal democracy weakens *thymos*-based conflicts because it removes the basis of discrimination and abolishes hierarchical differences.

Reflections about other ends—work[27] or class divisions—can also add diagnoses of lessons in social ontology: an atrophy of the "nation" and nation state,[28] but also of the state as such, since globalization and supranational structures, such as the EU, limit its autonomy. The diagonal in political diagnoses of the end was drawn by Jean Baudrillard, who argued that in contemporary Europe and America we can no longer speak of a *demos* in the sense of a sovereign subject with respect to authority. When masses take the place of people, "there is no longer any social referent ... to lend force to effective political signs" and "the only referent that still functions is that of the silent majority."[29] This means that present-day political parties simulate representation of social diversity, and present-day execution of power consists of simulated decision-making. There are no people and no power, only silent masses and a political class focused on short-term problem-solving.

These concepts should be regarded as a functional context for deliberations on Sarmatism. In order to reflect on its mass version at the turn of the twenty-first century, one must take into account the challenges of late modernity. And it turns out that the list of these challenges is rather long: the end of history understood as a unilinear process determined by a shared goal, the disintegration of sense, the disappearance of collective subjects such as nation or social

---

27   Rifkin, *The End of Work*.
28   Cf. Chodorowski, *Czy zmierzch państwa narodowego?*; Iha, *The Twilight of the Nation State*; White, "Globalization and the Mythology of the Nation State," 257–84; Colomer, *Great Empires*.
29   Baudrillard, *In the Shadow of the Silent Majorities*, 19.

class, and the crisis of "the people" understood as a political subject. It is only in confronting these problems that the vitality of Sarmatism can be gauged.

For obvious reasons, the position I take in the above confrontation is not that of a political scientist or sociologist. My reflection will be limited to an analysis of books because I believe that they invent our reality. Books—fictional and documentary, essayistic and scientific, are sketches of real-world plots just as important as political programs or plans of collective activity. Moreover, the end of history described by Fukuyama in fact resulted from a standstill in the contemporary political imagination, which was not able to transcend the concept of liberal democracy. The more serious this aspect of the end turns out to be, connected with decrepitude in political imagination, the greater the significance of narratives.

As an example of narrative, I selected Jarosław Marek Rymkiewicz's tetralogy[30]: *The Hanging* (*Wieszanie*; 2007), *Kinderszenen* (2008), *Samuel Zborowski* (2010), and *Reytan* (2013), since in them I see a version of Sarmatism that is the most consistent, attractive, and predisposed for political applications.

All four books dealt with dramatic events in the history of Polish society. *The Hanging* recalled the outbreak of the 1794 uprising in Warsaw and a series of executions by the capital's inhabitants of traitors collaborating with Russia (Russia in 1772—together with Austria and Prussia—partitioned Poland, occupying the central-eastern part of the country). *Kinderszenen*—a book combining a historical essay with autobiography—examined the Warsaw Uprising

---

30 Jarosław Marek Rymkiewicz (1935–), as a young man, was a communist supporting the actions of the regime aimed at the opposition. From the early 1980s onward he himself was associated with the opposition; author of a dozen volumes of poetry (his *Zachód słońca w Milanówku* [Sunset in Milanówek] was awarded a Nike Prize in 2003, the most important literary prize in post-1989 Poland); as a poet he was an opponent of the avant-garde and a proponent of classicism (this was expressed in the volume of essays *To jest klasycyzm* [This is classicism], 1967). However, he chose and introduced a renewed tradition of Baroque to Polish culture. He refreshed the formula of a scientific biography with books combining historical and essayistic considerations (*Aleksander Fredro jest w złym humorze* [Aleksander Fredro is in a bad mood], 1977; *Juliusz Słowacki pyta o godzinę* [Juliusz Słowacki asks about the time], 1982; a series of books devoted to Adam Mickiewicz). Since 2010 (the time of the Smolensk air crash, in which among the dead were President Lech Kaczyński and his wife; the last president of Poland in exile Ryszard Kaczorowski; members of parliament and senators; representatives of the Polish government) strongly associated with the nationalist right in Poland.

of 1944, launched against the Germans occupying Poland from 1939. The author paid special attention to massacres of civilians perpetrated by the Nazis and proved that the insanity of the uprising was a rational response to the madness of mass murder perpetrated by the occupiers. *Samuel Zborowski* tells the story of a nobleman who was beheaded in 1584 per order of the king. According to Rymkiewicz, execution is a symbolic moment of the birth of Polish freedom, understood as the right to renounce obedience to unjust authorities. *Reytan: The Fall of Poland* describes the protest of parliamentarian Tadeusz Reytan, who in 1773, during the Partition Sejm, lay down in front of Sejm hall, blocking the way for traitors leaving the room after consenting to the partition of Poland. In Rymkiewicz's view, Reytan's attitude symbolized the need to accept madness as a component (and maybe even a foundation) of patriotism.

A common feature running throughout the entire tetralogy is a sharp opposition to the Enlightenment. According to Rymkiewicz, the defeat of the Enlightenment occurs when the state is in danger of collapsing, when history cannot be negotiated during talks, and when the defence of freedom requires irrational action. These three moments dominate history, and the Enlightenment must therefore be rejected. The participation in history proposed by the author requires giving voice to what is dark, prerational, prelinguistic in man, that is, everything that the European Enlightenment tried to civilize. Therefore, what emerges from Rymkiewicz's deliberations can be called a dark, endarkening[31] Sarmatism.

Rymkiewicz fights Enlightenment in both its cultural and technological forms. Enlightenment of the legal and moral kind (modernity) is fought because it mediates reality and cuts off access to emotions. In times of peace, it interposes institutions (courts, parliament, government) between people, as well as legal codes, which mediate between citizens. Because of these media, instead of influencing the other person directly, we go to court or send a petition to a member of parliament. Enlightenment also develops technologically (modernization), so that even in times of war, when forms of interpersonal mediation are suspended, people turn into killing machines. In order to regain influence over history, one must regain access to oneself, and this can be accomplished through the rejection of Enlightenment. For Rymkiewicz, this is what the majority wanted. And he gives us evidence: Robert Ritter von Greim, commander of the Luftwaffe Sixth Division, proposed mass air raids as the simplest method of suppressing the uprising and destroying Warsaw in 1944. As a last resort, the Germans chose direct combat:

---

31   Cf. Ventura, "The Age of Endarkenment," 44.

> Employing technology, using impeccable tools, leads to the disappearance (hiding) of the executors of the massacre, as well as its organizers; and with them disappear faces and feelings; sentiments, thoughts, anything that could be on their minds—their fury, anger, hatred, satisfaction, and something else also disappears, that which is dark and cannot be named (we cannot name it; I cannot). In other words, a Greim-style massacre deprives the murderers of the pleasure they could take in murdering.[32]

Thus, when people have a choice between manual and technology-mediated massacre, they choose direct contact with a victim because only then can they feel a direct agency. It is only then, too, that they regain access to their darkest inner selves.

The motif of "that which is dark" allows us to more fully explain the cultural aspect of Enlightenment, connected with civilizing various behaviors. Seen from this point of view, the Enlightenment is a network of institutions and forms that mediate between people: the law. Manners or proprieties result from the assumption that it is possible to introduce security guarantees into interpersonal relationships. Civilizing progress manifests itself in a growing acceptance of the authority of codes (social and legal) that designate permitted forms of behavior. Thus, the processes of "civilizing" and "modernizing" are aimed at plugging a hole oozing "that which is dark." This was what Father Meier, a proponent of the Enlightenment, did when "civilizing" Poles by urging them to maintain personal hygiene. However, "at one point, Father Meier got bored with such modernization—that is, with the arduous conviction of his readers that they should become more modern and more European—and he took to hanging."[33]

Father Meier went from mediated "modernizing" to direct hanging, just as the Germans decided against air raids in favor of destroying Warsaw man to man. As can be seen, for Rymkiewicz both aspects of the Enlightenment share a mediating function: technology mediates between man and killing while law mediates between man and living. They both work toward covering up "that which is dark" by hiding the meaninglessness of life and death. On the whole, Enlightenment develops as a firewall against awareness that in life there is only life, and in death there is only death. The counter-enlightened man is one who knows that he stands over a hole of meaninglessness and carries this within him. However, human life and death can be endowed with meaning but not through faith in a messianic pact with God or in naturalistic reproduction. The chance

---

32   J. M. Rymkiewicz, *Kinderszenen*, 212.
33   Ibid., 57.

lies in bringing transcendence down to this world and rebelling against biologism. The only transcendence available to an individual is the republican community, and it is only possible to give meaning to the relationship between an individual and the republic, that is, to establish this relationship, when someone dies in the name of this community.

It is on this (metaphysically ungrounded) basis that Rymkiewicz based his concept of modern Sarmatism. His vision is not only because *Samuel Zborowski* is set at the beginning of the Sarmatian formation (sixteenth century) and *Reytan* at its end (eighteenth century). Above all, Rymkiewicz translates the characteristics of the old formation into present-day conditions. The author does justice to historical realities only to a limited extent: he marginalizes the idea of the "noble estate" as representative of the nation. He ignores the link between social status and birth—a connection crucial for the class-based system—and denies the soundness of eastern expansion, regarding the colonization of Ukraine as Poland's civilizational mistake. Nevertheless, his idea is Sarmatian since it is based on sacralization of the Republic, on associating citizenship with a readiness for sacrifice for the common good, and finally, on deeming the "right of rebellion" a condition for freedom.

Hence, like the other forms discussed above, Rymkiewicz's Sarmatism is egalitarian, but it cannot be called unconditional. Anybody can be a member of the community, but nobody becomes one by right of birth or based on the place of residence or daily practiced social norms. Inclusion depends on the readiness to fill your life with meaning. However, it cannot be done either by content with biological duration or by committing your life to God. Vegetative life, life as such, is meaningless, and transcendence is not concerned with the human order of things. If man is to give meaning to his life, he must create a form of existence between passive vegetation and indifferent transcendence. Such existence is the transgression of individual life in an act of sacrifice for the community. It connects the individual with the community and creates the republic—the only political system in which the individual, giving meaning to his life, defends the freedom of the community.

This does not exhaust the meanings of "murkiness" in Rymkiewicz's Sarmatism. "Darkness" concerns not only motivations of protagonists participating in history ("that which is dark, which cannot be named") but also the narrator's motivations in telling his story. His narrative activity is stimulated by extreme yet ambivalent experiences from the past: a case of renouncing obedience to the authorities and the ensuing political murder committed by them (*Samuel Zborowski*), treason committed by the rulers and the bloody revolt of the people of Warsaw in 1793 (*The Hanging*), the threat of biological annihilation and, in response to it, an armed uprising (Warsaw 1944—*Kinderszenen*), the threat of the disappearance of the state, and an individual's protest (*Reytan*).

Thus, on every occasion the author tells us about a would-be trauma of vanishing, obliteration, falling into the black hole of nothingness. He presents protagonists who, carried away by patriotism, saved Poland from annihilation. This aspect gives Rymkiewicz's proposal a strong affective trait: the Sarmatism that emerges from his essays is a temporary state of patriotic elation, conditioned and legitimized by powerful emotional stimulus not lending itself to full explanation, counter-modern, prerational, and manifesting itself in ecstatic acts of killing or self-sacrifice. This gives Rymkiewicz's concept an unbearable similarity to the historiosophy of Sienkiewicz. They both promote patriotism as an emergency action, which becomes necessary only when things have gone too far.

Affective Sarmatism—a moment of patriotic excitement—is made possible thanks to the regaining of directness. And this regaining, in turn, enables the author to move from the eighteenth century to the present. In such a juxtaposition, direct Sarmatism turns out to be a (diminished) version of direct democracy. Both of these types of political activity are aimed at influencing the authorities to adopt the form of alternative parliamentarism—social committees, rallies, demonstrations, blockades, or rebellions. There is one clear difference, though: direct democracy strives to secure, for as large a portion of society as possible, the opportunity to participate in the exercise of power, whereas direct Sarmatism conceived by Rymkiewicz does not retain the right to vote. It wants to temporarily abolish the distance between the rulers and the ruled. When affects erupt violently, Sarmatism does away with the mediating links between the authorities and society, creating conditions whereby authority can be touched directly. This is why, according to the author, the Kościuszko Uprising was a victorious moment because anybody could touch the dead body of Primate Michał Poniatowski: "All were equal. Complete anarchy. If there is still something to be loved in Poland, it is this—its wonderful insurrection".[34]

Thus, the political features of Rymkiewicz's Sarmatism are derived from the affective sphere: republicanism, that is, the belief that the state is the only entity that transcends individual life, stems from the experience of the core meaninglessness of life. Activism is born in response to the premonition of a traumatic vanishing of Poland. Anarchic directness—manifested in rebellious efforts to touch authority—results from the desire to regain access to one's own emotional sphere, partly disconnected by modern mediations. This explains the instant response to Rymkiewicz's books and their prompt application to politics. The reason behind this is the fact that they cocreate the present-day process

---

34   Ibid., 160.

of political emotionalization.[35] His essays not only illustrate this phenomenon but also legitimize and enhance it with fascinating narratives. They confront the contemporary Pole with a traumatic emptiness, the only remedy for which is the republican-national community.

In this respect, Rymkiewicz can be situated vis-à-vis Benedict Anderson, who argues in *Imagined Communities* that nationalism is not an idea that gives cohesion to an already existing nation but rather a narrative that calls a nation into existence. He also reveals the characteristic loop where nationalism tends to get stuck when attempting to hide the fact that what it defines as its empirical basis is actually its very own creation. In Rymkiewicz's writings, it is precisely this moment that is obscenely put on public view and transformed into an act of communal and ethical awareness. In order to exist, a nation must be preceded by an idea, and the idea is then born as a projection of collective obligation onto the past. We are grounded in the past by every death that took place so that our present can exist. In this sense, our heritage burdens us with the obligation to make little of the life that was given to us. Our forefathers' death chooses us, even though it is we who define it.

But we should ask: what for? After all, an important test for any form of politicalness is its power of agency: the ability to achieve planned results and control their continuation. Faced with this problem, Rymkiewicz's Sarmatism will behave strangely. Samuel Zborowski's attack on castellan Andrzej Wapowski, the patriotic lynching committed by the people of Warsaw during the Kościuszko Uprising, Reytan's desperate act of protest, or the unprecedented sacrifice of civilians who fell in the Warsaw Uprising constitute very different actions yet share a structural resemblance. They all effect a suspension of the normally binding law in the name of higher necessity and initiate a time of anomie unleashed in the name of order. They also mark a moment in which everyone participates in the execution of power, albeit remaining aware of the exceptional nature of this moment. In ancient Rome, such a state was referred to as *tumultum*—a caesura that enabled taking "exceptional measures" and at the same time applying these measures. With the appearance of this caesura, "every citizen seems to be invested with an *imperium* that is floating and 'outside the law.'"[36]

Rymkiewicz's ecstatic actions with contradictory legal classifications do not trigger new history, however. Instead, they serve to arrest current history. Their task is to introduce a civil state of exception. This is Rymkiewicz's way of showing his readers the road to reclaimed subjectivity—a road that leads

---

35 Cf. Illouz, *Cold Intimacies*.
36 For an explanation of *tumultum*, also with respect to other cases of "necessity," see Agamben, *State of Exception*, 45–46.

though affective (justified by emotions rather than arguments) direct paralyzing of authorities. If contemporary society wants to be "a continuation" of historical events, it needs to shed the Enlightenment and awaken the inner affective Sarmatian. Only this Sarmatian, awoken from its slumber, will be able to bring about a *tumultum*. The problem is, however, that such "tumult," understood as calling the authority to order, cannot achieve anything beyond a direct touch or beyond the threat of physical proximity. Rymkiewicz does not give us any concrete idea as to the order to which authority could be called. In this respect, all books by this author say almost the same thing: "If the people who rule Poland break the law in any way, if they disobey the law, if they violate my personal rights—I am free from obedience. If the people who rule Poland in any way limit my freedom—I am free from obedience.... This is what you must bear in mind, Mr President, Mr Prime Minister, you, gentlemen, who are here in power now".[37]

This is not so much a set of principles as a set of performatives: any authority can provoke a rebellion, and any rebellion can prove lawful. This specifies one more aspect of the "darkness" of the kind of Sarmatism advocated by Rymkiewicz, namely a lack of proposals for political, legal, or moral order in the name of which the tumult has been incited. The narratives of *The Hanging* or *Reytan* cast glaring light on cases of rebellion but keep us in the dark about the order that is being defended.

As can be seen, this concept has some blank spots. Perhaps it is thanks to these holes, though, that the author is able to maintain the performative radicalism of his demands and proposals. Among them one can also find suggestions for solving dilemmas of late modernity and the turn of postmodernity: a response to the end of history. According to Fukuyama, the end of history entails a transition to dispersed time, multidirectional history, politics of negotiation, unimportant museum culture, and to a society that does not fight for recognition. For Rymkiewicz, an end of history understood in these terms is tantamount to losing democracy and the autonomy of the state. He counters this with a vision of a nation capable of threating its authorities and the state as a monad isolated from other states. In response to the diagnosis of the end of the *demos*, postulated by Baudrillard, Rymkiewicz writes about the return of a sovereign people, which does not reach for the right to vote but for the power to suspend law. In response to the threat of *sensus communis* (Lyotard) disappearing, the author presents protagonists who take charge of creating such common sense themselves. He constructs a narrative of a community that, through a founding murder or collective sacrifice, becomes a nation and constitutes a republic.

---

37   J. M. Rymkiewicz, *Samuel Zborowski*, 101–2.

Thanks to the sum of these gestures, in Rymkiewicz's essays the empty Sarmatian slings are refilled. The author managed to combine the fight for recognition with a political demand. He addressed his texts to the elite but also ennobled political grudges of the masses and reconciled political emotions with the concept of politics of emotions. Finally, he revitalized patriotism and alarmed the authorities. Although one may regard Rymkiewicz's Sarmatism as the wrong answer, it would be hard to not notice how his questions are the right ones.

An Open Ending

Rymkiewicz's essays constitute an ecstatic, if illusory, proposal for overcoming the problems of Enlightenment and independently breaking through to post-Enlightenment. These books conclude my deliberations on the twentieth-century forms of mass Sarmatism. Such forms would not exist if Sarmatism were not so prone to adopting ever more modern characteristics. Neither would the last project discussed exist if it were not for the troubles of late modernity, resulting from the weakening of political power and the increasing difficulty in defining social agency.

In this chapter, I discussed three forms. Plebeian Sarmatism (1960s and 1970s) comprised the phase of accelerated appropriation of signs of noble culture by socialist mass society, which did not manage to develop a new identity and made up for this deficiency with images of nobility devised by socialist mass culture. Populist Sarmatism (Solidarity movement, late 1970s/early 1980s) took over Sarmatian signs and filled them with their own meaning—a subjectivity defined by the demand for care from the state combined with the demand for the right to social rebellion. Finally, post-Enlightenment Sarmatism, constructed by Rymkiewicz (late first/early second decade of the twenty-first century), redefines politicalness: the author identified Sarmatism with regaining direct influence over authority, which can be accomplished through acts of collective execution of power.

Rymkiewicz's concept—according to which the *demos* only exists in moments of rebellion and the limits of a republic are those of meaningful political activity—strangely concurs with processes observable today across Europe and even in the United States. In both we can see "the people" taking to the streets; however, instead of going from rebellion to direct democracy, they support a "strong man." The "strong leader" accumulates political agency in his hands and transforms the political order into a state-of-exception democracy, persuading the voters that it is necessary to tighten borders. To a certain extent, the world is becoming more and more Sarmatian and Poland more and more globalized. Everywhere, however, this is just a reaction to crisis, not a solution.

Bibliography

Adorno, Theodor W. "Culture Industry Reconsidered." In *The Culture Industry: Selected Essays on Mass Culture*, 98–107. London and New York: Routledge, 2001.

Agamben, Giorgio. *State of Exception*. Translated by Kevin Attel. Chicago: University of Chicago Press, 2005.

Baudrillard, Jean. *In the Shadow of the Silent Majorities or the End of the Social*. Translated by Paul Foss, Paul Patton, and John Johnston. New York: Semiotext(e), 1983.

Beauvois, Daniel. *Trójkąt ukraiński. Szlachta, carat i lud na Wołyniu, Podolu i Kijowszczyźnie 1793-1914* [The Ukrainian triangle: Nobility, tsarist rule, and the people in Volhynia, Podolia, and Kiev Region 1793–1914]. Lublin: Wydawnictwo UMCS, 2005.

Beauvois, Daniel. "Nowoczesne manipulowanie sarmatyzmem—czy szlachcic na zagrodzie był obywatelem?" [Modern manipulations of Sarmatism: Were the landed gentry citizens?] In: *Nowoczesność i sarmatyzm* [Modernity and Sarmatism], edited by Przemysław Czapliński, 121–140. Poznań: Wydawnictwo Poznańskie Studia Polonistyczne," 2011.

Błoński, Jan. "Polak jaki jest każdy widzi" [You can tell a Pole when you see one]. *Znak* 198, no. 12 (1970).

Chodorowski, Jerzy. *Czy zmierzch państwa narodowego?* [The twilight of the nation state?] Poznań: Wers, 1996.

Colomer, Joseph. *Great Empires, Small Nations. The Uncertain Future of the Sovereign State*. New York and London: Routledge, 2007.

Czapliński, Przemysław. *The Remnants of Modernity: Two Essays on Sarmatism and Utopia in Polish Contemporary Literature*, translated by T. Anessi. Frankfurt am Main: Peter Lang, 2015.

Garton Ash, Timothy. *The Polish Revolution: Solidarity 1980–82*. London: Jonathan Cape, 1983.

Honneth, Axel. *The Struggle for Recognition: The Moral Grammar of Social Conflicts*. Translated by Joel Anderson. Cambridge, MA: MIT Press, 1996.

Illouz, Eva. *Cold Intimacies: The Making of Emotional Capitalism*. Cambridge and Malden, MA: Polity Press, 2007.

Jha, Prem Shankar. *The Twilight of the Nation State. Globalisation, Chaos and War*. London: Pluto Press, 2006.

Klimowicz, Mieczysław. "Sarmatyzm Oświecony." *Prace literackie Uniwersytetu Wrocławskiego*, 11–12 (1970): 195.

Klimowicz, Mieczysław. *Oświecenie*, Warsaw: PWN, 1972.

Kłoskowska, Antonina. *Kultura masowa. Krytyka i obrona* [Mass culture: Critique and defense]. Warsaw: PWN, 1980.
Kowalski, Sergiusz. *Krytyka solidarnościowego rozumu. Studium z socjologii myślenia potocznego* [A critique of Solidarity reason: A study in the sociology of colloquial thinking]. Warsaw: Wydawnictwa Akademickie i Profesjonalne, 1990.
Laclau, Ernesto. *On Populist Reason*. London: Verso, 2005.
Lyotard, Jean-François. *The Postmodern Condition: A Report on Knowledge*. Translated by Geoff Bennington and Brian Masumi. Minneapolis: University of Minnesota Press, 1984.
Majmurek, Jakub, "Dlaczego Wajda?" In *Wajda. Przewodnik Krytyki Politycznej*. Warsaw: Krytyka Polityczna, 2013.
Nyczek, Tadeusz "Sarmacka awangarda, czyli opis obyczajów Mikołaja Grabowskiego," *Teatr* 9 (1991): 4–7.
Ost, David. *Solidarity and the Politics of Anti-Politics*. Philadelphia: Temple University Press, 1990.
Parkitny, Maciej. "Oświecenie Sarmackie—próg nowoczesności w Polsce?" In *Polonistyka w przebudowie: literaturoznawstwo—wiedza o języku—wiedza o kulturze—edukacja*. Edited by Małgorzata Czermińska. Vol. 2. Kraków: Universitas, 2005.
Rifkin, Jeremy. *The End of Work: The Decline of the Global Labor Force and the Dawn of the Post-Market Era*. New York: G. P. Putnam's Sons, 1995.
Rymkiewicz, Jarosław Marek. *Wieszanie*. [The Hanging] Warsaw: Sic!, 2007.
Rymkiewicz, Jarosław Marek. *Kinderszenen*. Warsaw: Sic!, 2008.
Rymkiewicz, Jarosław Marek. *Samuel Zborowski*. Warsaw: Sic!, 2010.
Rymkiewicz, Jarosław Marek. *Reytan. Upadek Polski*. Warsaw: Sic!, 2013.
Sowa, Jan. *Fantomowe ciało króla. Peryferyjne zmagania z formą* [The king's phantom body: Peripheral struggles with form]. Kraków: Universitas, 2011.
Tazbir, Janusz. "Początki polskiej ksenofobii" [The Beginnings of Polish Xenophobia]. In *Sarmaci i świat* [Sarmatians and the world], 367–406. Kraków: Universitas, 2001.
Tischner, Józef. "Chochoł sarmackiej melancholii" [The straw man of Sarmatian melancholia]. *Znak* 196, no.10 (1970).
Toeplitz, Krzysztof Teodor. "*Potop*, czyli o rzetelności." *Miesięcznik Literacki* 11 (1974): 89.
Ventura, Michael. "The Age of Endarkenment." *Whole Earth Review* (Winter 1989).
White, Philip L. "Globalization and the Mythology of the Nation State." In *Global History: Interactions Between the Universal and the Local*, edited by A. G. Hopkins, 257–84. Basingstoke, UK: Palgrave Macmillan, 2006.

Chapter Thirteen

The Polish Connection

Lithuanian Music and the Warsaw Autumn Festival

Lisa Jakelski

A group of singers stands in a circle as the final section of Bronius Kutavičius's *Last Pagan Rites* begins. One vocalist starts to repeat a short, simple phrase that glorifies a sacred oak tree. Gradually, her companions begin to sing the same melody, staggering their entrances so that the sonic texture builds in layers of repetitive material. The music is simultaneously static and mobile—constantly circling back to its beginning, while slowly increasing in density. Kutavičius's canonic procedures are simultaneously modern and archaic—similar to the gradual processes devised by American minimalist composers Philip Glass and Steve Reich, while also reminiscent of polyphonic practices in Lithuanian folk singing that had nearly disappeared from oral tradition before their revival in the 1960s.[1] The work's Lithuanian texts, by contrast, point in only one direction: they identify a circumscribed community through the distinctive sounds of its language.

Kutavičius allows the adoration of the oak to unfold over several minutes. Then another process begins; like the music that precedes it, this passage also uses aural signifiers to reinforce links between sound, religious confession, and national identity. Quietly, an organ plays a phrase that has been likened to the Bogurodzica ("Mother of God"), a monophonic thirteenth-century chant that is considered Poland's oldest hymn.[2] As if the melody and the instrument itself

---

1   Šmidchens, *The Power of Song*, 266.
2   Droba, Program Notes for Kutavičius, 140.

were not enough to evoke the world of Christianity, Kutavičius recalls the texture of chorales by harmonizing the organ's melodic line with vertical block chords. The organ plays its phrase once more, this time slightly louder; although the singers have now exited the performance space, the sound of their voices persists in a recording. Each time the organ repeats the phrase it increases in volume, and, by its seventh entrance, the recording of the singers has become barely audible. Thus, the organ's Christian rites ultimately engulf the singers' pagan ritual. This prolonged crossfade is the sole instance of stark contrast in a work that otherwise avoids sharp juxtapositions.

Last Pagan Rites is part of a set of four oratorios in which Kutavičius explores facets of Lithuanian history and identity.[3] Kutavičius, adhering to the career trajectory of many (formerly Soviet) composers of his generation, gradually developed the compositional approach these works exemplify. Born in 1932, he was educated in Vilnius at the Lithuanian Academy of Music, where he was trained to emulate Soviet Russian heavyweights Dmitry Shostakovich and Sergey Prokofiev; after graduating in 1964, he went through a period of abstract, "twelve-tonish" experimentation. The style and subject matter of *Last Pagan Rites* cemented Kutavičius's mature voice, which melds allusions to Lithuanian folk music with the extreme repetition characteristic of late twentieth-century minimalism.[4] Composed in 1978 for soprano, choir, organ, and four horns, the piece includes poetic texts by Sigitas Geda. It consists of four movements, each an invocation to symbols of Lithuania's natural landscape: a grasshopper, sacred mountain, serpent, and, as described above, an oak. Many Lithuanian musicologists consider it to be the most important composition produced in their country after 1945.[5]

As its title suggests, *Last Pagan Rites* dramatizes Lithuania's Christianization in the late fourteenth century—an event that was both the outcome of negotiations between Lithuanian Grand Duke Jogaila and the Polish nobility, as well as the start of a centuries-long political alliance. Inhabitants of what became known, from 1569 to 1795, as the Polish-Lithuanian Commonwealth developed concepts of identity during a period in which modern, ethnic notions of "the nation" did not yet exist.[6] Rather, identities in the Commonwealth were flex-

---

3   Lampsatis, *Bronius Kutavičius*, 62.
4   Ibid., 29–52. My account of career trajectories in the Soviet Union is indebted to Schmelz, *Such Freedom, If Only Musical*.
5   Ibid., 62.
6   "Polish-Lithuanian commonwealth" is itself a problematic term. For a discussion of the name's complexities, pitfalls, historical usage, and connection to notions of federalism, see Augustyniak, *Historia Polski 1572–1795*, 25–27 and 31–32.

ible, the product of what Urszula Augustyniak describes as a cross-pollination of cultures.[7] The sight of Catholics, Calvinists, Lutherans, Orthodox Christians, Uniate Christians, Jews, and Muslims living and working together in apparent harmony dazzled visitors in seventeenth-century Wilno. The city's inhabitants spoke a variety of languages: predominately (a hybridized form of) Polish, as well as Ruthenian, German, Yiddish, Lithuanian, and Tatar, which likely were hybrid, too.[8] David Frick cautions that this relatively peaceful coexistence of confessions and ethnicities was the result of toleration rather than tolerance, and it depended as much on continuous litigation and regulated violence as it did on neighborly goodwill.[9] Yet this is not how early modern views of identity in Poland-Lithuania would come to be remembered and preserved, most influentially by Adam Mickiewicz. Works such as *Pan Tadeusz* characterized Poland's eastern borderlands as an arcadia in which diverse ethnic groups, languages, and belief systems thrived alongside each other, rooted in a common soil.[10] Mickiewicz's nostalgic filter colored the perceptions of many subsequent generations of Poles, including the musicians who sought to understand Lithuanian composition in the late twentieth century.

Mickiewicz articulated his views at a time when nineteenth-century ethnic nationalism was transforming notions of identity in both Poland and Lithuania. Rejecting the fluidity of earlier conceptualizations of belonging, Lithuanian nationalists defined themselves against Poland—privileging their Baltic ancestry and the ancient pedigree of their language, while dreaming of a modern revival of the lost medieval past.[11] Polish nationalists in turn came to understand the Lithuanian awakening as inimical to their own aspirations.[12] By the early twentieth century, Polish-Lithuanian relations were often fueled by acrimony—negative stereotypes, bitter recollections of the past, and contestation

---

7   Augustyniak, "Wielokulturowość Wielkiego Księstwa Litewskiego i idea tolerancji, a praktyka stosunków międzywyznaniowych w XVI do XVIII w.," 90–93.
8   Frick, *Kith, Kin, and Neighbors*, 105–6.
9   Ibid. See especially pages 400–418.
10 For a further exploration of Poland's borderlands (kresy), refer to Kathryn Ciancia's chapter in this volume.
11 Snyder, *The Reconstruction of Nations*, 15–102.
12 For an example of this in the realm of symbolic culture, refer to Waligórska, "On the Genealogy of the Symbol of the Cross in the Polish Political Imagination," 497–521.

over Wilno/Vilnius.[13] Soviet intervention determined the city's fate: Stalin granted Vilnius to Lithuania in 1939.[14]

The shift from early modern to modern views of identity formed the backdrop to *Last Pagan Rites* and its performance at the Warsaw Autumn International Festival of Contemporary Music on September 21, 1983. With its emphasis on paganism, language, and folk culture, *Last Pagan Rites* portrays Lithuanian national identity in modern, ethnic terms. This identity further coheres through its juxtaposition in the piece with a threatening, external force that is implicitly Polish in origin. How did this work come to be performed in Poland? What did it mean there, and who was constructing these meanings? We will see that Polish musicians were strongly affected by the composition's insider view of Lithuanian selfhood and its outsider take on Polish identity. As they grappled with *Last Pagan Rites* and the version of history it projects, Polish musicians reflected on the roles Polish culture had played in Lithuania; this reflection helped to shift their self-perceptions. Moreover, the collaborative effort to bring *Last Pagan Rites* to the Warsaw Autumn suggested an alternative to combative modes of Polish-Lithuanian engagement. While interactions in the realm of art music could not entirely obviate prejudices and memories of conflict that, according to Krzysztof Buchowski, continued to linger long after their early twentieth-century origins, musical performances did contribute to the formation of significant cross-border ties between Poland and Lithuania in the late socialist period. These ties reconfigured old Polish-Lithuanian cultural connections; viewed in hindsight, they presaged the bonds of the postsocialist era.

This case study therefore demonstrates how the movement of people, cultural artifacts, and ideas contributed to processes of identity formation in late twentieth-century Eastern Europe. Some of this motion occurred across state or geopolitical borders and can thus be understood as spatial. Other border crossings were temporal, as historical phenomena bled into and were reconfigured in the present.[15] Polish and Lithuanian musicians traversed boundaries of both space and time when they circulated music between their countries, creating various identities in the process.

Polish-Lithuanian cultural engagement has received little attention in previous efforts to understand border crossing in the Eastern Bloc and Soviet Union. Many prominent studies trace encounters across the systemic boundary that

---

13   Buchowski, *Litwomani i polonizatory*.
14   Snyder examines the transformation of Wilno into Vilnius in *The Reconstruction of Nations*, 52–89.
15   My thinking on this point has been informed by Schneider, *Performing Remains*.

separated socialist East from capitalist West.[16] Investigations of mobility in Eastern Europe often focus on relations between the Soviet Union and its satellite countries.[17] In shifting the focus away from the superpowers and examining interactions between Poland and one of the Soviet Socialist Republics (SSRs), this chapter sheds light on ties that were obscured by the glare of East-West encounters and interaction with the Soviet center but were vital to the formation of identities and the cross-border circulation of contemporary art music during the Cold War. Focusing on Polish-Lithuanian musical relations also reveals the persistence of historical patterns and relationships that predated the Cold War, as well as how these patterns and relationships changed in response to the Cold War's pressures.

More broadly, this case study provides an example of the ways in which music making, as a social activity, can create, concretize, destabilize, and disseminate identities. Music has the potential to draw boundaries around communities, facilitating perceptions of a group's distinctiveness both from without and within. Music's power as a medium of communication and its efficacy in building social relationships have made it a vital component of nationalist movements, particularly in eastern-central Europe.[18] These same qualities, however, also give music the capacity to connect people across borders, as a growing body of scholarship compellingly demonstrates.[19] Jessica Gienow-Hecht emphasizes that music "constitutes one out of many devices by which individuals,

---

16   They include Clark, *Moscow, the Fourth Rome*; David-Fox, "The Implications of Transnationalism," 885–904; David-Fox, *Showcasing the Great Experiment*; Péteri, "Sites of Convergence," 3–12; Reid, "Who Will Beat Whom? 194–236; and Tomoff, *Virtuosi Abroad*.

17   See, for instance, Babiracki, *Soviet Soft Power in Poland* and several of the chapters in Babiracki and Zimmer, *Cold War Crossings*. A useful exception is Mëhilli, "Socialist Encounters: Albania and the Transnational Eastern Bloc in the 1950s," 107–132.

18   The literature on music and European nationalism is vast. Classic studies include Beckerman, "In Search of Czechness in Music," 61–73; and Taruskin, *Defining Russia Musically*. Some notable recent studies are Applegate and Potter, *Music and German National Identity*; Bohlman, *Music, Nationalism, and the Making of the New Europe*; Hooker, *Redefining Hungarian Music from Liszt to Bartók*; Tochka, *Audible States: Socialist Politics and Popular Music in Albania*; and Willson, *Ligeti, Kurtág, and Hungarian Music during the Cold War*.

19   Refer to Ahrendt, Ferraguto, and Ferguto, *Music and Diplomacy from the Early Modern Era to the Present*; Fosler-Lussier, *Music in America's Cold War Diplomacy*; Gienow-Hecht, *Music and International History in the Twentieth Century*;

regions, nations, and unions can be either united or driven apart."[20] I nuance Gienow-Hecht's argument in this chapter by showing how music making can contribute to unity and division simultaneously, creating identities that are at once national, international, and transnational. For centripetal and centrifugal forces were both in play when Kutavičius's *Last Pagan Rites* was performed at the Warsaw Autumn Festival in 1983. Music making provided individuals in Poland and Lithuania with an opportunity to come together in common cause, mitigating aesthetic differences and state borders in the process. While the Warsaw Autumn fostered boundary crossing in general, the long, complex history of Poland-Lithuania made this specific entanglement in the early 1980s particularly meaningful. At the same time, *Last Pagan Rites*—the piece itself, and Polish responses to it—also strengthened perceptions of Poland and Lithuania's national distinctions.

Festival Identities, Festival Relations

The specific interactions that brought *Last Pagan Rites* to Poland took place within a larger context of Polish-Soviet cultural exchange. Some of the most significant of these encounters occurred through the Warsaw Autumn festival. Launched in 1956 during the post-Stalin Thaw, the state-supported Warsaw Autumn was a unique zone of aesthetic liberalism and cross-border contact during the Cold War: its concerts brought together a range of people, musical works, values, and ideas from both the socialist and the capitalist spheres of influence. As such, the festival contributed to a particular kind of Polish identity in contemporary art music: one that was recognizably modern to Western observers, participated in the formation of a global musical avant-garde, and supported various kinds of aesthetic (and national) aspirations in musical life throughout Cold War Eastern Europe.[21]

Gienow-Hecht, *Sound Diplomacy: Music and Emotions in Transatlantic Relations, 1850–1920*; and Mikkonen and Suutari, *Music, Art and Diplomacy*.
20   Gienow-Hecht, "Sonic History, or Why Music Matters in International History," 5.
21   I discuss the festival at much greater length in *Making New Music in Cold War Poland*, 34–62. Further discussion of the specific identity of contemporary art music in Poland can be found in Jakelski, "Górecki's Scontri and Avant-Garde Music in Cold War Poland," 205–39; Vest, *Awangarda*.

In being an important site of identity formation, the Warsaw Autumn is typical of festival environments.[22] Multiple actors, with various agendas, continually make and remake identities through their festival participation. And, at music festivals like the Warsaw Autumn, identity formation takes place in multiple locations. Messages about identity might be conveyed within musical works as well as a festival's overall programming. Notions of belonging emerge through performers' interpretive strategies as well as audience responses to the music on offer. Identities also arise through a festival's relationship to the location in which it occurs, the composition of its audiences, the weight of its history, or its connections to other institutions—to name just some of the possibilities.

The kinds of cross-border relationships the Warsaw Autumn engendered were similarly multiple. International ties tended to reinforce existing state borders and prevailing notions of East-West opposition; transnational connections, by contrast, blurred divisions and mitigated differences between states and systems. Formal, state-level exchanges of observers, performers, and compositions coexisted (and overlapped) with informal contact that occurred in festival participants' personal networks. Polish-Soviet interaction at the Warsaw Autumn took place at all of these levels—international and transnational, formal and informal, official and unofficial.[23]

Formal negotiations via Moscow- and Warsaw-based state agencies determined which Soviet performers would appear at the festival and what music they would play, decisions that shaped perceptions of the individual SSRs and their place in the Soviet Union as a whole. Festival organizers did not equally desire all Soviet music and performers. But they did not always have a choice. Because ensembles and repertoire were typically selected without their input, the Polish composers and musicologists who did most of the Warsaw Autumn planning often found it frustrating to negotiate with the Soviet Union through formal channels. Soviet state agencies did not send musicians and compositions from the various republics to Poland with equal frequency, and the Lithuanian SSR was rarely represented in the 1960s and 1970s compared to the Estonian, Latvian, and especially the Caucasian republics.[24]

The Lithuanian Chamber Orchestra's 1978 performance at the Warsaw Autumn was therefore unusual because it was only the third time that an

---

22   Bennett and Woodward, "Festival Spaces, Identity, Experience and Belonging," 11–25.
23   Jakelski, *Making New Music in Cold War Poland*, 86–138.
24   Stanevičiūtė, "Reception of the Warsaw Autumn Festival in Lithuania," 83.

ensemble from Soviet Lithuania had appeared at the festival.[25] In terms of the dissemination of Lithuanian composition, the concert was also noteworthy because it was the Warsaw Autumn's first presentation of Kutavičius's music: *Dzūkian Variations* was part of a program that also included the Polish premieres of Alfred Schnittke's Concerto Grosso no. 1 and Arvo Pärt's *Tabula Rasa*.[26] At this concert, however, Kutavičius's national identity was not the sole—or even the main—point, as it would be in an important strand of *Last Pagan Rites*' reception in 1983. By showcasing music from Estonia, Lithuania, and Russia, the concert program subsumed Kutavičius's national identity within a panoramic overview of recent Soviet composition. While Polish reviewer Olgierd Pisarenko noted Kutavičius's use of ethnographic field recordings of Lithuanian folk music, he was just as keen to discuss how Kutavičius molded these source materials using avant-garde approaches to manipulating sound, and he was eager to connect all of the composers on the program to postmodern trends prevailing throughout the transnational art-music world of the 1970s.[27]

This particular concert, of course, represented only one perspective on Soviet music, and it was in tune with the ambiguities of Soviet musical culture in the late 1970s: the Lithuanian Chamber Orchestra's journey to Warsaw required official approval, which was granted even though some Soviet cultural officials thought at least one composer on the ensemble's program was politically questionable.[28] As important as these official encounters were, moreover, they were not the only form of Polish-Soviet encounter at the Warsaw Autumn. In the 1960s, for instance, personal connections and the advocacy of Eastern European performers had enabled the westward dissemination of "unofficial" Soviet music—that is, music subject at the time to official suppression or neglect due to the modernist techniques with which it was composed.[29] The chain of influence also ran from West to East: along with their thoughts and impressions, Warsaw Autumn attendees transported scores, recordings, books, and other publications back to the Soviet Union, where the festival's ongoing

---

25   The other instances were in 1965 (Lithuanian String Quartet) and 1971 (Lithuanian Chamber Orchestra).
26   Kaczyński and Zborski, *Warszawska Jesień—Warsaw Autumn*, 317.
27   Olgierd Pisarenko, "Neobarok lat siedemdziesiątych," 13.
28   That composer was Arvo Pärt. See Karnes, *Arvo Pärt's* Tabula Rasa, 94.
29   Schmelz presents an in-depth study of unofficial Soviet music in *Such Freedom, if only Musical*. The first performance of an unofficial Soviet composition at the Warsaw Autumn was in 1964. See Jakelski, "Pushing Boundaries: Mobility at the Warsaw Autumn International Festival of Contemporary Music," 189–211.

ripple effects facilitated personal and professional bonding among musicians while also changing their aesthetic outlooks.

The Warsaw Autumn's impact in Lithuania conformed to the general trend of Polish influence on Soviet musical life. Lithuanian musicians responded in concrete ways to news from Warsaw, not least because their contact with Poland, a vital conduit of information about music from Western Europe and the United States, facilitated access to avant-garde and modernist works that were otherwise difficult for them to obtain. After Vytautas Landsbergis, musicologist and future head of an independent Lithuanian state, attended the Warsaw Autumn for the first time in 1963, he used the materials he acquired there to write his first article on music that employs aleatoric procedures and graphic notation.[30] Polish experiments with texture and timbre influenced compositions by their neighbors.[31] Kutavičius may have been shocked in 1969 when he heard a recording of a viscerally gritty string quartet by Krzysztof Penderecki,[32] but he was also inspired by the Polish composer's ability to meld a modern sound-world with national sentiment, an example he would follow in *Dzūkian Variations*.[33] The Warsaw Autumn left some of its deepest marks on Lithuanian musical discourse and self-perception: critics, composers, and musicologists in Lithuania continually confronted the Polish example when they debated the development of modern music in their home country.[34]

While similar conversations took place in many parts of the Soviet Union in the 1960s and 1970s, in Lithuania they also marked the persistence of historical patterns. The Warsaw Institute of Music educated many Lithuanian composers in the late nineteenth and early twentieth centuries.[35] Most prominent among these was composer and painter Mikolajus Konstantinas Čiurlionis, the acknowledged father of modern Lithuanian music. Poland's cultural influence in Lithuania was older still: Timothy Snyder contends that, in the Polish-Lithuanian commonwealth, Lithuania typically gained access to Western

---

30   Gruodytė, "Lithuanian Musicology in Historical Context: 1945 to the Present," 43–44.
31   Parulskienė, "Onutė Narbutaitė and Other Lithuanians at the Warsaw Autumn."
32   Goštautienė, "The Reception of Penderecki's Music in Lithuania, Latvia, and Estonia,"158.
33   Braun, "Reconsidering Musicology in the Baltic States," 8.
34   Stanevičiūtė, "Reception of the Warsaw Autumn Festival in Lithuania," 88.
35   Daunoravičienė, "Exiled Modernism: Lithuanian Music through the Second World War," 113.

European ideas through Poland.[36] With this access had come hierarchies: a perception of Polish as the language of the elite, which slowed the codification of the Lithuanian language and the development of Lithuanian literature.

Thus the channel that the Warsaw Autumn opened was nothing new. What were new were the historically specific constraints that affected the circulation of information, people, music, and ideas between Poland, the Soviet Union in general and the Lithuanian SSR specifically. Because Polish-Soviet cultural exchange was routed through Moscow, it was difficult for musicians to establish direct—that is, official—contact with their colleagues in the Soviet republics, even if their countries shared a border.[37] Limits on formal channels of interaction compelled Polish and Lithuanian musicians to seek other routes.

Bringing *Last Pagan Rites* to Warsaw

Kutavičius's first Warsaw Autumn performance might also have been his last, were it not for the development of informal Polish-Lithuanian connections that bypassed official channels. Personal contacts were key to the dissemination of Lithuanian music in Poland starting in the 1970s, when works by Lithuanian composers began to appear at venues outside the Warsaw Autumn. In time, a series of interpersonal, informal interactions would bring Kutavičius's music to the Warsaw Autumn once again.

How did these connections come to be? In many respects, this is a story of musicological activism. Krzysztof Droba is the key figure on the Polish side. Droba's involvement with Lithuanian music started in the 1970s, when he was a lecturer at Kraków's State Higher School of Music and, from 1975 to 1980, the director of the Young Musicians for a Young City Festival (*Festiwal Młodzi Muzycy Młodemu Miastu*) in Stalowa Wola, Poland. Held annually, the three-day festival featured the works of young or underplayed composers and served as a kind of counterweight to the Warsaw Autumn.[38] Aesthetically, the Stalowa Wola festival is associated with "new tonality" and "new Romanticism," through which it contributed to the emergence of a new identity in contemporary Polish composition.[39] It was also the first venue in which Droba promoted works by Lithuanian composers.

---

36 Snyder, *The Reconstruction of Nations*, 19–20.
37 Interview with Krzysztof Droba, Warsaw, Poland, June 5, 2011.
38 Bylander, "Charles Ives and Poland's Stalowa Wola Festival," 43–47.
39 Thomas, *Polish Music since Szymanowski*, 290.

This began in 1976, when Droba decided to add works by Čiurlionis to the 1977 Stalowa Wola festival program.[40] As part of this project, Droba came into contact with Landsbergis, a Čiurlionis specialist. Landsbergis, with a group of Lithuanian musicians, traveled to Stalowa Wola for the 1977 festival, where he gave a lecture on Čiurlionis's output and, in an article for a local newspaper, considered the composer's connections to Poland.[41]

Beyond contributing his expertise on Čiurlionis, Landsbergis acquainted Droba with the music of postwar Lithuanian composers. Landsbergis's musicological work, as encapsulated by Rūta Stanevičiūtė-Goštautienė, emphasizes "charismatic personalities, cultural figures, or 'maverick composers'" such as Kutavičius, Osvaldas Balakauskas, and Feliksas Bajoras—precisely the composers Droba would come to advocate.[42] One listen and Droba was hooked. He remembers that, in the late 1970s, Lithuanian music was "downright exotic in Poland," and it was heard "in the aura of fascination that accompanies the discovery of new, unknown worlds."[43] He soon programmed Kutavičius's music in Stalowa Wola: a composer-portrait concert took place on May 14, 1979. Droba and Landbergis's connection was therefore mutually beneficial. Through Landsbergis, Droba gained access to an appealingly distinct, unfamiliar musical realm. In Droba, Landsbergis discovered a receptive collaborator, eager to arrange performances in Poland of music by the composers he championed and to further disseminate his views of Lithuania's essential national difference from the prevailing official musical culture of the Soviet Union.

Droba's contact with Lithuanian musicians in the late 1970s was, in some senses, unidirectional: while he readily hosted his Lithuanian colleagues in Stalowa Wola, he initially refused their invitations to visit their home country, a decision he later explained as motivated in part by his shame when he discovered just how little he (and Poles more generally) knew about contemporary Lithuanian history and culture. "Refusing their invitations," he rationalized, "was a form of penance or fine for my—for our Polish—ignorance."[44] Eventually, though, Droba's fascination with contemporary Lithuanian composition took him to Vilnius, where he heard a recording of Kutavičius's *Last Pagan Rites* during a public listening session in 1981. The music's effects were

---

40   Droba, "Ku pamięci," 4.
41   Bylander, "Charles Ives and Poland's Stalowa Wola Festival," 48.
42   Stanevičiūtė-Goštautienė, "Narratives of Lithuanian National Music, 32.
43   Droba, "Ku pamięci," 4.
44   Droba, "Dar kartą apie 'Apeigas.'" I am grateful to Dr. Stanevičiūtė for sharing this material with me.

so powerful they brought Droba to tears, a visceral response he would go on to describe as: "a kind of physical reaction ... to experiencing the very essence of tragedy."[45] He decided that the work should be disseminated more widely, and, to that end, he finagled a copy of the score and recording, which he then smuggled over the Polish border. Once he was back in Poland, he passed these materials on to Olgierd Pisarenko, a friend who was part of the Warsaw Autumn's Repertoire Commission.[46] At the time, the commission was planning the 1983 festival concerts. During their meeting on November 17, 1982, commission members listened to the recording, reviewed the score, and added *Last Pagan Rites* to the festival roster.[47] They pinned down the details of the performers in March 1983.[48]

The apparent ease with which *Last Pagan Rites* traveled to Warsaw could suggest that interpersonal communication through informal networks enabled music and musicians to flow between Poland and Lithuania unimpeded. But there were barriers, typically understood by both sides as party-state obstruction. Kutavičius has recalled that listening to music by Polish avant-garde composers in the 1960s carried with it the danger of imprisonment.[49] Political authorities had reportedly disbanded a group that gathered clandestinely in Vilnius to hear Landsbergis's account of his experiences at the 1963 Warsaw Autumn,[50] and the article he wrote in response to that year's festival would not be published in full until 1990.[51] The spectrum of possible styles and techniques had widened in Lithuania by the late 1970s, when Lithuanian composers gained recognition both locally and internationally for their idiosyncratic, national approach to musical modernism.[52] Greater aesthetic flexibility, however, did not necessarily mean that it was easy for a Polish citizen to cross the

---

45 Ibid.
46 Krzysztof Droba, "Pamiętam, była 'Jesień' ..." *Ruch Muzyczny* 51/18–19 (September 16, 2007): 18.
47 WAF, Postanowienia z zebrania Komisji Programowej WJ w dniu 17 listopada 1982 r.
48 WAF, Sprawozdanie z zebrania komisji repertuarowej WJ w dniu 17 marca 1983 roku.
49 Goštautienė, "The Reception of Penderecki's Music in Lithuania, Latvia, and Estonia," 157.
50 Gruodytė, "Lithuanian Musicology in Historical Context," 44.
51 Stanevičiūtė, "Reception of the Warsaw Autumn Festival in Lithuania," 79.
52 Rūta Stanevičiūtė-Kelmickienė, Lithuanian Music Modernisation Discourse (1960s-mid 1980s) Summary of the Doctoral Dissertation (Vilnius: Lithuanian Academy of Music and Theatre, 2011), 54.

Soviet state border and enter the Lithuanian SSR, especially after the advent of Solidarity.[53] Looking back on 1970s and 1980s from the vantage point of 2005, Droba stressed the former difficulty and precariousness of cross-border interaction between Poland and Lithuania:

> It is worth remembering that during the time of the PRL [*Polska Rzeczpospolita Ludowa*, Polish People's Republic] our contacts with Lithuanians were not official, because official contacts would have required the agreement of the political authorities. And in that case someone else would have come and maybe we would have come to know an entirely different kind of Lithuanian music. So we had to devise various subterfuges to arrange our not entirely law-abiding meetings. How funny this all seems today! But it was not nearly so funny back then.[54]

In other words, key players in these informal networks not only promoted views of Lithuanian cultural difference; they also understood their activities to be politically charged. Politics and identity would be the axes of the coordinate system in which Warsaw Autumn participants would plot their responses to *Last Pagan Rites* in 1983.

Familiar Difference

More than a year before the performance of *Last Pagan Rites* at the Warsaw Autumn, the Polish musical press began to set the terms of the work's reception by the festival audience. A review in *Ruch Muzyczny*, Poland's oldest music magazine, primed listeners to understand the piece as exotic—populated with woodland nymphs and spirits, who divulge a strange and secret history. Romuald Twardowski, reporting on the Festival of Lithuanian Music that took place in Vilnius in 1982, told readers that *Last Pagan Rites* had put the audience "into a trance." Twardowski was particularly affected by the work's conclusion: as the singers slowly began to leave the performance space, they had seemed to become "ghosts conjured from the depths of history." He remained under the work's spell after it was over, gushing that Kutavičius himself had agreed with Twardowski's conviction: "The pagan mysterium would sound best performed during the middle of the night of Kupala."[55]

---

53 Droba, "Dar kartą apie 'Apeigas,'" 1–3.
54 Droba, "Ku pamięci," 4–5.
55 Twardowski, "Podróż na Litwę," 15.

Though the performance circumstances at the Warsaw Autumn were somewhat tamer, festival organizers did what they could to heighten the work's numinous atmosphere. Listeners were put into a mystical frame of mind by the first piece on the program: a luminously static concerto for reeds and percussion by Romanian composer Stefan Niculescu. *Last Pagan Rites* was then performed near midnight in a church decorated with flickering candles. The vocalists in the chorus were Polish girl scouts, who were wearing flowing white dresses adorned with Lithuanian folk patterns as they sang the work's Lithuanian texts.[56]

This was intoxicating stuff for the Warsaw Autumn audience in 1983. It is no surprise, then, that one strand of the Polish critical reception fixated on the work's exotic spirituality. One reviewer described the configuration of the singers as "reminiscent of an ancient ritual circle."[57] Musicologist Tadeusz Kaczyński characterized *Last Pagan Rites* as a "strange, secret celebration, which is probably familiar to Lithuanians because of the stylization of Lithuanian folk music, whereas to us it seems downright exotic (*egzotyczna*)."[58]

Exotic, of course, is a loaded term laden with colonialist and Eurocentric connotations. Inextricably entangled with power relations, the designation *exotic* entails Othering—a split into center and periphery, division into "us" and "them." Within the context of Polish-Lithuanian relations in the twentieth century, the Othering of *Last Pagan Rites* in the Polish critical reception was significant, not least because the piece so clearly projects a modern, circumscribed view of Lithuanian national identity. Responses that highlighted the work's exotic qualities could, on the one hand, reinforce Polish stereotypes of Lithuania as a primitive land of myth and magic in need of Polish intercession to overcome its backwardness. At the same time, these responses also recognized and perpetuated understandings of Lithuania as distinct from Poland, thereby helping to concretize the cultural borders of the modern Lithuanian nation-state (even before this state regained its independence). Or, to put it another way: when Kaczyński contrasted the presumed reactions of Polish and Lithuanian listeners to *Last Pagan Rites*, he tacitly acknowledged that the notions of belonging that predated nineteenth-century ethnic nationalism were now lost—that neither the Romantic fantasy of community in Mickiewicz's poetry, nor the complex realities of identity in Poland-Lithuania on which this poetry was based, had persisted into the present.

---

56 Tumiłowicz, "Ucha się nie rozciągnie"; *Ruch Muzyczny* 27/23 (November 13, 1983): 3 (photograph of Last Pagan Rites in performance).
57 Cegiełła, "Dzień szósty."
58 Kaczyński, "Niculescu i Kutavičius," 12.

Yet the relations of the past continued to linger, blurring boundaries that separated one nation from another. Kaczyński went on to say that Kutavičius's piece was not so strange that it prevented Polish listeners from evaluating it positively, a contrast to the more negative responses of some Western European audience members. He concluded, "This means that this Lithuanian music is considerably closer to us, in spite of all its 'exoticism.'"[59] Bronisław Tumiłowicz brought the work even closer to home, likening it to "the second part of Mickiewicz's *Dziady*."[60] That is, for Polish listeners *Last Pagan Rites* could simultaneously be both self and other.

For many Polish commentators, the political implications of *Last Pagan Rites* also spoke to the closeness of the Polish and Lithuanian situation in the early 1980s. While they appreciated the work's ingratiating surface qualities, these critics highlighted the work's narrative of loss and hinted that it might relate to contemporary politics as well as historical events. These readings focused on the climactic moment that occurs at the end of the work (which I described at the beginning of this chapter), when the organ chorale gradually overwhelms the singers' adoration of the oak tree. Droba primed his audience to perceive this moment negatively. In his extensive program notes, he described the end of *Last Pagan Rites* as a "tragic situation ... in which one value annihilates another." Attempting to encapsulate the emotional impact of this conclusion, he continued: "when the organ, the Vilnius Jesuit Baroque organ, blares and when triumph is corroborated for the seventh time—I am very sorry ... sorry for the innocent childhood of mankind."[61] These thoughts surely influenced Tumiłowicz, who interpreted the organ finale as having a "sad and cold effect, as though it were taking place after the loss of something dear to us."[62] In his review of the piece, critic and musicologist Andrzej Chłopecki added a politically suggestive gloss to Droba's reading, contending that the parable of values *Last Pagan Rites* dramatizes is "bitter," "tragic," and a "testimony from a part of our native realm (*danie świadectwa z części naszej rodzinnej Europy*)."[63]

These responses could mean a number of things. One way to understand them is as attempts to grapple with the historical legacies of power, dominance, and cultural imperialism in eastern-central Europe. Polish critics acknowledged and took seriously the Lithuanian nationalist view expressed in *Last Pagan Rites*

---

59 Ibid.
60 Tumiłowicz, "Ucha się nie rozciągnie."
61 Droba, Program notes for Kutavičius, 140.
62 Tumiłowicz, "Ucha się nie rozciągnie."
63 Chłopecki, "Jesień odzyskana," 9.

of what it had meant for Lithuania to enter into political alliance with Poland. For Tumiłowicz, the piece provided an opportunity to engage in "historiosophical reflection."[64] For Chłopecki, the piece represented a watershed that had transformed "our entire image of music." Kutavičius's work, he stressed, gave the impression of being both necessary and inevitable: "It seems as though someone had to compose the *Rites*, that [the piece] had been waiting to be spelled out clearly, and that it was necessary for the way we think about our culture."[65] The composition of *Last Pagan Rites*, that is, had the potential to recalibrate Poles' self-perceptions and their understandings of the past.

Whereas Chłopecki's comments specifically concerned the place of Kutavičius's work in music history, his reassessment aligned with a rethinking of Polish-Lithuanian relations that was occurring throughout Poland's intellectual circles in the 1970s and 1980s. Chłopecki's reference to a "native realm" (*rodzinna Europa*) suggests that he had Czesław Miłosz in mind as he reflected on the Warsaw Autumn performance of *Last Pagan Rites*: Miłosz's *Rodzinna Europa*, typically translated into English as *Native Realm*, criticizes insular, prejudicial, right-wing manifestations of Polish nationalism as the poet reflects on his early life in Lithuania.[66] Chłopecki was in good company in early 1980s Poland, where Miłosz was being (re)discovered by the intelligentsia at large. Publications in the independent press further encouraged Poles to recalibrate their views of the country's former eastern borderlands when they characterized Belarusians, Lithuanians, and Ukrainians not as enemies blocking the reconstitution of the interwar Polish state but as brothers who deserved Poland's support in their struggles for national self-determination. A passage from *Lithuania*, a two-volume history produced by Poland's independent press in 1984, reads almost as a summary of the sentiment that underlay Droba's views on Lithuanian art-music composition, and that were further disseminated, albeit quietly, in the positive reviews of *Last Pagan Rites* that appeared in state-run media outlets: "We have to forget about our mutual trauma and stop treating Lithuania as a part of Poland. Every nation has a right to an independent existence and if we ourselves want to be a sovereign and free nation someday, then we must respect the aspirations to independence of those peoples with whom we are bound by historical and cultural ties."[67]

---

64 Tumiłowicz, "Ucha się nie rozciągnie."
65 Chłopecki, "Jesień odzyskana," 9.
66 Miłosz, *Native Realm*, 90–107.
67 Quoted in Buchowski, *Litwomani i polonizatory*, 387–88, fn. 17.

Buchowski links the Polish intelligentsia's "vogue for the borderlands" with opposition to communist authority.[68] Classical musicians in Poland, driven by Romantic notions of their art form's autonomy, had complex and often tenuous investments in oppositional activity.[69] Within the particular circumstances of the 1983 Warsaw Autumn, however, the potential link between resistance and Lithuania is suggestive. The Polish Composers' Union had canceled the festival in 1982 in response to the ongoing fallout of martial law. And the 1983 festival was hardly a triumphant return.[70] Significantly for a state-sponsored event, that year's Warsaw Autumn featured few state symbols. Gone were the flags that typically hung at the National Philharmonic Concert Hall, one of the festival's main venues, to announce the state affiliations of the composers whose works comprised the Warsaw Autumn program. In a departure from long-standing tradition, the 1983 festival did not begin with a rendition of Poland's national anthem. Witold Lutosławski, Henryk Mikołaj Górecki, Tadeusz Baird, Wojciech Kilar, Kazimierz Serocki, Włodzimierz Kotoński—virtually none of Poland's leading composers had works performed at the 1983 Warsaw Autumn, a notable absence at a time when actors and musicians throughout Poland protested against martial law by refusing to appear in certain public venues, and "collaborator" performers were applauded off the stage. "We are in the graveyard of contemporary music," one journalist reported after the inaugural concert, which featured music shadowed by the aura of the dead: Pierre Boulez's *Rituel (in memoriam Bruno Maderna)* and Edison Denisov's *Requiem*.[71] Most of the works on the 1983 festival program were lamentations in one way or another, *Last Pagan Rites* included. None of these pieces were about Poland per se. But, in conjunction with the silence of Polish composers, they suggested an identity through implication: the civil society that understood itself in opposition to the Polish party-state.

Nor was mourning limited to a particular nation: as one Polish reviewer put it, "We have the right to be sad, but we do not have a monopoly on sorrow."[72] Suffering, that is, had the potential to be transnational. At the 1983 Warsaw Autumn, Kutavičius's *Last Pagan Rites* could be understood not as a specifically

---

68 Buchowski, *Litwomani i polonizatory*, 387.
69 Bohlman, *Musical Solidarities*; Jakelski, "Witold Lutosławski and the Ethics of Abstraction," 169–202; Bylander, "Responses to Adversity, 459–509.
70 For an expanded discussion of the 1983 Warsaw Autumn Festival, see Jakelski, "The Changing Seasons of the Warsaw Autumn."
71 Lampart, "Jesienny smutek."
72 Ekiert, "Skąd ten smutek?"

national tragedy but as one evocation of loss among many. Or, to put it another way, the work's overtones of domination and loss could be understood as a metonym for the plight of all peoples subjugated to Soviet Russian power in the early 1980s. Joachim Braun has noted that compositions melding folk music with modern techniques were produced in the 1970s throughout the Baltics, where they were interpreted as veiled forms of resistance.[73] *Last Pagan Rites* certainly had powerful political connotations in Lithuania, where it was heard as a protest against the Sovietization—that is, the enforced Russification—of national cultural life.[74] Droba was aware of these connotations and shared his Lithuanian colleagues' point of view.[75] Many Polish reviewers' emphasis on suppression, tragedy, and loss in their responses to *Last Pagan Rites* suggests that, in 1983, these subtexts were operative in Poland, where they acquired additional significance: in commenting obliquely on Lithuania's contemporary political situation, Polish critics and musicologists could also speak about their own. It is just as noteworthy in this context that one of the rare negative Polish responses to Kutavičius's work appeared in *Gazeta Krakowska*, a local party newspaper: Zbigniew Lampart dismissed *Last Pagan Rites* as a "pseudointellectual" and "embarrassingly naïve little piece"[76] in a series of reviews that lambasted the 1983 Warsaw Autumn as a whole for its insularity, lugubrious atmosphere, and lack of national pride.[77]

Whereas the political implications of loss were meaningful within the broader context of the Eastern Bloc, *Last Pagan Rites* became transnational at the Warsaw Autumn in yet another way. Critics readily connected the ritualized lamentations on offer that year with globe-spanning aesthetic phenomena. The festival's gloomy atmosphere, Kaczyński suggested, was not just a reflection of the prevailing local mood: "It would be easy to accuse the festival Repertoire Commission of giving this year's festival this kind of character, but it would be just as easy to deflect this accusation, because both Polish and foreign composers, in both the East and the West, have recently been writing precisely these kinds of works."[78] Kaczyński hesitated to provide a reason for the trend, but

---

73   Braun, "Zur Hermeneutik der sowjetbaltischen Musik," 86–90.
74   Lampsatis, *Bronius Kutavičius*, 65–66. See also Gaidamavičiūtė, "Die Idee der Freiheitsbewegung und ihre Geschichte im Werk von Bronius Kutavičius," 296–307.
75   Droba, "Mit Litwy w oratorynej twórczości Broniusa Kutaviciusa," 162.
76   Lampart, "Deszczowe pożegnanie."
77   These culminated in Lampart, "Warszawska Jesień czyli umarłemu kadzidło."
78   Kaczyński, "Gra na trzech tonach."

Janusz Ekiert hazarded a guess: the advent of postmodern aesthetics in music. "From a purely aesthetic point of view," he told his readers, "it is interesting to compare how composers are expressing sadness at the turn of the 1970s and '80s," continuing on to posit that "perhaps this lamentation is just tears over the emptiness that has been left behind after the irretrievable passing of the great Romantic tradition and the great avant-garde of the 1960s?"[79] Critics therefore blurred the specifically national identity of Kutavičius's *Last Pagan Rites* when they counted it as yet another expression of sorrow—as just one more sign of the postmodern aesthetic shifts that were affecting creative activity in a far-reaching, border-spanning art-music world. The articulation of this national identity was itself a part of larger trends: in drawing on folk motifs and cultivating a specifically national relevance, *Last Pagan Rites* mirrored the late-socialist emergence of postmodernism throughout the Eastern Bloc.[80]

This apparent contradiction speaks to the many complexities of *Last Pagan Rites*' performance at the Warsaw Autumn in 1983. The piece traveled to Poland on the basis of sustained, informal ties between nonstate actors—precisely the kinds of connections Steven Vertovec identifies as the basis for transnational relations.[81] Yet one of the first Lithuanian works to circulate informally to the Warsaw Autumn—where one strand of its reception viewed the piece as a part of a transnationally funereal milieu—also had the potential to reify the cultural borders of the modern Lithuanian nation-state. Polishness, with respect to *Last Pagan Rites*, turned out to be paradoxical. In the composition, Polish influence is depicted as a constraint on Lithuanian cultural expression; but in the late 1970s and early 1980s, the overwhelming majority of Polish musicians responded positively to the piece and made efforts, in concert with their Lithuanian colleagues, to promote it. Routed through the self-consciously modernist institution of the Warsaw Autumn, Polish-Lithuanian musical engagement also referenced a fundamental tension in Polish culture, in which aspirations to be modern and Western have coexisted uneasily with ongoing attachments to what is often understood as the "backward" East.[82] And, while *Last Pagan Rites* was interpreted in Lithuania as resistance to Sovietization, Snyder has suggested that

---

79   Ekiert, "Skąd ten smutek?"
80   Erjavec, "Introduction," 43.
81   Vertovec, *Transnationalism*, 3.
82   Further analyses of Polish discourses on "the East" can be found in Zarycki, "Orientalism and images of Eastern Poland," 73–88; and Mayblin, Piekut, and Valentine, "'Other' Posts in 'Other' Places: Poland through a Postcolonial Lens?," 60–76.

the modern notion of Lithuanian identity (which Kutavičius's work projects) was realized in part due to Soviet involvement, which forced an answer to the Vilnius question, contributed to the formation of ethnically homogenous states through deportations and facilitated the ascendance of Lithuanian language and culture in Soviet Lithuania's urban centers.[83]

Interactions, Ongoing

Interactions between Polish and Lithuanian musicians in the late 1970s and early 1980s exemplify what Patricia Clavin has called "one of the central paradoxes of transnationalist studies: that transnational ties can dissolve some national barriers while simultaneously strengthening or creating others."[84] By disseminating music, values, and ideas across borders, the Warsaw Autumn helped integrate both Poland and Lithuania into an increasingly globalized world of new music creation, performance, distribution, and consumption, thereby facilitating the development of transnational identities in both countries. The sustained informal, interpersonal ties that enabled the performance of *Last Pagan Rites* in Poland mitigated the Soviet state border and centralized procedures that otherwise limited direct contact between Polish and Lithuanian musicians. Meanwhile, Polish responses to *Last Pagan Rites* loosened the work's ties to a singular, defined national context as critics and musicologists connected it to Polish conceptions of self and implicated it in political and aesthetic contexts that were relevant far beyond Lithuania. Yet the critical reception of *Last Pagan Rites* in Poland also acknowledged and thereby helped to concretize perceptions of Lithuanian national difference from Poland, an important step in consolidating the cultural borders of both the Polish and the Lithuanian modern nation-states.

Moreover, the Polish-Lithuanian interactions that have been my concern in this chapter testify to the importance of individual actors and informal, nonstate communication channels in circulating music (and ideas about it) across borders. Peter Schmelz contends that, although "unofficial, personal transnational networks between the USSR and the West" have received comparatively less scholarly attention than state-level cultural diplomatic exchanges, these ties are worthy of study because "they formed a crucial nexus for information exchange,

---

83 Snyder, *The Reconstruction of Nations*, 88–98.
84 Clavin, "Defining Transnationalism," 431.

and especially for music, during the Soviet thaw of the 1960s."[85] Such ties were just as crucial starting a decade later in Poland and Lithuania. The informal, interpersonal connections musicians forged in the 1970s and 1980s were noteworthy at a time when there were few venues for official Polish-Lithuanian contact and there was a glut of sentimental, Mickiewicz-influenced portrayals of Lithuania in Polish popular culture.[86] These connections did more than disseminate information about Poland and Lithuania's latest musical trends; they also contributed to the emergence, consolidation, and maintenance of particular notions of identity. Personal ties among musicians reconfigured older Polish-Lithuanian cultural connections, presaging a post-Soviet, multinational eastern-central Europe in which differences between ethnic groups tend to be confirmed by state borders. Despite the ongoing reality of Lithuania's status as a Soviet republic in the 1970s and 1980s, Droba, Landsbergis, and others acted as though the country were already sovereign when they brought music by Kutavičius and his compatriots to Poland. Significantly, figures on both sides promoted symbols of Lithuanian national aspirations, such as *Last Pagan Rites*. Within the specific circumscribed world of art music, this promotion shaped identities in Poland, too, suggesting an alternative to conceptions of Polishness that attempted to downplay the history of Polish dominance in Lithuania, or that subsumed Lithuanian into Polish culture.[87]

The Warsaw Autumn has continued to promote composers from Lithuania, including Kutavičius; as of 2017, the most recent presentation of his music was in 2011. New works by Lithuanian composers have been commissioned specifically for Warsaw Autumn performance. The 1987 world premieres of Osvaldas Balakauskas's *Tyla* (*Le Silence*) and Kutavičius's *Die stille Stadt* were important early instances of a trend that has persisted into the twenty-first century.[88]

Droba continued to champion Lithuanian difference in his musicological work until the end of his career. In an influential article from 1984, he declared that composers from Poland and Lithuania were not interchangeable: "We have no analogues to Kutavičius and Bajoras, and, vice versa, Kutavičius and Bajoras

---

85 Schmelz, "Intimate Histories of the Musical Cold War," 191–92.
86 Buchowski, *Litwomani i polonizatory*, 388.
87 Compare to Augustyniak, "Wielokulturowość Wielkiego Księstwa Litewskiego," 104; Buchowski, *Litwomani i polonizatory*, last chapter.
88 For a more in-depth exploration of Lithuanian responses to the Warsaw Autumn after 1990, see Stanevičiūtė, "Reception of the Warsaw Autumn Festival in Lithuania," 86–88.

are not analogues to -*skis* or -*ckis*."[89] He lauded a rising generation of Lithuanian composers (Onutė Narbuitaitė, Mindaugas Urbaitis, Vidmantas Bartulis, and Algirdas Martinaitis) for crafting antiacademic music suffused with the spirit of their country's native culture and natural landscapes. Expressing a view that was in keeping with postmodern tastes for cultural diversity, he applauded the group for providing local alternatives to the forces of globalization and technological homogenization. In Lithuania, Droba's article brought these composers both recognition and official condemnation.[90]

Before the late 1980s, ongoing interactions between Polish and Lithuanian musicians depended on the unofficial, personal contacts that had been so important in the Warsaw Autumn's production of *Last Pagan Rites*. This changed in the aftermath of a 1987 Polish-Soviet cultural exchange agreement that aimed to strengthen relations between Poland and the Belarusian, Lithuanian, and Ukrainian SSRs in the service of fostering a larger socialist unity.[91] Consequently, Droba's Lithuanian ties became official: delegated by the Polish Composers' Union, he traveled to Moscow in 1988 to arrange the first joint Polish-Lithuanian musicological conference.[92] By this time, however, his network of Lithuanian contacts was already well developed, and soon the Lithuanian SSR would become a thing of the past, removing the barriers that had shaped interactions among Polish and Lithuanian musicians for several decades. The informal Polish-Lithuanian connections that contributed to national identity formation and transnational music making during the late-socialist period laid the groundwork for what would come after.

Bibliography

Ahrendt, Rebekah, Ferraguto, Mark, Ferguto, Damien, ed. *Music and Diplomacy from the Early Modern Era to the Present*. New York: Palgrave Macmillan, 2014.

Applegate, Celia, Potter, Pamela, ed. *Music and German National Identity*. Chicago: University of Chicago Press, 2002.

Augustyniak, Urszula. *Historia Polski 1572–1795*. Warsaw: Wydawnictwo Naukowe PWN, 2008.

---

89 Droba, "Młoda muzyka litewska," 104. Reprint of an article originally published in *Ruch Muzyczny* in 1984.

90 Budraitytė, "Młoda muzyka litewska w latach osiemdziesiątych—i później," 109–15.

91 Bohlman, "Where I Cannot Roam, My Song Will Take Wing," 227.

92 Droba, "Ku pamięci," 5.

Augustyniak, Urszula. "Wielokulturowość Wielkiego Księstwa Litewskiego i idea tolerancji, a praktyka stosunków międzywyznaniowych w XVI do XVIII w.". In *Lietuvos Didžiosios Kunigaikštijos tradicija ir tautiniai naratyvai*, ed. Alfredas Bumblauskas and Grigorijus Potašenko. Vilnius: Vilniaus Universiteto Leidykla, 2009.

Babiracki, Patryk. *Soviet Soft Power in Poland: Culture and the Making of Stalin's New Empire, 1943–1957*. Chapel Hill: The University of North Carolina Press, 2015.

Babiracki, Patryk, Zimmer, Kenyon, ed. *Cold War Crossings: International Travel and Exchange across the Soviet Bloc, 1940s–1960s*. Arlington: University of Texas at Arlington, 2014.

Beckerman, Michael. "In Search of Czechness in Music," *Nineteenth-Century Music* 10, no. 1 (1986): 61–73.

Beckles Willson, Rachel. *Ligeti, Kurtág, and Hungarian Music during the Cold War*. Cambridge: Cambridge University Press, 2007.

Bennett, Andy, Woodward, Ian "Festival Spaces, Identity, Experience and Belonging". In *The Festivalization of Culture*, edited by Andy Bennett, Jodie Taylor, and Ian Woodward. Farnham: Ashgate, 2014.

Bohlman, Andrea. *Musical Solidarities: Political Action and Music in Late Twentieth-Century Poland*. New York: Oxford University Press, 2020.

Bohlman, Andrea. "'Where I Cannot Roam, My Song Will Take Wing': Polish Cultural Promotion in Belarus, 1988." In *Music and International History in the Twentieth Century*, edited by Jessica C.E. Gienow-Hecht. New York: Berghahn, 2015.

Bohlman, Philip V. *Music, Nationalism, and the Making of the New Europe*, 2nd ed. New York: Routledge, 2011.

Braun, Joachim. "Reconsidering Musicology in the Baltic States of Lithuania, Latvia, and Estonia: 1990-2007". In *Baltic Musics/Baltic Musicologies: The Landscape Since 1991*, edited by Kevin C. Karnes and Joachim Braun. London and New York: Routledge, 2009.

Braun, Joachim. "Zur Hermeneutik der sowjetbaltischen Musik. Ein Versuch der Deutung von Sinn und Stil," *Zeitschrift für Ostforschung* 31, nos. 1–4 (1982): 86–90.

Buchowski, Krzysztof. *Litwomani i polonizatory. Mity, wzajemne postrzeganie i stereotypy w stosunkach polsko-litewskich w pierwszej połowie XX wieku*. Białystok: Wydawnictwo Uniwersytetu w Białymstoku, 2006.

Budraitytė, Daiva. "Młoda muzyka litewska w latach osiemdziesiątych—i później". In *W kręgu muzyki litewskiej: rozprawy, szkice i materiały*, ed. Krzysztof Droba. Kraków: Akademia Muzyczna w Krakowie, 1997.

Bylander, Cindy. "Charles Ives and Poland's Stalowa Wola Festival: Inspirations and Legacies," *The Polish Review* 59, no. 2 (2014): 43–47.

Bylander, Cindy. "Responses to Adversity: The Polish Composers' Union and Musical Life in the 1970s and 1980s," *Musical Quarterly* 95, no. 4 (2012): 459–509.

Cegiełła, Janusz. "Dzień szósty," *Rzeczpospolita*, September 23, 1983.

Chłopecki, Andrzej. "Jesień odzyskana," *Ruch Muzyczny* 27/25, December 11, 1983.

Clavin, Patricia. "Defining Transnationalism," *Contemporary European History* 14, no. 4 (2005).

Clark, Katerina. *Moscow, the Fourth Rome: Stalinism, Cosmopolitanism, and the Evolution of Soviet Culture, 1931–1941*. Cambridge, MA: Harvard University Press, 2011.

Daunoravičienė, Gražina. "Exiled Modernism: Lithuanian Music through the Second World War." In *Baltic Musics/Baltic Musicologies: The Landscape Since 1991*, edited by Kevin C. Karnes and Joachim Braun. London and New York: Routledge, 2009.

David-Fox, Michael. "The Implications of Transnationalism," *Kritika* 12, no. 4 (2011): 885–904.

David-Fox, Michael. *Showcasing the Great Experiment: Cultural Diplomacy and Western Visitors to the Soviet Union, 1921–1941*. Oxford: Oxford University Press, 2012.

Droba, Krzysztof. "Dar kartą apie 'Apeigas.'" In *Krzysztof Droba. Susitikimai su Lietuva* [Krzysztof Droba: Encounters with Lithuania], edited by Rūta Stanevičiūtė. Vilnius: Lietuvos kompozitorių sąjunga, Lietuvos muzikos ir teatro akademija, 2018.

Droba, Krzysztof. "Ku pamięci." In *X. Polsko-Litewska Konferencja Muzykologiczna, Kraków, 14-16 grudnia 2006. Sesje naukowe i koncerty. Program*. Kraków: Akademia Muzyczna w Krakowie, Katedra Teorii i Interpretacji Dzieła Muzycznego Zakład Analizy i Interpretacji Muzyki, 2006.

Droba, Krzysztof. "Mit Litwy w oratoryjnej twórczości Broniusa Kutaviciusa," *Konteksty* 3–4 (1993).

Droba, Krzysztof. "Młoda muzyka litewska." In *W kręgu muzyki litewskiej: rozprawy, szkice i materiały*, edited by Krzysztof Droba. Kraków: Akademia Muzyczna w Krakowie, 1997.

Droba, Krzysztof. "Pamiętam, była 'Jesień.'" *Ruch Muzyczny* 51/18–19, September 16, 2007.

Droba, Krzysztof. *Program notes for Kutavičius, Last Pagan Rites in Warsaw Autumn '83 26th International Festival of Contemporary Music Warsaw September 16–25, 1983*. Warsaw: Polish Composers' Union, 1983.

Ekiert, Janusz. "Skąd ten smutek?" *Express Wieczorny*, September 28, 1983.

Erjavec, Aleš. "Introduction." In *Postmodernism and the Postsocialist Condition: Politicized Art under Late Socialism*, edited by Aleš Erjavec. Berkeley: University of California Press, 2003.

Fosler-Lussier, Danielle. *Music in America's Cold War Diplomacy*. Berkeley: University of California Press, 2015.

Frick, David. *Kith, Kin, and Neighbors: Communities and Confessions in Seventeenth-Century Wilno*. Ithaca, NY: Cornell University Press, 2013.

Gaidamavičiūtė, Rūta. "Die Idee der Freiheitsbewegung und ihre Geschichte im Werk von Bronius Kutavičius." In *Litauische Musik. Idee und Geschichte einer musikalischen Nationalbewegung in ihrem europäischen Kontext*, edited by Audrone Žiūraitytė and Helmut Loos. Leipzig: Gudrun Schröder Verlag, 2010, pp. 296–307.

Gienow-Hecht, Jessica C.E. *Music and International History in the Twentieth Century*. New York: Berghahn, 2015.

Gienow-Hecht, Jessica C.E. "Sonic History, or Why Music Matters in International History." In *Music and International History in the Twentieth Century*, edited by Jessica C. E. Gienow-Hecht. New York: Berghahn, 2015.
Gienow-Hecht, Jessica C. E. *Sound Diplomacy: Music and Emotions in Transatlantic Relations, 1850–1920*. Chicago: University of Chicago Press, 2009.
Goštautienė, Rūta. "The Reception of Penderecki's Music in Lithuania, Latvia, and Estonia." In *In The Music of Krzysztof Penderecki: Poetics and Reception*, edited by Mieczysław Tomaszewski. Kraków: Akademia Muzyczna, 2005.
Gruodytė, Vita. "Lithuanian Musicology in Historical Context: 1945 to the Present." In *Baltic Musics/Baltic Musicologies: The Landscape Since 1991*, edited by Kevin C. Karnes and Joachim Braun. London and New York: Routledge, 2009.
Hooker, Lynn M. *Redefining Hungarian Music from Liszt to Bartók*. Oxford: Oxford University Press, 2013.
Jakelski, Lisa. "Górecki's Scontri and Avant-Garde Music in Cold War Poland." *Journal of Musicology* 26, no. 2 (2009): 205–39.
Jakelski, Lisa. Interview with Krzysztof Droba, Warsaw, Poland, June 5, 2011.
Jakelski, Lisa. *Making New Music in Cold War Poland: The Warsaw Autumn Festival, 1956–1968*. Berkeley: University of California Press, 2017.
Jakelski, Lisa. "Pushing Boundaries: Mobility at the Warsaw Autumn International Festival of Contemporary Music," *East European Politics and Societies* 29, no. 1 (2015): 189–211.
Jakelski, Lisa. *The Changing Seasons of the Warsaw Autumn: Contemporary Music in Poland, 1960-1990*. PhD diss., University of California, Berkeley, 2009.
Jakelski, Lisa. "Witold Lutosławski and the Ethics of Abstraction," *Twentieth-Century Music* 10, no. 2 (2013): 169–202.
Kaczyński, Tadeusz. "Gra na trzech tonach," *Tygodnik Powszechny*, October 30, 1983.
Kaczyński, Tadeusz. "Niculescu i Kutavičius," *Ruch Muzyczny* 27/22, October 30, 1983.
Kaczyński, Tadeusz, and Andrzej Zborski. *Warszawska Jesień—Warsaw Autumn*. Kraków: Polskie Wydawnictwo Muzyczne, 1983.
Karnes, Kevin. *Arvo Pärt's Tabula Rasa*. New York: Oxford University Press.
Lampart, Zbigniew. "Deszczowe pożegnanie." *Gazeta Krakowska*, September 26, 1983.
Lampart, Zbigniew. "Jesienny smutek." *Gazeta Krakowska*, September 22, 1983.
Lampart, Zbigniew. "Warszawska Jesień czyli umarłemu kadzidło." *Gazeta Krakowska*, October 5, 1983.
Lampsatis, Raminta. *Bronius Kutavičius: A Music of Signs and Changes*. Vilnius: VGA Publishers, 1998.
Mayblin, Lucy, Piekut, Aneta, Valentine, Gill. "'Other' Posts in 'Other' Places: Poland through a Postcolonial Lens?" *Sociology* 50, no. 1 (2016): 60–76.

Mëhilli, Elidor. "Socialist Encounters: Albania and the Transnational Eastern Bloc in the 1950s." In *Cold War Crossings: International Travel and Exchange across the Soviet Bloc, 1940s–1960s*, edited by Patryk Babiracki and Keynon Zimmer, 107–32. Arlington: University of Texas at Arlington, 2014.
Mikkonen, Simo, Suutari, Pekka eds. *Music, Art and Diplomacy: East-West Cultural Interactions and the Cold War*. Farnham, UK: Ashgate, 2016.
Miłosz, Czesław. *Native Realm: A Search for Self-Definition*. Translated by Catherine S. Leach. New York: Doubleday, 1968.
Parulskienė, Daiva. "Onute Narbutaite and Other Lithuanians at the Warsaw Autumn," *Lithuanian Music Link* 15 (2007). http://www.mic.lt/en/discourses/lithuanian-music-link/no-15-october-2007-march-2008/onute-narbutaite-and-other-lithuanians-at-the-warsaw-autumn. Accessed December 21, 2017.
Pisarenko, Olgierd. "Neobarok lat siedemdziesiątych." *Ruch Muzyczny* 22/24, November 19, 1978.
Péteri, György. "Sites of Convergence: The USSR and Communist Eastern Europe at International Fairs Abroad and at Home." *Journal of Contemporary History* 47, no. 1 (2012): 3–12.
Reid, Susan E. "Who Will Beat Whom? Soviet Popular Reception of the American National Exhibition in Moscow, 1959." In *Imagining the West in Eastern Europe and the Soviet Union*, edited by György Péteri, 194–236. Pittsburgh: University of Pittsburgh Press, 2010.
Schmelz, Peter J. "Intimate Histories of the Musical Cold War: Fred Prieberg and Igor Blazhkov's Unofficial Diplomacy." In *Music and International History in the Twentieth Century*, edited by Jessica C. E. Gienow-Hecht. New York: Berghahn, 2015.
Schmelz, Peter J. *Such Freedom, If Only Musical: Unofficial Soviet Music during the Thaw*. Oxford: Oxford University Press, 2009.
Schneider, Rebecca. *Performing Remains: Art and War in Times of Theatrical Reenactment*. London: Routledge, 2011.
Snyder, Timothy. *The Reconstruction of Nations: Poland, Ukraine, Lithuania, Belarus, 1569–1999*. New Haven, CT: Yale University Press, 2003.
Stanevičiūtė-Goštautienė, Rūta. "Narratives of Lithuanian National Music: Origins and Values." *Musikgeschichte in Mittel- und Osteuropa*, Heft 12 (2008).
Stanevičiūtė-Kelmickienė, Rūta. *Lithuanian Music Modernisation Discourse (1960s-mid 1980s). Summary of the Doctoral Dissertation*. Vilnius: Lithuanian Academy of Music and Theatre, 2011.
Stanevičiūtė, Rūta. "Reception of the Warsaw Autumn Festival in Lithuania: Cultural Discourse and Political Context." *Musicology Today* 14 (2017).
Šmidchens, Guntis. *The Power of Song: Nonviolent National Culture in the Baltic Singing Revolution*. Seattle: University of Washington Press, 2014.
Taruskin, Richard. *Defining Russia Musically: Historical and Hermeneutical Essays*. Princeton, NJ: Princeton University Press, 1997.

Thomas, Adrian. *Polish Music since Szymanowski*. Cambridge: Cambridge University Press, 2005.
Tochka, Nicholas. *Audible States: Socialist Politics and Popular Music in Albania*. Oxford: Oxford University Press, 2016.
Tomoff, Kiril. *Virtuosi Abroad: Soviet Music and Imperial Competition during the Early Cold War, 1945–1958*. Ithaca: Cornell University Press, 2015.
Twardowski, Romuald. "Podróż na Litwę." *Ruch Muzyczny* 26/2, June 27, 1982.
Tumiłowicz, Bronisław. "Ucha się nie rozciągnie." *Argumenty*, October 9, 1983.
WAF. *Postanowienia z zebrania Komisji Programowej WJ w dniu 17 listopada 1982 r.*
WAF. *Sprawozdanie z zebrania komisji repertuarowej WJ w dniu 17 marca 1983 roku.*
Waligórska, Magdalena. "On the Genealogy of the Symbol of the Cross in the Polish Political Imagination." *East European Politics and Societies* 30, no. 2 (2019): 497–521.
Vertovec, Steven. *Transnationalism*. London and New York: Routledge, 2009.
Vest, Lisa Cooper. *Awangarda: Tradition and Modernity in Postwar Polish Music*. Oakland: University of California Press, 2021.
Zarycki, Tomasz. "Orientalism and images of Eastern Poland". In *Endogenous Factors in Development of the Eastern Poland*, edited by Marian Stefański, 73–88. Lublin: Innovatio Press, Wydawnictwo Naukowe Wyższej Szkoły Ekonomii i Innowacji, 2010.

Chapter Fourteen

Performing Polishness Abroad

(Non-)Polish Actors and the Construction of (Trans)National Identities in European Cinema

Kris Van Heuckelom

Introduction

Claiming that the experience of emigration has been crucial in shaping Polish national identity is little more than stating the obvious. As Izabela Kalinowska has noted, "Exile, a banishment from one's place of origin, presents one of the central problems around which modern Polishness was built."[1] This statement holds true not only because various forms of expatriation—from partitions-era exile over wartime displacement to economy-driven migration—have affected the lives of millions of Poles throughout the nineteenth and twentieth centuries but also because many of these expatriates—in particular the country's political and cultural elites—actively engaged in discussions about what it means to be a Pole (at home and abroad). While the roots of these émigré discourses on national identity can be traced back to the writings of Adam Mickiewicz in the early years of his Parisian exile—especially *Księgi narodu polskiego i pielgrzymstwa polskiego* (The books of the Polish nation and of the Polish pilgrimage) (1832) and *Pan Tadeusz* (Mr. Thaddeus) (1834)—the rapid revival and adaptation of this quintessentially romantic paradigm within the changing geopolitical parameters of post–World War II Europe ultimately came to a close with the

---

1   Kalinowska, "Exile and Polish Cinema," 107.

downfall of the communist regime in 1989 and the subsequent disappearance of exilic institutions and networks.

Taking the historically rooted connection between emigration and Polish national identity as a point of departure, this chapter turns its focus to filmmaking as a field of cultural production that has attracted relatively little attention in discussions of expatriate Polishness—especially when compared to the long-standing and continued academic interest in Polish exile literature and migrant writing. Only recently, efforts have been made to explore and examine the interconnectedness between the national and the transnational in the artistic output of Polish and Polish-born film professionals, including the work of internationally mobile filmmakers such as Jerzy Skolimowski, Roman Polański, Krzysztof Kieślowski, Agnieszka Holland, and Paweł Pawlikowski.[2] Meanwhile, however, as Ewa Mazierska has rightly observed, "A much less explored phenomenon is the presence of Polish actors and actresses in international cinema."[3] In this chapter, I intend to extend this line of inquiry by concentrating on the contribution of Polish (and non-Polish) performers to constructions of expatriate Polishness in foreign (European) feature film. As such, the two principal questions that lay at the root of this research are: which actors have been cast in the role of Polish expatriates in European filmmaking? And how does the on-screen Polishness impersonated by these performers intertwine with other identity markers (such as class, gender, ethnicity, generational affiliation, religion)? Although the primary focus will be on productions and performances from the past four decades (1980s–2010s)—when the subject of Polish migration gained increasing cinematic prominence across Europe—reference will also be made to some earlier films featuring Polish expatriate characters. As I will show, whereas interwar and early postwar cinema tended to offer ossified (and increasingly anachronistic) representations of (predominantly female) aristocrats of Polish extraction (typically played by non-Polish actresses), the political crisis of the early 1980s helped to recontextualize and update the onscreen treatment of expatriate Polishness—not without the creative involvement of some prominent Polish film practitioners—and shifted the thematic focus to the dilemmas faced by (predominantly male) dissident artists and intellectuals in the exilic space. The post-1989 era, finally, has seen a significant rise in cinematic portrayals of blue-collar labor migrants from Poland (usually played

---

2 See, for instance, the following edited volumes: Mazierska and Goddard, *Polish Cinema in a Transnational Context*; Jagielski and Podsiadło, *Kino polskie jako kino transnarodowe*.

3 Mazierska, "Train to Hollywood: Polish Actresses in Foreign Films," 153.

by Polish performers). As I will indicate with the example of the professional trajectory of two prolific actresses—Alicja Bachleda-Curuś and Agata Buzek—this expanding corpus tends to redefine expatriate Polishness along two lines of thematic development: interethnic romance (as a form of Europeanization) and intergenerational conflict (as a form of antipatriarchal resistance).

One could object, of course, that the films under discussion in this chapter have little or nothing to say about actual processes of Polish identity formation throughout the long twentieth century, especially if one takes into account that the productions involved were predominantly realized outside Poland and did not primarily target Polish audiences. Following this line of argument, a much more productive (but conservative) approach toward the interplay between feature filmmaking and Polishness would be to focus on a body of "distinctly" Polish pictures that has been massively consumed by Polish cinema-goers over the past few decades, namely high-budget heritage film (usually adapted from the national literary canon).[4] By way of contrast, this chapter brings into view a much less prominent but nonetheless significant category of European film productions that portray Polish characters beyond the borders of the nation-state and, while doing so, engage in destabilizing fixed notions of Polishness. Importantly, while some of the film projects involved derive their transnational character first and foremost from the considerable creative involvement—on and off screen—of Polish-born film professionals, many of the recent productions also involve significant cross-border flows in terms of production, distribution, and consumption (including financial input from Polish funding bodies).[5] Last but not least, new modes and technologies of film exhibition—such as VOD and online streaming services—have been equally instrumental in making the productions involved easily accessible for audiences across the continent. Therefore, without dismissing the enduring importance of the traditional nation-state perspective, this chapter acknowledges the relevance of transnational networks, ties, and interactions and their considerable impact on the identities of individuals and communities alike. This approach pertains in

---

[4] See, for instance, Haltof, "Adapting the National Literary Canon: Polish Heritage Cinema," 298–306.

[5] As I have argued elsewhere, this shift toward coproductional activity has become particularly prominent after the establishment of the Polish Film Institute in 2005 (which, as one of its main missions, has been strongly stimulating international collaboration. See van Heuckelom, *Polish Migrants in European Film 1918–2017*, 206–8.

particular to the salient topic of migration as the transnational subject par excellence in contemporary European cinema.

The Protohistory of Expatriate Polishness in European Filmmaking

As ensues from Jerzy Maśnicki's analysis of Polish motifs and figures in European cinema of the presound era (from the late 1890s through the late 1920s), early cinematography privileged two major lines of identification with Polishness (both of which were firmly rooted in nineteenth-century representational practices): musical genius and noble origins.[6] While the first association rapidly disappeared in the postwar period—Jan Kiepura's 1948 musical *Valse brillante* (Brilliant waltz) perhaps being its final manifestation—the close identification between expatriate Polishness and a noble background turned out to be more resistant to change and retained much of its prominence well into the Cold War era, as films like Jean Renoir's costume drama *Elena et les hommes* (Elena and her men, 1956) and Billy Wilder's French-West German coproduction *Fedora* (1978) exemplify.[7] One of the typical hallmarks of this long-standing (and increasingly anachronistic) engagement with nobly born Polish exiles is the cinematic focus on physically attractive but highly capricious female aristocrats of Polish (or vaguely Slavic) extraction. In the heydays of French classical cinema, this paradigm was initiated (and incarnated) by the Romanian-born star actress Elvire Popesco, most notably in popular comedies such as *Ma cousine de Varsovie* (My cousin from Warsaw, 1931) and *Ils étaient neuf célibataires* (There were nine bachelors, 1939). Not only in terms of casting but also in terms of narrative, productions like these tended to conflate various surface markers of exilic Polishness with a composite portraiture of Eastern Europeanness. In terms of characterization, the female protagonist's "romantic" state of mind did not so much rely on her nostalgic longing for the lost Polish homeland or the involvement in the collective struggle for national independence—as it used to be propagated by Polish romanticism—but rather on her passionate engagement with heroic foreigners fighting for a good (and equally noble) cause.

The long-standing—gender- and class-inflected—cinematic association of exilic Polishness with whimsical upper-class femininity gains even more prominence when compared with the far less frequent onscreen appearances of male

---

6   Maśnicki, *Niemy kraj*.
7   Van Heuckelom, *Polish Migrants in European Film 1918–2017*, 71–75.

Polish expatriates (who were typically associated with a working-class background). The gender imbalance that characterizes these early cinematic representations indicates that female figures of Polish (or vaguely Slavic) extraction were privileged as the nostalgic impersonations of a social order which had irrevocably disappeared (as a result of the Bolshevik Revolution and the post–World War II Sovietization of eastern-central Europe). This state of affairs is also reflected on the level of genre: inasmuch as Polish "ladies" came to occupy centerstage in various costume dramas, Polish "tramps" occasionally appeared in (more or less exotic) adventure stories. These rare masculine performances include, for instance, the role of a wandering Polish sailor played by Horst Buchholz in J. Lee Thompson's police thriller *Tiger Bay* (1959). Importantly, although Thompson clearly attempted to imbue his crime story with a sense of neorealist authenticity—for instance by giving the German lead actor long dialogues in Polish—the makers of *Tiger Bay* remained strongly indebted to the widespread strategy of cross-ethnic casting (which was undoubtedly facilitated by the fact that Poles do not constitute a visibly different ethnic group). No less indicative of the viability of such casting practices in postwar European filmmaking is the professional trajectory of Polish actors and actresses such as Anna Prucnal, Władysław Sheybal, and Barbara Kwiatkowska-Lass (who left the Polish People's Republic in order to embark on an international acting career): rarely if ever were these performers cast in the role of Polish expatriates (although they happened to play characters with an Eastern Bloc background).

The "Polish Crisis": The (Male) Icons of Polish National Cinema Going Abroad

A major shift in terms of casting strategies and representational practices took place in the early 1980s, when the rise of the Solidarity movement and the subsequent introduction of martial law drew increasing international attention to the critical situation in the Polish People's Republic. Within a span of only a couple of years, no less than seven European film productions featuring Polish expatriate characters made it to the screen. The list of pictures involved includes two British films by the Polish-born director Jerzy Skolimowski (*Moonlighting* from 1982 and *Success Is the Best Revenge* from 1984), Jean-Luc Godard's acclaimed masterpiece *Passion* (1982), Charles Nemes's French-spoken romantic comedy *La fiancée qui venait du froid* (The fiancee who came from the cold) (1983), the Greek poetic drama *Roza* by Christoforis Christofis (1982), the Belgian-Tunisian migration drama *Traversées* (Crossings) (Mahmoud Ben Mahmoud,

1982), and the French TV production *Mariage blanc* (Paper marriage) (Peter Kassovitz, 1986). If, in the preceding decades, expatriate Polishness had been treated either anachronistically or in a highly decontextualized manner, the Polish background of the lead characters now became firmly grounded in the reality of Cold War Europe and its geopolitical tensions. Moreover, the widespread practice of cross-ethnic casting—Polish roles being typically played by non-Polish actors—now gave way to an increasing involvement of Polish film professionals in Poland-themed foreign productions. This pertains in particular to the roles performed by two acclaimed Polish actors of the day, Daniel Olbrychski and Jerzy Radziwiłowicz. After a stream of successful leading roles in the late 1960s, Olbrychski reached the pinnacle of his acting career in the mid-1970s with memorable appearances in two Oscar-nominated historical films, Jerzy Hoffman's *Potop* (The deluge) (1974) and Andrzej Wajda's *Ziemia obiecana* (The promised land) (1975). Radziwiłowicz, in turn, became the iconic (male) face of Solidarity cinema, thanks to his impressive performances in Andrzej Wajda's political diptych *Człowieku z marmuru* (Man of marble) (1977) and *Człowiek z żelaza* (Man of iron) (1981). As a side effect of the international attention generated by the Polish films in which they starred, both Olbrychski and Radziwiłowicz received invitations to take part in foreign (predominantly Francophone) film productions. Undoubtedly the best-known example is Radziwiłowicz's performance in Jean-Luc Godard's *Passion*, where he plays the role of a Polish director (Jerzy) employed in Switzerland to shoot an art film composed of historic *tableaux vivants*.[8] With the action being set in December 1981 and January 1982, *Passion* subtly references the ongoing political crisis in Poland and at least partly relates Jerzy's lingering artistic crisis (epitomized by his failure to finish the film within the film) to the spatial and mental separation from his home country (where real "action" is being taken) and culminates in his apparent return to Poland. What is more, Godard draws further on Radziwiłowicz's Polish on-screen persona by exposing the romantic appeal that the politically committed and dedicated director holds for some of the female characters that surround him (even to the extent that each one of them is eager to join Jerzy on his return trip to martial-law Poland). In a similar vein, Daniel Olbrychski's roles as a Polish expatriate in two foreign productions of the early 1980s—Christofis's *Roza* and Kassovitz's *Mariage blanc*—explicitly build on the on- and off-screen persona the actor developed in the Polish phase of

---

8   For an in-depth discussion of Radziwiłowicz's "Francophone" career, see Smith, "Polish Performance in French Space," 174–93; Mazierska, "Train to Hollywood: 153–73.

his career. In contrast to Radziwiłowicz, however, who created his acting profile and image by starring in topical films dealing with the tense political climate in the Polish People's Republic, Olbrychski imported into foreign cinematic space some features (and props) of his performances as a dedicated national hero in Polish period films, most notably his role of the hot-tempered but patriotic nobleman Andrzej Kmicic in Hoffman's *Potop* (about the Polish-Swedish war in the mid-seventeenth century). The Greek production *Roza*, to begin with, features Olbrychski in the role of a Polish refugee (Andrzej Kominowski) who ends up in a remote boarding house in Trieste inhabited by an international group of political refugees. In terms of mise-en-scène, the Polish expatriate embodied by Olbrychski is usually framed in two different spaces. The isolation to which Kominowski succumbs in the dark and claustrophobic interiors of the Italian boarding house is repeatedly contrasted with a series of oneiric images that serve to evoke memories of his Polish homeland. In these intercut frontal shots, the viewer sees Kominowski approaching the camera while riding on a white horse, dressed in white clothes and strolling through a warm, sunlit forest.[9] In Kassovitz's *Mariage blanc*, in turn, Olbrychski plays the part of a dissident Polish architect (Feliks Radziszyński) who escaped from imprisonment in martial law Poland (thanks to the support of some French intellectuals) and then attempts to settle in Paris. Significantly, one of the few personal belongings that accompany Radziszyński on his peregrinations through the French capital is an antique saber, which—apart from being a family heirloom—comes to serve as a particular form of intertextual baggage transferred from Polish into French cinematic space. As historically loaded signifiers of the struggle for the Polish cause, both the horse-riding trope in *Roza* and the prominent saber motif in *Mariage blanc* not only resonate with Olbrychski's "heroic" roleplaying in Polish cinema (most notably his performance as Kmicic) but also help to expose the contrast between the main character's primary identity as a Polish "freedom fighter" and the growing lack of agency that befalls him in the exilic space (without losing, however, his magnetizing effect on foreign women—not unlike the seductive aura that surrounds Jerzy in *Passion*). Quite obviously, of course, what makes Olbrychski stand out from Radziwiłowicz as the male

---

[9] Apart from evoking associations with Olbrychski's role playing in Polish historical films, the horse-riding motif and its spatial configuration can also be read on a more general level. As Ewa Mazierska has indicated with regard to the function of landscape in Polish cinema: "Often the image of idyllic country life or battle is adorned with the figure of a perfectly shaped white horse—symbol of the Polish fight for independence." Mazierska, *Masculinities in Polish, Czech and Slovak Cinema*, 29.

incarnation of Polishness is the energetic and athletic masculinity that typifies his on- and off-screen personality (in striking contrast with the more pensive and slower mood embodied by Radziwiłowicz's intrusive gaze and massive physical appearance).

In the same year that Radziwiłowicz and Olbrychski made their on-screen debut as Polish expatriates in foreign film, Jerzy Skolimowski released the first of two feature films dealing with the harsh experiences of Polish newcomers in the UK. While the award-winning *Moonlighting* focuses on the predicament of a crew of Polish construction workers stuck in London at the time of the introduction of martial law, the second part of Skolimowski's British Solidarity diptych—*Success Is the Best Revenge*—shifts focus to the exilic fate of a dissident Polish artist (Alex Rodak) who (not unlike the characters embodied by Radziwiłowicz and Olbrychski) struggles with the romantic dilemma of sacrificing personal and private interests for the sake of the collective cause. Skolimowski, for his part, however, decided not to cast a Polish actor—or himself, as Roman Polański did in his psychological thriller *The Tenant* (1976)—in the leading Polish role but gave preference to two high-profile (and commercially more attractive) English actors (respectively, Jeremy Irons and Michael York). By way of contrast, most of the supporting Polish roles in Skolimowski's London-set films were played by non-professional Polish actors (including some close relatives and acquaintances of the director).

The Kieślowski Effect (and its Aftermath)

If expatriate Polishness in European filmmaking of the 1980s became the almost exclusive reserve of male dissident artists and intellectuals struggling with the legacy of Polish romanticism (as embodied by Polish national cinema of the 1970s and early 1980s), then the demise of communism and the fall of the Iron Curtain led to a far much diversified screen portrait of Polish migrants (not least in terms of gender identity). Moreover, whereas the international career of Radziwiłowicz and Olbrychski in the early 1980s was at least partly linked to their close collaboration with Andrzej Wajda, the second half of the decade saw the emergence of what may be called "the Kieślowski effect." The continent-wide success of Krzysztof Kieślowski's *Dekalog* (Decalogue) (1988)—especially the two "short films" about "love" and "killing" that grew out of the original TV series—helped to put not only the director himself but also some of his favorite Polish actors on the international radar. This pertains, first of all, to Mirosław Baka who broke through as the lead actor in *A Short Film About Killing* (the theatrical version of *Dekalog V*). At the turn of the decade, Baka's performance as a young, homeless drifter roaming urban space and ultimately resorting to criminal activity was continued in a series of German-language films that cast him in the role of an erratic Polish labor immigrant, first of all in Michael Klier's diptych about preunification Berlin—*Überall ist es besser wo wir nicht sind* (The grass is greener everywhere else) (1989) and *Ostkreuz* (1991)—and then followed by Uli Schuppel's TV film *Vaterland* (Fatherland) (1992). Only a couple of years later, another young Polish actor who made his breakthrough in Kieślowski's *Decalogue*—Olaf Lubaszenko—was given his foreign screen debut in the social realist drama *Les amoureux* (Lovers) (1994), in the role of a Polish jobseeker traveling through northern France. Portrayed throughout the film as a timid but tender and caring lover, Lubaszenko's character takes pity on a young local woman who leads a wild and dissipated life. In a somewhat similar vein, Grażyna Szapołowska (Lubaszenko's female costar in *A Short Film about Love*) was offered the leading role (of an undocumented Polish labor migrant who becomes the love interest of her German neighbor) in Franziska Meletzky's drama *Nachbarinnen* (Neighbors) (2004). Quite evidently, inasmuch as these foreign roles are at least partly reminiscent of the characters Baka, Lubaszenko, and Szapołowska incarnated in Kieślowski's cycle about the Ten Commandments, the Polishness they embody is much less historically and politically circumscribed than in the case of the Solidarity-era performances of Radziwiłowicz and Olbrychski.

As a celebrated European arthouse director, Kieślowski not only had an impact on the career of some of the Polish actors with whom he collaborated in the late 1980s, but he also made his own substantial contribution to the cinematic portrayal (and renegotiation) of expatriate Polishness, most notably in *Blanc* (White) (1994), the second installment of the acclaimed "color trilogy" (which came into being as a French-Swiss-Polish coproduction). As Izabela Kalinowska has rightly observed, *Blanc*'s focus on the marginalization of a hapless Polish émigré residing in Paris (Karol Karol) and his subsequent return to early postcommunist Poland cannot be separated from the central (and symbolic) role that the French capital came to play in the development of romantic mythology among nineteenth-century Polish exiles. As she notes, "At first glance, Karol Karol is not a likely heir to the tradition of romantic heroism. But the choice of character and the circumstances of his French residency do underscore the amazing vitality of those Polish national myths that were born in the nineteenth century and which survived throughout the twentieth century."[10] In terms of casting and characterization, it is undoubtedly significant that Kieślowski refrained from engaging an actor with the heroic stature of Olbrychski or Radziwiłowicz in the leading role. Instead, he picked the more "ordinary" Zbigniew Zamachowski (with whom he collaborated on the tenth part of *Decalogue*) and provided him with the features of a Chaplinesque, downtrodden antihero. On the level of representational practices, Karol Karol's return to his native Warsaw (where he refashions himself into a powerful business tycoon) symbolically coincides with the advent of a new cinematic paradigm of expatriate Polishness, in which the exile's romantically inspired engagement with the national cause gives way to the predicament of average Poles trying to make ends meet in the socioeconomic constellation of the New Europe. As I have written elsewhere, the representational shift from romantically connoted exile toward the topical subject of labor migration revealed itself first "in major European countries such as France, the UK, and Germany. Soon after, the cinematic interest in Polish labor migrants also spread to Austria, the Netherlands, Denmark, Sweden, Norway, and Switzerland, which indicates the almost continent-wide nature of the phenomenon."[11] Shortly after his memorable performance in Kieślowski's *Blanc*, Zamachowski himself quite literally came to embody this turn toward economy-driven expatriation by taking up the role of an undocumented Polish construction worker in the French TV production *Le clandestin* (The illegal) (1994).[12]

Starting from the early 1990s, not only blue-collar workers but also film professionals from the former People's Republic became increasingly internationally mobile, which is exemplified by the fact that the lion's share of Polish immigrant roles in post-1989 filmmaking have been given to actors with a Polish background.[13] At the same time, however, the overwhelming visibility of Polish actors and actresses in expatriate film roles does not imply that the

---

10   Kalinowska, "Exile and Polish Cinema," 110.
11   Van Heuckelom, "Londoners and Outlanders, 211–12.
12   See Van Heuckelom, "From Dysfunction to Restoration," 71–93.
13   Apart from the already mentioned "Kieślowski actors" Baka, Lubaszenko, Szapołowska, and Zamachowski, the list of performers contracted over the past three decades to play a Polish immigrant role in a foreign production includes known (and lesser known) TV, film and stage actors and actresses such as Lesław Żurek, Łukasz Garlicki, Ireneusz Czop, Artur Steranko, Aleksandra Justa, Agnieszka Grochowska, Przemysław Sadowski, Andrzej Chyra, Dorota Zięciowska, Joanna Kulig, Dagmara Bąk, Natalia Rybicka, Magdalena Popławska, Alicja Bachleda-Curuś, Agata Buzek, Jakub Tolak, Cezary Pazura, Renata Dancewicz and Agnieszka Czekańska.

long-standing tradition of casting across ethnic boundaries has entirely lost its viability. As ensues from the massive body of post-1989 European films dealing with Polish labor migration, certain genres—such as the comedy, with its looser adherence to a mimetic logic—continue to display a stronger inclination to employ domestic actors in the role of expatriate protagonists.[14] Film productions that deal with intergenerational relations (and conflicts) in the diasporic space, in turn, tend to attribute the roles of the parental generation to Polish-born actors, whereas the generation of their offspring is typically impersonated by local actors.[15] As another side effect of the changing mobility practices after the fall of communism, the past two decades have also seen a growing number of hyphenated film professionals (and amateurs) who are typically cast in the role of Polish expatriates, such as Redbad Klijnstra (who regularly appears in Poland-themed Dutch productions) and the Dublin-based Natalia Kostrzewa (who has been repeatedly cast as a Polish immigrant in Irish film). In terms of representational practices, finally, the perhaps most remarkable (and persistent) casting strategy may be called "cross-ethnic East European casting" and brings to mind Elvire Popesco's performances as a Polish aristocrat in classical French cinema. Based upon the alleged interchangeability of Slavic (and other Eastern European) identities across ethnic lines and the assumption that local audiences are not able to distinguish the differences between these ethnic affiliations (in terms of language and phenotype), this strategy is in line with the well-established homogenizing treatment of other cinematic minorities (such as Asians and North Africans) and (re)produces a monolithic concept of Eastern Europeanness. This is, for instance, the case in two recent Dutch productions—*Shocking Blue* (2010) and *De verbouwing* (The renovation, 2012)—both of which feature an actor of Yugoslav descent (Serbian and Croatian, respectively) in the role of a Polish immigrant worker. Obviously, what sets the onscreen homogenization of Eastern European characters apart from examples of Asian and North African typecasting in European fiction film is the fact that the former are not visibly different from other (European) whites—which, arguably, invalidates the need to cast nondomestic actors in these roles.

---

14 See, for instance, films such as *Caruso Pascoski di padre polacco* [*Caruso Pascoski, son of a Polish father*] (1999), *Heirate Mir* [*Marry me*] (2001), *Was nicht passt, wird passend gemacht* [*If it don't fit, use a bigger hammer*] (2002) and *Coursier* [*The courier*] (2010).

15 See, for instance, *Small Time Obsession* (2000), *Lena* (2011) and *Crache-coeur* [*Raging rose*] (2015).

Some particular cases, however, defy such a reading and shed a different light on the practice of "cross-ethnic East European casting." The most intricate example is offered by Costa Gavras's Paris-set tragicomedy *La petite apocalypse* (A minor apocalypse, 1992). A French-Polish coproduction loosely based on Tadeusz Konwicki's eponymous novel, the film features the famous Czech actor-director Jiří Menzel in the role of a formerly dissident Polish writer who— not unlike Karol in *Blanc*—suffers from social (and marital) marginalization in early 1990s France. Seen from the perspective of the historically different development of Czech national cinema—in particular the "incompatibility of "proper heroes" with Czech culture that has been "signified by casting foreign actors, including Polish, in heroic roles"[16]—the submissiveness, clumsiness and lack of heroism impersonated by Menzel in Gavras's film may be seen as a dose of "Czechness" consciously injected into the cinematic portrayal of expatriate Polishness (not the least because Menzel's body language strongly contrasts with the agility of forthright Polish "heroes" such as the ones incarnated by the horse-riding and sabre-fighting Olbrychski).

"Wanda Who Did (Not) Want a German": Post-1989 Polishness and Interethnic Romance

As I have indicated earlier, the fact that Olbrychski and Radziwiłowicz were cast in foreign film productions in the early 1980s (as well as the kind of roles they were expected to play) cannot be separated from the onscreen persona they developed in Polish filmmaking of the 1970s and from the international attention these performances evoked. With some exceptions (Zbigniew Zamachowski perhaps being the most notable example), quite the opposite seems to be the case for post-1989 performances of expatriate Polishness. As Ewa Mazierska has observed in her discussion of the international careers of four generations of Polish actresses, the post-1989 cohort—including prolific performers such as Alicja Bachleda-Curuś and Agata Buzek—paved the way to an international career not by passively waiting for proposals from abroad but by joining acting agencies and regularly taking part in international auditions.[17] Moreover, along with the diminishing international attention for Polish auteur cinema (especially after the untimely death of Krzysztof Kieślowski), the rapid commercialization of Polish filmmaking after the fall of communism and

---

16 Mazierska, *Masculinities in Polish, Czech and Slovak Cinema*, 24.
17 Mazierska, "Train to Hollywood: Polish Actresses in Foreign Films."

the industry's growing dependence on imported generic formats (such as the action movie and the romantic comedy) have led to a much more fragmented and diversified cinematographic landscape. In this regard, it is undoubtedly telling that the two performers who became the most prominent filmic faces (and bodies) of Polish masculinity and femininity in the early postcommunist period—Bogusław Linda as the cynical tough guy and Katarzyna Figura as the voluptuous blonde sex bomb—have drawn little (if any) attention from filmmakers and producers abroad.

From the perspective of representational practices, the fact that the casting of Polish actors and actresses in the role of expatriate Poles has become largely detached from their position (and roleplaying) within Polish cinematography allows one to disclose the significant disparity between constructions of Polishness in national and transnational cinematic space. A case in point is offered by the professional trajectory of the aforementioned actress Alicja Bachleda-Curuś, who made her silver screen debut in 1999—at the age of sixteen—starring in Andrzej Wajda's long-awaited adaptation of Mickiewicz's *Pan Tadeusz* (commonly called "the Bible of Polishness"). Significantly, after playing the role of Zosia Horeszko—a "quintessential beautiful Polish maiden with blonde hair and blue eyes"[18]—she was cast again in the role of a virtuous Polish virgin (also with the name "Zosia") in another Polish period film devoted to the historically strained relations between Poland and Russia, namely Jerzy Wójcik's *Wrota Europy* (The gateway of Europe) (1999). Her function within the narrative brings to mind the romantic model of Polish femininity (and motherhood)—according to which "falling in love with someone of the wrong nationality" was considered "in terms of national betrayal"[19]—and leads us back to "the centuries-long stereotype of the "proud Polish woman" who rejects the advances of a foreign man, thereby preserving the purity of Polish blood and culture."[20] In the Polish cultural imagination, one of the legendary stories typically evoked to support such a patriotic model of womanhood and motherhood—referred to as "Wanda, co Niemca nie chciała" ("Wanda who did not want a German")—is that of the Cracovian princess Wanda who refused to marry her German suitor and—in the various versions of the myth—either committed suicide or remained a virgin till death. Bachleda's double onscreen performance as a "virginal patriot" in Polish historical productions of the late 1990s gains additional significance when compared with

---

18   Falkowska, *Andrzej Wajda*, 2.
19   Szwajcowska, "The Myth of the Polish Mother," 31.
20   Mazierska, "Train to Hollywood: Polish Actresses in Foreign Films," 169.

some of the Polish expatriate roles she played in the 2000s. Two years after the release of *Wrota Europy*, she starred in the German coming-of-age film *Herz im Kopf* (Heart over head, 2001), where she plays the role of a young Polish immigrant (Wanda) employed by a German couple as an au pair for their two children.[21] The coming-of-age story centers around Wanda's romance with an erratic German teenager (Jakob) who has just lost his mother and who is in desperate need of balance in his personal life. The Polish girl's function within the narrative is similar to that of many other Polish immigrant characters featured in post-1989 European film: while becoming the love interest of an emotionally (or otherwise) troubled representative of the immigrant-receiving society, these vigorous newcomers are functionalized on screen as problem-solvers and redemptive agents. Although probably not intended by the makers of *Heart over Head*, the surrogate maternal role that Wanda/Bachleda-Curuś comes to fulfil in German cinematic space—as an au pair and as the love interest of a homeless and motherless German teenager—can be read as a symbolic reversal of the romantic myth of the Polish Mother (and the Wanda legend as one of its medieval sources of inspiration). Significantly, only a couple of years later, Bachleda-Curuś appeared in a somewhat similar configuration in the Francophone Swiss production *Comme des voleurs (à l'est)* (Stealth) (2006). Its main protagonist is a homosexual Swiss radio journalist (Lionel Baier) who goes through a personal crisis and becomes obsessed with his family's distant Polish roots. Along the way, Baier gets romantically involved with a Polish au pair living and working in Lausanne (Ewa, played by Bachleda-Curuś). By bringing into view the main character's performative "heterosexualization"—under the influence of his female Polish love interest—the film adds an undeniably parodic twist to the widespread trope of interethnic coupling (and its allegedly redemptive impact on the local protagonist). At the same time, it imbues Polishness with a sense of moral conservatism: as it appears, being Polish (or being of Polish descent) is incompatible with queerness.[22]

On a more general level, the trope of interethnic romance as it unfolds in post-1989 migration-themed European filmmaking cannot be separated

---

21   As an exclusively German production, the film did not have a theatrical release in Poland. It did come out, however, on DVD (under the Polish title *Z miłością nie wygrasz*). Moreover, viewing statistics on the popular Polish streaming site www.zalukaj.com indicate that the film has been viewed more than fifty thousand times (data from June 2019).

22   For an in-depth analysis of the film, see van Heuckelom, "Changing Sides. East/West Travesties in Lionel Baier's 'Comme Des Voleurs (à l'est),'" 37–50.

from the geopolitical reshuffling of Europe that took place after the end of the Cold War and also lends itself to be interpreted as a familial metaphor of Europeanization. Read along these lines, the multitude of mixed relationships in which Polish labor migrants engage on screen is indicative of Poland's return into the "European family," after decades of being caught behind the Iron Curtain. As such, the Polishness as it is portrayed in these interethnic romance films points, first and foremost, to a re(dis)covered European identity and is indicative of these newcomers' transformation from outsiders to insiders (e.g., in the European Union, the Schengen zone).[23] And along with the changing position of Poland on the geopolitical and cultural map of Europe, the cinematic inclusion of Polishness in an overarching European identity coincides with the exclusion of more distant ethnic Others (such as Russians, Belarussians, and Ukrainians) from the European identity space.[24] Therefore, whereas some productions still adhere to the practice of "cross-ethnic East European casting," many more film projects are at pains—both on the level of casting and on the level of narrative—to differentiate Polish characters (and other "New Europeans") from those who remain on the outside.

Returning to Bachleda-Curuś's double performance as a "virginal patriot" in post-1989 Polish cinema, the fact that the ideal of Polish womanhood represented by her character has been staged within the narrative and aesthetic framework of a period film may suggest that its historically circumscribed views on Polish femininity and motherhood—including the long-lasting taboo surrounding intermarriage (especially when it involves "archetypical" enemies such as Russian and German men)—bear no significance whatsoever for contemporary Poland. Upon closer examination, however, such a diagnosis does not seem to be entirely tenable, especially if we take into account recent pop-cultural treatments of interethnic coupling and out-group marriage in the diasporic space. Its most telling example is, undoubtedly, the high-budget serial *Londyńczycy* (Londoners) which ran on Polish public television in 2008–2009 and which brings into view the ups and downs of a heterogeneous group of young Poles moving to the UK in the postaccession period: while the final episode of the first season closes with the announcement of the engagement between two of the Polish lead characters, the second season ends with a double Polish wedding

---

23 See van Heuckelom, "From Dysfunction to Restoration: The Allegorical Potential of Immigrant Labor."

24 See van Heuckelom, "Londoners and Outlanders."

in a London church (in addition to the fact that four other major characters end up in a Polish-Polish relationship as well.)[25]

Polish Patriarchy and Intergenerational Conflict: Expatriate Daughters in European Film

If the promotion of in-group relationships in *Londyńczycy* reveals a patriotic agenda reminiscent of partitions-era discourses on the "conservation" of Polishness (at home and abroad), then the serial is decidedly more progressive and balanced in its assessment of the opportunities offered by emigration. The second season features two very similar sequences in which a young Polish migrant—the characters played by Lesław Żurek and Rafał Maćkowiak—is urged by his future father-in-law—respectively, a Polish farmer and a Solidarity-era exile—to leave Britain and return, out of moral and economic duty, to Poland (where the "Polish daughter" will be able to "live like a queen"). The intergenerational disagreement that unfolds in both scenes exposes two conflicting views of Polishness: the patriarchal and patriotic notion of a stable national identity and a fixed "fatherland" versus the younger generation's embracement of a more fluid, transnational identity (which can be lived out and developed beyond Polish territory). In the corpus of films under scrutiny, the significance of familial and intergenerational relationships in the Polish migrant experience finds apt expression in a couple of roles played by Agata Buzek, who was by far the most prolific embodiment of expatriate Polishness in contemporary European film.

At the age of twenty-two, after making her Polish screen debut (in a minor role) in Robert Gliński's *Kochaj i rób co chcesz* (Love me and do what you want) (1998), Buzek was cast in the Italian production *La ballata dei lavavetri* (The ballad of the windscreen washers) (1998). Set in the late 1980s, the film tells the story of a Polish working-class family that arrives on a pilgrimage to the Vatican and then decides not to return to the Polish People's Republic. While the paterfamilias Janusz, his brother Zygmunt, and his son Rafał try to earn a living by washing windscreens at busy crossings in the Italian capital, his wife Helena and his teen daughter Justyna (played by Buzek) work as domestic aids for the Roman upper class. Unable to cope with the professional and social degradation he faces in Rome, Janusz soon vanishes without a trace (and is supposed to have thrown himself in the Tiber). After the father's disappearance, the entire

---

25   See van Heuckelom, "Londoners and Outlanders," 231.

family disintegrates, including the optimistic and somewhat naïve Justyna who dies after a rape attempt by two local adolescents.

The 2006 German production *Valerie*, in turn, transposes Buzek to a completely different environment (and she plays a character some ten years older). Set in the vicinity of the remodeled Potsdamer Platz—during the Cold War a no man's land between East and West Berlin—the film revolves around a transnationally mobile fashion model of Polish extraction ("Valerie" Adamczyk) who tries to relaunch her modeling career (and maintain her cosmopolitan lifestyle) by doing photoshoots and auditions in the German capital. Although the main character's umbilical cord with the Polish homeland has not completely severed—as Valerie's occasional phone calls to her mother in Poland suggest—her sense of belonging is decidedly transnational rather than national. In a variety of ways, the film reflects and reproduces the new reality of postunification Germany and postenlargement Europe in which the long-standing East-West divide has been pushed into the background (without disappearing altogether). Moreover, with its prominent focus on casting practices in Europe's creative industries, the film may be said to take Buzek's professional position as a transnationally mobile (and polyglot) Polish actress to a reflexive level.

In the 2011 Dutch coming-of-age film *Lena*, in turn, Buzek appeared in a supporting role, as the morally suspect mother (Danka) of a Polish-Dutch teenager (Lena) who lives in one of Rotterdam's working-class districts. As the viewer learns over the course of the narrative, the generational conflict that drives Danka and her revolting teen daughter apart (and urges the latter to move into the—equally dysfunctional—middle-class household of her Dutch boyfriend) at least partly ensues from the Polish mother's own problematic childhood. Time and again, the woman is framed by the camera while talking on the phone to her sister who stayed behind in Poland and complaining about their tyrannical father. Quite symbolically, the statement "Nie mam ojca" ("I don't have a father") runs like a mantra through the film.

The 2013 British action-drama *Hummingbird*, finally, features Buzek in the role of a Polish nun (Krystyna) who runs a food kitchen for poor and homeless people in London.[26] One of her clients is a traumatized alcoholic ex-serviceman (Joey), with whom Krystyna romantically engages. Toward the end of the film, the viewer learns that the Polish nun is equally haunted by a traumatic past: her

---

26 It is noteworthy that both *Lena* and *Hummingbird* have been made accessible for Polish viewers on the popular streaming service http://www.zalukaj.com. While the former has attracted almost twenty thousand viewers, the latter has been watched by no less than three hundred thousand people (data from June 2019).

childhood dream of becoming a world-famous ballerina was cut short by her despotic Polish father who decided to send her to gym class instead of ballet. Repeatedly sexually abused by her gym instructor, the girl eventually killed the man, after which she ended up in a convent because she was too young to be sent to prison. As it turns out, rather than serving as a superficial symbol of her Polishness, the woman's—imposed rather than self-chosen—Roman Catholic identity is inextricably linked with a story of patriarchal oppression that needed to be covered up.

Taken together, these films not only epitomize the breadth of Buzek's acting range in foreign films but also reveal the subsequent guises of her performance as an expatriate "Polish daughter." While her on-screen persona develops and matures over the course of time, the position of the Polish father in the subsequent narratives changes as well, from his untimely disappearance in *La ballata dei lavavetri* to his very much welcome absence in the more recent films. Therefore, although it may seem a broad interpretive stretch, the tropes of intergenerational conflict and interethnic romance that recur in cinematic representations of post-1989 expatriate Polishness may be seen as the opposite sides of the same coin: if the former serves to reconfigure Polishness from a position of resistance and contestation (against paternal and patriarchal authority), then the latter does the same from a distinctly positive and constructive perspective (as it epitomizes a return to the "European family" through a form of transnational reconciliation).

Conclusion

Over the course of only a few decades, Polish performers have increasingly contributed to the construction of expatriate Polishness in European feature film. Along with the proportionally diminishing prominence of cross-ethnic casting practices and the growing mobility of Polish film professionals, the 1980s saw a turning point in the onscreen treatment of Polish expatriates. Against the backdrop of the Solidarity era, some of Polish cinema's most iconic (male) faces of the day made their appearance in foreign cinematic space, although not without bringing along some substantial elements (motifs and requisites) drawn from the country's romantic mythology. Somewhat paradoxically, along with the growing involvement of Polish actors and actresses in foreign film projects, the 1990s and 2000s have been marked by a substantial degree of incongruity between expatriate and domestic performances of Polishness (as the different treatment of interethnic coupling aptly indicates).

With some simplification, the body of films discussed in this chapter allows us to discern three paradigms of (trans)national belonging: from Polishness as something spatially and temporally distant and vaguely "Eastern European" (prior to the 1980s) over the emergence of distinctly national signifiers of Polish identity (in the Solidarity era) to the gradual Europeanization of Polishness (after the fall of communism). Using the familial metaphor from the analytical part of this chapter, the first stage is aptly represented by Elvire Popesco's performance as the strange, distant "cousin from Warsaw" in the eponymous French film from the early 1930s. The most prominent signifier of the second phase is, undoubtedly, the saber used as a prop by Daniel Olbrychski in *Mariage blanc*—a heirloom of his "Polish family" (both in the literal and the metaphorical sense). At the center of the third paradigm, finally, lies the issue of familial reconfiguration, which is given narrative shape through the interrelated tropes of interethnic coupling and intergenerational conflict (as the performances of Alicja Bachleda-Curuś and Agata Buzek reveal).

Ultimately, when taken together, these three paradigms are indicative of the growing importance of feature film production as a vehicle of Europeanization, along with the increasing involvement of Polish (and hyphenated) film professionals in these transnational identity constructions (which serve to imbue Polishness with a sense of European belonging). Therefore, apart from reflecting the changing mobility practices on the East-West axis after the fall of the Iron Curtain and the increasing coproductional activities of Polish film studios and companies, the post-1989 portion of the corpus may be said to partake in a process of imaginative reconfiguration (the object of which is post–Cold War Europe and its geopolitical, economic, and cultural parameters). Along the way and in spite of some persisting tensions (old and new), the very notion of "expatriate Polishness" has taken a distinctly new shape: while the condition of expatriation is now conceived of in terms of gains rather than in terms of losses (as opposed to the particular discourse surrounding exile in Polish romantic mythology), Polishness itself has shifted from being something vaguely Eastern European to becoming a constituent feature of Europeanness.

Bibliography

Falkowska, Janina. *Andrzej Wajda: History, Politics, and Nostalgia in Polish Cinema*. New York and London: Berghahn Books, 2007.

Haltof, Marek. "Adapting the National Literary Canon: Polish Heritage Cinema." *Canadian Review of Contemporary Literature* 34, no. 3 (2007): 298–306.

Jagielski, Sebastian, and Magdalena Podsiadło, eds. *Kino Polskie Jako Kino Transnarodowe*. Kraków: Universitas, 2017.

Kalinowska, Izabela. "Exile and Polish Cinema: From Mickiewicz and Słowacki to Kieślowski." In *Realms of Exile: Nomadism, Diasporas, and Eastern European Voices*, edited by Domnica Radulescu, 107–24. Lanham, MD: Lexington Books, 2002.

Maśnicki, Jerzy. *Niemy kraj. Polskie motywy w europejskim kinie niemym (1896-1930)*. Gdańsk: Słowo/obraz/terytoria, 2007.

Mazierska, Ewa. *Masculinities in Polish, Czech and Slovak Cinema: Black Peters and Men of Marble*. Oxford and New York: Berghahn Books, 2008.

Mazierska, Ewa. "Train to Hollywood: Polish Actresses in Foreign Films." In *Polish Cinema in a Transnational Context*, edited by Ewa Mazierska and Michael Goddard, 153–73. Rochester, NY: University of Rochester Press, 2014.

Mazierska, Ewa, and Michael Goddard, eds. *Polish Cinema in a Transnational Context*. Rochester, NY: University of Rochester Press, 2014.

Smith, Alison. "Polish Performance in French Space. Jerzy Radziwiłowicz as a Transnational Actor." In *Polish Cinema in a Transnational Context*, edited by Ewa Mazierska and Michael Goddard, 174–93. Rochester, NY: University of Rochester Press, 2014.

Szwajcowska, Joanna. "The Myth of the Polish Mother." In *Women in Polish Cinema*, edited by Ewa Mazierska and Elżbieta Ostrowska, 15–33. Oxford and New York: Berghahn Books, 2006.

Van Heuckelom, Kris. "Changing Sides. East/West Travesties in Lionel Baier's 'Comme Des Voleurs (à l'est).'" In *East, West and Centre: Reframing Post-1989 European Cinema*, edited by Michael Gott and Todd Herzog, 37–50. Edinburgh: Edinburgh University Press, 2015.

Van Heuckelom, Kris. "From Dysfunction to Restoration: The Allegorical Potential of Immigrant Labor." In *European Cinema after the Wall: Screening East-West Mobility*, edited by Leen Engelen and Kris Van Heuckelom, 71–93. Lanham, MD: Rowman & Littlefield, 2014.

Van Heuckelom, Kris. "Londoners and Outlanders: Polish Labour Migration through the European Lens." *The Slavonic and East European Review* 91, no. 2 (2013): 210–34.

Van Heuckelom, Kris. *Polish Migrants in European Film 1918–2017*. New York: Palgrave Macmillan, 2019.

Chapter Fifteen

"Poles—Their Own Portraits" Revisited

Taking a Critical Stand

Ryszard Koziołek

Understanding Backward

On October 5, 1979, the National Museum in Krakow launched an exhibition that showcased nearly a thousand exhibits featuring images of Poles produced over a thousand years of history. Organized by Marek Rostworowski, who was director of the museum at the time, "Poles—Their Own Portraits" enjoyed enormous popularity. It is estimated that the exhibition was visited by three hundred thousand people, mostly by those who did not regularly partake in exhibition culture at large. In the aftermath of John Paul II's election to the papacy and just a few months before the August 1980 strikes in Poland, the context of those events was significant for the success of the exhibition. Its sheer scale was reason enough to attract visitors: it was one of the first Polish "blockbuster" exhibitions. These exhibitions are not meant to be aesthetically attractive; rather, they seek to collect and display a particular kind of artifact. From the point of view of its visitors, viewing an exhibition like that is testimony to their democratic participation in culture.

Paweł Leszkowicz writes that in the Poland of the 1970s (under Edward Gierek's rule) there were other homely "soc-blockbusters." And yet the most important of these was the patriotic-historical "Poles—Their Own Portraits" in the National Museum in Krakow, which was visited by people from all over Poland. They went there to see themselves in the portraits of their forefathers and in the mirror that was placed at the end of the exhibition.[1] Leszkowicz stresses that these blockbusters prove their own egalitarianism in an unmistakable way: "Most of them are scheduled to be open for three months and they should be visited by 250,000 people to reach the status of class B atop the Olympus of museum exhibitions. A quarter of a million is then a threshold. We are dealing here with big, even very big, and popular exhibitions. Secondly, there is the quality of the museumgoers to be taken into account. Blockbusters are visited by the sort of people who usually do not visit museums and are not interested in art. In this particular case, however, they voluntarily join long queues, and even buy more expensive tickets."[2]

Two elements made the "Poles—Their Own Portraits" a broadly popular exhibition: an unprecedented number of exhibits with rationalistically appealing content and a uniquely condensed package of historical portraits and self-portraits of Poles from the Middle Ages to the 1970s. It aimed to prompt a sudden collective self-recognition or, at the very least, to instigate in the visitors a nascent desire to make the exhibition a kind of essential collective portrait of their own so that, according to *Linde's Dictionary*, "they fashion their own design, shape and ideal after the image."[3] Marek Rostworowski, the exhibit's creator, made its intended effect crystal clear in his declaration to bring out into the open a suprahistorical and class-transcending community of Poles:

> It does not matter whether we define our cultural heritage as noble, plebeian, bourgeois, romantic or positivist; today all those elements are contained there and there is no telling them apart.[4]

Rostworowski's point was upheld by Aleksander Gieysztor, who wrote:

> A Polish community that was presented to us had been born in the eyes of artists of varying ages and talents but it is also a community on the strength of its cumulative inheritance. That transcends any kind of genetic materiality or inspiring spirit because it consists in an act of choosing cultural values, renewed over and over again, from one generation to another.[5]

---

1 Leszkowicz, "Blockbusters. Sztuka wypełniania sal muzealnych."
2 Leszkowicz, "Blockbusters."
3 S.B. Linde, *Słownik języka polskiego* [A Polish Language Dictionary], Lwów 1860, 6:343.
4 M. Rostworowski, in: *Polaków portret własny* [*Poles—Their Own Portraits*], ed. M. Rostworowski, Warszawa 1983, part I, 21.
5 A. Gieysztor, "Wielkie zwierciadło przykładów" [A huge mirror of examples], in *Polaków portret własny*, part 1, 5.

Accordingly, "a thrust of several hundred images provokes the sense of a peculiar hominess and togetherness."[6] Many reviewers' testimonies (a full list of those is available at the end of this essay) confirm this particular aspect of the exhibition's reception by visitors (i.e., a sense of evident belonging to an iconographic universe). Even one of the critics from *Trybuna Ludu* (a communist daily), obliged to take a skeptical stance, expressed his surprise at the ado while confirming the visitors' relationship to the displayed images:

> After all, what is so interesting that this exhibition exposes? Is that anything that we have not been familiar with yet? Well, nothing like that is going on here; whatever it says has been well known.[7]

The visitors' responses, recorded and collected on the spot, confirmed the dialectic between a chaotic excess of exhibits and discovering the secret unity of images and their viewers, separated by a historical distance and social class. The paradox is amplified by the entries in the visitors' book, especially where they express their dislike of contemporary portraits of Poles. They find it easier to identify with images of the First Republic gentry than with images of their contemporaries. Here are a few emblematic entries to illuminate further discussion:[8]

> "The last hall makes a depressing impression. What a decline of art and spirit. All of it is spectacular: it makes you proud of your ancestry."
>
> "Look here, Poles, here is who you were. And who are you today?"
>
> "There is a tremendous power in all of this. I feel powerfully Polish."
>
> "Man—how proud it sounds! And to be Polish sounds even prouder."
>
> "The ground floor with contemporary images ruins the charm of the entire exhibition."
>
> "In every portrait, there is a particle of myself. I did not know I was like that."
>
> "An exceptional exhibition, except for the last hall. Do we really look like that, and are we like that?"
>
> "The 'We' mirror is the best exhibit."

---

6   Gieysztor, "Wielkie zwierciadło przykładów," part 1, 5.
7   Jaworski, "Dowód zbiorowej tożsamości."
8   Quoted in Magdoń, "Między wzniosłością a płotem," 38–46.

The last entry mentions a key exhibit crucial to my entire argument. It was a framed mirror in front of which, heading for the exit, every visitor had to pass. As a form of performative engineering, by placing visitors in front of a real mirror, the exhibit creators forced them to take a stance in defining their position in a boldly simple manner, ostentatiously inviting analogies by having them confront "their own" face. The simplicity of that "quasi-Lacanesque" trick is striking. Upon viewing almost a thousand "portraits of their own" the viewer is truly confronted with their own reflection of a Pole. Their genuine individuality transcends expression. The only visible (discursive, signifying) thing is the gargantuan palimpsest that covered the actual faces of the visitors as soon it starts talking about its "Polishness." This is not an archaeological process. The exhibition as such, despite the claim made by the poet character in Wyspiański's *Wesele*, demonstrates that Poland does not reside "in the heart", as a motherlode of blood and affects, but is their symbolic extrapolation. This Poland is always and already external, which makes me adopt a subjective position. I must be *some* subject, after all!

Critical Hubris

The point of this analysis is not to reconstruct or critique the exhibition on the basis of documents and testimonies focusing on its reception. It is to reflect on determining factors of a research position that I call "a critical stand." In short, it could be described as a methodologically buttressed suspicion, although the stand could be allegorized by references to stands or positions in ballet or fencing.

In principle, the transition from a situation to a position offers the subject more sovereignty than what is offered to a participant in the exhibition who is not burdened with the obligation to entertain analytical suspicions. By simplifying things at the beginning, then, we may put forward claims that taking a critical stand requires disillusionment. The condition does not necessarily entail an advantage of knowledge or theoretical competences characteristic of the critic over the participant but does require taking a critical stand, which includes, as its sine qua non, reflections over restrictions and limitations of the freedom of choosing a particular discursive *lieu* to continue with the critique. That means that by posing questions about the limitations of the critical *geste*, I am questioning my own limitations defining the place that will constitute a foundation for my critical claims concerning the exhibition, especially in context of the exhibition "Poles—Their Own Portraits" to which I adopted a critical position and explored the construction of an identity message.

In the spirit of full disclosure, I did not attend the exhibition; and yet, like its numerous visitors, I feel as if I had attended and never left it (or kept coming back to it). Its inimitable completeness brings to mind a possibility of collecting and absorbing Polishness as a commodity available to everyone because we carry the completeness within ourselves, as members of the cultural community called Poland. What this retroactive recognition of our own cultural and historical determination means is, as Clifford Geertz puts it, "Ex-post interpretation, the main way (perhaps the only way) one can come to terms with the sorts of lived-forward, understood-backward phenomena anthropologists are condemned to deal with."[9] Besides a mildly self-centered need to understand oneself, a more general problem arises here. Namely, this is about questioning the sort of placelessness of a critical stance that transpires from an attempt to hide the place from whence one can offer a critical exploration of the performative performance that the exhibition involved.

And that is what I wanted to do first, that is, demystify the exhibition's ideological framework by following the trail of Andrzej Leder and Jan Sowa's discursive practices. My expected outcome was to expose the suppressed and thereby unrepresented peasant and proletarian genealogy of the majority of visitors who attended the exhibition. With the imminent launch of the Solidarity movement, in place of that genealogy and its images, the visitors are offered a powerful injection of phantasmic steroids distilled from a national-nobiliary synthetic culture. A thousand exhibits purport to constitute a single narrative of a universalist occidental culture emerging from some tribal magma. Then a universal Polishness emerges, represented by figurative images of nobility and post-nobility intelligentsia. It was imperative to inquire into the absence of images among those who expressed themselves physically but not politically; they had no means of expression to articulate their aspirations to be represented by such images. Then, once they acquired the prerogative to speak, their voice could not significantly contribute in any significant way, to the spectrum of representations predominant in symbolic culture.

Several of my attempts to do justice to those absences proved futile, so I abandoned that particular project.

Analytical problems occur at the level of a subject's model that is meant to emerge from the processes of compensation for the lack of its own symbolic representation and suppression of "one's own"—real and not expressed—Polishness, those processes being reactivated by the very participation in the

---

[9] C. Geertz, *After the Fact: Two Countries, Four Decades, One Anthropologist.* (Harvard, London: Harvard University Press, 1995), 167.

exhibition. With no adequate symbolic representation, the citizen of Poland under socialism is prone to accept a genealogy alien to their class, yet instilling vigor in their harassed psychology. Andrzej Leder claims that "the deeper, less conscious sediments of contemporary Polish imaginary feed on a grange tradition, with its brutal division into <the lordlike> and <the boorish>, rather than on an emphasis on being <chained to our sacrifices>."[10] A matrix for that imaginary is found in the eastern borderlands, which, for millions of forcibly relocated Poles, was established as "lost" by the political order following World War II. Extermination of the Jews by the Nazis, not to mention a physical and political liquidation of Polish nobility and intelligentsia by the communists and the introduction of socialism, created a vacuum resulting in nostalgia, which was additionally amplified, as Leder has it, by "the weakness of the symbolic justification of the newly established social order."[11] It turns out that the peasant and proletariat subject, forcibly emancipated by Nazis and communists, took over elements of the nobility's imaginary and kept perpetuating them till the present day. "A strange concoction of these three elements—abhorrence of the lords, bourgeoise aspirations and traditional religiousness—may be found in the mindsets of many contemporary inhabitants of Polish cities and towns."[12]

Following that logic, in 1979 descendants of the "yahoos" swarmed into an exhibition that, for the most part (around 90 percent), showcased images of their oppressors. They recognized the images as components of "their own" symbolic universe. Lacan's mirror offers a convenient model whereby a postwar member of the Polish proletariat (no matter whether an actual one or a degraded descendant of nobility), deprived of their own cultural representations, integrates their scattered and disintegrated cultural body by means of hundreds of hallucinatory images. They are relieved to recognize them as their own because the images offer an opportunity to self-identify as members of a symbolic community. However, what Leder fails to explain in any satisfactory way is the mechanics of the takeover.

Jan Sowa offers an incisive description of the problem concerning the emergence of a permanent quality of the hallucinatory identification of a real face with its "other" reflection recognized in the mirror of culture. Since the Lacanian model focuses on the child with no capability of reflection on the process of their own "symbolization," what follows is that identification with the reflection is not "a performative effect of some imaginative and symbolic

---

10   Leder, *Prześniona rewolucja*, 16.
11   Ibid., 33.
12   Ibid., 172.

jiggery-pokery.... This is about a certain effect of <carving> the neuronal matter that is done by the signifiers."[13] The quotation marks (the less-than and greater-than signs) are justified because they symbolize—rather than explain—the inscrutability of the process. I do not think it is explained by Lacan's "psychophysical parallelism" between physical phenomena occurring in neurons and the subject's perception.[14] That is because, when it comes to the visitors who saw the exhibition, we are dealing with grown-ups, educated subjects influenced by egalitarian socialist ideology. Rather, the subject's evolution enters a further stage, which involves confrontation with the return of the real. The real, in the context of the Polish historical experience, turned out to be inexorable and unyielding to the descendants of Sarmatians. It could not be bent in any way. The real returned to its own position proving thereby that Poland did not exist.

That is what could emerge from a description of Poland's modern history along psychoanalytic lines. The republic has never existed; or, to be more precise, "the republic" does not designate a *real* positivity but a fundamental deficit.[15]

By relating a model to the exhibition itself, we may identify its enormous popularity (evident in the attendance figures) as a symptom of the visitors' becoming aware of the deficit as a deficit, that is, of a twofold loss of "Poland" in real and symbolic terms. They still do not have their own sovereign state, but unlike our ancestors, they have not developed their own symbolic representation of that—either traumatic or compensatory-mythographic—experience. A condition like that may lead to the disintegration of the subject—their implosion—when they do not have any exterior anymore. It is also possible to construe the exhibition as a collective psychosis whereby the visitors are incapable of distinguishing between reality and imagination.

At this point we part ways with Leder and Sowa because I am principally preoccupied with the critical stance from which they develop a description or a model of historical phenomena. Both Leder and Sowa place their own insights outside the locus of psychosis and in a place of critical "awakening," where one is liberated from hallucinations and may perform a psychoanalysis of the Polish psyche. At the same time, as members of the Polish cultural community, who think and write in Polish, are also part of this Polishness as "a deficit", masked by symbolizing hallucinogens. Nevertheless, one can hardly identify the place

---

13   Sowa, *Fantomowe ciało króla*, 379–380.
14   Ibid., 380.
15   Ibid., 382.

from where they deliver their critical assessments; it seems that they emerge from a nonplace and certainly not from in front of the mirror. Placelessness seems to be inscribed in the sovereign critical position of the subject, a position that the subject owes to their prerogative to use or create metalanguage. The subject, however, falls into the trap of counter-transference when a real object of their analysis coincides with their psychoanalytic model. Under such circumstances, the researcher explores their own theoretical products.

Let us return to the visitor's position as an indispensable stage in taking a critical stand. This requires making the assumption that we are affected by the same forces that led to the identification with images showcased during the exhibition. My suggestion is to pick up a performative dimension of symbolization rejected by Jan Sowa. Furthermore, I want to emphasize the somatic effects of symbolization without having recourse to biology-based metaphysics or neuronal jiggery-pokery. Verbal and pictorial violence, recurring over centuries, leaves literal scars on the body.

A simple illustration should suffice here. Let us think of the embodied materialization of a story in which one is referred to by means of a hurtful and offensive name: how the name enters the limbs, fashions one's gestures, and bends one's back. It is worth calling to mind how racist or sexist insults continue to live within the addressee's body and as their body:

> how those insults accumulate over time and, by concealing their story, acquire the semblance of being natural. Consequently, they come to shape and define the limits of the *doxa* that counts as "reality."[16]

Likewise, my body and mind have been shaped by the words used to refer to myself and the world. Nested within the Polish language, I am incapable of taking a critical stand in any other language, or in any other supradiscursive position from where I could conduct a supremely revisionist deconstruction of the peculiar laboratory of embodied symbols that the exhibition constituted. A critical stand—even a safe one, detached from the performative violence of the concentrated assault of images—occupies a circumscribed position, too. Where is that other position to bolster my critical stand on the absence that has shaped me? No critical detachment comes into play here. That is not because, as Adorno puts it, "The detached observer is as much entangled as the active participant; the only advantage of the former is insight into his entanglement, and the infinitesimal freedom that lies in knowledge as such."[17] Each position

---

16 Butler, *Excitable Speech*, 159.
17 Adorno, *Minima Moralia*, 26.

I take to pronounce the exhibition belongs to a territory it has already marked as symbolic.

Critique's Mirror

There is plenty of evidence showing how the concerted force of the exhibition affects not only those visitors who had no critical competences. Despite a plurality of critical languages and individual distinctions among critics themselves, they all end up where the original visitor faced the mirror containing a palimpsest of their face and a thousand others. Here are five examples illustrating the process of language being anatomized, that is, when that process parts ways with the critics' declared endeavors and alienates their critical efforts by coming back to its source symbolized by the showcased exhibits.

Marek Rostworowski

A two-volume album documenting the exhibition is the most exhaustive and fundamental publication of its kind.[18] Not only do descriptions of the illustrations contained in the second volume offer information about each image, but they also constitute interpretative essays that, whether by design or inadvertently, homogenize the images by reading them as a unified identity framework for Poles' collective portraiture. The poetics of those descriptions are adequately exemplified by Marek Rostworowski's passage commenting on Tadeusz Brzozowski's 1950 painting "Kuchenka" [A small cooker]:

> "A man with a mug in his hand, sitting by a small cooker in 1950: this could be virtually anyone. At that time our society had a prewar "superstructure," but it had no prewar "base," destroyed by the juggernaut of the war. It must be added, however, that compared to today, a larger section of our intelligentsia would subscribe to left-wing positions, and the living standards, minor exceptions notwithstanding, were bleak. The man by the cooker could then be a railwayman or a penman—a laborer but certainly not a functionary.
> And yet it is not the status of the man that matters here but the ambience: it does not even matter that he is alone with his tea, broken doorbell, and little rags drying on a line. People happen to be lonely in all sorts of situations. This man's teenage years were consumed by the Nazi occupation; he boasts considerable

---

18   *Polaków portret własny.*

sensitivity and consciousness, having awoken from a nightmare, though with no courage to go out and acknowledge that the reality is different now. He looks like a sick person still in need of recovery.

Without a shadow of a doubt, this is a Pole's—and the artist's (though not literally)—self-portrait.[19]

What is comic about this interpretation is its arbitrary volte-face, occurring when its historically contingent focus on the man in the picture is radically transformed and turned into a universalizing conclusion. The thesis that the figure in the painting is Polish does not manifest itself in argumentation but in a sudden eruption of revealed gnomic truth, which emerges unexpectedly and appropriately, under a "Polish" banner—existentially universal and aesthetically idiomatic.

Tadeusz Chrzanowski

Another, more interesting example, illustrates a serious problem. Tadeusz Chrzanowski's article "Polaków portret—jubileuszowy czy codzienny" ["Poles' Portrait, Festive or Casual"][20] offers one of the best "spontaneous" responses to the exhibition. In the very first sentence, the author draws attention to the tautological aim of the whole exhibit:

> The exhibition is meant to be a manifestation of The National Museum in Cracow, the oldest one in our country, and celebrating its centenary at the moment.[21]

Thus, the exhibition becomes, first and foremost, a spectacular gesture of self-engendering on the part of an institution established to document and codify Polishness, a mission attested to by exhibits showcased in the National Museum. Those objects—remnants of an unavailable wholeness of the past—are collected and synthesized by the power of synecdoche to represent wholeness and make it promptly accessible to the visitor capable of spending just a few hours in the museum. Temporal and spatial dispersal is nullified or, rather, camouflaged. Thereby Polishness thickens; there are no gaps since it fills up the museum space with a luxury of excess replicated by the crowds of visitors. The museum speaks to itself and about itself: "Here is Poland for you."

---

19   M. R., *Polaków portret własny*, 141.
20   Chrzanowski, "Polaków portret—jubileuszowy czy codzienny," 1.
21   Ibid.

Chrzanowski writes, "Upon entering the museum the visitor is supposed to feel that they enter <a Polish universe ranging from long-bygone days to today>." He is critically astute here, not deceived by the excessive nature of the exhibit nor any inconsistency between tradition and contemporary times. He notes that "[t]here is a seeming confusion around Wanda Wasilewska and Father Kolbe, Bierut and <A Pole> by Leszek Sobocki." The closer he gets to his conclusion, the softer his suspicion-driven revisionist criticism becomes. It transmogrifies into the banality of a borrowed phrase, testifying, as it seems, to a critical paralysis in front of the mirror where the best you can do is reflect (on) quotations and paraphrases. As a consequence, he concludes his piece with a quote from Szymon Starowolski: "Rough Sarmatians carry within themselves seeds of divinity."[22]

Janusz Tazbir

Unlike Chrzanowski, Janusz Tazbir begins his essay with a critique of simplifications prevalent in amateurish approaches to national characterology. He notes that many publicists, writers, and historians have already delivered pronouncements on the subject of Polish nature. Most of them, however, have oscillated between foggy philosophizing on history and registering statements about Polish nobility's customs and character.[23] Then Tazbir goes on to discuss the diversity represented in Polish identity in the prepartition periods. Again, the closer he gets to his conclusion, the more his diverse argument narrows until it reaches a predictable deduction. When summarizing the historiography of the partition period, Tazbir reduces his multifaceted argument to an uncontested position. A rich repertoire and multiplicity of Sarmatian faces are subsumed in a single angelic/earthy type. Like the powerful forces of gravity, something twists and standardizes the critical discourse here.

Jan Błoński

Błoński begins with a dose of irony by mocking the issue of images of Poles in twentieth-century literature. Distrustful of his own position, Błoński deconstructs, in his own writing, any potential predilections for aesthetic ideology by

---

22 All quotations here come from Chrzanowski, "Polaków portret—jubileuszowy czy codzienny," 1.
23 Tazbir, "W zwierciadle trzech epok," 33.

emphasizing that the value of a literary portrait "is, at best, tantamount to the value of a symptom in a testimony."[24] However, he soon yields to the temptation of synthesis:

> I guess the literary Pole has never spoken about themselves in worse terms than during the three post-war decades. It is all the more peculiar that never before had they articulated their own sufferings more loudly (and more effectively).[25]
>
> Acceptable evidence of Polishness has become unimaginative: it comes down to an identification with the raison d'état and, more frequently, blood and language bonds.[26]
>
> Polishness, then, fares particularly well among signs of culture rather than in reality by culling its own substance from historical documents and works of art. It seems that Polishness is particularly comfortable in "a national church of relics", i.e., a museum.[27]

For Błoński, that is closely connected with the popularity of the eastern borderlands theme. The lands, so nostalgically described by Iwaszkiewicz, Kuncewiczowa, Rymkiewicz, and Konwicki, include Ukraine, Polesie, Samogitia (Pol. Żmudź) and Vilnius. The privileged position of the east (and the south—Galicia) confirms the persistence of the theme of "a national imaginative self-portrait."[28] Błoński himself is drawn into that powerful current of native symbols. His critical stand starts losing its firmness while his ironic affirmation of difference and incompatibility, so clearly pronounced at the beginning, is gone: "Is that supposed to prove that the tellers of those ironic and comic stories believe themselves to be someone else than society holds them to be ... and yet they come to question their own otherness?"[29]

Eventually, much to our chagrin, we are left with the perception that all the wild diversity of contemporary literature is reduced to a single, uniform symbolic train, which, like a chain, pulls Błoński to a place we already know so well—in front of the mirror:

Possibly, the opposition between an "All together now, kind sirs!" attitude and an attitude that was defined by the catchphrase involving a nobleman and

---

24   J. Błoński, "Kto ty jesteś?," 103.
25   Ibid.,106.
26   Ibid., 110.
27   Ibid., 113.
28   Ibid., 114.
29   Ibid., 121.

his prerogatives within his homestead is not entirely gone. It is common knowledge that the opposition was symptomatic of Poland's entire cultural past.[30]

Mateusz Halawa

Of all the critics I discuss here, Halawa is the only one who did not attend the exhibition. He makes no effort to conceal his position by acknowledging that he has to "reconstruct" the exhibition. He describes his approach as follows:

> In this text, I am looking at "Poles—Their Own Portraits" in the context of a notion of society. It is worth paying attention to the fact that, in the eyes of its visitors, the exhibition was an embodiment of an imagined national community. One can even say that "Poles—Their Own Portraits" was part and parcel of an attempt, characteristic of the times of the "Solidarity" movement, to cement together collective existences—i.e., society and nation—that had recently gone their separate ways.[31]

Halawa's professional detachment and objectivity promise a different perspective, but once we read that the exhibition finds society as "what is visible and external to us and yet it permeates us through and through," it is clear that Halawa is already there, in front of the mirror, contributing his own professional reflection. It is fair to note that he has no intention of hiding his agenda, discussing the inclusion of expert research and its results in the development of society's self-knowledge. A scientific discussion of social behaviors proves to be a metanarrative that blends meaning and commentary into an indissoluble whole. Halawa writes that

> what constitutes a characteristic quality of contemporary reflection is that those meanings, rather than acquiring a local nature, rooted in current experience, are abstract and dependent on expert systems.[32]

In other words, both discourses—mythographic and debunking—join hands in the same practice of alienating individual experience and its history. Finally, aware of his own involvement, Halawa seems to be tired of the similarity that he himself has discovered so he postpones the exploration of the problem:

> A description of this problem, whereby "society" and its statistical models and rep-

---

30   Ibid., 121.
31   Halawa, "Tylu Polaków naraz widzieć, 35.
32   Halawa, "Tylu Polaków naraz widzieć," 57.

resentations mutually bring each other to life, constitutes a challenge consisting in producing a theory of theory's effects. Its criticism may become a starting point for a richer and more diverse "self-portrait."[33]

Nothing like that is going to happen; one can only reiterate Zbigniew Herbert's words from his magnificent poem "Mr Cogito Looks at His Face in the Mirror": "I lost the tournament with my face."[34]

A critical position, that is, a methodologically bolstered suspicion, does not set critical discourse free or sovereign in relation to symbolic violence perpetrated by the language being critically assessed and used for the assessment. Making pronouncements about Poland, and in Polish, the critic is instantaneously transferred, like a chess piece, to the front of the mirror filled with images of signifiers. The place belongs to the Polish language and only the Polish language is lord and master of the place, temporarily leased, as it may be, by individual utterances delivered in the same language.

Polishness—Scissors of Interpellation and Performance

The spot in front of the mirror may be identified with an X, a sign whose location is determined by the intersecting vectors of two forces governing identity statements that, in this particular case, are questions about Polishness. One of the forces is performative and the other one interpellating. I use these notions in the senses we owe to Austin[35] and Althusser.[36] Performative agency and felicity of utterances results from the emergence of authoritative language that, in turn, is contingent on convention or the context of violence (as in the case of "excitable speech"[37]). Interpellation renders identity suspicious. Andrzej Staroń, who translated Althusser into Polish, discusses, in a footnote, all the relevant meanings of interpellation in French:

> Althusser uses the term "interpeller" which has the following meanings in French: 1. turn to sb abruptly and demand sth; 2. Inquire about sb's identity; 3. To detain or question sb; and, of course, 4. Interpellate sb.[38]

---

33 Halawa, "Tylu Polaków naraz widzieć," 66.
34 Herbert, *Wiersze zebrane*, 365–66.
35 Austin, *How to Do Things with Words*.
36 Althusser, "Ideology and Ideological State Apparatuses."
37 See Butler, *Excitable Speech*.
38 Althusser, "Ideologie i aparaty ideologiczne państwa," n. 20.

The first force allows me to utter my name as "my own"; the other inquires who I am or, immediately identifies me without asking. At the X spot, in front of the exhibition's mirror, both forces operate simultaneously like two cards being shuffled in order to determine how to effect a transformation. They force the subject to rearticulate a performative response to the original interpellation: "Hey, you?!" (implicitly meant to convey the idea of: "Who are you?").[39] Images from the exhibition are instruments of symbolic violence that shove me in front of the mirror so that I constitute myself as a Pole. Still, an inevitable difference between my face and its image provokes a regulatory interpellation: "Who are you, really?" The subject's individual willingness to answer the question is of no consequence. My refusal to answer makes me vulnerable to the discourse of images, or else my identity is defined by state-owned birth registries and personal records.

As Michał Paweł Markowski explained when discussing Foucault, whose views are strikingly relevant here, the subject signifies a certain *position* to be taken by an "I" that decides to speak.[40] Markowski concludes:

> A human being's transformation into a subject assumes, then, that human beings and subjects are not the same: a human being becomes a subject by entering into language, which the subject uses to speak about themselves and others use to speak about the subject. A human being becomes a subject once they are required to do so by the institution of speaking.[41]

Polishness, as an issue, requires that one stands on the X. What emerges is a cross between performativity and interpellation. Polishness works by virtue of that dialectic agency, even without a tangible symbolic corpus. Both discourses constitute me as a subject speaking Polish about my own identity, its absence or contestation. Beyond the Polish symbolic universe, I am speechless. Revisiting the exhibition affirms Polishness as my only language. It is not my own, but I do not have another one. More than that, I desire to succumb to its universalizing

---

39 Althusser puts it as follows: "I shall then suggest that ideology 'acts' or 'functions' in such a way that it 'recruits' subjects among the individuals (it recruits them all), or 'transforms' the individuals into subjects (it transforms them all) by that very precise operation which I have called interpellation or hailing, and which can be imagined along the lines of the most commonplace everyday police (or other) hailing: 'Hey, you there!'" Althusser, "Ideology and Ideological State Apparatuses," 174.
40 Markowski, *Polityka wrażliwości*. 134.
41 Ibid., 134–35.

power and give up my individuality, distinctiveness, stigma, and exception present in my accent and vernacular inflections. The distinctiveness is a common experience of a particular individual fate. It keeps summoning me and paves the way for injustice by shoving me beyond meaning and into the arms of biopolitical engineering governing "life." It is an illusion to think that the living face of the visitor can resist the lifeless images.

"It seems that the only living image in the exhibition hall is the mirror undergoing transformations effected by passing crowds. Every now and then someone else takes a look at themselves in the mirror: pale, pink, content, indifferent, sweating, or as fresh as a daisy. And yet alive, yet alive":[42] this universal quality is a longed-for exception. The phantasmal Polishness that the exhibition radiated was a catalyst for the desire to break away from one's own unwritten history and join the ranks of those happy members of the showcased Polish community. And even if I myself—as a commoner, a Lutheran, an inhabitant of a periphery with frequently changing state allegiances—was not a good fit there, at least, against the background the exhibition, I became visible as an "other."

The objections, raised by Leder and Sowa that Poles are quick to yield to hallucinatory mythography, rests on an unspoken assumption that it is possible to think of a collective critical subject that will strike out for independence in relation to their own culture and language. Meanwhile the only possible critical position that readily comes to mind boils down to a regressive phrase used by Bartleby the scrivener: "I would prefer not to."

Another critical position may arise only from the same symbolic interior that sucks up and absorbs any attempt at taking a sovereign position that would be external to language. Above all, the power of the performative exonerates the subject, as Gorgias put it in his classical encomium of Helen:

> And if persuasive discourse deceived her soul, it is not on that account difficult to defend her and absolve her of responsibility, thus: discourse is a great potentate, which by the smallest and most secret body accomplishes the most divine works; for it can stop fear and assuage pain and produce joy and make mercy abound.[43]

By exonerating Helen from any responsibility of unfaithfulness, Gorgias exposes the power of the word, not so much in its seductive as divine (i.e., creative) capacity. Rather than for naming or describing, human beings, just as gods, make use of *logos* for its performative power to create reality and endow it

---

42   Rodziński, "Refleksje o wystawie," 3.
43   Gorgias, "Encomium of Helen."

with value. This is what happens every time language captures and overwhelms objects or constitutes them in a performative act.

That power was appropriated and exploited during the exhibition. Empowerment, or a sensation of being overwhelmed by "Polishness," does not seem to have been merely a transpassive bliss generated by the discovery of an unauthorized affinity with synthetic "Polishness." The performative action of the exhibition was a practical and appetitive critique of ontology. It did not really matter whether the Polish state and the subject inheriting a millennium-long cultural heritage existed or not, since it was the accumulation of the symbols that constituted both in front of visitors' eyes. Enthusiastic participation in the exhibition also meant responding to an interpellation of the communist regimes' political institutions in Poland: "Hey, you, who are you?" That is an aspect of the exhibition that Kazimierz Kutz drew attention to:

> The Sarmatians! Those nasty, abhorrent mugs! Let's party like there's no tomorrow but.... Everything was on display in those mugs: boundless drinking, arrogance, and stupidity. We went to see the "Poles—Their Own Portraits" exhibition out of sheer animalistic curiosity. We wanted to see what a true Polish monstrosity looked like; what features it had; what it wore and whether it resembled the contemporary monstrosity. That was a wonderful, all too wonderful Polish tissue; a natural element; raw flesh. No pretending and laying it on thick.... We relished the opportunity to take a closer look at ourselves; we relished our freedom. It was close at hand: in the Poles' experience and history going three, two or one hundred years back. While before the exhibition we had originated from nowhere, now we came from some place.[44]

A Critical Parade

Literature alone is capable of supporting criticism in its attempt to multiply possible positions. For potential versions of identity discourses, even the traditional historical epic is a welcoming heterotopia rather than an exclusively performative-interpellating oppression. What I have in mind is not only Sienkiewicz, whom the new, plebeian reader at the turn of the nineteenth century recognized as "their own" writer. They did so not only because of his hallucinogenic force but on the strength of the emancipatory power of the *Trilogy*'s language, which made it possible to denounce school, law, annexationists, illiteracy, etc. Modern historical novels from Scott (*Waverley*) to Lampedusa (*The Leopard*) have offered the reader a kind of refuge from constraints imposed

---

44 Radłowska, "To było lustro. 25 lecie wystawy."

by modernization. Namely, they showed possible worlds in which evolutionary discontinuities and cultural nonsimultaneousness were natural. Cultural peripheries are an inalienable, integral ingredient of historical processes, rather than objects to be liquidated in the name of modernization.[45] Although *Waverley*'s eponymous character must choose between the manliness of rebellion (Fergus, the Highlanders, and Flora) and the manliness of duty and responsibility (Colonel Talbot, "Englishness," and Rose), both cultural forms remain permanently undecidable there.

Jacques Derrida's advice is to incapacitate unidirectional performatives by drawing on their dynamics inherent in literary language, which are easier to recontextualize.[46] Revitalizing dynamics of the signifier, Derrida reveals his own position involving speaking "from within" the text, that is, as an actor of the symbolic field who is a holder of the rules of symbolic dictionary and grammar. And yet, without relinquishing a responsibility for objectivity, why not "turn up" meaning's potentiality and activate literature as an affective and semiotic event? For a limited duration: for the duration of a single reading, a conversation, the stage of reception? All the same, this will affect a reorganization of the symbolic field.

A critical utterance that is not founded on the institutional distinction between criticism and literature takes over qualities of the latter, thus putting at risk, at least initially, the authority of criticism. By relinquishing a distanced description, a critical statement like that acquires the prerogative to act as performative, that is, to produce an event by placing the text in a new, often alien context. Images from the exhibition, detached from their original context, are *usurped in the act of iteration* even though they no longer work as a conventional utterance instituting Polish identity. They lose their performative power, that is, their power "to communicat[e] a force through the impetus (impulsion) of a mark."[47] They become utterances that describe a singularity; synecdoches bereft by an inaccessible totality.

In search of a figure to stand as the critical subject in front of the interpellating mirror, I go for the word "parade" in its famous artistic implementation. On

---

45 Spatiotemporal differentiation of modernity, as encoded in European novels, is discussed at length in Welge, *Genealogical Fiction*. In the context of my discussion here, the chapter on *The Leopard* is particularly relevant: "Death of Prince, Birth of a Nation: Time, Place, an Modernity in a Sicilian Historical Novel (G. Tomasi di Lampedusa)," 170–93.
46 Derrida, "Signature Event Context," 9.
47 Derrida, "Signature Event Context," 13.

May 18, 1917, in the Théâtre du Châtelet in Paris, *Parade* premiered. It was a ballet performance by Diagiliev's Ballets Russes, with music by Erik Satie and a one-act scenario by Jean Cocteau, with costumes and sets designed by Pablo Picasso, choreography by Léonide Massine (who danced), and an orchestra conducted by Ernest Ansermet.[48] Let us put the music aside. Cocteau's scenario and Picasso's costumes were involved in staging new art (a modern situation), which was defined by a radical liberty to create within a tightening field circumscribed by the market and the tastes of mass consumers. A high demand for avant-garde art that is shocking, inventive, and "modern" transfers it from a zone of noble exclusion right to the middle of mass interest and economic exchange, which seemed reserved for easy (i.e., commercial, conventional, or popular) art. *Parade*, as a title, is what Cocteau took from the Larousse dictionary, aiming for one concrete meaning, as his own notes indicate. He jotted down the definition of parade as a burlesque performance staged outside the entrance to a theater in order to attract an audience to the performance.[49] Meaning is conveyed by two groups of characters. The first consists of three stock figures borrowed from entertainment shows and cinema: a Chinese illusionist, an American dancer, and acrobats. The other consists of directors whom Picasso dressed in gigantic (nearly three-meter-high) Cubist costumes. With grotesque obtrusion, they pitch the show given by the first group all the while degrading its attractiveness by their own gross promotional activities, which overwhelms the artists' show largely because of the directors' monstrous costumes, inspired by advertisements of "walking" hot-dogs and animated street ads in general.[50]

Parade showcases a position that avant-garde modernism may take within the tightening art field. At the same time, it fills us with the hope that, though forced to speak from a place designated by the institutions of language (outside the theater or inside), the critical subject is capable of reorganizing the symbolic dictionary and its articulation in such a way that the results are destabilizing, inducing a kind of disorientated awe. That is due to the use of the most worn-out clichés, taken over from various modes of entertainment: circus, vaudeville, musicals, and cinema. They are paraded in front of the audience's eyes, in

---

48   History of surrealism notes a scandal caused by the conflict between the composer, Eric Satie, and a critic, Jean Poueigh, who took Satie to court. The court sentenced Satie to a week in prison and a fine. See Davis, *Eric Satie*, 119–20.

49   Volta, *Satie As Seen through His Letters*, 110. Some crucial information on the ballet and its contexts is to be found in Doyle, "Erik Satie's Ballet Parade." (It includes a very useful bibliography.)

50   See Rothschild, *Picasso's 'Parade'*.

the generalizing and self-deconstructing figures of actors and directors, failing to respond to interpellation (Is this art?) and refusing to seek to—performatively—constitute themselves as new art. Instead, they produce a constructive aesthetic event, which aim is to keep, for as long as possible, the institutions of art in limbo without being certain about their own part played in the event. And that is what the critical dimension of the event is all about.

Before I proceed to outline the possibilities of a critical parade in relation to the exhibition in the title of this essay, let me offer the reader a simple, truly ascetic example. What exemplifies critical parade is an entry made by Szczepan Twardoch in his online profile, in which the writer articulates his disappointment with a decision taken by the Supreme Court in Poland. The decision dismissed the possibility that the Association of People of Silesian Nationality would be officially registered, thereby questioning the very existence of Silesian nationality. Twardoch's entry said: "Fuck you, Poland!" For Twardoch, a Silesian, the court ruling was an interpellating question: "Who are you?" (not a Silesian after all, as those do not exist). His answer does not respond polemically to the ruling; it fails to provide new arguments for the existence of Silesian nationality. It speaks "astray," "off topic," and yet it succeeds in attracting both readers' and the media's attention. His derogatory words do not address the nub of the matter, but their articulation becomes a critical parade in the context of quarrels over Silesian nationality and the Silesian language. In an interview with Anita Czupryn, Twardoch expressed his disappointment with the fuss that, in his opinion, his entry did not deserve:

> It makes me sad that you even want to talk to me about that, like all the media people, by the way. I cherish no illusions about the condition of the media in Poland and yet I find it very funny that you must say "Fuck you, Poland" to be heard in the context of a matter that I have discussed for at least 5 to 10 years now; one I have discussed at length in my journalism, in my literature and in many other ways.[51]

Indirectly, Twardoch's disapproval indicates the workings of a parade whose showy quality lures the addressees of criticism. This is just a brief moment because, confused for a while, the powers responsible for managing identity soon resume their operations. For example, a lawyer from Poznań, Michał Boruczkowski, citing Article 133 of the Penal Code, reported, with the police, an alleged crime perpetrated by Twardoch. The article concerns public

---

51 See https://dziennikzachodni.pl/twardoch-pierl-sie-polsko-prokuratura-rejonowa-w-poznaniu-wszczela-postepowanie/ar/3345225 (accessed 8 October 2022).

defamation of the Republic of Poland. In reply, Twardoch reminded everyone of his declared nationality: "More than 800 thousand people declared Silesian nationality [in the 2011 census], and almost half of those declared their Silesian identity as the only one they had. So did I."[52] A declaration of one's allegiance (a national identity) brings us back to the spot in front of the mirror.

How can those allegorical models inspire academic humanities today? In the humanities, a necessary step in any research procedure involves reflecting how a critical gesture is determined and being aware that academic freedom (concerning themes and methods) will not, by itself, translate into criticism's inventiveness and creative license. Only then is it possible to take a considered critical position, which, in academic terms, must not come down to what my friend, Stefan Szymutko, described in one of our conversations as "putting a piece of theory side by side with a piece of writing". The criticism emerging from the experience of a text's performative operation, like literature, affirms "the principal right to say everything, even if it be under the heading of fiction and the experimentation of knowledge, and the right to say it publicly, to publish it."[53]

Since there is no escaping the dictionary and grammar of symbolization, which are inevitable and not of my own making, what I am left with are practices that destabilize the liquid sequence of interpellation and performativity. They fix subjects in a place where they can only say/respond: 'I am this', pointing beyond themselves, i.e., saying 'yes' to the signifiers assigned to them by symbolic violence. If language and its inherent symbolic violence always reroute my answer to the question beyond me—beyond my singularity—the gesture of "exclusion" may be anticipated by speaking without responding; by parading instead. What I have in mind here is parade in its simultaneous (and aggressive-defensive) meanings of an exhibition, a display of wealth, a ceremonial assembly, a formal review of marching military troops, and an ostentatious show. In Polish, parade ('parada') has some additional meanings. It may refer to 'parrying a blow or hitting your opponent in response to their blow' or 'saving the goal by throwing one's body to either side in order to catch or deflect the ball' (a diving save). Even a goalkeeper who parades their skills impresses the fans not so much with their athletic efficiency as with a sudden and surprising showy thrust that may make little sense but it draws our attention to its performance.

---

52 See https://dziennikzachodni.pl/twardoch-pierl-sie-polsko-prokuratura-rejonowa-w-poznaniu-wszczela-postepowanie/ar/3345225 (accessed 8 October 2022)

53 Derrida, "The University Without Condition," 205.

Forced to stand in front of the mirror, the parading critic neither asks nor answers questions about meaning but "performs artistic tricks." They use language to affect language so that it displays its own ostentatious wealth and power according to an old Greek performative mode known as *epideiktikós* (showing power, parading).[54] An epideictic critical parade involves theory affecting the text in such a way that a performative power of language is shown, extracted, and demonstrated in action; thus making the verbal parade visible to the addressee of the critical utterance.

"The force of the event is always stronger than the force of a performative,"[55] says Jacques Derrida in a lecture delivered at Stanford University in April 1998. A critical parade is an infelicitous performative: it does not work as a force; it does not become something new. What it does is abolish the sign that depends on some original context, a fixed routine, a law of convention or the authority of power. A critical parade affirms play in the sense an effect on the restored freedom of a sign by endowing it with the right to mean something else, while the parade performer refuses to articulate what it means.

Bibliography

Polaków portret własny: praca zbiorowa [Poles—their own portraits: a collective work]. Part 1. Warsaw, 1983.

Polaków portret własny: praca zbiorowa [Poles—their own portraits: a collective work]. Part 2. Warsaw, 1986.

Reviews and Discussions of "Poles—Their Own Portraits"

Bauman, Marzena. "Polaków portret własny" [Poles—their own portraits], *Głos Nauczycielski* 3 (1980): 8–9.

Borek, Wojciech. "Przyspieszony kurs historii" [A crash course in history]. *Student* 25–26 (1979): 18–19.

Burzyński, Roman. "Portretujmy!" [Let's portray!] *Foto* 3 (1980): 72.

Chruścicki, Tadeusz. "Polaków portret własny" [Poles—their own portraits], a conversation with Elżbieta Sadowska, *WTK. Tygodnik Katolików* 44 (1979): 11–12.

Chrzanowski, Tadeusz. "Polaków portret—jubileuszowy czy codzienny?" [Poles' portrait, festive or casual]. *Tygodnik Powszechny* 44 (1979): 1–6.

---

54 For a discussion of *epideixis* in Greek philosophy, see E. Apter et al., *Dictionary of Untranslatables*, 1037–39.

55 Derrida, "The University without Condition," 235.

Cieślińska, Nawojka. "Swojskie panopticum" [A familiar panopticum]. *Sztuka* 1 (1980): 3–12.

Grzybkowska, Teresa. "Przeszłość mą widzę ogromną" [Huge is my past in front of my eyes]. *Polityka* 44 (1979): 9.

Jaworski, Marek. "Dokument zbiorowej świadomości" [Testimony to collective consciousness]. *Trybuna Ludu* 275 (1979): 6.

Jędrzejczyk, Olgierd. "W polu widzenia: Polak" ["A Pole within my eyesight"]. *Tygodnik Kulturalny* 48 (1979): 14.

KG. "Kręgi wtajemniczenia" [Circles of initiation] *Kierunki* 50 (1979): 10.

KTT. "Nie będzie zapomniana..." [It will never be forgotten...]. *Kultura* 6 (1980): 16.

Koźniewski, Kazimierz. "Polaków portret własny—wystawa w Krakowie" [Poles—Their own portraits—the exhibition in Cracow]. *Muzea Walki* 14 (1981): 61–72.

Lisowski, Andrzej. "Polaków portret własny" [Poles—their own portraits], *Życie Warszawy* 261 (1979): 7.

Madeyski, Jerzy. "Polaków portret własny" ["Poles—Their Own Portraits"], *Życie Literackie*, no. 43, (1979): 1 and 11.

Madeyski, Jerzy. "Sztuka prawdomówna (O wystawie <Polaków portret własny>)." [A truthful art: On the *Poles—Their Own Portraits* exhibition]. *Zdanie* 4 (1979): 47–52.

Magdoń, Andrzej. "Między wzniosłością a płotem. (Wpisy do Złotej księgi na wystawie <Polaków portret własny>)" ["Between the sublime and the fence enclosure: Entries in *The Visitors' Book* during the *Poles—Their Own Portraits* exhibition]. *Zdanie* 4 (1979): 38–46.

Małachowski, Aleksander. "Pamiętnik współczesny" [A contemporary diary]. *Kultura* 44 (1979): 16.

"<MY> na wystawie. Wybór wpisów z <Księgi pamiątkowej> wystawy <Polaków portret własny> w Krakowie" [Exhibited *WE*: A selection of the entries from *The Visitors' Book* made during the *Poles—Their Own Portraits>* exhibition]. *Sztuka* 1 (1980): 13–18.

Najder, Zdzisław. "Autoportret Polaków" [Poles' Self-Portrait], *Twórczość*, 1, (1980): 131–135.

Nowak, Leopold R. "Jaki jest nasz portret?" [What is our portrait like?]. *Magazyn Kulturalny* 1 (1980): 6.

Osęka, Andrzej. "Między historią a lustrem"" [Between history and the mirror]. *Kultura* 51– 52 (1979): 15.

Osęka, Andrzej. "Sarmaci, powstańcy i my" [Sarmatians, insurgents and us]. *Kultura* 46, (1979): 11–12.

Osęka Andrzej. *"Polaków portret własny"* [Poles—their own portraits]. *Projekt* 3 (1980): 2–13.

Osęka Andrzej. "Wystawa <Polaków portret własny> trwa" [Poles—their own portraits exhibition continues]. *Kultura* 7 (1981): 16.

Piskor, Stanisław. "Polaków portret własny" [Poles—their own portraits] *Poglądy* 4 (1980): 18.
Raducka, Zofia. "Portret Polaków w dzieje narodu wpisany" [Poles' portrait inscribed in the nation's history]. *Tygodnik Demokratyczny* 46 (1979): 12–13.
Ratajczak, Mirosław. "Lustro" ["The mirror"], *Odra*, 4, (1980): 108–09.
Rodziński, Stanisław. "Refleksje o wystawie" [Reflections on the exhibition]. *Magazyn Kulturalny* 1 (1980): 1–3.
Rostworowski, Marek. "Szukać i znaleźć" [To seek and to find], a conversation with Nawojka Cieslińska. *Sztuka* 1 (1980): 1–2.
Roszko, Janusz. "Polaków legenda malowana" [Poles painted legend]. *Magazyn Kulturalny* 1 (1980): 4–5.
Starosta, Ewa. "Czym będziemy..." [What we will be...]. *Fakty* 6 (1980): 6.
Szemplińska, Ewa. "Między nami Polakami" [Between us, Poles]. *Tygodnik Demokratyczny*, 7, (1980): 7.
Wierzchowska, Wiesława. "Polaków portret własny" [Poles—their own portraits]. *Literatura* 50 (1979): 13.
Wilczek, Jan. "Lustro" [The mirror]. *Kultura* 4 (1980): 9–11.
Witt, Piotr. "Portretów mowa niewyraźna" [The portraits' inarticulate speech]. *Sztuka* 6 (1979): 46–52.
Wróblewski, Andrzej. "Nasz portret" [Our portrait]. *Życie Warszawy* 12 (1980): 3.

Afterword

Polishness: A Time of Deconstruction, a Time of Reconstruction

Paweł Rodak

As demonstrated by the essays collected in this volume, the notion of Polishness can be understood in many different ways. Polishness is dynamic and heterogeneous, changeable in time and space (e.g., Polishness differs across the nineteenth, twentieth, and twenty-first centuries in national or émigré contexts, or depending on the region or place of residence). Polishness is, to a large extent, likewise dependent on a given social group or class, as well as on its experiences and the languages in which these experiences were expressed—namely, in some of these encounters, the experience of Polishness was brought to the fore while in others it was completely marginalized. Thus, if the category of Polishness is to have any meaning, it is only when subjected to critical reflection, constant revision, and reconstruction processes that reveal its historical and social complexity. Such is also the purpose of the studies collected in this volume. At the same time, they are part of a broader phenomenon, that of the "reworking" of Polishness within Polish historiography and social sciences, which took place in the first two decades of the twenty-first century and has gained momentum in recent years. These efforts have become a context for the process of reconstructing Polishness as a challenge for the near future. I will thus try to point these out and briefly describe them by drawing attention to five issues, illustrating them in the context of the most recent publications. They can be classified with the following keywords: a people's history, women's experiences, Polish modernity, war and postwar, diaries and oral history. The first four concern changes in the perception of Polish history and its related discussions, the fifth regards changes in source materials that accompanies the former.

"A people's history of Poland" is a phrase that became, in a short period (2016–2021), distinctly present within Polish humanities and journalism. It was the title of an important special issue in one journal,[1] then it became the title of a comprehensive monograph,[2] and finally the title of a whole book series.[3] Besides three comprehensive historical and anthropological publications (which I will refer to here), the people's history of Poland comprises today an ever-growing constellation of literary, documentary, autobiographical, theatrical, musical, and artistic works.[4]

The people's history of Poland transfers the scrutiny of Polishness as an experience from the nobility and intelligentsia toward the "Polishness" of peasants, laborers, or craftsmen—Polishness being in quotes here because it does not usually constitute a valuable component of people's popular identity. Historian Adam Leszczyński and two anthropologists, Michał Rauszer and Kacper Pobłocki,[5] namely the three authors of the most important books on the matter recently published in Poland, all draw attention to the desire of bringing out the voice of those who have thus far been suppressed, ignored, or discredited despite the fact that they make up almost 90 percent of society. As seen by the three authors, the history of Poland and Polishness has so far been written predominantly from the perspective of a narrow aristocratic-intellectual group, whose tool of action was violence—be it physical or symbolic. Even though there is no lack of earlier, important studies that discuss "Polishness in the village," to borrow a phrase from the landmark book by Keely Stauter-Halsted,[6] they have not caused major shifts in conceptualizing history. Changing this situation and "[doing] justice to those who were ruled"[7]—this is the position of the three authors, whose aim is to alter the parameters of the debate on history and identity *within* and *outside* academic circles. At the same time, all three use emotionally charged language and stand on the side of an engaged history,[8] critical in the sense that it firmly rejects the existing models of Polishness but

---

1   See the special issue of *Czas Kultury*, entitled "Odzyskać pracę."
2   Leszczyński, *Ludowa historia Polski*.
3   See the series Ludowa historia Polski, edited by Przemysław Wielgosz. So far three books have been published in the series, including, as its first publication, Michał Rauszer's *Bękarty pańszczyzny*.
4   See the special issue of *Teksty Drugie*, entitled "Chłopskość."
5   Leszczyński, *Ludowa historia Polski*; Rauszer, *Siła podporządkowanych*; Pobłocki, *Chamstwo*.
6   Stauter-Halsted, *The Nation in the Village*. See also her contribution in this volume.
7   Leszczyński, *Ludowa historia Polski*, 16.
8   "This book was intentionally conceived as one-sided. The aim of this strategy is to create a new history by taking the side of the weak": Pobłocki, *Chamstwo*, 317; "A people's history of Poland must put the interests and needs of the subjugated

is far from the critical history postulated by Krzysztof Pomian, according to whom the most important stance of a historian would be "outside of any identity attitudes."[9]

Exploitation, violence, and resistance—these three categories appear, with varying degrees of intensity, as the most important accounts of Poland's people's history. Of these, violence is key. Physical violence was the basis of the serfdom system, which in its basic form closely resembled slavery.[10] Violence, however, was also one of the most effective ways of resisting enslavement, which—among others—took the form of peasant rebellions and uprisings. Rauszer devoted an entire book to this subject.[11] Thus, one of the most significant features of Polishness, irrespective of its subject, turns out to be the feature of violence taking the form of "obedience enforced by beating" or "revenge for suffered humiliation" (and so suffering and sacrifice) but also sexual violence or violence against strangers (including anti-Semitism). It must be added at once that, viewed historically, violence is not only a Polish affliction. This was best shown by Norbert Elias in his acclaimed work describing the process of civilization as one of denaturalization of human behavior and gradual elimination of aggression and violence.[12] Authors from the circle of Poland's people's history perceive this broader context, although perhaps they underestimate its significance. In our volume however, this context is clearly present.

The ultimate consequences of Polishness's violent features are drawn by Pobłocki, who supplements or even replaces the notion of serfdom with that of patriarchy. "Serfdom killed the human in the peasant, but patriarchy brought him back to life and showed him his place in the social order," he writes, "in order to become a lord, it was enough to crush someone who was inferior to him. Whom he could rule, manage, dispose."[13] Thus, Pobłocki proposes that a people's history should be perceived as women's history. For him, it is not the

---

people first and constitute a complete reinterpretation of national history from their perspective": Leszczyński, *Ludowa historia Polski*, 570.

9 According to Pomian's proposal, works from the people's history of Poland can be recognized as representing 'revisionist history', understood descriptively rather than in terms of value. See Pomian, *Historia urzędowa, historia rewizjonistyczna*, 188–98.

10 '[...] modern slavery was based on one universal practice. On beating.' Pobłocki, *Chamstwo*, 25.

11 Rauszer, *Siła podporządkowanych*. An abridged and more popular version of this work is the book *Bękarty pańszczyzny: Historia buntów chłopskich*.

12 See Elias, *The Civilizing Process*.

13 Pobłocki, *Chamstwo*, 104.

male peasant, the laborer, or the craftsman who is the actual embodiment of the "people," but the maid, countrywoman, and female worker:

> People's history is women's history. Not only because women are its main characters, but it is they who are the ones usually doing the most servile work. People's history is feminine because women are its guardians. The lordly story is made up of a procession of heroic figures who come, look around, and conquer. Peasant history comprises the legend of valiant resistance to the lord's tyranny. People's history, on the other hand, is everything that happened around. It is not the account of skirmishes and class struggles, but that of support, solidarity, and care.[14]

The originality and interpretative capacity of this approach—which allows the unveiling of mechanisms like patriarchal domination of cultural patterns and rules of everyday life in Poland while providing real premises for the establishment of alternative patterns and rules—does not change the fact that, once again, we are dealing with revisionist history, which is a consciously one-sided history instead of a critical history.

Pobłocki's poignant observations lead us to a discussion of the second tendency I mentioned, namely to what may be described as the recovery of the female experience. The restoration of women to their rightful place in our thinking about the past and the present involves the need for a completely new look at the relationship between Polishness and femininity. The list of works on this subject, written both in Poland and by authors working outside of Poland, is impressive. As a *pars pro toto* of sorts I will only mention one work by four authors—Katarzyna Stańczak-Wiślicz, Piotr Perkowski, Małgorzata Fidelis, Barbara Klich-Kluczewska, *Kobiety w Polsce 1945–1989. Nowoczesność. Równouprawnienie. Komunizm* (2020).[15]

The volume addresses the issue of women's empowerment, which during the postwar period took place in two ways: in the public sphere through the acquisition of labor and political rights (i.e., gender equality) and in the domestic sphere through a gradual change in the status of women within the family (i.e., emancipation). Both processes were at the same time significantly limited by the dominant traditional cultural patterns assigning women the role of wives, mothers, and "guardians of the hearth and home" (i.e., the figure of the "Matka-Polka" [Polish mother]). These models—which are somewhat surprising—turned out to be equally as resonant irrespectively of whether they pertained to the politics of the communist authorities, the position of the Catholic Church,

---

14 Pobłocki, *Chamstwo*, 247.
15 Stańczak-Wiślicz et al., *Kobiety w Polsce 1945–1989*.

or attitudes within opposition movements and Solidarity. A consequence of this was the phenomenon that the book calls "conservative modernity,"[16] in which the space for processes of equality and emancipation turned out to be the household. The household was ultimately "the site of modernization and its related processes negotiating roles within the family and more broadly the roles of women and men in society," thanks to which women could be called "agents of modernization."[17] Several essays in our volume contribute to these discussions, showing strategic adaptations of the domestic roles of female migrants (Pasieka), discussions on patriarchy and moral conservatism as a staple of national identity in cinematographic representations (van Heuckelom), and complex trajectories of Polish feminism (Grabowska).

"Conservative modernity" directs us toward another set of phenomena that is fundamental when it comes to discussions and disagreements on Polishness. Has Poland ever achieved its modern form, and if so, what is it? These questions are constantly recurring within these discussions. The formulated answers have essentially four possible forms, which can be best summarized as follows: (1) we have never been truly modern, Poland never crossed the threshold of modernity (although it is constantly approaching it), which is something desirable; (2) we had and have our own modernity, which however only partially resembles Western modernity, hence it needs clarification, most often revealing the contradictions inherent in it ("conservative modernity," "peripheral modernity," "unmodern modernity"); (3) we have not been and cannot be modern and, moreover, never had an initiation into modernity because Polishness and modernity, in the forms that we know, are both so distant from each other that only a radical reconstruction of one or both of them could enable some kind of synthesis; (4) Polishness does not need modernity, at least not in an obvious and necessary way because the value of modernity lies in its scientific and technological layers, not in its spiritual or moral ones.

Historian Tomasz Kizwalter has recently reconstructed the genealogy of Polish modernity, starting from the understatement that sees it as "a combination of the ideological influence of the Enlightenment and the economic impact of capitalism."[18] The author of *Polska nowoczesność* [Polish modernity] draws attention to a very important issue, namely, the fact that

> diverse, older and newer criticisms of the 'Enlightenment project' do not sufficiently take into account the fact that from the point of view of our life practice, modernity

---

16 Fidelis, *Równouprawnienie czy konserwatywna nowoczesność?*, 161–64.
17 Perkowski and Stańczak-Wiślicz, *Nowoczesna gospodyni*, 166, 190.
18 Kizwalter, *Polska nowoczesność*, 10.

primarily means building an environment that provides us with living conditions that our ancestors could not even dream of.[19]

This means that Polishness, seen from the point of view of life practice, is usually far more modern than we think and often cannot (or does not want to be) appreciated. At the same time, these modern practices are accompanied by traditional social ideas and attitudes passed down from generation to generation, in which Polishness is inscribed in a stereotypically understood romantic paradigm, possessing an evidently anticivilizational and often martyrological character.[20] That is why an outside perspective can be so important as, for example, the one that Brian Porter-Szűcs proposes in his book *Poland in the Modern World: Beyond Martyrdom* [21] (see also Porter-Szűcs in this volume).

Brian Porter-Szűcs pays special attention not only to what is exceptional but to what is ordinary, everyday, and related to the average Pole's experience. He does not agree with the version of history in which "the only genuine Pole ... is either a hero or a victim (or both)."[22] Referring to statistics showing Polish standards of living he underscores that it is lower than in many developed countries of Western Europe and North America but higher than in South American, Asian, or African countries. This allows him to conclude that Poles "are among the weakest of the mighty and the mightiest of the weak, among the poorest of the rich and the richest of the poor."[23] Moreover, Porter-Szűcs draws attention to something of fundamental importance:

> One might say that identity is something we *do*, not something we *are*. And it isn't something we do all the time, or even most of the time. This would become particularly evident as economic changes at the end of the 19th century introduced yet more competing forms of identity, and unsettled the ones that already existed.[24]

---

19   Kizwalter, *Polska nowoczesność*, 14.

20   Kizwalter: "Poland's peculiarity lies in the specific significance of the content opposed to modernity," 235. Andrzej Mencwel undertook a discussion with Kizwalter by drawing attention to the significance of the Enlightenment and positivist components of Polish modernity, and in particular to the role of associationism, "the question of self-governing social organization.'" See "Oświecanie nowoczesności," 98.

21   Porter-Szűcs, *Poland in the Modern World* (citations from the English edition). Polish edition: Porter-Szűcs, *Całkiem zwyczajny kraj*.

22   Porter-Szűcs, *Poland in the Modern World*, 4.

23   Porter-Szűcs, *Poland in the Modern World Beyond*, 3.

24   Porter-Szűcs, *Poland in the Modern World*, 29–30.

As we show in this volume, precisely this way of looking at Polishness—one that is not from the perspective of fixed patterns of behavior but from dynamic and diverse practices—allows one to see what Polish is in all its complexity. It creates a network of tensions between the exceptional and the commonplace, the sublime and the mundane, the military and the civilian, the heroic and the shameful: all connected with the struggle and daily toil of work, sacrifice for others or for the common good, and with aggression against others that makes the common good an alibi. This outlook turns out to be very important to understanding the complexity of nineteenth-century (not to mention twentieth-century) Polishness, especially during World War II and the years immediately preceding and following it.

It is no coincidence, then, that in contemporary discussions on Polishness a special place is held for World War II, perceived more broadly than just the 1939–1945 period but also encompassing the preceding 1930s and the second half of the 1940s. War—as a "never-ending history"[25]—increasingly becomes the central experience of the Polish twentieth century as well as an important element in the process of deconstructing and reconstructing Polish identity. Three processes can be noticed here. In one we see the process of consolidation of the "heroic" model of Polishness—very strongly supported by state historical politics—which referred to romantic and insurrectionary traditions, ranging from the Kościuszko Uprising to the Warsaw Uprising, and the activity of the anticommunist underground in the immediate postwar period, the so-called żołnierze wyklęci (cursed soldiers). The second constitutes the process of restoring the memory of everyday experiences during and just after occupation, including women's and children's experiences, as well as the experiences of "insignificant people," "powerless people," and "people destroyed by the war machine" (the sick, lonely, living in poverty, the victims of sexual violence, the disabled or concentration camp prisoners).[26] The third instance is the difficult process of uncovering and initiating a discussion on a broad spectrum of behaviors of Poles during the war, especially of ethnic Poles' attitudes toward (Polish and non-Polish) Jews, where aside from help often requiring exceptional bravery and heroism (and aside from passivity and indifference), we see many examples of blackmailing, denouncing, and murdering Jewish neighbors and fellow citizens, as well as seizing their property both during and after the war.

Given the weight of this debate, it is impossible to do justice to a growing and diverse body of literature on the subject. The breakthrough book *Neighbors*

---

25   See the special issue of *Teksty Drugie*, entitled *Druga wojna światowa*.
26   Dauksza, *Wojna bezsilnych*, 9–20.

by Jan Tomasz Gross and the discussions and polemics around it[27] were followed by numerous works of the Warsaw-based Polish Centre for Holocaust Research[28] as well as historical and philosophical works on the postwar period.[29] All these show how diverse Polish attitudes were and how important it is not to perceive Polishness in an idealized and one-sided way. Violence and cruelty, which Poles experienced during the war, were also their actions. Thus, if heroism can and should be regarded as a component of Polish identity, it should not be heroism treated in an unconditional and uncritical manner. As Poles were neither only heroes or victims but were often also perpetrators of shameful and criminal deeds, the concealment of this fact falsifies the image of Polishness and deprives it of its self-critical potential and ability to work on itself. This ultimately results in the increased presence of a "phantom anti-modern identity,"[30] increasingly detached from reality and its pressing problems. At the same time, however, the reception of and heated debate around the works mentioned above are a good illustration of what Geneviève Zubrzycki calls a "narrative shock,"[31] emphasizing that the new—more complex—narrative about what happened during the war and in its aftermath brings about discussion on Polish national identity. Time will show to what extent the difficult process of reckoning with the knowledge of war can alter dominant conceptualizations of Polishness (on the role of Jewishness in this process see also Grudzińska-Gross and Zubrzycki in this volume).

The last issue I want to draw attention to concerns sources on which contemporary research on Polishness is based. A clear shift can be observed from various official sources— documents, press, and literary sources—toward ones of an autobiographical nature, like personal diaries, letters, memoirs, autobiographies, various kinds of everyday records, and oral history. Almost all of the works I have cited are evidence of this. So are numerous chapters in our volume (Ciancia, Galbraith, Grabowska, Grudzińska-Gross, Pasieka, Stauter-Halsted, Zubrzycki). I think we can even speak of a change from a literary-centric to an

---

27 Gross, *Sąsiedzi. Historia zagłady żydowskiego miasteczka*; Gross, *Wokół "Sąsiadów"*; *Jedwabne. Spór historyków wokół książki Jana T. Grossa "Sąsiedzi."* See also Machcewicz, *Spory o historię 2000–2011*.
28 Among the many important works of this research center, the following volume requires particular mention as one of the most extensive and significant publications: Engelking and Grabowski, *Dalej jest noc*, 8. See also Kichelewski et al., *Les Polonais et la Shoah*.
29 Zaremba, *Wielka Trwoga. Polska 1944–1947*; Leder, *Prześniona rewolucja*.
30 See Bielik-Robson, *Polska: wspólnota fantazmatyczna*, 89.
31 Zubrzycki, "Narrative Shock and (Re)Making Polish Memory," 95–115.

autobiographical-centric paradigm of perceiving Polishness. The consequences of this change are very significant. Until recently, Polishness was primarily constructed as a space of ideas and values, and if experiences appeared within this space, it was mainly those devoted to ideas. Everyday life and the individuality of singular human fates were of much less importance and this fact was symbolically highlighted by the periodization of Polish history that emphasized "historical events"—partitions, uprisings, wars, revolutions. Along this anthropological turn, we see varied attempts to experiment with different sources that shed light on experiences and understandings of Polishness, as illustrated in this volume by exploration of musical compositions (Jakelski), exhibitions (Koziołek, Litwinowicz), and films (Czapliński, van Heuckelom).

The consequences of the five tendencies described above are numerous and significant. First, Polishness is now perceived not from the point of view of exceptional attitudes—most often frozen in myth or stereotype and thus avoiding critical judgment—but from the perspective of everyday varied practices and behaviors, rooted in experiences. Second, it is a personalized and polyvocal or even multientity Polishness, in which the voice of those who have so far been deprived of their voice (or were barely heard in the past) is becoming more and more clearly present: that is, the voice of peasants, workers, women, children, national minorities, and sexual minorities.[32] Third, this is not a monolithic Polishness but rather a dynamic sphere of relations, tensions and conflicts, encounters and experiences, which constitute a combination of lofty and down-to-earth, heroic and despicable, worthy of emulation and worthy of condemnation. Polishness, which is not an idea but a practice, is shaped over and over again in every single biographical experience.

Thus, the process of deconstructing and reconstructing Polishness is an ongoing one,[33] mutually coupled with the everyday practices of Poles and the critical diagnoses of researchers and publicists. We very much hope that our volume will likewise contribute to this process.

---

32 I have written about this at greater length in my essay "*Poland's Autobiographical Twentieth Century*," 627–41.

33 As we are finalizing this volume, the presence of few million Ukrainian refugees in Poland—victims of Russian aggression on Ukraine—provokes new questions on the Polish identity: especially on whether it is possible to stretch the boundaries of national community (cf. Zubrzycki, this volume) and on the hierarchies that mark Polish-Ukrainian relations (cf. Ciancia, this volume). Time will show what impact the new geopolitical context will have on identity processes in and beyond Poland.

Bibliography

Bielik-Robson, Agata. "Polska: wspólnota fantazmatyczna." In *Kim są Polacy*. Kraków: Uniwersytet Ekonomiczny w Krakowie, 82–95. Warsaw: Agora, 2013.

Dauksza, Agnieszka. "Wojna bezsilnych. Niekończąca się historia," *Teksty Drugie*, no. 3 (2020): 9–20.

"Druga wojna światowa: niekończąca się historia." Special issue of *Teksty Drugie*, no. 3 (2020).

"Chłopskość." Special issue of *Teksty Drugie*, no. 6 (2017).

Elias, Norbert, *The Civilizing Process. Sociogenetic and Psychogenetic Investigations*. Oxford: Blackwell, 2000.

Engelking, Barbara, Grabowski, Jan, eds, *Dalej jest noc. Losy Żydów w wybranych powiatach okupowanej Polski*. Warsaw: Stowarzyszenie Centrum Badań nad Zagładą Żydów, 2018.

Fidelis, Małgorzata, "Równouprawnienie czy konserwatywna nowoczesność? Kobiety pracujące." In *Kobiety w Polsce 1945–1989: Nowoczesność. Równouprawnienie. Komunizm*, edited by Katarzyna Stańczak-Wiślicz, Piotr Perkowski, Małgorzata Fidelis, Barbara Klich-Kluczewska, 103–64. Kraków: Wydawnictwo Universitas, 2020.

Gross, Jan Tomasz. *Sąsiedzi. Historia zagłady żydowskiego miasteczka*. Sejny: Fundacja Pogranicze, 2000.

Gross, Jan Tomasz. *Wokół „Sąsiadów". Polemiki i wyjaśnienia*. Sejny: Fundacja Pogranicze, 2003.

Jedwabne. Spór historyków wokół książki Jana T. Grossa „Sąsiedzi". Warsaw: Fronda, 2002.

Kichelewski, Audrey, Lyon-Caen, Judith, Szurek, Jean-Charles, Wieviorka, Annette, eds. *Les Polonais et la Shoah. Une nouvelle école historique*, Paris: CNRS Èditions, 2019.

Kizwalter, Tomasz. "Nienowoczesna nowoczesność?" *Przegląd Polityczny*, no. 165 (2021): 98–100.

Kizwalter, Tomasz. *Polska nowoczesność. Genealogia*. Warsaw: Wydawnictwa Uniwersytetu Warszawskiego, 2020.

Leder, Andrzej. *Prześniona rewolucja. Ćwiczenie z logiki historycznej*. Warsaw: Wydawnictwo Krytyki Politycznej, 2013.

Leszczyński, Adam. *Ludowa historia Polski. Historia wyzysku i oporu. Mitologia panowania*. Warsaw: Wydawnictwo WAB, 2020.

'Odzyskać pracę. Ludowa historia Polski'. Special issue of *Czas Kultury*, no. 3 (2016).

Machcewicz, Paweł. *Spory o historię 2000-2011*. Kraków: Wydawnictwo Znak, 2012.

Mencwel, Andrzej. "Oświecanie nowoczesności." *Przegląd Polityczny*, no. 165 (2021): 90–98.

Perkowski, Piotr, Stańczak-Wiślicz, Katarzyna, "Nowoczesna gospodyni. Kobiety w gospodarstwie domowym." In *Kobiety w Polsce 1945–1989: Nowoczesność. Równouprawnienie. Komunizm*, edited by Katarzyna Stańczak-Wiślicz, Piotr Perkowski, Małgorzata Fidelis, and Barbara Klich-Kluczewska, 165–216. Kraków: Wydawnictwo Universitas, 2020.

Pobłocki, Kacper. *Chamstwo*. Wołowiec: Wydawnictwo Czarne, 2021.
Pomian, Krzysztof. *Historia urzędowa, historia rewizjonistyczna, historia krytyczna*. In *Historia: Nauka wobec pamięci*, 188–98. Lublin: Wydawnictwo UMCS, 2006.
Porter-Szűcs, Brian. *Całkiem zwyczajny kraj: Historia Polski bez martyrologii*. Translated by Anna Dzierzgowska and Jan Dzierzgowski. Warsaw: Wydawnictwo Filtry, 2021.
Porter-Szűcs, Brian. *Poland in the Modern World: Beyond Martyrdom*. Hoboken: Wiley-Blackwell, 2014.
Rodak, Paweł. "Poland's Autobiographical Twentieth Century." In *Being Poland. A New History of Polish Literature and Culture since 1918*, edited by Tamara Trojanowska, Joanna Niżyńska, Przemysław Czapliński, and Agnieszka Polakowska, 627–41. Toronto: University of Toronto Press, 2018.
Rauszer, Michał. *Bękarty pańszczyzny: Historia buntów chłopskich*. Warsaw: Wydawnictwo RM, 2020.
Rauszer, Michał. *Siła podporządkowanych*. Warsaw: Wydawnictwa Uniwersytetu Warszawskiego, 2021.
Stańczak-Wiślicz, Katarzyna, Piotr Perkowski, Małgorzata Fidelis, Barbara Klich-Kluczewska. *Kobiety w Polsce 1945–1989. Nowoczesność, Równouprawnienie, Komunizm*. Kraków: Wydawnictwo Universitas, 2020.
Stauter-Halsted, Keely. *The Nation in the Village: The Genesis of Peasant National Identity in Austrian Poland, 1848–1914*. Ithaca, NY: Cornell University Press, 2001.
Zaremba, Marcin. *Wielka Trwoga. Polska 1944–1947. Ludowa reakcja na kryzys*. Kraków: Wydawnictwo Znak, ISP PAN, 2012.
Zubrzycki, Geneviève. "Narrative Shock and (Re)Making Polish Memory in the Twenty-first Century." In *Memory and Postwar Memorials: Confronting the Violence of the Past*, edited by Florence Vatan and Marc Silberman, 95–115. New York: Palgrave, 2013.

Contributors

Paweł Bukowiec is a literary scholar and professor at the Faculty of Polish Studies, Jagiellonian University in Kraków. He is author of the following monographs: *Dwujęzyczne początki nowoczesnej literatury litewskiej* [Bilingual beginnings of modern Lithuanian literature] (2008); *Metronom. O jednostkowości poezji "nazbyt" rytmicznej* [Metronome. On the singularity of "too" rhythmical poetry] (2015), *Różnice w druku. Studium z dziejów wielojęzycznej kultury literackiej na XIX-wiecznej Litwie* [Differences in print: Study of the history of multilingual literary culture in nineteenth-century Lithuania] (2017). Recent publications include: "Constraints of Canon Constructing: Research into the Paradoxes of Reception of Józef Baka's Poetry," in *Literary Canon Formation as Nation-Building in Central Europe and the Baltics* (2021), "Literature as a Performative Act, Nation as Literature: Nineteenth-Century Lithuanian Literature from a Slavonic Perspective," in *Das historische Litauen als Perspektive für die Slavistik* (2022).

Kathryn Ciancia is associate professor of history at the University of Wisconsin–Madison. Her first book, *On Civilization's Edge: A Polish Borderland in the Interwar World* (2020), situates interwar Polish attempts to "civilize" the multiethnic province of Volhynia within the entangled global frameworks of imperialism and postimperial state building. She has also published articles in *Slavic Review* and the *Journal of Modern History*, as well as a book chapter in *Enemies Within: The Global Politics of Fifth Columns* (2022). Her new book project explores how practices of law, territoriality, and citizenship intersected in the everyday work of the Polish consular network between 1918 and the early Cold War.

Przemysław Czapliński is professor at the Faculty of Polish and Classical Philology, Adam Mickiewicz University in Poznań, and director of the Open Humanities Center there. His fields of interest are history of modern and postmodern European and Polish literature; late modernity in Central and Eastern Europe; and the Holocaust in Polish literature. His recent publications are *Polska do wymiany: Późna nowoczesność i nasze wielkie narracje* [Poland to exchange. Late modernity and our grand narratives] (WAB, 2009); *The Remnants of Modernity: Two Essays on Sarmatism and Utopia in Polish Contemporary Literature* (2015); *Poruszona mapa. Wyobraźnia geograficzno-kulturowa polskiej literatury przełomu XX i XXI wieku* [The shifted map: Geo-cultural imagery of Polish literature at the turn of 20th and 21st century] (2016); *Being Poland: A New History of Polish Literature and Culture since 1918* (2018).

Marysia Galbraith is professor at New College and the Department of Anthropology at the University of Alabama. She earned her PhD in anthropology from the University of California, San Diego. Her research engages with issues of national identity, European integration, and Jewish heritage in Poland. She received the 2017 Bronislaw Malinowski Social Science Award for her book *Being and Becoming European in Poland: European Integration and Self-Identity* (2015).

Magdalena Grabowska, a sociologist, is professor at the Institute of Philosophy and Sociology of the Polish Academy of Sciences. She holds a doctoral degree from the Women and Gender Studies Department of Rutgers University and was a European Commission Marie Curie International Re-Integration Fellow at the University of Warsaw. She is the author of the book *Zerwana genealogia. Działalność społeczna i polityczna kobiet po 1945 roku a współczesny polski ruch kobiecy* [Broken genealogy: Social and political women's activism after 1945 and contemporary women's movement in Poland] (2018). Her academic interests span the history of emancipation movements in Central and Eastern Europe, postcoloniality and postsocialism, and the transnational feminist movement. She also conducts activist research on violence and sexual violence, reproductive rights, women's equality, and feminist and queer social mobilizations. She is a cofounder of the Foundation on Equality and Emancipation STER.

Irena Grudzińska-Gross is professor in the Institute of Slavic Studies of the Polish Academy of Sciences. She was involved in student movements and emigrated from her native Poland after the unrest of 1968. She resumed her studies in Italy and received her PhD from Columbia University in 1982. She taught courses in Eastern European literature and history at several universities and was a 2018 Fellow at the Guggenheim Foundation. Her books include: *Miłosz i długi cień wojny* [Miłosz and the Long Shadow of War] (Pogranicze Fondation, 2020), *Golden Harvest. Events at the Periphery of the Holocaust* [with Jan T. Gross] (2012); *Czesław Miłosz and Joseph Brodsky: Fellowship of Poets* (2009); *The Scar of Revolution: Tocqueville, Custine and the Romantic Imagination* (1991).

Lisa Jakelski is associate professor of musicology at the Eastman School of Music at the University of Rochester. Broadly stated, her research investigates the social, cultural, economic, and political dimensions of music making after 1945. Her areas of specialization include music in Poland, new music institutions, and Cold War cultural politics. She is the author of *Making New Music in Cold War Poland: The Warsaw Autumn Festival, 1956–1968* (2017), and coeditor (with Nicholas Reyland) of *Lutosławski's Worlds* (2018).

Ryszard Koziołek, a literary scholar and essayist, is professor at the Institute of Literature of the University of Silesia, Rector of the University of Silesia. His area of specialization is the Polish novel of the nineteenth and twentieth century. In 2010 he received the Gdynia Literary Award for the book *Ciała Sienkiewicza. Studia o płci i przemocy* (Sienkiewicz's bodies: studies on gender and violence) (2009). In 2017 he received the Kazimierz Wyka Award for outstanding achievements in the field of essay writing and literary criticism. His recent major publications: *Dobrze się myśli literaturą* (Thinking well with literature) (2016); *Wiele tytułów* (Multiple titles) (2019).

Krystyna Lipińska Illakowicz holds a PhD in comparative literature from New York University. She teaches Polish language, theater, and film at Yale University. She has published book chapters and articles both in English and Polish about Witold Gombrowicz, Bruno Schulz, Tadeusz Kantor, Andrzej Bobkowski, and others. Her work focuses on cultural exchanges between East and West, processes of modernization, issues of small cultures, provinciality, and the ethos of women in the Polish cultural discourse. She often writes on contemporary Polish theatre and coedits the theater journal *European Stages*. Currently she is working on a book tentatively titled *The Image of America in Poland in the 1920s and 1930s*.

Małgorzata Litwinowicz is associate professor at the Institute of Polish Culture, University of Warsaw. Her academic interests include Polish modernization dilemmas (especially relating to everyday experience) and questions of participation, aspiration, and imitation. She is author of books devoted to the experience of peripheries in Poland, including *Zmiana, której nie było. Trzy próby czytania Reymonta* [The change that wasn't there. Three attempts to read Reymont] (2019). She has also published work on the processes of national identity building in Lithuania: *O starożytnościach litewskich. Mitologizacja historii w XIX-wiecznym piśmiennictwie byłego Wielkiego Księstwa Litewskiego* [On Lithuanian Antiquities. Mythologization of History in the 19th Century Literature of the Former Grand Duchy of Lithuania] (2009). Litwinowicz is also coeditor of works devoted to such exhibitions as cultural phenomenon and inventions in the nineteenth century. She is currently working on a book about "incorporating" the Baltic Sea in the Polish collective imagination in the interwar period.

Agnieszka Pasieka is a sociocultural anthropologist. Her research explores the role of nationalism and religion in political mobilization and social activism. A recipient of numerous fellowships and research grants, she is currently Elise Richter Research Fellow at the Department of Social and Cultural Anthropology, University of Vienna. She is the author of *Hierarchy and Pluralism: Living Religious Difference in Catholic Poland* (2015) and numerous journal publications and book chapters on religious pluralism, national and ethnic minorities, multiculturalism, postsocialism, and, most recently, far-right politics and far-right movements. She is currently completing a book project on transnational activism of radical nationalist movements in Europe.

Brian Porter-Szűcs is an Arthur F. Thurnau Professor of History at the University of Michigan-Ann Arbor. His most recent book is *Całkiem zwyczajny kraj: Historia Polski bez martyrologii* (2021), which is a revised and translated version of *Poland and the Modern World: Beyond Martyrdom* (2014). His earlier works include *Faith and*

Fatherland: Catholicism, Modernity, and Poland (2010), and *When Nationalism Began to Hate: Imagining Modern Politics in 19th Century Poland* (2000). Brian Porter-Szűcs has been a professor at the University of Michigan since 1994, teaching classes on economic history, the intellectual history of capitalism and socialism, the history of Roman Catholicism, and the history of Poland.

Paweł Rodak is a historian of Polish culture and professor at the Institute of Polish Culture, University of Warsaw. Previously he was associate professor and director of the Center of Polish Civilisation at the Sorbonne University (2016–19) and head of the Institute of Polish Culture, University of Warsaw (2012–16). He is a member of the International Auto/Biography Association (IABA Europe). His main publications are *Wizje kultury pokolenia wojennego* [Visions of culture in the war generation] (2000); *Pismo, książka, lektura. Rozmowy* [Writing, book, lecture: Conversations with Jacques Le Goff, Roger Chartier, Jean Hébrard, Daniel Fabre, Philippe Lejeune] (2009); *Między zapisem a literaturą. Dziennik polskiego pisarza w XX wieku (Żeromski, Nałkowska, Dąbrowska, Gombrowicz, Herling-Grudziński)* [Between the written practice of everyday life and literature: Polish writer's diary in the 20th century] (2011).

Keely Stauter-Halsted is professor of history and Hejna Family Chair in the history of Poland at the University of Illinois at Chicago, where she serves as director of graduate studies and codirects programming in Polish studies. Her teaching and research examine issues of ethnicity, gender, and class in eastern-central Europe. Stauter-Halsted has published on topics ranging from peasant nationalism to Polish-Jewish relations, prostitution, and human trafficking. Her monograph *The Nation in the Village: The Genesis of Peasant National Identity in Austrian Poland* (2001) won the Orbis Prize in Polish History. Her book *The Devil's Chain: Prostitution and Social Control in Partitioned Poland* (2015) received the American Historical Association Joan Kelly Prize and the Association for Women in Slavic History Heldt Prize. Her recent work investigates refugees, border changes, and population movement in the Polish Second Republic immediately following World War I.

Kris Van Heuckelom is professor of Polish studies and cultural studies and vice dean of international policy at the Faculty of Arts of KU Leuven, Belgium. He specializes in late modern Polish culture, with a particular focus on comparative and transnational perspectives. His most recent books are *Polish Migrants in European Film 1918–2017* (2019) and *Nostalgia, solidarność, (im)potencja. Obrazy polskiej migracji w kinie europejskim (od niepodległości do współczesności)* [Nostalgia, solidarity, (im)potence. Images of Polish migration in European cinema (from independence to the present)] (2022). Over the past few years, he has contributed chapters to volumes such as *Being Poland: A New History of Polish Literature and Culture since 1918* (2018) and *The Routledge World Companion to Polish Literature* (2021).

Geneviève Zubrzycki is professor of sociology and faculty associate at the University of Michigan, where she directs the Weiser Center for Europe and Eurasia and the Copernicus Center for Polish Studies. She has published widely on national identity and religion, collective memory and national mythology, and the contested place of religious symbols in the public sphere. Zubrzycki is the award-winning author of *The Crosses of Auschwitz: Nationalism and Religion in Post-Communist Poland* (2006), *Beheading the Saint: Nationalism, Religion and Secularism in Quebec* (2016), and *Resurrecting the Jew: Nationalism, Philosemitism and Poland's Jewish Revival* (2022). In 2021 she was the recipient of a Guggenheim fellowship and was awarded the Bronisław Malinowski Prize in the Social Sciences from the Polish Institute of Arts and Sciences of America.

Index of Names

Adorno, Theodor, 259, 275, 331
Akielewicz, Mikołaj (Mikalojus Akelaitis), 38
Althusser, Louis, 337–38
Anderson, Benedict, 242, 272
Ansermet, Ernest, 342
Astaire, Fred, 138, 143
Augustyniak, Urszula, 8, 14, 278–79, 297–99
Austin, John Langshaw, 337

Bacciarelli, Marcello, 239
Bachleda-Curuś, Alicja, 306, 313, 315–18, 322
Badeni, Stanisław, 247
Baird, Tadeusz, 293
Bajoras, Feliksas, 287, 297
Baka, Mirosław, 311–13
Baka, Józef, 359
Balakauskas, Osvaldas, 287, 297
Baranowski Antoni (Baranauskas Antanas), 5, 39–49
Barrymore, Lionel, 143
Bartoszewicz, Joachim, 56
Bartulis, Vidmantas, 298
Basanavičius, Jonas, 39, 49
Baudrillard, Jean, 266, 273, 275
Bauman, Zygmunt, 214, 230, 345
Beck, Ulrich, 224, 230
Beecher, Harriet, 137
Ben Mahmou, Mahmoud, 308
Benjamin, Walter, 253
Beyer, Karol, 242
Biliński, Jan, 64–65, 68
Bjork, Jim, 8, 14, 107

Błoński, Jan, 261, 275, 334–35
Bona Sforza, queen of Poland, 243
Borowik, Irena, 28, 34, 109
Boruczkowski, Michał, 343
Boulez, Pierre, 293
Bourdieu, Pierre, 107–8, 214, 230
Branicki, Ksawery, 87
Braun, Joachim, 285, 294, 299–301
Broniewska, Janina, 168
Brown, Kate, 30, 34
Brubaker, Rogers, 1, 7, 15, 96, 108
Brzechwa, Jan, 76, 79, 90
Brzechwa, Krystyna, 76, 90
Brzozowski, Tadeusz, 332
Buchholz, Horst, 308
Buchowski, Krzysztof, 280, 292–93, 297, 299
Buchowski, Michał, 7, 15, 180, 186, 224–25, 231
Bukowczyk, John, 194–95, 197, 207
Bukowiec, Paweł, v, 5, 11, 37, 44, 49, 359
Buzek, Agata, 306, 313, 315, 319–22

Caro, Leopold, 113, 121, 130
Casimir the Great, king of Poland, 239, 248
Chaplin, Charlie, 142–43, 313
Chłopecki, Andrzej, 291–92, 299
Chmielarski, Jan, 81
Chopin, Frederic, 74, 83–85, 89–91
Chopin, Mikołaj, 84
Chopin, Tekla Justyna, born Krzyżanowska, 83–85
Christofis, Christoforis, 308–9
Chrysler, Walter, 150

INDEX OF NAMES

Chrzanowski, Tadeusz, 333–34, 345
Ciancia, Kathryn, v, 9, 11, 14, 50, 67–68, 279, 355–56, 359
Cicero, Marcus Tullius, 37, 46, 49
Čiurlionis, Mikalojus Konstantinas (Konstanty Mikołaj Czurlonis), 38, 285, 287
Clifford, James 241–42, 254
Cocteau, Jean, 342
Cooper, James Fenimore, 137
Crawford, Joan, 142
Czapliński, Przemysław, vi, 5–6, 12, 14, 256, 275, 356, 358–59
Czapski, Józef, 76
Czarnek, Przemysław, 90
Czupryn, Anita, 343

Dambrauskas, Aleksandras (Aleksander Dąbrowski), 38
Dawes, Charles G., 150
Deak, Istvan, 51, 69
Del Rio, Dolores, 142
Denisov, Edison, 293
Derrida, Jacques, 341, 344–45
Diagiliev, Siergiej, 342
Dmowski, Roman, 56, 58, 62, 66, 69, 120, 131
Dowkontt, Szymon (Simonas Daukantas), 38
Dowojna Sylwestrowicz, Meczysław (Mečislovas Davainis-Silvestraitis), 38
Droba, Krzysztof, 277, 286–89, 291–92, 294, 297–301
Drozdowski, Antoni (Antanas Strazdas), 38
Duda-Dziewierz, Krystyna, 114–15, 120, 128, 131
Dumas, Alexandre (father), 257
Dunn, Elizabeth, 223, 224, 231
Dziwisz, Stanisław, cardinal, 95

Earhart, Amelia, 137, 144
Edison, Thomas, 152
Ekiert, Janusz, 293, 295, 300
Elias, Norbert, 350, 357

Fairbanks, Douglas, 143
Fenger, Jakub, 86
Fidelis, Małgorzata, 162, 164, 167, 174, 186, 351–52, 357–58
Figura, Katarzyna, 316
Foucault, Michel, 186, 338
Fra Bartolomeo, 239
Frick, David, 279, 300
Friedan, Betty, 178
Fukuyama, Francis, 265–67, 273

Galbraith, Marysia, vi, 8, 11–12, 208, 211–12, 223–24, 231, 355, 360
Gavras, Costa, 315
Geda, Sigitas, 278
Geertz, Clifford, 328
Ghodsee, Kristen, 166, 179, 187
Giedroyc, Jerzy, 41, 49, 76–77, 90, 157
Gienow-Hecht, Jessica, 281–82, 299–302
Gierek, Edward, 324
Giertych, Roman, 89–90
Gieysztor, Aleksander, 325–26
Gish, Lillian, 143
Glass, Philip, 277
Gliński, Robert, 319
Godard, Jean-Luc, 308–9
Goetel, Ferdynand, 81
Gombrowicz, Witold, 89–90, 137–38, 143, 149, 152, 156, 157, 159, 362
Górecki, Henryk Mikołaj, 282, 293, 301
Gościmińska, Wanda, 176
Grabowska, Magdalena, v, 9, 12, 14, 161, 164, 175, 178–79, 187, 352, 355, 360
Grabowski, Mikołaj, 263, 276

INDEX OF NAMES   367

Graff, Agnieszka, 95, 108, 163, 164, 178, 181, 183–84, 187
Gregory XVI, pope, 23, 34
Gribauskaitė, Dalia, 41
Gross, Jan Tomasz, 78, 90, 104–5, 108, 355, 357, 360
Grudzińska-Gross, Irena, v, 9, 14, 74, 104, 108, 355, 360
Gumowska, Irena, 169, 171, 187

Halawa, Mateusz, 336–37
Halecki, Oskar, 56
Hannerz, Ulf, 211, 214, 218, 229, 231
Herbert, Zbigniew, 337
Herder, Johann, 44, 238
Herling-Grudziński, Gustaw, 76–77, 91, 362
Hoerder, Dirk, 116–17, 131
Hoffman, Jerzy, 259, 265, 309–10
Holland, Agnieszka, 305
Hoover, Herbert, 152
Horolets, Anna, 211, 217, 231
Hurley, Patrick, 153

Irons, Jeremy, 311
Iwanowski, Eustachy, 20, 34, 21
Iwaszkiewicz, Jarosław, 251, 254, 335
Iwiński, Wawrzyniec (Laurynas Ivinskis), 38, 47–48

Jackson, Michael, 14
Jakelski, Lisa, vi, 8–9, 277, 282–84, 293, 301, 356, 360
Janion, Maria, 75, 90, 188
Januszewska, Salomea, primo voto Słowacka, secundo voto Bécu, 82
Jaszczukowa, Maria, 176
Jemielity, Witold, 39–40, 49
Jogaila, Lithuanian grand duke, 278
John III Sobieski, king of Poland, 243

John Paul II, pope, 28–29, 35, 77, 90, 97, 99–100, 324
Judson, Pieter, 51, 67, 69

Kaczyński, Jarosław, 185
Kaczyński, Tadeusz, 284, 290–91, 294, 301
Kalb, Don, 224–25, 231–32
Kalinowska, Izabela, 304, 312–13, 323
Kalita, Tomasz, 89
Kassovitz, Peter, 309–10
Keaton, Buster, 143
Kiepura, Jan, 307
Kieślowski, Krzysztof, 305, 311–13, 315, 323
Kilar, Wojciech, 293
Kitowicz, Jędrzej, 263
Kizwalter, Tomasz, 352–53, 357
Klein, Julius, 149
Klich-Kluczewska, Barbara, 181, 188, 351, 357–58
Klier, Michael, 312
Klijnstra, Redbad, 314
Koczanowicz, Leszek, 211, 231
Kołomińska, Antonina, 83
Konopnicka, Maria, 89
Konwicki, Tadeusz, 76, 90, 315, 335
Kormanowa, Żanna, 166
Kościuszko, Tadeusz, 135, 158, 239, 243, 255, 271–72, 354
Kosiakiewicz, Wincenty, 248, 252
Kosiński, Józef Adam, 79–81, 90
Kossowski, Jerzy, 25, 35
Kostrzewa, Natalia, 314
Kotoński, Włodzimierz, 293
Kowalska, Izolda, 164, 173
Kozicki, Stanisław, 62, 63, 70
Koziołek, Ryszard, vi, 10–11, 324, 356, 360
Krasiński, Wincenty, 243
Krasiński, Zygmunt, 87

Krukowski, Franciszek, 239
Krzyżanowski, Jakub, 83–85
Kubiak, Zygmunt, 88
Kuczyński, Stefan, 83
Kula, Witold, 122, 131
Kuncewiczowa, Maria, 335
Kuroń, Jacek, 77–78
Kutavičius, Bronius, 277–78, 282, 284–89, 290–97, 300–301
Kutz, Kazimierz, 340
Kwaśniewski, Aleksander, 97
Kwiatkowska-Lass, Barbara, 308
Kwiatkowski, Eugeniusz, 150

Lacan, Jacques, 327, 329–330
Laclau, Ernesto, 260, 276
Lampart, Zbigniew, 293–94, 301
Lampedusa, Giuseppe Tomasi di, 340–41
Landsbergis, Vytautas, 285, 287–88, 297
Lange, Antoni, 84, 86, 90
Lechoń, Jan, 79–82, 89–90
Leder, Andrzej, 7, 11, 15, 182, 188, 328–30, 339, 355, 357
Lehrer, Erica, 93, 109
Lem, Stanisław, 89
Leo XII, pope, 21
Leśmian, Bolesław, 76
Leszczyński, Adam, 349–50, 357
Leszkowicz, Paweł, 324–25
Levy, Robert, 213, 232
Likowski, Edward, archbishop, 21
Linda, Bogusław, 316
Lindbergh, Charles, 152
Linger, Daniel, 215, 232
Lipińska Illakowicz, Krystyna, v, 133, 361
Lipski, Jan Józef, 29, 35
Lissa, Zofia, 84–85, 91
Litwinowicz (Litwinowicz-Droździel), Małgorzata, vi, 5, 9, 237, 254, 356, 361

Lloyd George, David, 58, 70
Łossowski, Piotr, 39–40, 49
Lubaszenko, Olaf, 312
Łukasiewicz, Ignacy, 244
Lutosławski, Witold, 293, 301, 360
Luxemburg, Rosa, 166
Lyotard, Jean-François, 265, 273, 276

Mačiulis, Jonas (Jan Maculewicz), 38
Maćkowiak, Rafał, 319
Majewska, Barbara (Barbara Mickiewicz), 75, 84, 86–87
Majewski, Ignacy, 86
Majewski, Michał, 87
Makowski, Bronisław, 39–40, 49
Makuch, Janusz, 101–2, 106–7
Malinauskaitė, Ludmila (Ludmiła Malinowska), 38
Mann, Maurycy, 23, 35,
Marczyński, Jacek, 83, 91
Markowski, Michał Paweł, 338
Martinaitis, Algirdas, 298
Maśnicki, Jerzy, 307, 323
Massine, Léonide, 342
May, Karl, 257
Mazierska, Ewa, 305, 309–10, 315–16, 323
Mazowiecki, Tadeusz, 77–78, 97, 189
Melcer, Wanda, 169, 189
Meletzky, Franziska, 312
Mellon, Andrew, 150
Mencwel, Andrzej, 353, 357
Menzel, Jiří, 315
Michnik, Adam, 97, 100, 109
Mickiewicz, Adam, 74–75, 82, 84–91, 243, 255, 267, 279, 290–91, 297, 304, 316, 323
Mickiewicz, Barbara, born Tupalska, 87–88
Mickiewicz, Mikołaj, 86
Mieroszewski, Juliusz, 41
Mieses, Mateusz, 78, 84, 91

INDEX OF NAMES 369

Miliauskas, Juozapas (Józef Milewski), 38
Miłosz, Czesław, 292, 302, 360
Morawska, Ewa, 119, 120, 121, 125, 131
Morris, William, 249
Moschitzker, Robert, 149
Musiałowa, Alicja, 168
Mussolini, Benito, 53, 67, 71
Mysłakowski, Piotr, 83

Namier, Lewis, 58
Napieralska, Emilia, 144
Narbuitaitė, Onutė 298
Narutowicz, Gabriel, 25
Nemes, Charles, 308
Niculescu, Stefan, 290, 301
Nikolai I, tsar of Russia, 245
Norwid, Cyprian Kamil, 237, 249, 254

Odrowąż-Pieniążek, Janusz, 82, 86–89, 91
Odyniec, Antoni Edward, 82
Okołowicz, Józef, 120, 131
Olbrychski, Daniel, 309–13, 315, 322
Orłowska, Edwarda 164, 166, 168, 170, 172, 175, 189

Paczkowski, Andrzej, 78, 91
Paderewski, Ignacy, 58, 135–36, 158, 160
Pajo, Erind, 210, 211, 232
Pasieka, Agnieszka, iii, iv, v, vi, 1, 6, 8, 16, 30, 35, 107, 100, 110, 191, 201, 207, 352, 355, 361
Pawlikowska-Jasnorzewska, Maria, 81–82
Pawlikowski, Paweł, 305
Paziński, Piotr, 90
Pedersen, Susan, 52, 57, 71
Pelczar, Józef, bishop, 29, 35
Penderecki, Krzysztof, 285, 288, 301
Perkowski, Piotr, 351–52, 357–58
Picasso, Pablo, 342

Piemiczna, Wanda, 173, 189
Pigoń, Stanisław, 86–87
Piłsudski, Józef, 56, 58–59, 62, 66, 68–69
Pisarenko, Olgierd, 284, 288, 302
Pobłocki, Kacper, 7, 16, 349–51, 358
Pokrywka, Józef, 114–15, 117–18, 120, 124–25
Polański, Roman, 305, 311
Pomian, Krzysztof, 238–39, 255, 350, 358
Poniatowski, Józef, 243
Poniatowski, Michał, primate of Poland, 271
Popesco, Elvire, 307, 322
Porter-Szűcs, Brian (Porter, Brian) ,v, 3, 8–9, 14, 16, 19, 23, 28, 35–36, 53, 56, 61, 71, 94, 97, 107, 109, 353, 358, 361–62
Potocki, Wacław 4
Pragierowa, Eugenia, 164
Prokofiev, Sergey, 278
Prucnal, Anna, 308
Pruszyński, Aureliusz, 249
Pulaski, Kazimierz 135, 158

Radziwiłowicz, Jerzy, 309–13, 315, 323
Rauszer, Michał, 349–50, 358
Reeder, Linda, 121, 132
Reich, Steve, 277
Renoir, Jean, 307
Reynolds, David, 51, 72
Reytan, Tadeusz, 267–68, 270–73, 276
Richmond, Winifred, 143
Ritter von Greim, Robert, 268
Rodak, Paweł, iii, iv, vi, 3, 4, 12, 243, 348, 358, 362
Rogers, Ginger, 138, 143
Rosiński, Bolesław, 85, 91
Rostworowski, Marek, 324–25, 332, 347
Ruskin, John 249
Rybczonek, Sergiusz, 86–87, 91

Rymkiewicz, Jarosław Marek, 267–74, 276, 335

Sartre, Jean-Paul, 96, 109
Satie, Erik, 342
Schmelz, Peter, 278, 284, 296–97, 302
Schnittke, Alfred, 284
Schulz, Bruno, 89–90, 361
Schuppel, Uli, 312
Schwartz, Theodore, 215, 233
Scott, Walter, Sir, 257, 340
Serocki, Kazimierz, 293
Sheybal, Władysław, 308
Shkriblak, Mikhailo, 252
Shkriblak, Vasyl, 252
Shostakovich, Dmitry, 278
Siemiradzki, Henryk, 239
Sieroszewski, Wacław, 152–53
Sikorski, Andrze,j 83, 84–85, 91
Skłodowska-Curie, Maria, 152
Skolimowski, Jerzy 305, 308, 311
Słowacki, Juliusz, 74, 82, 89–91, 209, 267, 323
Smuts, Jan, 57
Snyder, Timothy, ii, 51, 67, 72, 279–80, 285–86, 295, 302
Sobocki, Leszek, 334
Sokołowska, Karina, 98
Sowa, Jan, 7, 11, 16, 52, 72, 256, 260, 276, 328–31, 339
Spivak, Gayatri, 9, 16
St. Phalles, Francois de, 150
Stalin, Joseph, 174, 280, 299
Stańczak-Wiślicz, Katarzyna, 174, 190, 351–52, 357–58
Stanevičiūtė-Goštautienė, Rūta, 287, 300, 302
Staroń, Andrzej, 337
Starowolski, Szymon, 334
Stauter-Halsted, Keely, v, 5, 11, 14, 113, 204, 349, 355, 358, 362
Stolashchuk, Vasilina, 252

Stomma, Ludwik, 78–79, 91
Stronczyński, Kazimierz, 239
Swanson, Gloria, 142
Syrokomla-Bułhak, Andrzej, 87–88, 91
Szapołowska, Grażyna, 312–13
Szczerek, Ziemowit, 4
Sztachelska, Irena, 164, 167
Szymutko, Stefan, 344

Talko-Hryncewicz, Julian, 82
Talmadge, Norma, 143
Tarnowski, Stanisław, 24–25, 36, 87
Tatarkiewicz, Krzysztof, 78–79, 91
Tatarkiewicz, Władysław, 78
Taylor, Frederick Winslow, 145, 160
Tazbir, Janusz, 243, 255–56, 276, 334
Temperley, Harold, 57, 72
Terry, Alice, 143
Thomas, William, 115–16, 119, 124, 132
Thompson, J. Lee, 308
Titcomb, William, 244
Tocqueville, Alexis de, 136, 138, 150
Tomczyk, Zofia, 176
Traverso, Enzo, 96, 110
Tumiłowicz, Bronisław, 290–92, 303
Turner, William, 244
Tuwim, Julian, 81, 82, 91
Twardoch, Szczepan, 4, 343–344
Twardowski, Romuald, 289, 303

Urbaitis, Mindaugas, 298

Vachudova, Milada, 221, 233
Van Dyck, Anthony, 239
Van Heuckelom, Kris, vi, 6, 304, 306–7, 313, 317–19, 323, 352, 356, 362
Van Norman, Louis E., 149
Vertovec, Steven, 295, 303
Vincent, George E., 150

Wajda, Andrzej, 265, 276, 309, 311, 316, 322

Walaszek, Adam, 113, 118, 123, 128, 132
Walczewska, Sławomira, 161, 177–78, 180, 190
Walenowicz, Sylwester (Silvestras Valiūnas), 38
Wałęsa, Lech, 77, 97
Wańkowicz, Melchior, 76–77, 90
Wapowski, Andrzej, castellan, 272
Warchałowski, Jerzy, 250–51, 255
Warzyniak, Lech, 79–80, 91
Wasilewska, Wanda, 168, 334
Wasilkowska, Zofia, 164
Wierzyński, Kazimierz, 89–90
Wilder, Billy, 307
Wilhelm II Hohenzollern, kaiser, 21
Wilson, Woodrow, 50, 55, 57, 73, 136, 158
Witkiewicz, Stanisław, 248, 250
Władysław I the Short, king of Poland, 239
Wodziński, Marcin, 93, 110
Wójcik, Jerzy, 316
Wolf, Eric, 225, 233

Wołonczewski, Maciej (Motiejus Valančius), 38
Wood, Nathan (Nathaniel), 31, 36
Wujec, Henryk, 77–78
Wyspiański, Stanisław, 252, 327

York, Michael, 311

Zahra, Tara, 31, 36, 122, 132
Zamachowski, Zbigniew, 313, 315
Zborowski, Samuel, 267–68, 270, 272–73, 276
Żelwowicz, Józef (Juozapas Želvys-Želvavičius), 38
Żeromski, Stefan, 1, 13, 16, 157–58, 362
Znaniecki, Florian, 116, 119–20, 124, 131–32
Znaniecki Lopata, Helena, 195, 207
Zubrzycki, Geneviève, v, 8–9, 14, 16, 92–96, 99, 107, 110, 355–56, 358, 363
Żurek, Lesław, 313, 319

Index of Subjects

America, iv, 12, 114–15, 117–19, 121–28, 130, 132, 160, 171, 179, 193, 266, 300, 353, 361, 363; as a cultural model, 12, 126–30, 133–59
anti-Semitism: in contemporary Poland, 96–97, 106; as folk narrative, 97, 201, 204; historically, 3, 33–34, 63, 67, 97, 104, 305

Catholicism, 19, 23, 27, 29, 32–35, 80, 99–101, 109–10, 162, 167, 191, 216, 362; and migration, 32, 198, 279; and Polishness, 7, 16, 19–21, 23, 25–31, 33, 94–96, 106, 166, 257
civilization, 9, 37, 54, 56, 58, 61–66, 70, 217, 237–38, 350
Communism, 3, 93, 96–97, 118, 158, 163–65, 167–68, 174, 176–77, 180, 182, 217, 224, 226, 233, 265, 311, 314–15, 322; ethnic/national identity, ii, iv, vi, 13, 17, 19–20, 46, 96, 106, 161–62, 164, 192, 208–10, 220, 238, 249, 253, 277, 280, 290, 295, 298, 304–5, 344, 352, 355, 358, 360, 361–63; multiple, 205–6, 220, 284; transformation of, 106, 206, 213, 239, 243–44, 295, 319

Eastern Europe, 14, 21, 30, 53, 57, 72, 73, 119–20, 159, 177, 179, 181–82, 187–88, 190, 280–82, 291, 297, 302, 308, 359–60
Europe, ii, iv, 12, 27, 32, 38, 44, 45, 50, 53, 68–69, 71–72, 102, 109–10, 118–19, 121, 126, 131–32, 151, 166, 179, 186–89, 204, 213, 223–24, 227, 229–33, 244–45, 258, 265–66, 274, 285, 299, 302, 304, 309, 318, 320, 322, 353, 359, 361–63; discourses on, 8, 209–12, 214–19; and ideas of Polishness, vi, 11, 117, 208, 210–11, 213, 215–16, 220–21, 223, 227, 229–30, 305–7, 313, 316, 318–19, 321–22. See also West
exile, 20, 116, 304–5, 307, 312–13, 319, 322–23

gender, vi, 159, 162–63, 179, 184, 186–92, 241, 311, 351, 360, 362; and nation, 9–10 173–74, 183, 305, 307; roles, transformation of, 142, 165–67, 169, 171, 174–75, 182, 197, 205–6, 308

identity: Jewish identity, 98, 105–6, 109; Lithuanian identity, 40–41, 46, 277–78, 280, 284, 290, 295–98, 361; Ruthenian identity, 56, 60, 63, 198, 279; Ukrainian identity, 23, 56, 103, 318 (see also Ruthenian identity); ways of defining/expressing, 9, 20–21, 96, 134, 142, 149, 162, 173, 203, 205–6, 215, 220, 239, 243, 259–61, 274, 293, 304, 318–19, 338, 353, 355

Jews, v, 7, 25, 33, 35–36, 58, 62–64, 66–69, 73. 76, 80, 82, 84, 88, 92, 97, 99, 102–5, 108–10, 122, 172, 201, 204, 216, 279, 329, 354–55,

Jews (*continued*)
360, 362–63; as "others," 9, 78, 81, 95, 104–7, 191; and Polish culture, 74–90, 97–103, 105–6, 166, 175, 201–2; and Polish national identity, 8, 60, 66, 92–94, 96–97, 99, 103–6. See also anti-Semitism

landscape, 6, 103–4, 106–7, 129, 130, 156, 166, 248–50, 253, 278, 298, 299–301, 316
language, 10, 36, 38–41, 43–46, 49, 53, 55–56, 71, 108, 122, 128, 162, 178, 194, 197–98, 201, 204, 249, 277, 279–80, 286, 296, 312, 315, 331–32, 337–38, 340–42, 344–45, 349, 361; and identity, 10, 40, 42, 46, 59–60, 62, 68, 155, 163, 166, 184, 219–220, 253, 314, 335, 338–39, 343, 348; and translation, 40, 44, 87

martyrdom, 71, 142, 149, 353, 358, 361
migration, 12, 79, 113–22, 124, 129, 131–32, 207, 232, 306, 308, 314, 317, 323, 362; and identity, 6, 113, 115, 118, 120, 129–30, 304–5, 319; within Europe, 114, 119, 125, 313; to United States, 114, 117–19, 121–27
modernity, 3, 5, 10, 12, 14, 35, 103, 108–10, 137, 151–52, 159, 178, 190, 230–31, 259, 265–66, 273–75, 303, 359, 362; and Polishness, 239, 256–57, 264, 348, 352; visions of, 32, 54, 134–35, 143–44, 146, 150, 153, 155, 157, 257, 262, 268, 352

nation-state, 73, 99, 131, 183, 266, 275–76, 290, 295–96, 306; and empire, 50–52, 66–68, 70; after First World War, 249; visions of, 7, 238–39

peasants, 3, 10, 39, 44, 88, 134, 201, 248, 251–52, 253, 328–29, 349, 351, 356, 358, 362; and migration, 11, 118–19, 120–22, 124, 126–27, 128, 132; and serfdom, 124, 193, 257, 350
Polish People's Republic, 257, 259–62, 289, 308, 310, 319
Polish romanticism, 29, 49, 142, 231, 286, 307, 311
Protestants 15, 20, 26, 101, 207

right-wing populism, 2, 183, 225, 231–32, 261

Sarmatism, vi, 5–6, 12, 14, 256–76, 330, 334, 340, 346, 359
Second Polish Republic, v, 8, 9, 50–58, 66–68
Solidarity movement, 183, 274, 308, 328, 336

transnationalism, 3, 15, 68, 172, 187, 221, 228, 231–32, 284, 293–95, 298, 300, 302–3, 323, 360–62; and identity transformation, vi, 5–6, 129, 208–9, 213, 216, 229–230, 282–83, 296, 305–6, 316, 319–22; and migration, 6, 307; and modernization, 182, 211; and scholarship, 4, 10–11

Ukrainians, 53, 55–56, 60, 66, 97, 98, 103, 216, 292, 318, 356

West, 29, 53–55, 55, 57–58, 69, 72–73, 102, 120, 125, 192, 245, 282, 285, 291, 300, 307, 353; and feminism, 162–63, 171–72, 176–80, 182–83, 185, 187; images of, 14, 57, 97, 128, 163, 178–80, 227, 251, 352; migration to, 118–19, 322–23; as opposed to East, 8, 61–62, 65, 67, 121, 134, 179, 182, 211, 216–17, 224–25, 231, 231, 283–84, 294–96, 302, 320, 361

Printed in the United States
by Baker & Taylor Publisher Services